History Out of Joint

PARALLAX  RE-VISIONS OF CULTURE
AND SOCIETY

Stephen G. Nichols, Gerald Prince, and Wendy Steiner
SERIES EDITORS

History Out of Joint

Essays on the Use and Abuse of History

Sande Cohen

The Johns Hopkins University Press
Baltimore

© 2006 The Johns Hopkins University Press
All rights reserved. Published 2006
Printed in the United States of America on acid-free paper
9 8 7 6 5 4 3 2 1

The Johns Hopkins University Press
2715 North Charles Street
Baltimore, Maryland 21218-4363
www.press.jhu.edu

Library of Congress Cataloging-in-Publication Data

Cohen, Sande.
    History out of joint : essays on the use and abuse of history /
Sande Cohen.
        p.   cm. — (Parallax, re-visions of culture and society)
    Includes bibliographical references and index.
    ISBN 0-8018-8214-1 (hardcover : alk. paper)
    1. History—Philosophy. 2. Historiography. 3. Public
history. I. Title. II. Parallax (Baltimore, Md.)
    D16.9.C58 2005
    901—dc22   2005001868

A catalog record for this book is available from the
British Library.

Contents

▌ *Acknowledgments*

Thanks to Stephen Nichols and Michael Lonegro at the Johns Hopkins University Press, who evaluated this text and put it through review. I am grateful for their suggestions for revision. I also wish to thank the outside readers' helpful suggestions for changes to the arguments. For reading specific chapters and offering suggestions for revision, I wish to thank Gabrielle Spiegel, David James, Mario Biagioli, R. L. Rutsky, Tom Lutz, Kriss Ravetto-Biagioli, Vinay Lal, James Wiltgen, Joan Hugo, Sylvère Lotringer, Paul Zelevansky, Beatrice Dumin, Yuan-Huang Tsai, and Fandra Chang. Thanks to Cheng Shang-Hsi, S. K. Teng, and Dominique Nabokov for photo permissions. Chapters 2, 3, and 7 had earlier versions published in the journals *Emergences* and *Parallax*.

History Out of Joint

Philosophical Prelude

On the Difference between an Event and a Narrative

What operations do we perform on ourselves and others by the ways we use and abuse senses of history? Consider the term *posthistory* as usually contrasted with *history:* does it bring what its detractors insist is an "elitist, culturally pessimistic inversion of the optimism of progress," excessive concern with culture instead of social transformation? Does "posthistory" negate "the life-history of individuals . . . their experiences and failures . . . to tell others true stories . . . and to reach agreement with each other about the history that binds them together"?[1] Yet what is this "history" so aggressive toward "posthistory," here accused of crushing "history that binds," and thus killing storytelling? This book is not a defense of posthistory, as that is too simple. But the history of the attack on the term is interesting. Historical writing, following the chronology that places Herodotus and Thucydides as "founders," with precursors, is twenty four hundred years and going, yet can it authorize war on writing, representation, senses of temporality, life?

Our historians' verbal aggressions in support of "history" make for questions about the circulation of historical representations, questions about the structure and function of the historical profession, questions about thought and history, narrative and event.[2] Dominique Janicaud has argued that for the majority of Westerners, history as "tradition already *says* nothing," and asks "what will the 'historical' have become when it is no more than a gigantic 'data base'?"[3] Shouldn't we take the challenge, some might say "bait," and ask about our social life that is at once transitory, strangely immemorial, yet somehow "historical," a "time out of joint" where "before and after" and other stabilities of history might have shifted purpose and function?

I have much to say throughout these chapters on the difficulties of thinking history in today's cultural-political ecology, but this much seems clear: whoever speaks for the public(s) *historicizes*. For instance, "These are dark times," muses the cultural impresario Peter Sellars, invoking the present as history. These times require artistic engagement because "artists have to act . . . we're the people paid every day to follow our conscience."[4] In the confusion of giving artists an *eternal* (moral) role within *our* professional setups, history is both used and abused—how exactly is the "timelessness" of artistic engagement and the cash economy of current art production historical?

As this is a book of philosophical criticism, presuppositions are brought to the study of the "use and abuse of history." Here are the main ones.

First, the convergence of politics and culture, including the academicization of culture, can be seen in the ongoing culture wars over compensations, material and spiritual, for past injustices and present outrages—a hodgepodge of cultural slights, reparation movements, memory conciliations, blockbuster art shows. These different experiences are both cause and effect of current strife, riven by political agendas figured forth in cultural terms. Convergence of politics and culture shows itself in bitter disputes between artists and intellectuals (producers) over rankings that establish the future values of artifactual significance. The troubled status of mediation and cultural strife involves, then, discussion of sanctions, inducements, negotiations, zones of conjunction, and layers of exclusion, congealed in a first presupposition: *there is cultural warfare* at the level of mediation, as to whom and what should be represented as bodying forth signs and indices of cultural and intellectual *collective* importance. This conflict shows itself in selection decisions, from hiring teachers to textbook choices to competition for appearance in the "best" venues to issues of collective memory and ratios of obsolescence (people, concepts, things slip away at different rates).

The analysis of the uses and abuses of history also presupposes that competition, negotiation, and selection are active forces of social life that require "historical representation" but that such representation is secondary to the politics of culture. An institution changes the way it ranks, evaluates, and selects its objects of value according to internal professional rivalries (say, among curators) as well as offering various public things worth seeing (reading, thinking); "history" follows from competition even if it seems to drive it. In this tangle, *selection* is a highly contested term, but it seems clear that its various forms have become nearly ontological. *Ontological* means the ways in which empirical relations become almost unthinkable in any other way—imagine an "advanced" Western society without the "being" of universities; imagine social life in these universities if the schools did not provide rewards to "marginal" cultures, such as comic-book innovators. In what follows, competition, adaptation (negotiation), and selection are treated as practices and processes related to the myriad ways our social system reviews and evaluates objects, including cultural "states of value." We turn our things and processes into historical representations—we select, we choose, we eliminate, we evaluate. What are we doing when we make ourselves subject to a coherent history that "thinks" events in one register of sense and not another, or narrate with tools not developed for our existing social and intellectual arrangements? For example, if there is now an actual global "media state" and its opposite, a global "contestatory cosmopolitan public sphere"—"new radicals" versus the nearly omnipotent media—is it credible and plausible that these opposed tendencies are unified in some narrative dialectic? Does the formation of a media state automatically come with a "contestatory" or symmetrical other?[5] Or, from the art sphere: why have so many critics accepted equivalences between Warhol = Pop = popular culture = canonization of the marginal = normalization = social improvement? The specific object, the rare (e.g., Warhol's initial silkscreens), is made representative, an object stitched to a narrative of progress. To narrate is to give representative value: but how do our conflicting claims on such phenomena themselves, as claims, become selected? The privatization (= capitalization) of scientific knowledge (globally) is a fact; scholars of science now describe disjunctions over funding and research and intellectual property issues within science as a disturbing shift; which narrative "belongs" to Pop, which to scientific privatization?[6]

Selection, review, evaluation, ranking, inclusion, exclusion—these now seem necessary concepts for any kind of critical analysis of political and cultural convergence and strife, and come together around a second presupposition—there is such a thing as *historical selection or selection "for history."* This presupposition is a bit murkier than the first. In any case, historical selection discussed here is considered an agency that gives an entitlement—for memory, for social cohesion, for overcoming lacunae and gaps in knowledge. Taken together, historians and historical representation, and the far trickier historical "knowledge"—historiography—is understood below as an "externalized system of practices" trusted to "give normative force to the notions of memorizing and promising" and where "to change the system of social practices is to change the system of memory."[7] "Use and abuse of history" is then to study what happens—effects and consequences—when cultural production(s) are given a "fate" and "destiny" *as public significance informed by historical representation.* One simply keeps asking questions as to how history informs, shapes, gives public and institutional and affective continuities as other things and processes are rendered discontinuous.

Further, a cluster of presuppositions emerges the instant one brings the texts of *Nietzsche* into the open. The analysis offered here borrows from Nietzsche's theory that public life is also where *antiproduction* is an intrinsic practice, perhaps a superevent because so pervasive (like high blood pressure). In such practices as inflated estimations of cultural worth, elimination and scouring of rivals, dismissing possibilities, confirming a small or big canon of ideas that should remain disputable, antiproduction bureaucratizes culture and installs misrepresentation as public truth. For instance, it only takes a few dozen or few hundred words in the right place to make a name or concept or process something visible, a circuit in the strange information/misinformation cultural flux of these times. Why is even a "bad" review in a "visible" place worth more than a tauter, and more conductive review in a less-visible venue? *Such questions are acutely historical: how are the culturally "lasting" and "enduring" made? What are the relations between the "lasting" and our mobilization of a past?* A recurring focus of this book, then, is how history is made representable and affects "public life." Common processes of selection involve intellectual and academic judgments challenged here by a critical analysis that tries to build, so to speak, antiproduction into the analysis of contemporary life. Third presupposition: *antiproduction is not an accident—it is selected.*

The premise of asymmetry between history and culture and the study of their junctions stages an encounter between history and culture over the rank and value of things while no clear sense of "goals" is collectively sustained in terms of culture; this is a premise about current and collective normalization of disjunctions. Brian Rotman has written some sharp words on this. He has it that contemporary knowledge production has obliterated distinctions between public and private, so that our social world increasingly looks to be "disjointed and ultimately unconvincing . . . dizzying syncretism, the fibrillation of desire as we move back and forth across the boundary of an ongoing constructed real, and the wild promise of a future dance in the memories of the cyborged and robotized descendents of our body-selves."[8] Who can believe in the truth of any historical periodization today that would put us in narrative order—the "death" of modernism, the "affirmations" of postmodernism, the "dialectic" of history itself? If, collectively, Western social arrangements are less a matter of discipline than control—including new technologies that organize senses of the loss of control—can we expect more and more disjunctions to be incorporated by narrative rationalizations, the historian reduced to giving *reaestheticization* effects and new plausibility to social cohesion?[9] Is "public culture" more like a black hole of representation than it is like an agora of decision and choice? Again, in question form: what are the mechanisms by which artifacts are given equivalences as preparation for other distinctions? Did Pop survive some test of time? Is there actually a public that loves Pop in the same terms as Pop's reviewers, such as curators with a stake in cultural assessments? Intellectual disquiet about representing history raises questions of public historical consciousness—connections between the value of public-intellectual life and the circulation of "useable" history.[10] I am tempted here to argue that historical representation and "the public" are locked in an unfortunate dance: the high status accorded what the public is to find important, thinkable, is derived from the finalities offered by historical writing, scholarly and otherwise; in this the social distinction accorded to objects and things thus passes for cognitive significance, a leap in which the very public is left behind.[11] I read it in *Critical Inquiry* or *October:* just exactly how does such high-profile representation include public, value, norm, necessity, and hence come to mean public significance?

Part I of this book focuses on current yet persistent uses and abuses of history. Chapter 1 provides intellectual context to the readings made in chapters 2 through 5, and is a bridge to the second part of the book, which focuses on some recent French philosophers, where Nietzsche's impact is quite clear. Nietzscheist problematics are discussed so as to open a genealogy of pro- and antiskepticism toward the power of language to make illusions, a genealogy of the force of prose to generate statements that connect cognition, power, and obedience, elements of historical representation. This genealogy of skepticism about illusion, prose, public, and critical connections with historical representation includes writers such as Gorgias and Vico, who located the couple prose discourse / historical narration within a vexed social formation. In general, this first chapter focuses on language as it is turned into narrative thoughts, opinions, beliefs, and implications, or politico-logical offerings rendered in moral and aesthetic terms. Or language accepted as little more than a currency, the very point of its own exchange: public discourse as mostly order-words and command utterances, which include, here, the historian's professional uses of language.[12] Nietzsche's hypotheses concerning language are resistant to mainstream humanities and their claims to knowledge because Nietzsche complicated the arts and humanities by asking how and when they provide active knowledge at all. Too often, knowledge is a reduction to belief in judgment's authority, necessity, fatality.[13] Nietzsche's arguments about language and art in culture serve neither cultural "integrationists," where we are all said to share conditions of discourse—the so-called great conversation that never actually happens—nor the interests of "disintegrationists," a discourse that holds each social group finally turns and spins on its differences, which cannot be understood by outsiders. A Nietzschean workup of language makes it simultaneously impossible to believe in "normal history" as it makes it equally impossible to affirm the discourses of the periphery. Better to conceive language as opening onto divergences and decenterings that undercut representation. Better to conceive of language *at the outset* as a mixed system, reference on one side, possible madness on the other, the actual and virtual at once, with unresolvable problems of literalism, problems of delirium, problems of making meaning always *mean.* Can the humanities make concepts instead of political moralizations? When might scholarship *be* art? When and how might art realize scholarship? What are public words that make a difference in our redundancies over (about) already achieved differences and similarities?

Chapters 2 and 3 use reviews from the *Los Angeles Times* to launch questions about the effects of historicizing public life. The *Los Angeles Times* already has a well-documented, contentious history of representation. Given the fragmentation of knowledge and information that is itself part of public life, given the large readership of the *Times,* and its own attempts to influence public discourse (its sponsorship of political-cultural events), the materials chosen indicate what is at stake when an institution of representation takes it upon itself to selectively focus on matters said to be of interest to the broadest public, and then systematically makes one-sided political narratives, taking sides. In its pages, at least for the period discussed (1995–2001), Taiwan was turned into the "bad object" of a mythed Chinese history, Taiwanese history shrunk to the vanishing point of promoting fear of history. The deference to multinational capital at the center of the *Times'* urging its readers to accept the thesis of "One China" as historical "truth" is highlighted. Editorial demotion and narrative history is a study in how history is produced by one institution of representation. Does the public actually understand that One China is a political myth—with teeth—or that the editorial treatment of Taiwan as an illegitimate society is a negative model of how our own public life, as discursive life, is purged of thinking in terms of *legitimate contentiousness?* The Taiwan chapter is the only one where I directly counterread historicization by using "facts" and events. Chapter 3 takes up fulminations over the value of art reviewing and the image of an intellectual as gleaned from the *Book Review* and *Arts Review* sections of the *Times.* To put this philosophically and socially: the readings made of the *Times* argue that its editorials and reviews create a cosseting of political and aesthetic judgments, and in so doing, have also actually usurped the place of the involved audience.[14] Together, chapters 2 and 3 argue that the editorials suggest that the *reader is missing*—the editorials and reviews are more commands than invitations to analysis or the making of judgments on the part of readers. In the criticism offered here, these materials from the *Times* point toward an *antiproductive* confluence of relations between public life and history, with intellectuals, artists, and artifacts serving as the anchoring materials.

Chapters 4 and 5 shift to the more "placeless" but not less powerful instances of culture and narrative expectations. Chapter 4 asks a question—who is the historian when considered as a social agent, a producer of knowledge, a mediator of disputes, in short, a representationist? The historian is clearly a professional scholar: but what are the entanglements of the professional scholar with other roles, i.e., the connoisseur, mediator, and judge?[15] This chapter engages the *mediatization* of the historian's contemporary image-value, including literary self-conceptions. It examines such instances as obituary pictures, among other data, using the icon of Isaiah Berlin, insider/outsider par excellence. The political and cultural "who" of the historian (the historian as pure researcher, the historian as storyteller) is shaky, shifting between fixed norms and strange processes of cultural integration. I have tried here to use analyses of the type proposed by writers such as Corynne McSherry in her *Who Owns Academic Work?* McSherry's book probes how academics invent their own "property stories" authorized to legitimate our creative endeavors in relation to institutions and rivals, focusing on "boundary objects" such as copyrights. For instance, in chapter 4 the obituaries of Berlin are treated as a boundary object of a *propriety* narrative, the story of the historian's synthetic image-value.[16]

Chapter 5 concerns historical scholarship simultaneously connected to public persuasion through the use of anecdotes and to politics as such, since anecdotes operate across representation and the public world. It draws on Joel Fineman's investigation of the anecdote as a literary form, whose analysis plunged historical theory into literature and eros at once, so stunningly infrequent in Euro-American historiography. In Fineman's essay, theory sexualizes historiography and bruises the enabling premise of neoliberal political historiography, its sense of objectivity and nonrelativism. While offering a critique of Fineman's elevation of the anecdotal form as the sufficient condition for narrative, I analyze the anecdote-as-used in another historian's put-down of the sixties, that story a discrediting of the emergence of contemporary cultural studies (which I am not defending). The anecdote—an irruption of an event or incident within experience—may well be the metaphysical kernel of "historicity," forming time as integrated succession at the intimate level of perception, but the anecdote-at-work is highly political as well.[17]

In part II, chapter 6 opens with an analysis of Derrida's *Specters of Marx* treated as what it manifestly is, a deconstructive version of the philosophy of history. The reading here is a quarrelsome wrestling match with Derrida's premises and his intellectual offering of tasks that historical consciousness cannot perform. A detailed analysis of relations between the historical, the historial, and the "im-possible" are rendered. To the shaky "who" of the historian that emerges through study of abuse in part I, Derrida's "new scholar" is seen as more continuous than not with conventions pertaining to historians and their "curative" or mediational, classical role.

Chapter 7 is a synthesis of Jean-François Lyotard's theory of historiographic representation, offered, in part, as an antidote to Derrida's idealizing and, in another way, as a platform that keeps paradox ever sharp and the ambiguity of interpretation "present" when we represent history. This is the only chapter that veers toward an intellectual "homage," as I think that of all the so-called postmodern philosophers, Lyotard has the most acute things to say about historiography as what it most manifestly is, a modulation "in the family of narrative cultures," never separate from "savage, primitive, underdeveloped, backward, alienated, composed of opinions, customs, authority, prejudice, ignorance, ideology."[18] Chapter 8 sorts through the historiographic force of Deleuze and Guattari's *Anti-Oedipus,* their disjunctive-narration in which history is conceived less as retrospective finality and more as a series of paradoxical encounters, including how historical representation came to serve as a superpolitical cultural form or collective petitio principii. Chapter 9 focuses on Deleuze's *Difference and Repetition,* its metahistorical (pace Hayden White) philosophy of temporality in which Deleuze takes up the philosophical and cultural implications that "time is out of joint" in an entirely interesting and disturbing manner. For example, to the "passing present" of living, with its "successive instants" as well its coexistent temporal levels, how can one make a sense of "destiny" that is less narrative and more a question of selections created from different levels of existence? How to make goals less interesting than new processes of engagement with the world? Part II, as a whole, is an *affirmation* of conceiving history out of key, and stands in contrast to the readings made in part I, where abuse is fully brought out.

The remainder of this introduction focuses on issues of narration and event, bringing up the chapters on Lyotard and Deleuze, not as a defense of posthistory or to set philosophy of history against common sense, but to focus on narration and event, *the* contested terms of historiography today and, perhaps, of politicized culture-in-general. Their conceptual schemas about present-day cultural and political shifts in supercapitalized societies calls into question everything about traditional and conventional notions of *context*. In brief, for both writers, context is out of joint along with secure historical time.

Of the many thousands of articles and books concerning the historiographic topics of event and narrative—on their distinctions and modes of connection—there is a pragmatic acceptance that narrative constitutes the sense of events, a pragmatism that is confident about narrative. Narration has become a default drive; it absorbs events. R. G. Collingwood's comment in *The Idea of History* that facts and events are interchangeable allowed him to conclude that events are always *evidence* for the historian's present thinking of the past and provide for a narrative's coherence.[19] Arthur Danto's statement in *Analytic Philosophy of History* that a historical explanation "cover[s] the event with a general description and bring[s] it together with like instances,"[20] suggests just how commonplace it is for us to think of events as already stories, already "nested" in a medium that events seem naturally and socially to belong to. Narrative is that "written land" (Rancière) where, as historical representation, "a true body of words [is] substituted for erratic speech."[21]

Fifty years and more of directed criticism at various "narrative-effects" has not dislodged the pragmatism of historical narration, as is shown in the publication lists of university and nearly all commercial presses. Histories of every facet of, say, "design" proliferate today, appropriating events designated as neglected (a trope of giving "origins"), and resurrected out of a past, material world for present readers. We have transformed history into an "objectless singular," a container, a condition, a form of experience and expectation and can apply it to anything.[22] But in these transformations of "raw" material (no such thing?) into history, events are often purged of their differential elements, linearity (succession) preserved as a bulwark against chaos.

Modern semiotic theories of history have offered many conceptualizations about culturally inherited notions of history. For example, it has been argued that naming an event is shorthand for actions recognized, formally, "by a cognitive subject other than the subject of doing itself." An action becomes an event only if represented by someone else. An action requires recognition from another, not to be conceived, but to be believed, such belief embedded in ongoing narrations. Historical narration is not opinion, but quasi-argued belief. Linked to initial conditions and outcomes, "hard facts" are invoked to provide narrated results—Galileo made optic lenses which "tell the story" of science versus religious and philosophical ideologies of planetary motions. But every causal model is disputable, the basis of Claude Lévi-Strauss's famous remark that history is always "history-for" disguised as "history-of." Semiotic-driven analyses have argued that omniscient narration or the narrator construed as a "delegate" of the historian are devices of inducing belief-in-belief, saving the (naïve?) reader's commitment to social bonds said to be historical bonds because they are narratively intelligible—a petitio principii.[23]

Most historians insist that narratives are meant to elucidate events, to make the significance of events stand out as time-pivots. The historiographer Reinhart Koselleck is correct, I think, when he says that *periodization* is a necessary offering for any historiography. Microhistory, for example, made some previously neglected events dramatic. Carlo Ginzburg's well-received *The Cheese and the Worms* made the drama of the suppression of peasant ancestral criticisms of power turn on the myth of a "peasant origin" of resistance, dramatic details embedded in the myth of almost natural attributes of resistance read out of the history of the archaic but vivid past of Italy. The philosophically necessary thing to say is that perhaps historical narrative has its own, unique petitio principii—where the premise and conclusion of narration (an event *is* a story) are confused to the degree where narrative history *gives* premises and conclusions not warranted by events. Whatever we call the tribulations of narrative in our society, as in the loss of metanarrative coherence,[24] the shift to issues of use and abuse asks if historical narration can *beg questions in the very act of answering them*? Part I focuses on this topic.

In sum: contemporary Western societies have created multiple *effects of history*—synthesized as *to historicize,* infinitive form. The use and abuse of history is a critical study that tries to specify conceptual, linguistic, and philosophical mechanisms of such use and abuse. The difficulty of the "object," which is plainly the concept *to historicize,* stems from its strange but normal practice that individuals, groups, and institutions use to fuel as much legitimation as required so as to have credibility today and tomorrow. Narrative history, narrative thinking—is it now primarily set forth to remove claimants from the future? As will be argued, historical writing is different now as culture has become virtually a war over claimants in every zone recognized by some narrator of a subject, the narrators in combat over legitimacy. Claimants over names and processes, claimants to "firstness," claimants to intensity—*to historicize* also then means to lend time as a power to an existing claim. It is this sense of historical knowledge as deeply *selective* that marks *to historicize* as a transpolitical maneuver carried out in the very act of narrating.

First, Lyotard. It is unfortunate that his work has been denounced as "extremist" by historians.[25] His writings belong to resistance to post–World War II historicization, including writers such as Simone Weil, whose 1943 *The Need for Roots* was, among other things, an implied critique of Alexandre Kojève's notorious resuscitation of the dialectic of master/slave, Kojève having "eternalized" history *as* the repetition of master/slave. Weil was a writer for whom history was an obstacle to cultural affirmation.

Lyotard's most sustained elaboration of event and narrative occurs in the essay "The Sign of History." He has it that Westerners' attunement to historical experiences is based on a linguistic-social *infliction,* the name *common being.* Through this name, there circulates a pseudocognitive rule of telos, or finality. Acceptance of such common being—say toleration for capitalism's ordinary violence (e.g., of the workplace)—is signaled in subjective-teleological phrases, of the type in which some aspects of the present are judged narratively adequate or inadequate, acceptable or unacceptable. For example, one can say that capitalism does not mistreat its own national majorities *too* badly over time, but at issue is how "history" and "*too*" became common—a matter that involves normalization, language, and ideas of social reciprocity, among other social ties.

Lyotard presses into language—capital creates relays throughout the social system, names and definitions of things are subject to dissolve, replaced by the more fluid ambiguities of *interpretable signs.* As Vico foresaw, names come and go quickly in contested societies, with an upsurge of emotionalisms and legalisms. If all one has in making the present historical are signs, then the historian's *research* is no guarantee of objective sense, of common being, but only another *medium* of cultural filtering. We can say that common being gives the basis of intersubjective relations, but signs require assessment and at best *refer* to "an event, a deal (in the card-playing sense) . . . which would only indicate and not prove that humanity is capable of being not only the cause but also the author of its progress."[26] Whereas common being allowed *historical representation* to turn event/sign into a genetic or telic pattern and give the historian an anchor in providing coherence, "signs" resist this insofar as they are complex and ambiguous. Signs are *posthistoire*, even *ahistorical*, signaling the risks and dangers of interpretation, incessantly *re*historicized by recourse to new petitio principii.

Lyotard went still further. The pragmatic and moral dimensions of historical writing require Ideas of continuity and discontinuity, progress and decline. Typically, Western reliance on a pragmatic sense of morality requires that causes be thought of as somewhat *undetermined,* this to allow humanity or any cognitive subject to schematize history as freedom, will, and action distanced from explicit mechanistic causation. "Dark" histories affecting how we think about the future are still restricted to areas like ecology. Historians need to make what happened—incidents, events, processes—appear necessary but not determined by, say, human nature, social laws, or any other explanation that kills off the feeling for events. But narrative increasingly renders—or sorts out—"safe" events—what we call teachable history. Which events, if any, index the Idea of free causality today?[27] *Posthistoire* asks if a "feeling for history" is possible once *processes* elude "common understanding." Is there common understanding without common being? Lyotard asks us to consider event and sign as fissured, suspending the Kantian affirmation that the historical world exemplifies an Idea of progress, along with its premise of a "moral disposition within the human race." Of course Lyotard notes the risks of such aporias toward "moral disposition." But all that remains of Kantian optimism for history is the feeling of an incommensurability between Ideas and their presentation, a failure that acts as a subjective spur, "of having to supply a presentation for the unpresentable." We could ask, pushing Lyotard's analysis into our present: has enthusiasm-for-history given way to avoidance of events (choices) that could ruin the possibility of temporal continuity? Avoidance is a concept where Darwin and Nietzsche meet, in consideration of processes and practices of antiproduction. For example: a current plan to raze older buildings at the Los Angeles County Museum and deliver a Rem Koolhaus design (architect du jour) will attest to a now/new triumph of competition between the County Museum and other institutions of comparable rank and hierarchy in Los Angeles. The discourse in support of the building avoids intensive public discussion about the equation between "name" architect and public interests; the politics immersed in competition and selection remains mostly invisible.[28] What might avoidance plus enthusiasm equal or resemble?

It gets even more tense. In taking up Kant's arrangements about history and signs, Lyotard thus theorized history as potentially embedded in pathology, since enthusiasm, and a host of related terms, is an affection that can move toward a black hole, say, increasing social aggression, extensive and intensive, creating new genealogies of stigma. "Common being" could even come to signify nihilistic pragmatism—and this nihilistic pragmatism might be what resists "an energetical *sign,* a tensor," in which things and processes are both attracted and repulsed, or an "agitation on the spot" that adds new concepts for social consideration.[29] Narrative forms and social "tensors" are always potentially incommensurable.

As Lyotard reads Kant so as to doubt historical narration at every one of its hinges to productive knowledge, he asks why advanced social systems cannot maintain sublime feelings—the potential *unfigurability* of events and actions. *Signs*—the sense of or delivery of such unfigurability (or defiance of reason)—indicate that things have happened that require phrases that have not been said, and may not be sayable: a feeling, say, that middle-class America has voluntarily chosen formal democracy as a means of preserving economic self-interest, sacrificing Ideas of critique to their own social survival; could narrating such feelings *prove* their actuality, let alone satisfy a historical judgment that was "common" about such states of existence?

Quickly then, Lyotard worked back to that territory ploughed by Kant and Nietzsche, especially arguing that the public authority of historians should be challenged exactly at the point where common being is affirmed; philosophically, Lyotard, like other writers in recent French philosophy, argued that an event transmits an excess and surplus of sense and idea, and it is not clear *when* narration is the adequate mode of representing ambiguous events.

Gilles Deleuze's *Difference and Repetition,*[30] first published in 1968, is a fearsomely difficult book. Although Deleuze and Guattari are justly famous (or notorious) for their *Capitalism and Schizophrenia, Difference and Repetition* has not attracted the same attention, no doubt because it is a profoundly undramatic book by comparison to the hot theses of *Capitalism and Schizophrenia.* The latter work excoriated psychoanalysis on nearly every page, and claimed that intellectuals are often a "sellout," i.e., "that is to say, any literature that

takes itself as an end or sets ends for itself" panders to an existing audience instead of trying to create one. Very impolite. Of *Capitalism and Schizophrenia*'s
analysis of subject and temporality, many commentaries have been critical, to
say the least.[31] Such negative reception to *Capitalism and Schizophrenia* is
complemented with a hush attending to the historiography of *Difference and
Repetition* and its analysis of referential truth, chronology, or successivity, the
use of fictional devices in the service of "reality-effects," and the historian's all-
too-often acceptance of reality as-it-is.

Difference and Repetition unpacks linearization, sequence, the burden of
"before/after." It upends the concept of repetition, connecting it to "reflections, echoes, doubles and souls," to reciprocity and self-implication, as well as
to "theft and gift." Rigorously gnomic at times—temporality *not measured* by
narrative history—Deleuze is in effect saying that repetition is a kind of production. For a start, one could say: *repetition is additive*—reflection, theft, self-
implication, and possibility gather as something unrepeatable yet not over.[32]
Deleuze gives as the example a conjunction of the political and the festive that
carries a "first time to the 'nth' power." Diagrammed as a "universality of the
singular," this is where, say, the Fall of the Bastille itself "celebrates and repeats
in advance" all its commemorations. Historical narration obscures the past's
repetition-collision differences, their connections, however improbable. More
strongly: a *past is/was improbable* because of the force of repetition. Repetition
displaces concepts such as "beginning," the "finished," the "over," or telic origins and finalities. Such displacement is also threaded to what the American
philosopher Josiah Royce called "active thought," where "at any point in time
the returns so far as truth is concerned are not all in."[33] Events are not lost and
are never fully known—an event does not retrace patterns of law, equivalence,
or resemblance; in actuality the conjunction of past event and repetition is
closer to "transgression" and not "a single past that returns in the future." Negative repetition is "active" in relation to calls for "return," for the demand that
a previously unknown past be given its current equivalence, that it be recognized. Deleuze offers an event as disturbance of narrative containment, conflict between event and narration.

Repetition suggests the force of an event that suspends or at "times" defies
language; some events correlate with tropes such as prosopopoeia and apos-
trophe, or those slippery names that are part of the way events are sometimes
produced by agents. How to name/narrate the "singular, unchangeable, and
different, without identity," or events that somehow dissolve exchange or the
traffic of representation in favor of connections not bound by opposition,

negation, or false affirmations? If one makes the interpretation—evaluation, selection—that the Fall of the Bastille brought the Idea of the State to crisis in releasing and thus joining political prisoners and criminals at dynamic places that can be specified (e.g., Kant and de Sade are actually "wrestling"—if that is the right word—with each other), allowing criminals and politicians to freely mix for a while, then that event may "happen" every time politics and, say, certain qualities of social danger connect. Historians and present dangers: Deleuze asks that we account for neocapitalist culture, including left opposition that still believes it has a command discourse over history, by asking how we make events that slip politics.

Repetition as a positive act pertains to nonexclusive disjunctive experiences, as *Anti-Oedipus* put it, or in terms of *Difference and Repetition,* that an event's sense simply does not mesh with narration or succession (generality and equivalence). Hence, a Deleuzian historiography is rigorously against narrative politics, of any kind. An event is neither similar to nor equal to anything else: an event does not belong to law, to nature, to consciousness, but to the future. *Repetition is production. Difference and Repetition*'s great historiographical obsession is precisely with the future, not with the past or present. If, say, Americans have generally adopted narrative patterns that continue to legitimize "fuzzy" behavior (e.g., obesity patterns) and at the same time many of us pursue any number of specific narratives (e.g., the search for notable ancestors, exhuming the DNA of Jesse James so as legitimize family genealogy), it could be argued that this is due to negative, insecure obsessions with present and past—the future a negative continuity.

On the one hand, then, an event initiates difference and, from the perspective of knowing the past, focus should go to those events that functioned, in whatever domain of existence, as nonlaws *in their own time* (the untimely)—unexpected collisions and social and cultural adhesions no one could see coming. As with Lyotard, Deleuze goes further: he makes of historical thinking a present act that is uninterested in narrating the past for a third-party reader, usually the consumer/spectator (reader). Indeed, this affirms Nietzsche's proposition that those building a future should have strong claims to the past.[34] In sum, transgression by an event and in the writing of such events involves a break with narration and story. Events can become nonlaws, affirmations; and repetition, considered as event and concept, is thus a "test" for human beings—it places us somewhere "in-between" story and narration (7).

Now, consider the cultural implications of the above discussion. In a remarkable passage, Deleuze has it that "difference gives things to be seen and multiplies bodies; but it is repetition which offers things to be spoken, authenticates the multiple, and makes of it a spiritual event." Repetition as spirit does not mean mystical or invisible, but the persistence of *affirmations,* the effect of something once done capable of drawing us into its "subsistence," "its disquieting power," cultural attractions selected and distributed in myriad ways. In this, repetition is distinguished from habit and memory, because these relations are limited to acts that "recover the particulars dissolved in generality" (7). Instead, as production, repetition is active, intrinsic to a "forgetting [that] becomes a positive power" (7), or pertains to those acts of thought and will that go to the limit of what can be thought, felt, perceived, "making movement itself a work" (8). Philosophy activates repetition when it opens up new territories that convention would disallow. As *Anti-Oedipus* put it, repetition may belong to representation ("things spoken"), but it counteracts representation from the inside: "The theory of proper names should not be conceived of in terms of representation; it refers instead to the class of 'effects': effects that are not a mere dependence on causes, but the occupation of a domain, and the operation of a system of signs . . . the Joule effect, the Seebeck effect, the Kelvin effect. History is like physics: a Joan of Arc effect, a Heliogabulus effect—all the *names* of history."[35] No doubt some readers of historiographic theory will see in this a return to Gentile over Croce (action over mediation), or Nietzsche synthesized with Kant's theory of the "outrageousness" of the imagination: decisionism, selection, volition, drive, activating thought, taking thought to its limits. Deleuze will affirm making of consciousness itself a "theater," one that does not represent, but performs repetition, bypassing opposition and mediation—in short, *working* pastness for passage to the future (10).

Repetition is one of the boundaries of historical representation, for it is a concept that is surely a "terrible power," since it threatens our representations of history, in particular current *recanonization* of culture, at every level of its occurrence. How can we keep calling things masterpieces on nearly no basis at all? Repetition actualizes *nonconceptual differences* (13), that is, whatever can be said, or disputed and further interpreted, in an actual event or act of thought to escape "indefinitely continued conceptual difference" such as clichés overlaid on things (13). Again, certain events (processes) are not made for our memory-forms (retentions, forgettings)— they just produce more combinations and require methods of interpretation and connection that may not fit with conventions of various sorts. There are events "in which terror is closely mingled with movement of selection and freedom" (19). If we cannot stop writing the history of Hitlerism (negative repetition), is this not due to the fact that we keep on looking for the definitive mask that Hitlerism wore, instead of understanding the event called Hitlerism, what it willed and selected, its mixture of terror and freedom, which necessitated its constant change of masks and disguises, along with all the other masks made and dissolved in "the event"? If we cannot "settle" the intentions and roles of intellectuals in mid-1930s fascism and Nazism, isn't this because we could be loathe to figure forth the masks and disguises that the, say, teachers, bureaucrats, parents, artists, and intellectuals wore and circulated (wrote) so as to sustain themselves, to protect themselves, to . . . ? And is this not applicable to any present production of representations? History, according to Deleuze, is not about a present overcoming its distance from the past; it is about selections that are made to affect a future—how we make the past come to life, or any present's use and abuse of history, as we shrink, often, the future to our political and cultural "sizes."

Part I, then, is mostly critical of the tactics and strategies of normal historical representation; part II argues that we can conceive history so that its critical uses are transgressive, or a welcoming of events, which might involve activating public disputes that cannot be "returned" to narration. Part I is concerned with how various senses of the public are given history in ways that are actually abusive, culturally and intellectually speaking. Part II locates theory of history within changed conditions of capital, and stresses new uses of thought and criticism that are, perhaps, ahistorical.

PART ONE

On Reading History

1 | *Nietzsche and Us*

Last Readers

The purpose of this chapter is to embed the critical readings in chapters 2 through 5 in a genealogy of prose and skepticism. The active subtext concerns prose, historiography, and issues of the public, who become the audience for historical narratives. The continuity of historiographic representation, narrations in which readers move through a unified and mixed discourse—causal, descriptive, explanatory—and arrive at satisfaction and understanding, is part of the victory of prose over skeptical accounts of what is involved in belief-in-language. Narrative effect and power are based on the use and abuse of prose—achieved between uses of language that are freed from doubt. How does prose become stable enough to sustain historical narration?

Following up Michel Foucault's influential notion of biopower, the philosopher Giorgio Agamben has it that today "history" appears in applications of biopower: "to make die," as with State-ordered death; "to make live," or to sustain things while other things fade; and "to make survive" (endurance). These three "makings" mean that conceptions of history now pivot *on* conceptions of biopower, almost a conjunction of social physis with modes of discipline and control (structure and process). Agamben's idea is that Auschwitz—radical name—was a *moment* where "the impossible is forced into the real," a violent new process that carried itself beyond its immediate incarnation in the camps.[1] For Agamben, the consequences of this new process bear down on those who survive. The Nazi death camp does not come at the "end" of some historical process as much as it inaugurates the vicissitudes of survival within life and death, survival understood as neither intrinsically sutured to past or to

future, but only to remnants of time.[2] Survivor / to survive might even characterize the becoming-typical subject of Western societies—someone who just
goes on, a blend of the human and nonhuman.[3] Yet when *wasn't* survival the
"fate" of the vast majorities of peoples and milieus; what exactly does
Auschwitz mark? Agamben's inventiveness comes at the intellectual cost of interpreting the movement of modern history as a movement of overall destitution. I cite Agamben here to illustrate this point: none of us can think about a
present, any present, without invoking some sense of adequate representation,
poetic and prosaic language, to figure a sense of process and direction. The instant one makes the kind of judgment Agamben does, up for grabs goes any
present: exactly why is *this* event or process and not another the model for yet
other events and processes? If prose models and forms kinds of truths, what
are the forces of prose in historiography?

The modern author who inaugurated the strongest aporias toward modes of
historical representation was Nietzsche, particularly in his 1872 text, *On the
Advantage and Disadvantage of History for Life.* I would like to start with a few
extractions from this work. For Nietzsche, "history" goes into quotation marks
because it includes not only our discourse, but consideration of its fluidity of
form. Basic acts and processes such as subduing, reacting, self-defense, coun-
teractions, incongruous conjunctions, confusion of weak and strong reactions
are at work in cultural endeavors. Directionality is mixed: from the perspective
of asking as to which prognoses made in certain pasts turned out to be so,
"History is always new and replete with surprise."[4] As with politics, organized
by rivalry and competition, Nietzsche considered that every discourse of goal
is always partly incredible, once we consider rivalry and competition not as
means, but perhaps themselves "the goal" of culture and politics. Do goals
flow from one's means? Aporia toward goals: this is Nietzsche's project, which
is both the destitution of historiography and its necessity, for if historical discourse narrates with mythic goals, giving necessity to means confused with
ends, then we have confused both in the very act of thinking "historically."
    In the wake of such questions, how can historical discourse sort out present
claims and claimants if this historical discourse can only assert the very thing
that legitimizes it: common goals or some equivalent, i.e., the progression of
humanity? The goals are cloudy, and many persons show this today by their
disavowal of taking any position toward historical movement as such. But in
the spheres of culture and professional life, cloudy goals are not determinative,
for the means of cultural competition, however disputed, circulate in all their

intensity. It is the circulation of the means of having a future that concerns us as social beings. Nietzsche asks us to critique present *measures of evaluation,* to engage the forces that permeate existence and becoming, in particular to critique the forms of cultural evaluation we invoke to create hierarchies and other modes of order in any given present. We cannot but speculate on the metaphysics of goals and ends; but we can affirm alternative relations with the devices of cultural sorting, by first doubting them. Doubt can start anywhere; here is an opening that comes not from "ordinary" historical writing, but from an avant-garde line. In considering a "history of stupidity," we are told, "The temptation is to wage war on stupidity as if it were a vanquishable object—as if we still knew how to wage war or circumscribe an object in a manner that would be productive of meaning or give rise to futurity."[5] This opening tells its readers that history has established the futility of resistance to stupidity— war does not work and stupidity is ubiquitous ("circumscribe"), giving the reader a narrative starting point, not unlike what Agamben does with *to survive.* This reminder tells us that we must never relent in continuously adapting to stupidity, probably a good idea, but is this the same thing as making productive concepts for a critique of the present? Is the melancholy toward stupidity an evaluation that has become a prescription—an accepted story?

To call a concept productive for critical use vis-à-vis written history involves an act of invention. Invention to resist narrative: on the premise that the present is not completely determined by inherited discourse, some sense of a present's processes, as narrated, do not cohere with degrees of intensity that readers can bring to compare a historical text and their experience of worldly processes. Historical narration tends to close down this asymmetry between text and a reader's life instead of inviting readers to consider—invent—more signs and figures in relation to other concepts. It is not a question then of "lifting" Nietszchean categories such as the monumental, the critical, and the nostalgic and then measuring the present through these screens; it is a question of interpreting the present with concepts still somehow at war with world-weary bureaucratization of affect, where many people do not actually set goals as much as adapt to narrative linearizations, its "conductive" forms, where periodization sustains a prose narrative that removes a certain degree of skepticism about signs and selection practices.

The "Hard Case" Called Nietzsche

In a major essay on putting Nietzsche's work and life into context, an elusive and complex project, the scholar Allan Megill tells us that to historicize or locate Nietzsche's place in modern intellectual history is to be able to answer the historian's question: "What was the actual character of Nietzsche's project?" This Sartrean concept of finding the overarching coherence in any life-project is seriously doubted by Megill himself. For by the end of his essay, he asserts that Nietzsche, life and writings, gives us a "hard case," historicization suspended on the "complexity" called Nietzsche (life and writings). The "multiplicities of meaning" associated with much of Nietzsche's prose cannot be fitted to the historian's "authoritative account."[6] Nonetheless, Megill postulates four ways to read Nietzsche and, presumably, any other text offering similar complexities: (1) a straightforward reading results in believing Nietzsche a madman, for if read literally, the key texts show us the tragedy of a life severed from reality—Nietzsche's hallucinatory ideas undercut any epistemic import to his writings; (2) a parodic reading, so that Nietzsche's texts are not mad but informed by criticism, the parody recognized by ironic readers, presumably those in on Nietzsche's antipathy toward intellectuals and agencies of profundity, like "holy" books; (3) self-parody, a "great tragedy," or Nietzsche's writings give us something like the impossibility of conceptually fixed meanings, hence a defounding (deconstruction) of all things fundamental, which takes one to the emergence of cultural schizophrenia (see Deleuze and Guattari); and (4) Megill proposes the above three as possibly present in any particular text-scene of reading.

In addition, Megill offers four groups of Nietzsche readers: (1) those that share traditional notions of contextual studies, which relate "inner life" to work and to life-situation, exemplified in trying to figure out if Nietzsche was "gay" by today's criteria, his life and writings not reducible to the binaries of male/female, introvert/extrovert, and so on; (2) special studies, or those that remain continuous with Nietzsche's project of "effective history," so that we *contemporize* Nietzsche-words as a performative model of activism, which Megill also places next to edification, the "chief aim of any humanistic study"; (3) general studies, or those that stress Nietzsche's crossing of "disciplinary boundaries," and which result in acknowledging the "ambiguity of concepts and connectors" of the Nietzsche text-object; and, finally, (4) reception studies, which give us a Nietzsche in full irony, dissolving the very idea of a "Nietzsche legacy," since the amalgam of uses and abuses that Nietzsche's writings have given rise to has thoroughly obscured any basic meaning of the life and writings. In this age of "paradox and conjunction," but rich in cultural experiments, the historian's Nietzsche slips away in the face of Nietzsche-multiplicity. No single type of historical understanding can be sustained, and "rich history," "rich understanding," and "experiential richness" are what we should strive to make out of our hard case, this inability to historicize Nietzsche (life and text) without reduction. *Mutatis mutandis,* Megill's conclusions apply to any really difficult hard case.

Megill's treatment of Nietzsche as a hard case for use in contemporary criticism is altogether exemplary. But I do not think one can get even into the "hard" part without raising more questions. As noted above, Megill accepts that edification is the chief aim of any humanistic study, commonly associated with building character and spiritual improvement. It is unfortunate that edification, a straddle-concept, offered to mediate understanding, which can include both clarity of sense as well as tactical political force, is located in "special studies." The latter is a kind of intellectual and cultural ghetto. Can language be confined to special studies unless one believes it mastered, or thoroughly absorbed, brought under the control of speaking subjects? If the world is actually not built for our representations and idealizations of nature and society—nature as having a purpose, a harmony, society the outcome of a "contract" about goals—then surely it can be argued language in its various functions is more than "special"?[7]

Nietzsche's critical message was that to use language is always risky: at a certain point, our uses and abuses of language end up using and abusing *us,* an epistemic, affective, and political constant about the troubles that humans create with language. Nietzsche does not ask us to become burdened by language, but to instead work conceptual uses of language to their limits. Concepts span multiple discourses, as in phrases like "common being," which are political derivations that gradually, or not, become psychological and habitual; Nietzsche asks us to think the genealogy of a concept every time it is asked to make a difference. It doesn't much matter which method one applies, so long as one does not shut down the process of analysis too quickly, by falling back into notions like analogy, resemblance, or likeness, obliterating the tiniest crucial differences. The genealogy of a concept is its uses, abuses, transformations, disappearances, returns, dissipations, and the like.[8] While all concepts differ from each other, none is transcendent; no superconcept ("globalization," "truth") can overcome a sense of the *asymmetry* between prose and reference, between sign and meaning—existing *disjunctions* between discourse and thing cannot be settled (for long), and are not secondary to some "first" solid value that we are constantly searching for. On such presuppositions, Nietzsche's conceptual disturbance of the "normalcy" of language makes disturbance itself a candidate for a model of critical language; it makes inquiries, for instance, as to why we have so many masks of naïveté (I didn't know = I couldn't pay attention) in reference to the sense *and* satisfying distortions of language?[9] How can knowledge made *aestheticized* be critical when answers are at once satisfying and an aggressive removal of a rival claimant's discourse? This interpretation of cognitive and aesthetic effects calls into question how and when any kind of critical knowledge is actually obtained, irritating those who believe that language makes our relations to the world more complete, more satisfying. Nietzsche carried metaphysical disjunction into the very structure of discourse, if indeed the latter is structured as much as worked.

What gives *Advantage and Disadvantage of History* its ongoing resonance, not assimilable to terms like *modern* or *postmodern,* is that it offered a semiosis of cultural processes. Concepts of modernism and postmodernism locate us before and after, and so acquire their strength via secondary constructs like progress and decline, new and old, archaic and emergence. But Nietzsche argued that what makes culture negatively "stick" are the processes of *psychologization* and *historicization,* which are at once forms of culture and subjectivization, each giving the other a sense of depth and time, including affective continuity. Social scientists tell us that today Germans judge their six-week vacations as part of their employment, while Americans construe vacation as a reward, a payoff—and each appeals to satisfaction and history to legitimize such expectations.

Nietzsche's texts tear us away from the sanctities of our mutable "inner world" and from objective delusions associated with "capturing" history and self. His work made the case for a will-to-skepticism regarding all things conceptual and linguistic, in effect reversing the dominant cultural theory of his day (which is still ours). The question became, in respect to the forces that had dissolved a will-to-skepticism, what to make of the will "as" a majoritarian passive history—how had a will-to-skepticism been turned from critical and healthy grounds to those of submission and fear? Why isn't affirmative and critical skepticism normal? Why is it that cultural endeavors, especially those of criticism, assume defensive attitudes, or otherwise fall into the trap of playing detective with culture, helping us become spectators at the putative mysteries of the world's unfolding? It was strange, for Nietzsche, that we are unable to grant a will-to-skepticism the same reality as desire, self-interest, utopia, to name only three other modes of worldly connection. In particular,

Nietzsche's texts ask us to think to criticism "constrained to return constantly into its own beginnings which was its end, and hence pitiless, pitiless toward [even] human sorrow"—Hermann Broch's phrase from *The Death of Virgil.* These phrases—"thinking-to," "thinking-through"—are very difficult to explicate and can easily suggest that critical truths are achieved by *possessing* some depth or profundity. Not at all: such phrases offer language imaged as "carrying-case terms," concepts to "open a new set of questions," proximate concepts, a process of thinking that is not entirely inviting, since such thoughts are often unwelcome.[10] Highly developed cultural and political systems do not invite mythoclasm, or the critic for whom utopia is dead in its tracks.[11]

The riskiness of language, the internalization of psychologization and historicization, the ambiguous place of skepticism—these are notions from *Advantage and Disadvantage of History* that offer some conceptual openings in a critique of historical representation and, ultimately, address questions of the proliferation of culture and the contest between criticism and historiography. Genealogy works backward only to elucidate a present it wishes to challenge. In the next section, I offer a genealogy of prose that has been all but suppressed in present-day thought, and that informs the later readings of contemporary historians.

Genealogy of an Impossible Relation

Was there ever a time in the West when ideas about criticism and language were free of strife? It is not a mystery that language's sound-to-object connection was already a relation of some ambiguity in the ancient world. Gorgias (550 BCE), in Sicily when it was a frontier—undoubtedly an interloper contested by the then "natives"—made some moves with language that veer toward the (l)edge(s) of writing. One of his fragments proposed something radical about language and thought, addressing *spells,* when language serves unnecessary and, strangely, antipragmatic identifications. The fragment of Gorgias is as follows: "The inspired incantations of words can induce pleasure and avert grief; for the power of the incantations, uniting with the feeling in the soul, soothes and persuades and transports by means of its wizardry . . . persuasion by speech is equivalent to abduction by force . . . what is incredible and invisible appears before the eyes of the mind."[12] Gorgias's proposition is a warning about language transportation. "Inspired incantations" opens onto the figure of a potentially foolish listener, the addressee of "inspired." It is unclear if it is foolish *not* to go along with the comings and goings of a misused conventional or public language. Indeed, Gorgias has recently been paraphrased by Alain Badiou, who insists we think in terms of force, convention, and linguistic authority, not "the revelation or production of the true," philosophy yet again set against Gorgias and skeptical genealogy.[13]

Gorgias's "abduction" does not tell us enough about this interpretation of persuasion, how it might suppose foolishness and its opposite, parody and satire, or laughter toward the effects of "word-spells," satire's response to seriousness. But Gorgias's citation emphasizes the reality of verbal nihilism in the extreme of what happens when discourse is severed from parody and mockery: when all one has is discursive fraternization instead of mobile and mutating interpretations, each vying for credibility and further connections. This fragment tells us that *language brings the "incredible" and "invisible" against the ambivalence of renewal and destruction.* It suggests prose harms concept growth, as Heidegger thought,[14] and Gorgias's warning concerns the success of "incredible and invisible" objects—prose and poetic—becoming part of an expanding prosaics, installed as enduring truths of the social world.

The Greek institutionalization of writing as something lawful, official, and a weapon at the disposal of proper claimants swept aside "dances" such as Gorgias's. As soon as Pindar, for example, could exult in the capacity of words to erect immortality, where "the word lives longer than the deed,"[15] there was already a politics of writing, a becoming-cabal of language, State-sponsored use of prose for the cultural initiation of political values. It will be necessary *to believe* in language, infinitive mode, for participation in anything resembling public life. And there will be no belief without accusations aimed at an unbeliever. In different ways, writing has been a socially approved device of scapegoating, where the vicarious substitutions of words suppress other terms believed to be divisive, or assaults on sanctified belief.[16] Roy Harris has written some stimulating words on the suppressive triumph of the belief in the "likeness" of language to different experiential realms, its installation continuous with the impositions of word-identifications, of which the alphabet is paradigmatic.[17] Scapegoating is an extreme congealing of aggression and identification, political-moral judgments exploiting the vicarious or the capacity to make substitutions of terms; in fact, the modern valoration of public prose brings scapegoating without limits, parody mostly removed as a syntactic possible, where aggression and satisfactions of writing fuse in cult-effects among the most varied groups. Gorgias was calling attention to a sense of captivity brought into being with language, *doxa* as a blockage of thought, persuasion as suppression, language as a social narcotic.

What was required for opinionated belief ("it is so") or believable opinions ("in all likelihood") was acceptance of an underlying fit between grammatical form and social sense, writing reduced to a "ditto device" (McLuhan) or a strange amalgam of repetition, privilege, "no trespass" (Kenneth Burke), and negation. Any profession of writing, like the "discipline" of history, perforce existentializes such relations. From Gorgias on out, contentious arguments about whether or not prose helped or hurt human memory have come and gone, often displaced on the marvel(s) of so much "fine" writing in Western history (the repetition of canon wars). Conflicts between sound and ideas, between ideas and Ideas, between grammars and syntaxes and ideas and sounds, and so on were sequestered by the schools, social groups, political formations, and now, professions, so as to positivize different "intensities of adherence," a modification of all sorts of "nerves," language a resource in the provision of cultural-social expansion and safety.[18] In this genealogy, the very concept of the "word" comes to disclose relational significance between "rumor, fame, reputation, oracle," and also "personal" and "impersonal speech," the "portent," in which social demands connect "divine and imperative words" to basic notions of subjectivity.[19] A critical genealogy of language would at least have to try to demonstrate language's permeability in relation to the ceaseless "unreason" of language. Contemporary causal and inferential notions of language do not account for social passivity toward language, although such accounts do make sense of language interests.[20]

When does prose *give thought* to new beings? When does it serve to "transform our accustomed ties to world and to earth . . . to restrain all usual doing and prizing, knowing and looking, in order to stay within the truth that is happening"?[21] Some historians of rhetoric such as Barthes, in his magisterial "The Old Rhetoric: An Aide-Memoire," wondered if prose was not always "mass communication," the sway of the generally held view. Barthes showed that the medium of prose dominated events of public discourse, restricting poetry, sloganing, psalms, prose routed (in forming various educational matrixes) into eloquence and moral-memory conjunctions. Elaine Scarry has offered that Boethius's *Consolation* joined aesthetic rigor and metaphysical conviction, and stands as a model of prose that helps its readers love even death.[22] Political-cognitive rankings that support durative values have continuously been used to suppress prose's own nonidentity with the likeness of rational discourse. *What is prose "like"*—or is that a Derridean impossible question? How does prose determine matters of intellectual import if it cannot be purified of its own not-so-latent ambiguities with situation, context, authorization, legitimation, play? No one in contemporary criticism has pursued these matters further than Gérard Genette, arguing that a certain "insipid . . . aesthetic of resemblance" undergirds prose's aggression toward other discursive modes.[23] In this sense, prose adds to nihilism when it employs negation as commands and not as disruption, or officiates over an idealization, or devalues in the very name of defending values.[24] The sentences I have just written are extremely close to idealizing a deidealization of prose. Nihilism in language is not negation *simpliciter* but negation stripped of its own death and renewal.

Nietzsche's "On Truth and Lies in a Nonmoral Sense" asked us to consider that prose was not made for transparency, but for conflict—camouflage, tactic, move, shift, jump. Genealogically, it seems necessary to say none of this bespeaks a "wild time" of prose, for the meeting place of "persuasion" and "abduction" already assembled the "obedient specters" of signs, as C. S. Peirce had it, and it has its highs and lows, pleasures, evaporations, commitments, and fixations, none of them "natural." The infrequency of histories of rhetoric—certainly a candidate for "common knowledge"—is probably enough of an indication that idealized models of language must predominate, the alternative something unthinkable: a constant "defounding" of the "founding delusions" of public life if the social bonds are contested by too much pressure on rhetoric. How much energy has been expended in defense of a "social contract," despite all the evidence to the contrary? Gorgias said of writing that it "soothes, persuades and transports." What is at work to sustain and accept the pleasure of force and abduction? Man is a sign, wrote Peirce, talking to Gorgias some twenty-four hundred years later, after mountains, deserts, and oceans of words were divorced from skepticism in the face of forced equivalences between prose and propriety. Contemporary ideas of language as storage, as competence, or as use-value still draw a share from the Western reduction of prose to propriety. What Deleuze called the constant of Platonism is the latter's grafting of the propriety of thought to time: every idea must satisfy its "own time." We should not underestimate the tremendous scope of this compound called propriety, at once a legitimizing and censorious function, which has its own genealogy in the histories of ridicule written and not. Gorgias launched this genealogy of discourse, as can be seen in Vico's argument that the triumph of prose signals an Alexandrine collapse, which also flows into Bakhtin's insistence that the preposterousness of prose is offset by wit, or even close reading, which inquisitors learned very early to master.[25]

There *is* then both intellectual instability and discursive political centerings at the very "start" of recorded Western notions of language. There is more.

Gorgias's fragment also offered that speech or articulation did not "give any information about perceptibles," so that prose or descriptive language belonged to the conceptual *and* to feigned effects, as in the famous ghost in the machine called thought itself. Language and thought are asymmetrical, which is why Gorgias postulated that "reality is not the object of thought" and the "pure mind . . . is a myth,"[26] propositions that emphasized that language brings into being existents whose being is inseparable from language, including hallucinations, deliriums, or less dramatic types of imaginary objects. Effective nihilistic prose, e.g., a sentence of the type "there will always be . . ." does give meaning a function of control, which Barthes made the centerpiece of his reading of discourse on discourse.[27] More often, feigned discourse allows subjects to avoid pinning themselves to language, leaving an escape hatch from the said, where something like a Darwinian command intercedes for the sake of self-protection. We could hypothesize that such an escape is not built in to language as an "engineering excellence" of a technological sort, as Pinker, following language into DNA asserts, but arose as a specific capacity for language-war, which must itself be "feigned" in everyday life, as bluff, raising the ante.[28] It seems to be a distinctive feature of prose discourse that it belongs to crafty skills, more "wet brain" than engineering excellence, but who can say? The genealogy of feints has mostly not been written, but it would have to include feigned necessity ("history calls us"), concern ("our children are the most precious resource"), interpretative models (a hundred years of psychologization of the self), the alignment of *to feign* and cultural voices certified to speak for others, or proprieties of the representative function of language. A prosaic feint is first of all a space to maximize what is said in any here and now; to deploy prose is like any tactical weapon (which can blow up in one's face, as in legal depositions), giving oneself temporal potency, saying and receiving language in accordance with the rule of installing what one can do next. This figure/trope of language as making-a-move crosses discourse at every angle that discourse is joined to reality and truth.

The reign of prose marks the ascendancy of what Vico called the society of contracts, this explicit legal form an extension of grammar and logic, contracts formed on analogical notions of language. *You have promised to pay, a commanding command,* which Nietzsche's *Genealogy of Morals* laid out as a conjunction of sense, scents, and cents, or thinking, tasting, purchasing. Prose became one of the conditions of possibility of concepts offering up models such as generalization and equivalence to authorize states of mind such as completion and resolution, obsessively narrativized and capitalized since the seventeenth century. Like logic and grammar, contracts regulate the production of more determinations (and indeterminations), and, as Deleuze suggests, the contract (of writing) has since become a statute, the danger and ambiguity of prose neutralized as it expands its attractions and repulsions.[29] Vico insisted that prose intertwined self and other, a social nexus mediating exchange and reciprocation, and he compared regimens of phrasing to a mesh, suggesting that language is not a place, but a series of forces internally heterogeneous yet also capable of great containments. Vico tells us that "all the fictions of ancient jurisprudence were truths under masks . . . verbal safeguards or formulae," at times little more than expressions of penalties realized in blood.[30] A lot of mayhem *and* reduction helped convert Gorgias's what is "incredible and invisible" into Vico's sense of language as "eyes of the mind," normalized through cliché and stereotype, and today expressed, among other ways, in the politeness of, say, so much professional discourse.

What Gorgias construed as being "transported" by writing, Vico called the "firm traces" left by the command of nouns in language, compression of "all feasible things" to the imperative mode. As imperative, this indicated a sense of terror about language—when does anyone's words matter by comparison to the delivery of a great "No!"? Why are there extensive rules to protect a few words at any given time in every important area of cultural-political conflict? For Vico, the imperative mode was carried over from fathers to civil society, the "legitimate succession" of human relations, in which one adheres to the "communication" of the imperium, the "making of testaments."[31] An "it will be remembered so" fell over things, delivered by words that could not be taken back. Nietzsche will call this memorialization in and as language the transformation of sensation and image into concept, where the latter merged with the "cool breath" of logic and the rigor mortis of metaphor, a kind of intellectual stagflation.[32] After Vico, many of the feints of the humanities are ever present—to recode needs and disciplines—since skepticism itself was successfully overcoded as acts of withdrawal and alienation, something to avoid.

The conjunctions between "wizardry" and "force" raised by Gorgias are a constant refutation of the humanities' claim to offer finality. Everything can be made to disappear through wordedness (Foucault). For Vico, there is a cycle that involves the ruin of contracts, an exhaustion and disgust with contracts, linguistic or otherwise. Prose, Vico continued, was formed by the imposition of the mechanism of contraction—the "innumerable diverse articulate sounds" of language reduced to "intelligible genera" so as to make relations of all sorts imposable (the taming of divergence). Disruption of orders and commands, especially by ridicule and humor, logical gaming and raising of the ante, was channeled into the vicariousness of verbal satisfactions. In remarkable passages, Vico tells us that domestication absorbed the relations between words and things, words and words.[33] Recently, this domestication has been cast again by Harold Bloom. He insists that one who would write something worth reading must accept a Scene of Belatedness, where the to-be-said by any new text must show its indebtedness to the authority of the already-written (the canon, of which Vico noted that it meant both church law and *rents*). Bloom, as befits a psychoanalytic critic, makes the concept of belatedness, Nietzschean latecomers, equivalent to "the fear of time's revenges . . . the dungeon for the imagination." A social arrangement, this aesthetics of belatedness is turned by Bloom into a "fatality" for every subject, an imperative to control forces of writing that might be indifferent to the Western canon, of not accepting that writing is a "debt." How do you pay the dead(bt)? By joining with them: Bloom's ideas are made of self-abduction and wizardry, joining internalization of dread to not being "out-of-scene." An incarnated sense of loss drives the articulation of Bloom's terms. Utterly prejudiced by the hallucinogenics of the word *loss,* Bloom rampages on his readers, insisting that immortality is the only poetic stake, the only worthy stake of writing, another piece of the Higher Melancholy of Western thought.[34]

Vico was convinced that interrogative modes, question and answer, mixed with "solemn words," rendered an imperium of discourse, a "contract of receiving under one's power clothed with solemn words in which certain and precise stipulations were conceived . . . symbolized by a feigned force." Imaginative universals were put to the work of providing "verbal safeguards and formulae."[35] When interrogation is not a question but the suppression of an answer, there is cause for wondering how skepticism toward prose could be effective.

Why I Read Nietzsche (1): Last Writing

The critic and historiographer Michel de Certeau emphasized that today "the real now jabbers away." The animate and inanimate freely mix, as in the ubiquity of testing ourselves with things as much as with words. Giving reasons for various pretenses, or the many rationalizations of interest, makes our discourses add to symptomatology, not truth. The "cynicism and piety" that Deleuze and Guattari insisted is a condition of intellectual evaluations in mature capitalism has become a norm of public life. The "real" that "jabbers away" belongs to social physics, where production, consumption, structure, and event blend, as in the common "tie-in" between newspaper, book, commodity, and their timing for *impact.* There is no getting away from *to jabber,* infinitive mode. In this, critical uses of language are kept to minimal functions, with obvious exceptions (some literature, some literary theory, etc.). In a capitalist social order, discourse becomes an object of fear if it installs meanings that are reversible *and* unwithdrawable—if people mean what they say. A reign of pragmatism brings perpetual recoding of change under a stipulation of reactivity, as Nietzsche put it. Discourse is ceaselessly devalued, overvalued, undervalued, and revalued, reiterated as the figure of a "conversation of the public" that seems to have no effect on social transformation.[36] For intellectuals, professional discourse becomes what Nietzsche called "border patrolling," a mode of elite "intellectual housekeeping," a *last writing,* which has no date.

A "last writing" is not just an historical succession or phase of development, signaling collapse of bourgeois heroics. More strongly, last writing involves a ruinous self-contradiction brought to public and large slices of intellectual, professional life. Michel Haar has written that the "last man" so prominent in Nietzsche's imagery figures forth an agent *comfortable with absences,* a subject type that requires acceptance of absence as constitutive of experience of the real. "Last writing(s)" are comfortable with weak signification, and they show when a reader can detect that it is *in the name of an absence that one writes.* Added to a larger indifference, absences extend into adjacent experiences, or grow oxymoronically, analogous to an increase in debts owed to an imaginary past and nonrealized future. Last writing seems extraordinarily suited to contemporary America. The contention over Murray and Hernstein's book on IQ in 1995, *The Bell Curve,* suggests some of what is at stake. Denouncing it as unscientific and racist, shoddy, illogical, etc., the reviewing processes, from the *New York Times* out, made the book *sayable,* positive as an object to be refuted, valuable as part of the visibility of antiracism, ensuring not only that *race* remained a word in force, in circulation, but calling forth more absence—of the question as to why race can spell us so thoroughly. Last writings include those "important" books that seem to make available the very public conversations we are to want and need, but it is difficult to think of any such public text that does not add an absence to the inventory of cultural debt, or to needs that simply disappear according to no one knows what timescale.

I read Nietzsche because I am besieged by words of command. The most dangerous commands are rendered in a conjunction of aesthetic and rational judgments, in conceptual unities that issue absences that serve as injunctions, delivered in propositions that obey the rules of the unsaid.[37] "We must work hard to give to students what we were given," the command-word of a teacher, and a last word too because predicated on nonbeing. Last words are the ones that place things *under command*. These commands are now so vast as to nearly defy classification.

The demonization of Paul de Man and canonization of Derrida are merely the extremes of the normal processes of intellectual purification once last writing is at work in the changed and hypercharged circumstances of our collective oxymoronics. We live out, collectively, a period Barthes quite rightly called fascist in its language, meaning much of what passes for public discourse knocks us down. Institutions radically prosify themselves, wrap themselves in new "validities" (Barthes), while the public swears off its connection to any "indigence" of signification (Nietzsche), as it simultaneously elides its own intellectual comprehension. Academia itself has become part of gossip, where its leading trade magazine, the *Chronicle of Higher Education,* offers a weekly column on whining about the unfairness of academic employment; in another register, the Getty Institute solidifies in Los Angeles a newer institution that lays claim to building the best archive of contemporary art and so moving even closer to objects that will enable the Getty to market recent art as history. Nietzsche gives a cogent sense of this whirl of value and negation of indigence in a discussion of language conceived as a peace treaty: "This art of dissimulation reaches its peak in man. Deception, flattering, lying, deluding, talking behind the back, putting up a false front, living in borrowed splendor, wearing a mask, hiding behind convention, playing a role for others and for oneself . . . as if hanging on dreams on the back of a tiger . . . This peace treaty [language] brings in its wake . . . a uniformly valid and binding designation invented for things, and this legislation of language likewise establishes the first laws of truth . . . Is language the adequate expression of all realities?"[38] Pushing on a line that runs from Gorgias to Vico, that connects order and chaos, command and surprise, Nietzsche frames signification as incessant politics, evoking a last reader only competent enough to displace language-trouble. Life becomes a busy exhaustion of representation, the mental expenditures required to save the "necessary," to keep belief in obedience alive. The idea of a last reader here means the search for stability and territory: protection of boundaries inclusive of practices, rights, transmission of present to future. Think of words that American universities cannot abandon, like *excellence* and *quality,* that blackbox possible upheaval about themselves. Everyone is a last reader of something and someone. For example, under pressure to reform rigid boundaries that seal history departments off from the practices of other disciplines, some historians do not speak to a discipline of history now but rather to an "enclosure," more permeable than a discipline, with its exclusive undertones (see chapter 5). For Nietzsche, out of language's capacity to legislate (authorize) and to dissimulate, discourse is always involved in "playing a role," language intrinsically mask and disguise, interwoven with various peace treaties. Barbara Johnson, for example, has argued language is inclusive of both "complexities of fact" and "impulses of power," language at once conditional knowledge and social injunctions.[39]

The reverberations of writing figured as peace treaty suggests discourse is also a component of a war machine. As a peace treaty, discourse is less an expression of things to be settled by negation than it is a symptom and form of the variations of power. We are enjoined today to consider current retrospectives about Jackson Pollack the Westerner, Pollack the Psyche of America, Pollack the almost "unsubject," and each of these locations places Pollack at different angles to peace and war—high art and Pop (which quickly dissolved as a distinction), a new norm for art history to narrate, even if the end of norms. Simply: why is it so difficult to acknowledge links between social and cultural violence (exclusions, restrictions, blacklistings) and language? Further, Nietzsche's sense of language valued its micrologic capacity for making ever finer differences, hence more interesting conflicts, and not language's capacity to provide answers. When sociobiologists like Pinker inform us that language is "impression management," they are renaturalizing language—making it continuous with a clear function and purpose; yet "management" already implies war/peace over representation, as do concepts of reflection and coming-to-terms with various recalcitrant realities. Language, according to Nietzsche, can be controlled: but the controls always "stick out," i.e., as metaphorical repetition, as arbitrary classification, as rigid designators (Kripke). Despite the genealogy of taming prose, all modes of signification involve an "overleaping of spheres," where a statement combines logic, time, and sense that enables us to jump from demand to proofs to assertions to innuendo to . . . a genealogy, again, that involves language in soothing, dominating, and resisting at once.[40]

In sum, Nietzsche asks us to think when and how discourse/language can be said to matter, no mean feat since language both represses, often as metaphor, and sublimates its own repressions, for instance, "in the form of ideals of social justice."[41] Shibboleths, euphemism, cliché are not accidental to language's capacity to represent, but are intrinsic to the creation of self-satisfying, self-consuming conceptual unities. Genealogical probes have to notice that metaphors (of limits), satisfactions (of recuperating some "lost" past), or the ranking of claimants involves each subject in the mesh of multilayered processes of selection. And that notice opens onto Darwinian competition, questions as to language's role in cultural and political selection, how artists and intellectuals can make selection an event of intensity. Nietzsche: "thou refusest to stand still and dismiss thy thoughts before an ultimate wisdom, an ultimate virtue, an ultimate power,—thou hast no constant guardian and friend in thy seven solitudes—thou livest without the outlook on a mountain that has snow upon its head and fire in its heart—there is no longer any requiter for thee, nor any amender with his finishing touch . . . art opposed to any kind of ultimate peace."[42] Yes, Nietzsche's imagery is caught itself in the emotion of "celibacy" ("no constant," "without"), using grammatical tropes/figures; here, art *is* a mode of critical signification, so that "without any ultimate peace" hardly then constitutes language as a "special study," in Megill's classification, cited at the outset of this chapter. This art, of war-in-language, involves an existentialism of language and art—art is not peace but the techniques of making more interesting selections, preparations for conflict, becoming armed for different purposes. Much of this is transferred, as we will see, more or less directly into historiography.

Language, Visibility, and Intellectuals

Here, I want to bring the foregoing comments to bear on contemporary life by considering newer cultural-political forms "tested" through some basic senses of a "public intellectual." The latter is discussed because it is a boundary object—a whirl of media, institutional, and subjective interests difficult to resist, as well as a political index with "communicative" functions that relate "public" to intellectual production, a mode and object of credibility. Though "public" and "intellectual" are at some point allergic to the other, or should be, according to Pierre Bourdieu, the phrase, Fredric Jameson insists, is predicated on a "single white lie," that of scholarship's claim of distance from its objects. Jameson says there is no such distance other than the rhetorical and negative one of trying to withhold one's prejudices from exposure: writing as sheer skill in giving and withholding. Without this lie and skill, scholarship would lose its few advantages over other types of writing, notably its use of research to make archival-type referents, giving truth to policies. Without this illusion of distance, "public intellectual" dissolves into identity and/or interest-politics. At least Jameson acknowledges lie as constitutive of what passes for truth. It is worth asking why intellectuals cannot publicly affirm the pretensions of public Enlightenment, that the latter rests as much on wish and error as anything else?[43] Again, consider that in *Advantage and Disadvantage of History,* Nietzsche wrote about a certain "aura" required to produce an art object (critical artifacts, literary texts), an aura in maximum distance from the meddler's gaze, from the paranoia as well as ecstasies of others, from verbal overlays of all sorts. Nietzsche was suggesting that "public" had come to name a process that destroys all aura and nuanced atmosphere, which might be glimpsed in today's ubiquitous evocation of visual "wonder" to reimpart what passes for aura.

Of the interstices between public and intellectual, Nietzscheist ruminations reach a conceptual threshold that is nothing less than dizzying. As public culture is reduced to a politics of satisfaction, Nietzsche called for a writing entirely experimental, in the sense of overthrowing the author as the subject of writing, proposing what Roland Barthes would later call a middle voice. That is, to make writing a variation that allows for all sorts of effects and affects, conjunctions of cognitive strangeness with less-than-satisfying aesthetic moods—to crack up the glaciers of the public. Further, intellectual work is caught in a vicious game: the more we interpret, the more visible we make some "it and this," and much representation/writing actually puts to death the very things that allowed an "it" to come into being. Deleuze frequently referred to this process as the *death of the outside:* an active unconscious began to fade exactly after psychoanalysis "discovered" it; liberal capitalism's current social responsibilities dried up exactly after they were exposed—witness Clinton's insistence on passage of a violent antiwelfare law. Is this another way of saying that what becomes public is a series of replaceable absences? "Public" comes to include, if not mean, little more than a moment's entertainment. For intellectual work to mean something, it must become *positively metaphysical* in facing this scene, cultural production inseparable from the destruction of experience, part of even an *entropology,* as Lévi-Strauss put it. If social dilemmas pile up without disruptive conceptual discourse, a point is reached where language has virtually nothing to say—the more it says all the "its" of the world. The savagery with which some contemporary artists berate language is not entirely anti-intellectual; they know all too well the disasters of visibility.

Is there a discernable process that establishes a public intellectual? Thomas Pavel believes that there are three markets or domains of visibility for intellectuals: the first is made up of the couple specialist-peers, where works are judged valuable or not within a narrow community devoted to the solving of problems; then come those works valuable or not to larger groups (politicians, marketeers, et al.); and then there is a diffuse public taste, which can incorporate texts that testify to its own ruination as well as to its possible enlightenment. For Pavel, no cultural or political process should short-circuit the first market, and Pavel is upset that certain writers, e.g., Lyotard and Deleuze, have stepped outside of the only market which should judge them, other specialist-peers.[44] Philosophers like Quine should decide whether or not Deleuze's use of logical forms is adequate to philosophy. The question of the visibility of the intellectual-as-expert—consecrated dissident, loyal oppositionist, innovator, and so on—is complicated and even perverse.[45] What are the mechanisms by which peers evaluate each other if they themselves are rival claimants for the same intersections of prestige and authority as those they evaluate? Stanley Katz, president of the American Council of Learned Societies, a group that knows about prestige and authority, writes that "institutions and individuals today are looking for the main chance. They want to be rich and they won't let anything distract them from that." Pavel's model works only if we attribute to the first market a space of thinking beyond language and interest. The demands placed upon scholarly writing, to be accessible, appropriate, timely, necessary, are demands of the visible, a process the functions and effects of which are troublesome; it is at times unclear how visibility and knowledge coexist.

For Nietzsche, public and intellectual life was an oxymoron, since "public" filled the slot of "the eye of the witness,"[46] to ensure that representation *has* an other: "We leave ourselves at home when we go to the theatre; we there renounce the right to our own tongue and choice, to our taste, and even to our courage as we possess it . . . No one takes his finest taste in art into the theatre with him, not even the artist who works for the theatre: there one is people, public, herd, woman, Pharisee, voting animal, democrat, neighbor, fellow-creature . . . there stupidity operates as wantonness and contagion."[47]

Why I Read Nietzsche (2)

Now comes *impact-time*. The most visible texts are power markers instead of intellectual transformers. In bringing the objects of writing under control, knowledge is forced to magnify its interest in satisfaction, an aesthetics within knowledge, but which increasingly threatens to consume its critical aspects. Knowledge is supposed to oppose illusion but needs it in the forming of public credibility—but Apollonian illusion has a way of absorbing criticism and truth, as in the case of Lacanian psychoanalysis, where the "style" enveloped its conceptual "edge." Visibility and the slippery image of a public intellectual rely on metaphor and substitution, both also caught up in the forgetting of public life that may have become a *simulation* of the public, an aesthetics of illusion.[48] Paul de Man: "All rhetorical structures are based on substitutive reversals, and it seems unlikely that one more such reversal over and above the ones that have already taken place would suffice to restore things to their proper order."[49] Only a nihilist would take de Man's statements as pessimistic. Is the "community of historians" based on more than "common methods and aims" which cannot even be stated?[50] Should we speak of a generalized aesthesis—a *je ne sais quoi* effect? Don't the humanities ride on the back of the tiger, where any day may bring an obsolescence undreamed of?

As Sarah Kofman has argued, Nietzsche worked from the hypothesis that thought and word-phantoms are inseparable, which makes cultural telos (or antitelos) strange. Metaphor offers us a truth so that we do not "die of truths" that are too paradoxical to digest. *How to experiment and not serve the visibilities of representation* that are instant fodder for soon-to-disappear public contentions? It is these experiments in language that matter, it being *unsettled* just what these experiments "look like." Nietzsche emphasized that language is life enhancing when it brings into being thoughts that abandon overt communicative functions, to effectuate an "exhilaration of language," adding to the "capacity for the apprehension of incorporeal transformations; an aptitude for grasping language as an immense indirect discourse" (Deleuze and Guattari).[51] Apprehension is not to be confused with connoisseurship. This is tangled business. Millions of former Soviet citizens were caught up, by many accounts, in the exhilaration of the name Stalin, almost a psychological engraving of positive experience and memory; yet that very exhilaration suppressed the concept of a society that was outside the reach of the State. Don't we have just as dangerous metaphorical/illusion/truths with our own "triumphant" capitalism? The aim of Soviet "communication" was that name = truth; now consumption is an aim of American communication—to consume the visible, giving a role for artists, the humanities, the schools. In the name of what should one resist?[52]

Human suffering and pain are today unchallenged as determining the need to write—recall Agamben's argument, discussed above. But to make pain and suffering sustain criticism involves a restriction of choice and selection, stitching them to psychological distress, where new incantations can force a larger indifference. Nietzsche endeavored to think through this coagulation of forces, "needs" and aestheticization, knowledge and misrepresentation. He thought that at the point where language comes to psychologize and historicize, there also comes "the will to infect and to poison the fundamental basis of the universe with the problem of punishment and guilt, in order to cut off once and for all any escape out of this labyrinth of 'fixed ideas,' [a] will for rearing an ideal . . . The ascetic ideal in the service of projected emotional excess."[53] Our hard case wrote hard words. Because word and debt are as much related as word and representation—there are genealogical relations between *to promise* and *to continue* a memory,—when words become statutes, they do so as a conjunction of the "speaking voice, the marked body, and the enjoying eye."[54] To speak, to mark, to enjoy—the eyewitness has the advantage, but again, how does this matter in terms of intellectual-public life? Visible "stamp[s] of the sign" engulf cultural relations with "memorable" words, which, in turn, block submergence, or "going down" with words. Our best universities can give students a sample of this going down—juxtapose, as we do, styles and genres from radically different experiences—but prefer to emphasize promises of identity and fulfillment. There is plenty of retreat to "ontological priority of the sensuous object" (de Man), or belief in a necessary relationship between word and world: each can choose their own prison-house of representation.[55] In this regard, the contemporary psychoanalytic model of an "inevitability of disappointment" makes sense: it offers a restricted economy of satisfaction so as to lessen social friction.[56] As de Man noted in his analysis of Adorno's fragmentary style, Adorno's choice to use the fragment as a literary device to mimic the world's fragmentation supposes a finality of form, negative unity. Should artists and intellectuals deprive their works of satisfaction? Is that possible?[57]

Why I Read Nietzsche (3): The Last Reader

A last reader comes when reading is nearly finished as a creative and joyous destruction of what is read, including one's most possessive thoughts. Especially the latter. The "metamorphosis of the world into man" (Nietzsche) has, as consequence, drawn language into a created humanistic void, the "hardening" and "congealing" of metaphor, now one of the triumphant modes of figuring a nihilism we can live with. Nietzschean epistemology is a matter of taking distance when language settles into such rhetorical satisfaction; it tries to be rigorously sensitive to the possessive and holding operations of language and logic, a continuation of Gorgias's insights about wizardry and the social. A last reader is exhausted by epistemology, to the detriment of intellectual and social transformation, for to bypass epistemic problems is a symptom of linguistic politics, i.e., the imposition of common meanings that are highly disputable.[58] Last readers are driven to moral and aesthetic choices with only enough epistemology to quiet the scandal—of the potential groundlessness of the most deeply held beliefs and premises. When the national Republican Party invoked the figure of the contract (1994) in pursuit of its political, financial, and moral aims, "contract" idealized and aestheticized; it withers if epistemics get near it—how could the model of a contract evaluate social fairness or cultural waste, which are part of the political game? Intellectuals of all sorts need such phrases to sort ourselves, objects, places, memories, but is this already "a will satisfied with meaninglessness . . . having found a certain comfort . . . and a certain happiness" in nihilism?[59] I read in the *New York Times Book Review* that Benjamin Franklin biographies are said to be at the point of bursting with redundancy, "whatever the source of our current fascination with the founding generation," but what else is it but pleasant nihilism when I learn from this review, as "fresh information," that Franklin "investigated ways to make flatulence less odorous"?[60]

A last reader consumes words and images as the audience, and its easy consummation of language, come first. When discourse is driven by lastness, then values, interpretations, and beliefs are severed from *amor fati,* or chances for difference. A last reader works language with the sensibility of one for whom the burden of selecting and choosing has become defensive and self-protective. The professor, curator, gallery owner, publisher enact these relations, however progressive they may be. Nietzsche thought the aggravation of antagonisms alone allows us to continue to will, and is not helped along when prose is subjected to a fusion of economics-politics and fashion at every turn, including the fashion of antifashion. Claims, say for cultural identity, can be installed by last readers as the fear of an affirmative renunciation: who is brave enough to say, in relation to all things Nazi/German and Jew, that coming-to-terms-with-Nazism never actually happened, and many of its cultural effects that claimed to come to terms were as much moralistic self-satisfaction, and that careers in representation are made there, or that it is an epistemic scandal to claim that representation serves the victims? The shadow of the last reader reaches into the mind's relation to language whenever, as Nietzsche argued, interpretation confuses what is "individual and actual" with a concept that is neither,[61] where words are the master and the subject their puppet (Gorgias: "wizardry" and "abduction"). For example, Michael Berube calls for intellectuals to "talk regular" in matters public and critical, because intellectuals "have to be willing to restate other people's work and forgo the pleasure of producing the new."[62] Such is the acceptance of prosaic passive nihilism—the public must be raised to the threshold of an Enlightenment that does not, must not, overstimulate, overthink.

As noted above, Nietzsche argued language cannot wear an "expression of indigence" when it is offered to the public—it does not evoke a poverty of its means, appear insolvent, or inadequate.[63] Highly public and publicized words on Frank Gehry's titanium-covered museum at Bilbao displaces Bilbao as a colony of New York's Guggenheim juggernaut, but why not name Bilbao a "beautiful colony" as its chief name? Apollonian style or love of the appearance for the sake of appearance overdetermines writing: style may be said to precisely kill off intellectual individuation and tangles of thought—they go together—and in its reduced state, "style" is inseparable from "civic mediocrity," the removal of the "drunken satyr" from the public realm.[64] The public sphere enacts rhetorics of satisfaction, the writing of the lasting and the monumental—impact-value, but without dates. What criticism could open the ground where problems are posed that cannot be answered without changing the stakes of the problems?[65] There is already a lifetime of reading on what happened to Elvis Presley—each book trying to give some saving nomination, resolving theory—what it was *like* to be so infamous and so dumb, so talented and so inept; to what end such writings but more lastness (here melancholia and cynicism)? The equation between desire and disappointment, already mentioned, its "realism," words-up an "inner world" as having a form of representation structured by a philosophy of failure. Are Pascal's questions better: "Who dispenses reputation? Who makes us respect and revere persons, works, laws, the great?" We "pursue the phantom[s]" of our "imaginary sciences" and stake belief on the "glitter of metaphorical intuitions . . . this immediacy of deception." Pascal knew about the attraction of thought for diminished affect, the safety of conventions, the price to be paid for repressing "continually inflowing illumination," or language-turbulence.

The last reader's rampant and immediate will-to-knowledge and power, control and use, even in "writing the void," is immodestly *timely:* relevant, within the scene, part of the contest for meaning. What is judged timely in criticism is the pressure of the compulsion to know something right now; but in doing this, what is known is turned into comfort and recognition.[66] The history of the dissemination of Pop art in the United States has thoroughly saturated it in the rhetorics of the commonplace, an art without danger. Timely are those command-words that stamp a date on things, short to long, the sayable and the writable falling under the spell of the acceptable imposition: Pop art is nothing but "you" up close, Mr. and Mrs. and Ms. Last Reader. Something must be said now—the collapse of writing into provision and supply, hardly different from going to the store, not different from shopping.[67]

So the last reader is part of the extinction of writing and reading—an intensity and continuation of prose; as writing succumbs to the timely, countless sentences add raw material for a nihilism of the present—the Iraq war (2003) has spawned countless words, all conceivably pointless in relation to what that event becomes as used in future global political wrangling. The theological underpinnings of writings are thereby strengthened: always a few words are sent upward to serve as transcendental signifiers, saving us from the consequences of the dissolution of our discourses. Words like *globalism, multiculturalism, market discipline,* new singular universals assume one's agreeable sense, even if it is mad. Or perhaps because it is so. Consider some recent history. The writer Slavoj Žižek has insisted that post-1989 Eastern European societies wanted to acknowledge their long-suppressed desires. With the fall of the Soviet system, their liberated "desire," he insists, fell under the swoon of a new transcendental signifier, a "most sublime image," an "enthusiasm" over the "hole in the flag."[68] After the Fall, East European societies felt the absence of a genuine symbolic order, hence their enthusiasm had to void the symbolics of one system (Soviet vacuity) and only then could these Easterners understand what was happening to them. Are we unable to describe without such transcendental supports, without reliance on absence and transcendental signifiers? But what if this type of signifier comes with the last reader, in this example, the theorist's discourse and its insistence on maintaining imbecilic desire beneath the social and the cultural?[69]

The last reader is a manner of preserving ourselves once we have already given in—each preserves an image of something "higher" (lower) instead of something effectual, this in support of a larger *adiaphoria* or indifference to life. To survive? Denis Hollier, in his superb reconstruction of the College of Sociology in Paris (1937–39), introduced a collection of readings from these French intellectuals by saying, "One thinks a lot when afraid. And even more when one is afraid of being afraid. And even more when one is afraid of what one thinks. Afraid to think. Afraid of the thought."[70] Hollier directs us away from last readers and toward these intellectuals who tried to become "an impassioned subject that disrupts its own cognitively and programmed statements . . . [and] such a discursive subject can also interrupt and shift its own narrative rationality, and follow a passional pathway, or it can even perturb it with discordant pulsations."[71] That is an accurate statement of Nietzscheist formalism. Any such "positive disequilibrium" must be invented and cannot be separated from "the agonies of individuation . . . dismemberment," even a metempsychosis, "to see oneself transformed before one's own eyes and to begin to act as if one had actually entered into another body, another character."[72] This is not Gorgias's abduction, but rather to make becoming.

A dominant linguistic function correlated with the properties of discursive reactivity is the imaginary being of a present *third-party* perspective, where, in addition to the "sufferer and the spectator," the third person considers experience for the advantage to be gained from presentifying it: judges and justice, scholars and truth, the clergy that soothes the way. This third party, figure of mediation and transition, connection and network, installs within discourse a "brakeshoe," as Nietzsche put it, *truth-in-reception,* the discussable reduced from the speaker to the hearer: "the person who does not act considers that he possesses a natural light over action, that he deserves to derive advantage or profit from it."[73] The world is now brimming with these third-party perspectives, the new prose of the world. Do new centers of representation void the possibility of introducing difference into representation, as much as they entice us to represent? This third person has been installed as a social necessity, as an historical inevitability, a bit of transcendental judgment within immanence, but often serves to dissolve multiple perspectives, canceling the errant and wayward thought. Recourse to idealized mediators and representations limits the differential element of action, restricts selection, so as to salvage an advantage—experience delivered by prose decisions of "we must, we should." Giving an economy of the signifier, turning multiple contentions into the form of settling a debt, writing in the grip of third parties makes the fewest words say the most; force is quantified, as when someone says that "debt is a prison" or "art is irresponsible," where a piece of transcendence is made available for reassurance. For example, in a review of Francis Fukuyama's book *Trust,* the follow-up to his *End of History and the Last Man,* Richard Kaplan summarizes Fukuyama's assertion that, as to world conflicts, "cultures where suspicion reigns cannot create the necessary organizational links that fuel economic growth. Japan's industrial policy . . . derives organically from Japanese culture." Evaluated as to the force involved in this, one immediately notices a vast but simple assertion: no culture has a future if it is suspicious, a rationalization for the suppression of suspicion. Those who suppress suspicion have a future.[74] This shaky rationalization is normalized by the grammar of acceptance, which is the sense of "derives organically." Can this be outwritten when it comes with institutional leverage (I read it in . . .)?

Why I Read Nietzsche (4)

I started by considering a scholar's superb synthesis of how Nietzsche (life and writing) has been assembled by contemporary intellectual history. The argument has been that, concerning language and its practice as discourse, Nietzsche's texts are still ahead of us. Alone of the "masterthinkers," a hideous concept, is the truth that Nietzsche's texts cannot be mastered, and for a very good reason—this thinker kept making concepts difficult to absorb as normal representation. His texts do not offer "moral abrogation" or some "abolishing negation" (of what pains us, of what we must endure) but rather open to "an intelligent body that . . . accelerates itself in the course of its composition of self toward language, toward the intellect, and toward justice in a manner that is stringently perspectival, 'constructive,' 'eliminating,' and 'destructive.'"[75] We should try *to deneuroticize our relations to language.* But most of the time, we use discourses that give finalities and loopholes at once; we anthropomorphize it in the hope of making it reflect ourselves, but reflection has no end—or better, perhaps no referent that is not already partly fictive. I started with goal-doubt: it is time to ask if there are goals of language. Language is said to be "for" communication, "for" resolving problems, "for" cultural agreement. But one can also say of language and culture exactly what Kant affirmed of the concept of the sublime: "it is a point of excess for the imagination . . . like an abyss in which it fears to lose itself."[76] Is it language fear that supports the installation of unformalizable interpretations that we never stop trying to institutionalize?[77] It is crucial, then, that attempts to establish language on some foundation or other like "communication," "persuasion," "syntax," "form," "unity" be seen as political impositions, with cognitive determinations, emotional affects, cultural reverberations, and more.

In cultural terms, public language—as in a newspaper editorial—serves as a template regulating disputes by circulating aestheticizing satisfaction and cannot activate linguistic-formed problems for this public. This is not a question of putting mystery back into a disenchanted world, but of speaking in the world. We have had two hundred years of various types of Enlightenment as to how to use language for resolutions of one type or another, and every one of them has crashed in a heap of simultaneous cynicism and piety.

Nietzsche's ruminations on language and force oppose all mechanistic interpretations, as well as unprivilege metaphor: all of his energy was expended in supporting "new laws of motion of force."[78] Force contends with the passive-aggressive mode. The latter is language's "columbarium," or vault that holds the ashes of cremated sense—our public life. If language allows for the "imitation of temporal, spatial, and numerical relationships in the domain of metaphor," then critique *tears* the "web of concepts," opens language, "pairing the most alien things and separating the closest," offering the most "unheard-of combinations of concepts." This should not be reduced to an imitation "of the impression of the powerful present intuition."[79] Thus, in the perspective of extreme contention within today's humanities and arts, Nietzsche's writings point the way to a job: that of working the impasse posed by last readers, to subvert conjunctions of aesthetics and politics or remain permanently suspicious of language, with variable relations to it. The genealogy of prose distances one from word-spells, and, in this sense, what could today be more comic than Nietzsche as epistemologist—but that is exactly where this hard case transports us. The next four chapters discuss prose and its historiographic use and abuse.

2 ■ *How to Make an Ahistorical People*
The Island Taiwan

*It is not a matter of identifying with various historical
personages, but rather identifying the names of history with
zones of intensity.*

Deleuze and Guattari, *Anti-Oedipus*

Ahistorical does not mean to lack history—it designates those times when a
people or group cannot be assimilated to Western narratives without such narratives exposing their political biases. To narrate, to politicize, to historicize—
to call something ahistorical is to ask about existing politics of discourse,
which includes institution and public.

Names designate, denote, and associate at once and so are peculiar objects:
names are transits for innumerable actions and events, at once full and empty,
or can be, and are always loaded, even if their contentiousness has momentarily slipped below the line of fight.

Taiwan and *Taiwanese* are fully contested names. Outside Taiwan, these
names do not have the historical value that *Asia, China,* or even *Hong Kong* are
said to embody. In most Western discourses, *Taiwan* and *Taiwanese* are bound
to analogies and comparisons, incorporated by association with China and the
current hegemony of American-European-led globalization and China's latest
"leap" forward. Taiwan is caught between mainland China's drive for historical legitimacy—the governing fiction of "One China"—and America's drive to
financial, technical, and cultural outlets and cash inflows. In one sense, mainland Communist Party and American policies move to the same beat over Taiwan. Their mutual, if diverging interests of realpolitik are crystallized in
China's internal shoring up of State credibility by making the "renegade
province" return to its place, complemented by America's need for markets in
China. *Taiwan* and *Taiwanese* are also contested in Taiwan, this along a number of fault lines. There are political groups that disagree about the form of in-

clusion with the mainland; cultural groups disagree about how to sort out the legacies of all the peoples who have ventured to Taiwan, including strong aboriginal claims recognized by the U.N.; groups busy trying to capitalize on globalization, to avoid politics and culture and remain within Confucian family lines; and groups that embrace Taiwan's specific current social relations, of which its contemporary film and literature give numerous examples. In short, *Taiwan* and *Taiwanese* are not stable names.

A first purpose of this chapter is to underscore the work of stable and non-stable historical representations about the names *Taiwan* and *Taiwanese,* which means to bring out representations in *opposition* to mainland China's narrative and American interests. Second, and more important, is to argue that the persistent instability of the names *Taiwan* and *Taiwanese* can be interpreted as a continuous *discontinuity,* even a *Taiwanese resistance to history*—something more affirmative than opposition. Third, I wish to offer this interpretation of Taiwan to American readers so that we might outfit ourselves with ways in which we can alienate ourselves from Westernizing "historical learning." The first section gives *context* omitted from the editorials critiqued. The epigram from Deleuze and Guattari, above, signals resistance to Western historiography, the all-too-smooth absorption of difference, where we Westerners ourselves always "win" because we deserve to. From a dissident Western perspective, Taiwan offers the idea of a Nietzschean "fight against history," not as an illusory chimera, but as a practical matter of an unsettled genealogy—we can learn that contention is increased in the void of a dominant narrative history instead of continuing our "subscriptions" to certain stories. In focusing on historiographic disputes about Taiwan, China, and their representation in the American media, using *Los Angeles Times* editorials of the past few years to typify the media, I argue that the case of Taiwan belongs to a critical and philosophical register, an "ahistorical history"—at any time, the Taiwanese can be lodged and positioned in a number of narratives. Yet the peoples of this island have been able to evade the history imposed on them; I bring this out by using history against history. If there is such a thing as Taiwaneseness, in the sense of a group ethos, it can be interpreted as resistance-to-history. "Ahistorical" is borrowed here from Deleuze and is not to be thought of in Hegelian terms, the ahistorical as *lacking* something.[1] As used here, "ahistorical" does not imply any lack of history, narration, or temporal movement. "Ahistorical" refers to the *tension* of Taiwan, whose very name, as we will see, can cause "language to tend toward the limit of its elements, forms, or notions, toward a near side or a beyond of language."[2] Taiwan/ness is a test of prose narratives.

One is not saying that the vast majority of Taiwanese do not want the overarching political question of Chinese mainland power settled, or that large numbers of people there resist globalization; one is saying that the political and cultural resistance offered by the "Taiwanese" over the centuries—events—is itself a real agency with some force. It is a place where politics and culture intersect in ways that we comfortable Westerners might learn from. Learn what? That our own oversettled narratives (of left, right, and center) are part of the problem of globalization, the dogmatism that "our stories" are necessary and incontestable, that "everyplace" awaits our narratives because everyplace wants what we have, wants to become what we are (the West is so powerful it can even export cultural dissidence).

History against history: Taiwan as subject-to-China-narratives have got it *historically as wrong as it gets,* and so I am using *history*—what is omitted from the public discourse that we get in the *Los Angeles* or *New York Times*[3]—to bolster a sense of the ahistorical, that is, Taiwan as a place with problems, relations, and so on that should be supported, an argument, in sum, for Taiwan's independence, even if that is a little misleading. (Since who am I to use Western distance for Western ideals?)[4] Hence this is a case study in the exact sense of trying to make a case, what the philosopher Jean-François Lyotard called working the materials of conflict into phrases that may constitute a *differend*—claims that cannot be settled without further injury.[5] Again, this is to say that with the Communist Party's installation in 1949, with its insistence on representing One China, the party has made claims that Taiwan has always or continuously been a part of China, an erroneous misfiguration, given the audacity by the party (and many nationalists as well) to represent a continuity it helped to shatter. Taiwan's more independent-minded groups use discontinuity, discussed below, not just 1945 and the withdrawal of Japan from the island, to claim that Taiwan is a new society and so no mainland phrases of inclusion—One China—are justified. Thus, in what follows, *Taiwan* is treated as a phrase in dispute.

I traveled to Taiwan in 1990 for a period of a month. In terms of vivid experiences, no doubt I carried some baggage of one or more versions of Orientalism, but one hopes that one's experiences are those of the type that belong to apprehending the East in a way to undermine the West and its self-certainties.[6]

Experiences: humidity in July, accompanied by a nonstop, two-day monsoon that turned the streets of Taipei into mud and invited uncountable flying roaches to come to life; the jerry-built factories and housing on the road from the airport to Taipei; the incredibly jammed streets; a restaurant north of Taipei, in a deserted Japanese gold mine in the hills of Jeifang (whose Taiwanese pun is "nine pieces of shit") overlooking the Taiwan Straits; the sounds of a language not understood; the yummy noodle houses; the snake shops crammed next to a building still wearing painted slogans from 1949 denouncing the mainland Communist Party, next to a lovely Buddhist temple next to a McDonalds, next to . . . My contact's family corrected my English as too American, but my interlocutor was born and raised in Hong Kong—we had a nice laugh over Taiwanese and Hong Kong rivalries concerning their respective use of English. I walked most of Taipei and the magnificent central highlands, especially the bamboo forests, that included some aboriginal zones. The radical physical montage of industrialized urban areas and the landscape in Taipei was striking. One should say that Taiwan is an island ninety-six miles off the coast of mainland Asia. It is subtropical, bisected by the Tropic of Cancer, with winds that blow across it from Siberia as well as the East China Sea, with rain patterns that are distinctive to specific areas of the island, a northern constancy of rainfall, a southern landscape sometimes in drought. The Western coastal plain has seen most of its natural vegetation and animal life eliminated by human settlements (now twenty-three million inhabitants), a loss that has intensified since the seventeenth century, with the Kuomintang "modernization" since 1949 accelerating urbanization. Half the island is forest, with a mountain chain running down the middle. One can walk in the bamboo forests under a canopy of light green shade for miles on end. Taiwan has severe ecological problems, including nuclear ones. It is the second most densely populated place on earth, second only to Bangladesh.[7]

I made a second trip to Taiwan in 1996, and for parts of May and June 1997 I had a visiting teaching position in the People's Republic, at Xiamen University, due west from Taipei. Xiamen is another island, connected to the mainland by bridge, and itself adjacent to a third island, Gulangyu, with its huge statue of Koxinga, hero of both Taiwanese and mainland nationalist "history." I lectured on French Theory and the American university scene, my hosts expecting me to deliver American neopragmatism (= globalization = privatization = autonomy); I turned Foucault's masterpiece essay on Nietzsche into a defense of Taiwanese independence. My Taiwan visit in 1990 coincided with the arrest of some Taiwanese dissidents by the Kuomintang Party (KMT), as these dissidents were subject to political arrest for unauthorized sojourns in China, among other reasons. Their arrest, carried in the *South China Daily News* as an instance of the fragility and instability of civil society so soon after

Cheng Shang-Hsi, *The Child after School.* Taipei, 1958. Reproduced by permission of Cheng Shang-Hsi.

the lifting of martial law (in 1987), was eerily paralleled by a story on the back page of a visit by progressive American intellectuals (Fredric Jameson, Peter Wollen, Susan Buck-Morss), sponsored by universities, who had come to discuss cultural studies in Taiwan and, by doing so, affirmed the KMT's new "openness." A strange first visit to this island—Western intellectual life on display as model for "local" intellectuals, and "local" political dissidents on the outs. On this note of Western intellectuals in Taiwan, with all its ambiguity, let me now turn to the senses of Taiwan in recent historiography, context-work for the historiographic criticism below.

China and Taiwan as Narrative Subjects (Origin/Resistance)

For most Westerners, particularly Americans, Taiwan exists, if at all, as the object of a metanarrative whose speaker is the Communist Party of mainland China. Taiwan belongs to China, period. The Kuomintang Party in Taiwan continues this metanarrative, only as a different sender and receiver of the same message, tracing its legitimacy to Sun Yat-sen and 1911. There is irony that both groups claim to embody the narrative of national unity, cultural identity, and political reunification. The question addressed to Western publics by many contemporary political and cultural analysts, and commentators about Taiwan's "historical place," take their cue from the Communist Party and KMT early twentieth-century fusion of modernization and nationalism; current disputes between the mainland Communist Party and Taiwanese political groups "date" from the defeat of the Japanese in 1945 and the "return" of Taiwan to a mainland government (in 1943 Churchill and Roosevelt recognized Chiang Kai-shek's KMT as the legal government of the island). For a period in the 1950s, when Western demonization of the mainland party reached an apogee, Taiwan made educational, military, financial, and imaginary connections with some American groups (e.g., academics). But since Nixon and Kissinger's 1972 infamous toast with Mao and Zhou, where they acknowledged One China, the phrase "two systems" later added for Hong Kong, Taiwan has slipped, for Americans, into the subject-position of *return* (with alternations: *to* China, *to* Han Chineseness).[8] Many Taiwanese are incensed that their legally constituted government is subject to American realpolitik, and its acceptance of a mainland system that is not-legal, but whose fiction of One China is not seriously challenged. History out of joint indeed. A primary activity of the KMT from 1949 to 2000 has been to delay if not block non-mainland-identified Taiwanese from calling for the KMT to push harder against American realpolitik. For American audiences, a narrative already exists for Taiwan, the narrative of fusion with the "continental motherland." Philosophically, Taiwan is like a Deleuzian "incorporeal [narrative] body," its name located in different places, but ultimately embodied for Americans in the wrong place—Americans' acceptance of a mainland narrative or its own dismissal of effective and critical knowledge. It is extraordinary that before 1947–49 and the conclusion of the civil war between communists and the KMT, there is no mainland narrative on Taiwan at all.[9]

Initial narratives about Taiwan have come from outside. When European and American missionaries, adventurers, and traders began to be interested in it, they tended toward narratives of "origin." For example, in 1889, a Dutch Indologist made the proposal, based on linguistic evidence, that Taiwan was peopled by Austronesian groups; the Canadian missionary Mackay proposed, in 1895, a non-Chinese origin of Taiwan's people, arguing that the largest aboriginal group in Taiwan, the Amis, were Malayan; the Japanese scholars who lived and studied in Taiwan, including the famous Mabuchi Toichi, also were convinced that Taiwan was "southern," not Chinese. In what is called the "politics of the southern origin theory," many Japanese and Western scholars agree that

Taiwan's aboriginals were not Chinese, an argument that suited the Japanese, who, from the 1870s, wanted a "wall" between their and China's claims on Taiwan. This southern theory was disputed by Han-identified Chinese of Taiwan (especially those who came over after 1945) as well as by mainland writers. In 1988, Taiwan scholars of the aboriginal origins published a journal called *Tai-yuan-jen* (Taiwan Indigenous People Alliance) and treated the non-Chinese origin theory as fact. The most comprehensive statement of this position, which at once rejects communist and KMT narratives, is that of Shih Ming who, in 1980, published his *Four Hundred Year History of the Taiwanese People* with the claim that communist and nationalist narratives were equally "the mythogenesis of a political agenda."[10]

A second narrative-grouping is that of the "northern origin" of Taiwan, of which the dominant version dates from 1929, written by the Chinese scholar Lin Hui-hsiang, from Amoy University. In this version of Taiwan and its aboriginal origins, Taiwan was not considered a lost province of China; rather, Lin tied the southern Min people of China to the Taiwanese through coastal migration and did not invoke China as motherland, a nationalist version that only became the standard after 1949 and the defeat of the KMT. It is important to note that, in 1929, mainland Chinese scholars of Taiwan made no *political* argument that Taiwan was part of China; Taiwan was of interest only as needed for a core ideology to resist Japanese imperialism. But by 1982, Lin's *Brief History of the Kao-shan Tribe* (*Kao-shan-tzu chien-shih*) made the *timelessness* or "eternality" of Taiwan as part of China a feature of mainland ideology.[11] With increasing frequency since then, mainland writers reached back to cite the court records of Emperor Wu in 239 AD, the "first" record of China's awareness there was an island called Taiwan, historicizing this date by blending it with the events of 1945 and after. Old mainland names for the Yueh people of southern China turned such groups into "relatives" of "Tso Chen Man," found in Taiwan, near Tainan, so that 30,000-year-old artifacts were made to cohere with "a branch of Peking man." Ideology always makes for poor science.

A third historiographic thesis on Taiwan postulates that Taiwan itself is the "source" of Austronesian languages, with speakers who continue to use three of its oldest branches (called "first order sub-groups" by linguists)[12]; adherents of this thesis accept a neolithic movement of people from southeast China— not necessarily Han Chinese—to Taiwan, but with a radical break: it is Taiwan that bodies forth the Austro-Tai language family, which predates Austronesian, making Taiwan an exporter of Austronesian to the Philippines, Borneo, Indonesia. This thesis is obviously favored by Taiwan's aboriginals, who in 1984 formed the Alliance of Taiwan Aborigines (*Yuan ch'uan hui*), and called their publication *The Aborigine,* a title rejected by the mainland-identified KMT government information office, who insisted that the Alliance call itself "mountain compatriots" or "mountain people" or "Formosan aborigines," or anything but *aboriginal people.*[13] The problem both mainland Chinese as well as some KMT Chinese–identified in Taiwan have with the name *aboriginal people* is that it portrays a group undivided in time and space—or continuous and too different, and so in radical discontinuity with the claims of other histories and stories, especially with the politics of Marxism and Chinese nationalism. If one takes the perspective of aboriginal self-identification at its most radical, understanding that some aboriginal groups and their leaders are well integrated in Taiwanese society, then this third model of origin gives to the name *aboriginal* "some political and empirical rights," or joins resistance to China to resistance toward Han Chinese into resistance toward any Taiwanese government that might treat its "own" people as someone else. Who is this "own"? "Own people" moves toward boundaries of identity. Of course leaning on affirmation of the aboriginals can push one to ask about *Taiwaneseness,* insofar as other groups in Taiwan recognize aboriginal claims as consonant with "independence" claims.[14] A scholar who happens to be from the Amis tribe has insisted that "even if one argues that ancestors of Taiwan[ese] aboriginal people came from the continent [the northern thesis], 'there was no Chinese mainland ten thousand years ago, only the Asian continent.'"[15] This aboriginal historian asks what happened to the Austronesian people of China such that *all of them* migrated to Taiwan, since there are no Austronesian peoples *in* southern China? This "Taiwan origin theory" does not depend on "native" myths of the aboriginals themselves, but on linguistic and artifactual interpretations. In short, Chinese claims to Taiwan based on Chinese origins have been, in the scholarly literature, thoroughly challenged by various critical investigations into origins.

Historical Continuity and Discontinuity

The name *Taiwan,* "terraced bay," is a Chinese corruption of the aboriginal term *tayan* or *tayouan.*[16] There are populated sites in Taiwan from at least 15,000 BCE. Headhunters existed into the last century, with accounts of their ferocity toward the Japanese after 1895. As noted above, the first mainland regard of Taiwan's existence came in 239 CE, in which the island was explored but not occupied.[17] One scholar of origins has argued that mainland dynastic records refer to Taiwan only twelve times between the third century BCE and 906 CE.[18] The expedition of 239 CE does not indicate that the Imperial system made territorial claims on Taiwan; under the Sui Dynasty there were two further expeditions sent to Taiwan, in 605 and 611 CE. Then nothing for eight hundred years. Between 1405 and 1430, large expeditions were sent by the Ming, under the direction of Cheng Ho, to Taiwan and other southern areas, but with no follow-up.[19] No mainland government made territorial claims until the Manchu overthrow of the Ming Dynasty in 1644, and those were not claims commensurate with those after World War II.[20] A persecuted non-Chinese minority from Hubei province in northern China, the Hakka, rejected Chinese foot-binding, and were a "first" cohesive mainland group to migrate to Taiwan during the Tang Dynasty. Hakka migration to Taiwan continued until the 1860s, when the Manchu (Qing) Dynasty, terrified by the slaughterhouse unleashed with the Taipeng Rebellion, which was led by a mainland Hakka turned son-of-Jesus, shut down the movement of people in southeastern China. Of the roughly 85 percent of Taiwan's population today that shuttles between calling themselves Taiwanese and Han/Chinese, the Hakka make up some 15 percent.

In 1622, the Mings gave the Dutch a treaty to trade in Taiwan, in the southern part of the island. A Spanish landing took place in the north, somewhat earlier, and fizzled out. It took the Dutch and their incursions in southern Taiwan after 1624 to stimulate mainland interest in the island, only as the Mings were in dissolve. Demographers have estimated that in 1600, perhaps 70,000 aboriginals lived on the island. Demographers have also noted that before this Dutch/Chinese connection in 1624, the aboriginals constituted some fourteen distinct groups in the west and north coastal plains, and nine more in the central mountains. Into the eighteenth century, European cartographers were better at showing these areas than they were in representing the Chinese mainland settlements.[21] After the 1680s, Han Chinese settlers from the mainland increasingly displaced the aborigines. In 1650 it is gauged that no more than 25,000 "Chinese" had settled in Taiwan, many only seasonally. This did not make Taiwan a Chinese "frontier" area, however; Dutch control between 1624 and 1664 involved their recruiting of Chinese mainland settlers, so that Chinese migration claims to historic rights are undercut by the fact that the first wave of Chinese mainland emigrants were in fact clients of the Dutch. In 1652, 15,000 of these settlers revolted against the Dutch overlords, participating in what one historian has called the "first Chinese anti-Western uprising in modern history."[22] Perhaps this is the kind of "fact" that mainland/Kuomintang

Chinese find disturbing—not assimilable to narratives of One China and two systems? This is not a fact, as we will see, that one finds in the American editorial writing on Taiwan.

The Manchu invasion did not produce a Chinese historicization of Taiwan. As the Ming generals were defeated in the north, the remarkable pirate, known as Koxinga (Cheng Ch'eng-kung), his Japanese name (his father was also a famous pirate, married to a Japanese woman) took control of the southern resistance to the Manchu. A mixture of fact and legend has it that starting with ninety followers in 1647, he raised an army that by 1661 was able to oust the Dutch from Taiwan and wreak havoc on the Manchu, with Taiwan serving as a place of "retreat" (and aggression) for the "legitimate" Mings—thus is set in play Chiang Kai-shek's "retreat" to Taiwan some three hundred years later, also wrapped in the legitimacy of resistance to an unworthy State.[23] Koxinga's family had effective control over parts of Taiwan (mostly the southern areas) until 1683, when Koxinga's son, Cheng K'e-shuang, surrendered to the Manchus. At this point Taiwan entered Chinese "national history" because it was the site of Ming defeat.

The Manchu exploited Taiwan. Between 1683 and 1843, there were some fifteen major rebellions against Manchu officials. The historiographic literature suggests the Manchu were worried that Taiwan was a place "too Chinese," a source of delegitimation of their rule.[24] (As said above, the Manchus were not even Chinese themselves, but descended from nomadic tribes to the north of China, the Nuzhen people.) The Qing Dynasty closed Taiwan to immigration between 1662 and 1722, but by the 1780s, Chinese immigration resumed. A rebellion on the island in 1786–88 required a hundred thousand troops to put down. Yet by 1862, some historians figure, Taiwan was out of all but Qing military control altogether, the island's economy and social structure an amalgam of recognized and illegal modes of authority.[25] So tenuous was mainland interest and control in Taiwan under the Manchu that in the 1850s there were schemes by the Taiwanese to come under American control, and in 1869, some aboriginal tribes even tried to sign their own treaties with the U.S. government. In 1886, under intense pressure to modernize, the Qing Dynasty made Taiwan a province, but shortly thereafter Taiwan was ceded to Japan "in perpetuity" by the Treaty of Shimonoseki.[26] The Japanese had modernized much more effectively than China, and territorial expansion was part of its self-assigned reward, part of the overall occupations by the major powers. Taiwan was not "lost" or even "taken" by the Japanese, certainly not a territorial humiliation along the lines of what happened in Hong Kong, for there was virtually no interest about Taiwan by Chinese governments until Japan's defeat in World War II. For those who insist that historical claims are the strongest of all, communist/Kuomintang claims to Taiwan as an inalienable part of China are less than weak.

Between 1895 and 1945, the Japanese determined the state of life in Taiwan. The Japanese made claims on Taiwan going back to 1593, and their national mythologies about Taiwan go further back. They occupied the island in 1874, on a trumped-up charge against Taiwanese Botan aboriginals (who killed half of a shipwrecked Japanese crew), withdrew, and then returned, triumphant, in 1895. On acquiring Taiwan, the Japanese managed to provoke a rebellion every other year, the Tapani Revolt of 1915, with many thousands killed, being the most severe. The Japanese occupation of Taiwan bears uncanny comparisons with the American occupation of the Philippines, with Japan and the United States rivals in bringing enlightened modernization to someone else's exploited and neglected colonies. The Taiwanese declared their independence in 1915— the twelve-day Tai Republic, the "first" Republic of Taiwan. This rebellion was suppressed by later mainland and Kuomintang writers (it was common until the lifting of martial law in 1987 that Taiwan education made nearly no references to Taiwan history; the KMT were terrified of history-as-delegitimation of themselves).

The Japanese presence in Taiwan is far too rich and complicated to go into here in any detail. Suffice to say that during the fifty years Taiwan was Japan's colony, where the Japanese population was never more than one-eighteenth of the total, the island was modernized. From a run-down island frontier, it was given an infrastructure (roads, gas lines, electrification, reform of the education system). Today, many Taiwanese over the age of sixty-five or so speak Japanese, since it was required for professional and public life, many not learning Mandarin until their teens, while the Taiwanese dialect, Hokkien, was suppressed (now, knowing Hokkien is a sign of cultural sophistication). No doubt the Taiwanese were a subjugated people under the Japanese, but in the 1930s, very few Taiwanese seemed to have identified with the Chinese-Japanese conflicts on the mainland despite the fact that over 200,000 Taiwanese were conscripted into the Japanese forces.[27] On the mainland side, in 1925, 1934, and 1936 Chang Kai-shek proposed constitutions for China that did not invoke Taiwan as a province of China. Unfortunately, most Westerners have little if any knowledge about these complexities.

Before World War II ended, it was arranged that Taiwan would be given to the Kuomintang regime on the mainland.[28] Indeed, with the end of World

Zhongshan Hall, Taipei, 1945. Photograph by Teng Nan Kuang. Reproduced by permission of S. K. Teng.

War II, the Communist Party had no interest in Taiwan, and the initial Kuomintang "liberation" of the island from the Japanese amounted to looting Taiwan's machines, tools, even plumbing and so on for their conflicts with the communists on the mainland.[29] The Kuomintang was so out of control as to induce the February 28, 1947, massacres (*er er ba*) in different areas of Taiwan, which made the KMT a more ironic or even perverse form of the Japanese occupation. With their defeat on the mainland in 1949, Taiwan became for the KMT what it had been for Koxinga—a site of resistance to a mainland regime, but anchored in the fantasy of overthrow, the unification of motherland, the restoration of symbolic unity, the usual hodgepodge of mythification, identification, and terror.

The infamous February 1947 Taiwanese Uprising against the KMT mainlanders is too complicated to engage here, but suffice it to say that this is an utterly neglected theme in the American media, and other coverage of China and Taiwan.[30] The KMT entered Taiwan self-congratulatory as one of the Four Powers that ended World War II, and many Taiwanese saw themselves passing from one authoritarian regime to another. Close to 40,000 officials were put out of work in 1945, 17 percent of the country's GDP was confiscated so as to fight Mao, and the leadership of Ch'en I, Chiang Kai-shek's governor, was a disaster, little more than warlordism. From 1947 dates the introduction of a Taiwan Independence Movement, or the beginning of the long dispersal of the KMT. While this process is not over yet, the elections of 2000 suggest that the KMT cannot easily retain hegemony, at least not in its standard ways of the 1950s through the 1980s. As said above, in terms of an American audience, the complexity of Taiwan was neglected by scholars and journalists after Nixon and Kissinger's Shanghai Communique in 1972. From then, America went on another binge of image circulation: as Taiwan disappeared from representation here, a code-switch was effected on China, which went from a sly and treacherous government to emphasis on its people as hard-working and artistic, a switch encouraged by geopolitical leaders, artists, business interests, fashion mavens, and academics. Meanwhile, in Taiwan the entire social system moved from martial law and a "white terror" against dissidents that lasted until the late 1970s, to the election of the opposition, the Taiwanese-identified Democratic Progressive Party (DPP); in short, Taiwan went from a situation where "all publications had to be approved before publishing by the censorship department of the Taiwan Garrison Headquarters" to a situation as fluid and mobile, trenchant and treacherous, as any political system could—one of the so-called Asian tigers, yet the only one hunted by outside regimes.[31]

The Los Angeles Times' *"Taiwan Policy": The Editorial as Intellectual Suppression*

I have argued that Taiwan's contentious past is strong enough that it conceptually leads to a kind of ahistorical situation, where this contention could dislodge Western metanarratives. This is a case where Taiwan is not historicizable without acknowledging the rivalrous politics of representation and resistance, which includes origin notions as well as senses of discontinuity.

Now I wish to shift to the sense of Taiwan in a segment of the American media, here *Los Angeles Times* editorials. My purpose in moving to the editorial is to show how these editorials do *not* lead to a grasp of Taiwan as a complicated place, or dehistoricize it. This involves a discursive prose economy of restriction, which favors the mainland narrative of Taiwan's return, which for Americans is the easy way out of confronting our own hegemonic interests. In short, representation for purposes of persuasion, as old as rhetoric (i.e., politics) itself, has become an Asia-for-Americans, where journalists as well connected as Edgar Snow and scholars as well established as John Fairbanks have made representations that saturate American readers in narrativized, prosaic *misfiguration*.[32] The latter is a persistent prose form.

Despite some outstanding reporting and event analysis on Asia by some *Los Angeles Times* writers,[33] construction of ideas and images of Taiwan through the more directed *editorial* page remains a paramount instance of misfiguration. The editorial mode is an everyday prose text that makes a mental image or concept of action and relationship. The usual editorial is close to a mode of persuasion and dissuasion when it brings current theories and politics to public discourse, giving prosaic figuration. For example, there have been, nationally, hundreds of editorial columns using the phrase "Asian miracle," a phrase that embeds Asian financial and cultural life in Western notions of economics, threaded to uncontested notions of growth and "take-off," conjuring senses of development, Asia simplified and corresponding to the type, Asians R Us. While an exhibit by a Taipei artist depicting Asian icons with Western pornography "growing onto" sacred Asian sensibilities requires its own terms, once described for an American audience as "bold" and "audacious," it acquires the historicizing functions of "the first show that did that," which feeds various senses that are potential misfigurations.

Further, my reading of the *Los Angeles Times* editorials on Taiwan borrows from the conceptual framework of Tzvetan Todorov's *The Morals of History* (1995), a book that takes great pains to set forth categories of figuring forth others in modern Western writing. Let me discuss Todorov's book as a conceptual point of entry to my "local" reading of the *Times*. In surveying the history of wordedness or interpretative and ideological relations between Spanish conquerors and what they did to Indian texts, using commentaries by opponents of the conquest such as Las Casas or apologists like Sepulveda, Todorov argues that Western assimilation smuggles in the premise of its own superiority; for instance, the rule of law is said to show our advanced development despite the political violence of Western history.[34] The West claims superiority as it tries to avoid tagging others as inferior. No one wants to admit to superiorism, Todorov continues, so we privilege dialogism, to "read myself in quotation marks," often favored when referring to others.[35] Our affective feelings for others, say admiration for "Asian loyalty," often accompanies nonknowledge, as in the case of Montaigne's regret for the slaughter of the Aztecs, which was based on a Western failure to live up to its own ideals, not on the intrinsic worth of Aztec life. Of course emphasis upon a culture or civilization's internal articulation of differences—their "theirness"—may make it impossible to understand them at all.

In Todorov's notion of Western wordedness, truth and misfiguration are always co-present. In addition to risks of superiorism, historical writing presupposes truth-disclosure, an intersubjective truth, not a referential one. When issues of fact are unsettled, we expect a "depth of penetration" to provide a collective interpretation that spans group interests, serving as the basis for further discussions. This kind of truth aims at "adherence among readers." Here things get sticky. For with intersubjective interpretations, we are interested not so much in adequacy of discourse to referent, but in reaching agreement. Adherence is often at odds with truth-adequation, with its epistemic atomism or regression to the facts, but insistence that some facts cannot be explained away. How does one get from "facts" to an inclusive discourse that actually absorbs each fact's adequacy without *distortion*? Of all the facts, including those about processes, available about Asian economies since 1970, how did the phrase "Asian miracle" arise? Further, depth interpretations, requiring adherence, giving intersubjective connections, can be coherent in one way, but can render a larger incoherence in relation to another interpretation. A coherent interpretation is bound to be reductive just because it smoothes and resolves contention. In sum, in those areas ruled by intersubjectivity—politics, culture, morality, aesthetics, and language—truth as adequation and truth as disclosure opens onto the consequence that coherence is not very intellectually stimulating; the possible incoherence is stimulating. Try as he may, Montaigne's denunciation of Eurocentrism in the name of equality also gave Eurocentrism a lease on life once Europeans used the ideal of equality, its irresistible coherence, to oppress Africans, among others, in the nineteenth century.[36]

Another way of putting Todorov's construal of history and misfiguration is just to emphasize that representation and resistance can collide in any *public claim to mediate representation.* Public newspapers such as the *Los Angeles Times* can be used to intensify, slow down, speed up, displace, etc. what "counts" as news, namely, decisions by governing bodies; in another register, this means that one is always caught up in privileging certain mediating roles, such as those of cultural guide, or political prophet, or existential naysayer, or the wisdom of the businessman. This also occurs in Taiwanese life. For example, in July 1998 a conference was held in Taiwan at Tsing-Hua University, with the title "Problematizing Asia." The conference continued lines of thought opened by cultural (mainly British) and postcolonial studies. In the announcement of the conference, via e-mail, the chief organizer said that a gathering is necessary because of the coming into dominance of the phrase "rise of Asia" (dated from the mid-1980s), specifically the fact that Asia was again an obsession of the West. Calling for an "intervention" so as to "fill the gap" in what the various Western and Asian discursive regimes have neglected, the "Problematizing Asia" conference asked questions so broad that their sheer scale dominated as rhetorical form. Citing "local, national, regional, international and global levels," the organizer asked, "How do we place 'Taiwan' in these contexts?" Here, a progressive group's immediate worry was over Taiwanese nationalism—pro-aboriginal/proindependence for Taiwan—a worry that seems to have England at the time of Thatcher's ascendancy in mind, where right-wing nationalism was revived, adding to the difficulties of establishing a new critical left. But should response to Thatcherist nationalism serve as a model for Taiwanese intellectual resistance to Taiwanese nationalism?[37]

The Editorial and Intellectual Suppression

One can certainly see what is at stake when it comes to concepts and images of Asia in the editorial page of the *Los Angeles Times*. As said above, there is more writing by the *Times* on Asia than the editorials. Apart from headline stories, Jim Mann's "international outlook" regularly gave a deep sense of the historical and temporal issues involved. The business section reports on the financial turmoil, from a persistently dreadful perspective of Asia as a place of lower costs and infinite needs. I am going to restrict my comments to the editorials written by Tom Plate, who in the period under discussion wrote all of the editorials for the *Times,* whose byline listed teaching in UCLA's communication and policy studies program, and who heads an Asia Institute at UCLA, an organization of schools and corporate sponsors that promotes globalization in its "moderate" form.

The editorials discussed are an active attempt by the *Times* to shape public opinion, the editorial itself timed to Asian "events" so as to be more immediate in its impact. Editorial practice often serves to anticipate the possibilities of a future event and because of this quality, its timing connects immediate and structural forces at once. An editorial, in short, is one of the forms in which readers do not grapple with problems so much as receive interest and motivation, immediate impressions, even if they are canceled the next day by another editorial. They are more or less consistent tapes of guidance for the uninitiated. These impressions naturalize the political and intellectual, giving it the form of the unquestionable (the "real" right now). An editorial aims not so much at instruction as at guidance—shaping consensus for tomorrow's conflicts, defusing the contentiousness of other perspectives, leading its readers to the necessity of what tomorrow is to look like. It is all about the making of coherence.

Let us start then with an editorial from August 1997. Plate writes that the "Pacific Rim community" is a real entity, required not just by the historical moment of a "Rise of Asia" nor by trade concerns, but by the need for a "brain-trust" of the "best universities" in the United States, Asia, and Latin America. The president of USC is cited, for whom "L.A. is the Rome of the [Pacific] Rim," a community of the best universities that are "brand names" in Asia, where "a U.S. degree is worn like a badge of honor."[38] There is said to be a "bond" between Pacific Rim universities, a "sunny optimism" underlying their "common challenges" concerning economic development, this positive model set against a right wing in California protesting China's rent of docks at Long Beach. There are Asians "like us" and there are Americans stuck in McCarthyism. In a few sentences the prose frees the West's global community from opposition to it. In the same sentence, Los Angeles, Tokyo, and Singapore are said to have replaced New York, Paris, and Rome as world centers, but this is put hysterically: "the university group aspires to be this new community's on-call brain cell," where "on-call" privileges economic managers, financial traders, dealers of all sorts, including those involved in the circulation of symbol, sign, image. None of this talk of corporate and university "brain-trusts" is connected to such past practices as what happened with U.S. professors advising, say, the Chilean military and business interests.

In August of 1997, the column "On Taiwan, Beijing Learns to Yawn" compliments Beijing over an impending visit from the president of Taiwan, a one-night touchdown on U.S. soil (Hawaii). Beijing's not going berserk is made a sign of its "maturity" and is opposed to the "latest, potentially trouble making" move by Taiwan. The "maturity" of 1997 corrects Beijing's being "ultratouchy" in 1996, when it lobbed missiles close to Taiwan. Beijing has earned the right to be touchy because "Beijing, as well as a lot of Chinese (and more than a few people inside Taiwan) regard Taiwan as an integral part of historic China." Rather than define "integral" and "historic," words with a large range of potential misfiguration, the article images Taiwan as provoking China, by having a "perceived campaign of clever resistance to the process of eventual reunification." "Clever" goes with "trouble making," giving those Taiwanese the quality "aggressive," while "maturity" and "touchy" gives the mainland government the quality of "provoked." This is the coherence of which Todorov speaks—the Taiwanese are given a totalizing, overly coherent, interpretation, in the negative. The next phrase reads: "In fact, the diplomatic reality is that tiny but economically over-achieving Taiwan is formally recognized as an independent government by only 30 countries, one of which is Panama, and not by either the U.N. or the U.S. But its feisty government and newfound democratic ways combine to create the effect of an independent state, which stations an army of loyalists and lobbyists in America."[39] Let us name each of the pejoratives ladled over Taiwan, or the use of coherent history to delegitimize. "Diplomatic reality" refers to governmental and U.N. acceptance of mainland Chinese claims over Taiwan. This omits the U.N. decision of 1952 that affirmed self-determination as a principle for nonstates. "Tiny" reduces and "over-achieving" goes with "tiny" to form the image of an aggressive group, with the insult or curse that Panama, alone of the thirty supporting governments mentioned, recognizes Taiwan. If Taiwan is supported by Panama, then Taiwan must be eccentric or worse, insignificant except as a problem. "Feisty" could be a nod to something affirmative about Taiwan, but "newfound democracy" undercuts that, depriving Taiwan's government of legitimacy, as if there is something suspect about Taiwanese democracy. Taiwan only looks like a country, but is not one really. The reduction is "confirmed" by the rhetoric of militancy: "stations" an "army" in this country raises the ugly specter of Taiwan buying its legitimacy. The Taiwanese are construed as illegitimately aggressive, hence closer to Libya than to mainland China's claim of historic rights. In a single editorial, the historiographics of complexity are ruined. It is the U.S. Congress that listens to Taiwan because of campaign contributions etc., but the State Department and presidency are, one hopes, smarter about the long-term interests of that PacRim community whose brain is "on-line" or "on-call." Rhetoric has eaten into any semblance of objectivity, devoured it. In Todorov's terms, this specific editorial repeats Sepulveda's mode of superiorism, rhetoric blocking any sense here that Taiwan has grounds to resist either China or America acting in China's interests.[40]

Taiwan is removed from the Asia called for to participate in Westernization/globalization. The Taiwanese should not derail the United States' ability "to work both sides of the Taiwan strait." The Taiwanese should be deprived of "leverage" that would "imperil Sino-U.S. relations." In effect, the prose issues warnings: if left to their own devices, the Taiwanese will "sabotage" the future, an ominous throwback to the visual imagery of the stealthy Asian spy out of anti-Japanese propaganda films of World War II. In another editorial,

Asians are cited to remind us of our own better selves, readers getting ideals from unobjectionable "others," but subject to negative images—Taiwan is close, negatively, to Malaysia, the prime minister of Malaysia is called "bush-league" for distinguishing between foreign capital and foreign rogue capital (i.e., currency speculators like George Soros).[41] The "PacRim community" would never have allowed Indonesia's disastrous forest fires to occur, for this group would have installed "Asian regionalization" or Western-style crisis management. Westerners need to pay attention to "face," no perspective allowed but from those Asians who are like us. The mayor of Shanghai, Xu Kuangdi, is quoted as saying, "We like Americans . . . [they are] easy to read and we Chinese appreciate that," this in the context of Xu's identification with Rudy Giuliani in New York or Richard Riordan in Los Angeles. Xu wants to build Shanghai according to the logic of an American film: "if we build it, they will come." Who is quoting whom and what in this hallucination of identities? A Western image exported to an Asian leader just like us returns as he is made to say what we approve of; the sense here, regular fare of the editorial, its antiproduction of questions and problems, preserves Westernization as it turns Taiwan and other places "into history" or out of the future.

The "on-call brain cell" of the PacRim community is mobilized in an editorial of May 1998 and set against East Coast newspaper columnists who oppose Clinton's appearance at Tiananmen Square in June of 1998. Plate calls his rival East Coast journalists "potentates," orientalized in the negative, and who have no sense, he says, of Tiananmen apart from June of 1989; they should understand that Chinese leaders ceremonialize with all foreign dignitaries in Tiananmen, so that its "historical" force, as opposed to its "historic" association with the murder of workers and students, is misunderstood by critics. Clinton should not miss the opportunity to look "like a champ" at Tiananmen, just as the Chinese leaders should not reject "a fabulous opportunity to look great." (Is all this Pop writing about Asia a little weird?) Taiwan returns in association with worries about India and Pakistan as nuclear powers, Taiwan used to provoke a nasty question—"what would technologically capable but tiny Taiwan start plotting to do" in its relations with the mainland if it had such weapons, "plotting" repeating the notion of aggressiveness, "tiny" a negative redundancy. In an editorial from May 26, 1998, over questionable Chinese funds slipped to the Democrats and funds from the Loral Corporation to the People's Liberation Army commercial division, the subject is dismissed with the comparison that "money from China . . . was clumsily emulating foreign lobbying operations like Taiwan's and Israel's." Taiwan is emulated when countries do negative things, hence Taiwan is encoded as demonic—it sets off "nocturnal intensities" (Deleuze and Guattari). Taiwan belongs to and participates in no dynamics but self-survival, and is illegitimate in making moral claims that Westerners might recognize. Even fright is proposed to the *Times'* audience: "are we really ready to risk a new cold war over this?"

The wrangle over China's entry to the WTO is turned into the fear that its defeat would produce a "new-age Maoism," depriving the "best and brightest" of China's university leaders of a "cosmopolitan vision of higher education," citing as "evidence" the president of Fudan University that "there isn't a single faculty member here who has adopted a negative attitude toward the Internet."[42] Not one? If Taiwan has no claim to an autonomous future, China should dread the return of its past. The March 2000 election of the Democratic Progressive Party candidate Chen Shui-bian intensifies all this misfiguration. In an editorial of May 24, 2000, the China Trade Bill is claimed to be of "historic" value, a tag withheld from the political elections in Taiwan—the first such elections in all of Chinese history—and if the China Trade Bill is passed (it was), this will "bind China ever more firmly into a new world order of peace, international process and political predictability," a line straight out of Francis Fukuyama, lauded in an earlier editorial.[43] History returns in that the leaders of the United States, China, and Taiwan should turn away from China's human rights actions—still no discussion of Taiwan actually becoming more democratic—this because Westerners should "grant China overdue recognition of its absolutely extraordinary and unprecedented economic climb out of Mao's misery that has raised more of its people out of poverty more quickly than any other government in recorded history."[44] As Taiwan goes to the obsolete bin of history, China goes into history as delirium: the absence of present disasters for Jiang Zemin et al. ("absolutely," "more quickly") separates present from past, legitimizing China's future, which is the same thing as legitimizing the present Chinese leadership. The Democratic Progressive Party's surpassing the barriers of KMT and Western interests is hauled into this history *only* because Chen Shui-bian's inaugural speech was "tremendous, historic," because he showed "respect [for] . . . Beijing's policy of 'one China' yet without selling Taiwan's people down the river." Chen's "respect" was understood in Taiwan as a tactical move, omitted here. Relying again on the PacRim's "insider" knowledge, the views of Wang Daohan, doyen of the People's Republic of China's Taiwan policy, are put forward as historical wisdom, "whose responses to our written questions are known to have been cleared by the all-powerful Central Committee in Beijing . . . [who] called for tolerance on both sides." Taiwan must reunify with the "motherland" and Taiwan will have an ever better deal than Hong Kong: "What a deal this is! [Daohan] is saying."[45]

Immediately after the election of the DPP candidate, a column took up China's "White Paper" on Taiwan, released just before the March 2000 elections. Here the party reaffirmed the 1949 One China principle, which was really, as noted above, a principle shared with the Kuomintang insofar as they trace their genealogy to Sun Yat-sen's reforms and the Republic of China of 1911. Why not discuss 1911? Citing mainland Vice Premier Qian Qichen, the "White Paper" is affirmed as the "time-honored Chinese way of saying that only the full course of history can correct an injustice built up over the course of time."[46] That is, China's *continuous* historical claims to Taiwan are presented as fact. The question of Taiwan's independence is nothing more, now, than a "negotiating point." In an editorial four days after the defeat of the KMT in Taiwan, the negative marker "tiny island" returns, this time not to affirm Taiwanese sovereignty, but only as an end to the KMT "behemoth": the Taiwan political transformation is not about independence, only the Taiwan middle class pushed the DPP into office; the election was really about "corruption," the voters said to be concerned with globalization (= anticronyism), not politics.[47] The discourse keeps on track the affirmation of China as embodying historical continuity, this via the motherland unity argument, a delegitimation of the autonomy of politics on Taiwan. Globalization here is used as a lever of anti*local* politics.[48] America should have a "Goldilocks" attitude toward China: a "just right" attitude of balance, which nonetheless is based on acceptance of Beijing's demand that Taiwan is a "disrespectful, wayward son that must—somehow—be returned to the family fold."[49] Taiwan has been Oedipalized (the time span of the editorials roughly correlating with the time it takes to manifest Oedipus in children). Citing yet another well-placed "source," a "contact" at the Rand Corporation, readers are told that Americans must try to make sure that China is not placed in the vise where they will invade Taiwan "if they have no choice," i.e., Taiwan's political life must be depoliticized. Hence American foreign policy must "avoid strategic intimacy" with Taiwan, or Congress must foreswear any "formal alliance" with Taiwan. As before, Taiwan must not be treated as sovereign. In fact, the American public must listen to our "wise" and enlightened think-tank corporate "players" for whom the "third way" toward China relations (here reduced to hawk/dove, containment/engagement) is "congagement," or "a little of this, a little of that; lean a little left, then to the right," this to pursue the inexorable aims of globalization.[50] Thus China's "leftist purists" who criticize Premier Zhu Rongji for *rushi* or "entry to the world" (globalization) and American conservatives or liberal-unionists should both get out of the way. So too must Taiwanese independence groups.[51]

All this lopsided "coherence" has the effect of making Taiwan disappear. Its history of continuous discontinuity with invaders of all sorts is removed from present discourse. That the KMT's fifty-year domination might now dissolve, be made into something else, is unthinkable, i.e., that the island's self-sorting out can be achieved in its own register. Taiwan remains pre-historical, and not out of choice. The editorial that calls Clinton and Zemin's meeting "historic" also declares, "A new order is descending on Asia. This is no historical accident." Thus, Jiang Zemin and Zhu Rongji are not "parochial";[52] one should be gleeful over Clinton's rejection in Beijing of independence for Taiwan (communism in China and neoconservative-liberalism in America locked into No Clauses); then a rhetorical question: whether Taiwan "suddenly finds itself on the wrong side of history. With but 21 million people [tiny, again] the offshore island is a democracy that will never be a superpower or threaten anyone militarily."[53] The "wrong side of history" is a phrase of pure terror—extreme disidentification with Taiwan's actual political transformation in March 2000. Again, the linkage to China always makes Taiwan disappear into historiographic oblivion— history used to denarrate. I call this a strong instance of historical narration in the restrictive mode, disturbing because it gives its readers the satisfactions of eliminating rival concepts and attending social and political arrangements.

In fact, these editorials complete the dehistoricization of Taiwan: "The United Nations and the United States refuse to recognize Taiwan as an official nation . . . But even if you find no pathos at all in Taiwan's plight . . . the manner of Beijing's resolution of this *grating rebuke* [March 2000 elections] to mainland Communism will reveal much."[54] What matters in this reduction of conflict, in which "historic" and "historical" and related terms are crucial stakes, is only how the mainland is perceived by the West—China should avoid violence. Those pesky and trouble-making Taiwanese should listen to Clinton, who passes into the voice of speaking for the Communist Party: "his administration no longer wants the Taiwan tail to wag the Sino-U.S. dog." Again: "Clinton, like it or not Taiwan, has forsworn U.S. support for formal Taiwanese independence." Perversely, the elections of 2000 are treated as if they were nothing but the KMT of 1949.

The editorials singled out here testify to what Roland Barthes called myth, the editorial form conducive to a particular mode of mythmaking, realized in proverbial type utterances, or figures of thought and image that aim at the universal and "the refusal of any explanation, an unalterable hierarchy of the world."[55] They are prose-myth where the narrative dimension has become a premise: restriction of history. Todorov's concerns about the ideological effects of rigid coherence seem confirmed by the editorials. The complex historicity of Taiwan and its conflicts with others do not transfer into productive representation for its readers because Westernization—globalization—makes focus on such local conflicts only instances of further pragmatic solutions. "One China, two systems" is such a pragmatic or Western mode of coming to terms with conflicted narratives/histories. In addition, the editorials belong to prose, myth, and don the mask of reflexive speech, maxims that "overlay a world which is already made, bury the traces of this production under a self-evident appearance . . . the decorous equivalent of a tautology." That is to say, the editorials discussed above never waver in their commitment to the rhetoric of extending some existing facts on the ground, dubious as history, and as such facts are attached and threaded to the institutions of this university-based "PacRim community," whose interests are confused with the public, then it seems fair to ask how such misfiguration does not convey pure politics, the politics of historical misrepresentation. The editorials feel aimed at satisfying last readers, as discussed in chapter 1.

Taiwan is an island at the edge of continental Asia. On political and cultural grounds—regimes and resistances, involving the use of origins and narratives—there is not any plausible historical argument for One China. One China is a fiction. It is this fiction that is now nearly impossible to speak to in the midst of a "new class" discourse, since one is immediately tagged as right wing, antiprogressive, and antifuture if one objects to American politics and multinational capitalism linked to Chinese State-Capitalism, among other things. But one can resist the associations by suspending "one story" and shifting in thought to the Taiwanese—the elections of 2000 as a watershed in that it shows Taiwan's difference in politics and historiography. Imposed on Taiwan is a "burden of history" that prevents us from knowing Taiwan—in Todorov's sense—hence from knowing about a specific force of dissidence, people not-like-us. In this sense, Westerners who venture to learn something of the present conflicts between the United States, China, and Taiwan, might borrow an idea from Jean Baudrillard, that Taiwan is not a matter of *finalities*—but a "society [that] is totally there at each instant," a society that makes its own "speech before history," a "speech against power."[56] Which means: an affirmation of the island Taiwan's resistance to history. It should be unthinkable to make Taiwan subject to the failures and power attacks of the Communist Party of China, as America, even if by omission, yokes Taiwan to the destiny of American-led globalization and China's other role, its new submission to the West, becoming "us."

3 | *Art Criticism and Intellectuals in Los Angeles*

Desperate Narrations

In September 1998 I sent a letter to the *Los Angeles Times* about an art review written by David Pagel, a *Times* staff writer. I thought his review a nearly private use of the *Times'* "public" prerogative. I used the word "cribbing" to specify that the review used phrases, without attribution, drawn from the writings of the artist under review. I also challenged why the *Times* printed a blurb from another *Times* critic, Christopher Knight, about his friend/associate's book, the writer Dave Hickey. My letter was not published, and shortly thereafter, I received a missive from the arts editor of the *Times,* defending the two reviews in question. I was asked to provide "evidence" of what I had called cribbing, namely, the art review and, as to the book review, it was asserted that it was unfair of me to challenge "a tribute from one writer to another."[1] I responded to the missive by saying that my letter could have been published, that the mix of a public/private tribute muddled the purpose of review. I learned, later, that the arts editor, Susan Freudenheim, was given a hefty acknowledgment in a book previously written by Hickey, the book referred to in the tribute—thus her missive and the review serving as public relations disguised as criticism. Historiographically, such muddles are small events already nested in narratives concerning rank and selection, involving subjects, institutions, economics, and symbolic capital.

Such "on the ground" entanglements are part of the stew of the recent L.A. art world, occurrences that belong to what Max Weber and Pierre Bourdieu called cultural distinction. In Weber's words, however vague this art world, it is part of "the barriers of education and of aesthetic cultivation [that] are the most intimate and the most insuperable of all status differences."[2] What I tried to "touch" via a letter about an imposition of a plus-value made from intimate associations ("tribute"), ended up reinforcing subjects and institutions, by recourse to politics: the force (validity?) of a tribute was presumed by Freudenheim as already "earned," and so nearly inviolable as a judgment. Distinctions blend with pressures, as when a tribute muddles public/private and the effect of it, big or small, is given a dose of aggression. In this, one is in an historiography of the trenches—an undeniable element of writing history, as disparate writers such as Thucydides and Momigliano knew well.

What follows is a small inventory of related occurrences; they are not infrequent in any active urban cultural art world, and they suggest we could use a Deleuzian demographer, one who would have the impulse to "quantify, always quantify," in this case cultural processes in Los Angeles. These occurrences are nested in various discursive and social spaces, affecting reader and object, and they are elements in defining Los Angeles as an art world, one with a future.

1. A critic who teaches at one of the more distinctive art schools argues that current Los Angeles–based painters use the computer to pursue aesthetic formalism. L.A. art making is nested in the history of modernist techniques threaded to contemporary devices of production (painting with software). L.A. artists continue to historicize, to plow the genre of formalism for new additions to it.[3] Some of the artists cited were taught by the writer, this nondistance between review and subject certainly familiar to art history as a continuous norm of its reproduction (a Clement Greenberg syndrome?).

2. The *Los Angeles Weekly* came up as an "alternative" paper, which recently joined with the *Los Angeles Times* to gobble up the advertising of a smaller alternative paper, the *New Times*. A recent editorial insists the vitality of the current L.A. art world revival can actually be found in an auction, which indexes "the sheer sprawl and giddy energy that have emerged from the mutant Modernist seed planted by [the artist] Macdonald-Wright."[4] As with number 1, a preexisting narrative, modernism, offers a sense of progress, where "giddy" and "seed" constitute terms of the current tableau. Can an auction tell us of the Dionysiac energy of this city?

3. As we will see below, history at the ground level of representation also needs to dissolve history; thus in a different review, the same *Weekly* writer hones in on objects that collect the fragments of a new utopia, an exhibit that casts off "the torturously drab emperor's new clothes of post-structuralist theory," relegated to obsolescence. Anti-intellectualism forms this small dissolve

of history, as it makes theory the evil object of the new story of art's current vibrancy in Los Angeles.[5]

4. *Artforum,* a prestigious art journal, sends a stringer to Los Angeles to check out the art school scene. The stringer is guided by an L.A. writer and UCLA Art school faculty member, partly because the UCLA writer managed to place five of his students in a show in the New York gallery, Boesky, "despite his snuff-film aesthetics as a fiction writer." There is allusion to underground "legend-craft" stuff at work in that quote, interpersonal impact. The work selected has an "it"—here, "lack of irony and cynicism"—i.e., L.A. artists can deliver the visually naïve, the refreshing, ingredients in the recipe of *epater le bourgeoisie,* historically considered.[6]

5. When future historians turn to the Getty Center and the way it has embraced contemporary art as a topic of scholarly pursuit, will they notice its shift to engage the market that is based on archiving recent art practice, intensifying historicization (ranking) of the now? Will they note that a recent Getty conference on Pop was reviewed in the *Times,* favorably overall, with statements such as "if words such as 'epistemology,' 'de-skilling,' . . . 'narrativize' . . . don't roll off your tongue and into your conversation, this was not a conference for you. During one particularly dry presentation, one of the few artists in the audience fell asleep and snored loudly."[7] Where will this type of anecdote go in such narratives—into the file on the truth and vitality of art against language? Will someone include the history of antiacademicism in Los Angeles, that serves as one of the fronts for anti-intellectualism?

6. Number 5 should be read with this: the *Los Angeles Times* quotes, two weeks later, the Getty's new director, Tom Crow, who avers that the Getty's turn to contemporary art history and its objects is not a major institutional shift because, "The way you think about art and culture of the recent past is bound to change when you go back to look at earlier periods because human life hasn't changed in its fundamentals."[8] Will such statements be read as the scrim through which the Getty's presentation of art is read, or contained, here through resignation, and is this a victory for the progressive left in L.A.'s institutional-cultural competitions, or its surrender to a market it can leverage?

7. At the juncture of graduate schools and the public, one reads that a show at L.A.'s *Museum of Contemporary Art,* which must figure in any coherent narrative, delivered an event called "Public Offerings." It presented the works of internationally recognized artists who "blasted out of art schools in the 1990's." Paul Schimmel of the Museum of Contemporary Art calls Public Offerings an "historical exhibition" about the nineties, and what makes the show

"historically" vibrant is the "early" success of the artists internationally, their work "fresh and pure." "What they were doing was insane," intones Schimmel, locating this group formation in otherness from the public, or at least where the public is differently insane from the insanity attributed to artists. In this, the show managed to relegate the catalogue essays to the backroom—again, Schimmel: "We have left the critical, theoretical underpinnings of the exhibition to the theoreticians."[9] To the mix of the demand for Los Angeles to be seen as "pure" and "insane," future historians will have to make new machines of interpretation.

8. A recent anthology, *Writing Los Angeles,* offered by the Library of America, is reviewed in the *Los Angeles Times* and shows another condition for future narrations. Everything about literary production in the history of Los Angeles comes in twos: the reviewer, who is the editor of the *Times Book Review,* insists that cultural Los Angeles is already historicized—known—so contained in writer's phrases such as "body-fetish" and "eschewing of the mind," "home and refuge," "affection and disdain." The volume under review is praised for culling into print writings on L.A.'s "elusive essence," almost an oxymoron, and is embedded in the great writer Calvino's sense of "desire and fear," Los Angeles "entirely an act of will." "Los Angeles has no right to exist. And yet, against all odds, it does." One cannot go wrong with such metaphysical history: "a world unto itself . . . a mythic city of both abundant promise and tragic disappointment."[10] Of course, any parent could say that of any child.

9. Number 8 goes with this announcement from a well-regarded Los Angeles gallery that an exhibit called "White Album," after the Beatles', and modeled on its ambivalent uses—Charles Manson heard it as a call to race war, while its mainstream audience took it as an index of the demise of politics—is nonetheless a "point of emergence for artistic desire."[11] What does this referencing of a cultural past presented in a commercial gallery venue suggest about the audience's desire here?

10. Finally, how will such different senses of history stack up when compared to the arguments of Susan Anderson, who notes that the history of African-American art and artists in and of Los Angeles is presently "shutout" because "so few L.A. based African-American artists are collected, or even exhibited, by the city's museums"?[12]

Given these instances of facts and processes that already narrate, historicize, what follows is a probe of the murky politics of distinction—sorting, ranking—concerning the sense and value of art and intellectual life. Focus goes to Los Angeles culture and the reviewing procedures that have turned such occurrences—or try to—into history. What are the political and intellectual patterns that consistently make up the sense of the public artist and intellectual? The newspaper reviews are treated as a continuous boundary object, saying something to us about where events and objects mix with private and public, and achieve a narrative impact through reviewing. As in chapter 2, the public receives the present-as-history, but to what end?

In the first section, I examine how the competency of an intellectual is set forth by the *Los Angeles Times Book Review.* The argument is that the *Book Review* conveys a definite narrative message—that an "intellectual" must affirm Enlightenment as the controlling device on writing, Enlightenment modeled as interpretations of history that make historical consciousness a progressive force of criticism. This same Enlightenment is also an historiography of local (neo)canonization. In the second section, I analyze art writing and its move to join neopopulism and formalism, a rejection of language unless the latter affirms the aesthetic and the visual over the critical. Now, this gets tangled: the art reviewers associated with the *Los Angeles Times* are in fact historicizing or making contemporary art *notable,* the condition for its exchange; the *Book Review,* "in the name of history," is actually defending a position that is publicly dominant, and projects the phantom of its own "extinction." Art discourse has moved to the enthusiastic, language made the object of anti-intellectualism; the book-discourse has moved to the apocryphal to defend Enlightenment. Both discourses historicize. As a tangle, my point of entry is the language of both camps, that the language on art historicizes or makes some contemporary art "historically significant," and that the progressive book review has retreated to a form of—oxymoronically—Pop Mandarinism that is questionable in the extreme. The politics here pivot on the similarity of turning *judgments into intuitions* and *historicizing the present.* Taken together, critical judgment is subverted in favor of intuition (of the target reader), or Enlightenment results in *desperate narration*—making the new art representative, defending what is threatened with scare stories of obsolescence.

A few more words are due on the kind of contact made with these reviewing materials. First, when I argue about *intuitive* schemas in art and intellectual life, this means the outfitting of roles, distribution of labor, images of performance. Roughly, the Enlightenment model associated with the book review makes intuitions that pitch the intellectual as someone who represents or speaks for others, where agreement has already been reached as to the methods and tactics of social improvement. Whatever the philosophical history as to the concept of intuition, it is used here to suggest a constriction of sense. The art discourse favors making intuitions that affirm art as an involuntary trigger of the emotions and so a resistance to language as such, the artist imaged as "irresponsible" toward form, a practice that does not contradict any existing mode or type of art. Any discourse tending toward intuitive schemas threatens to turn anti-intellectual, withdrawing from contention its own presuppositions. The circulation of opinion is often an effect of an implicit anti-intellectualism.[13] Opinion making, or the sabotage of further evaluations/selections, is threaded to an *historicization* of information—where it is the review that becomes a "fact on the ground" in a move toward canon-formation.[14]

One final introductory note. Visibility of what that public uses to make judgments is a prerequisite for the public validity of art and writing.[15] There has been a shift to linking validity of judgment to visible authority. Yet running through much of the art writing in Los Angeles is a ubiquitous confusion between anti-intellectualism and antiacademicism: sometimes the anti-intellectualism comes from the academics, sometimes the antiacademicism from the artists, with every combination between. Anyone with a casual experience of art higher education in Los Angeles and New York is well aware how easily discourse on art slides into hatred for the academies, unfortunately screening the serious operations of anti-intellectualism within the academy. The anti-intellectualism of art critics is just as common as anti-intellectual "intellectuals," both groups sharing a dread of language that cannot be controlled or used to bolster aggressive self-positioning. Moreover, the arts in Los Angeles are really dominated by the schools, and the galleries and museums now directly raid the studios of the schools in search of fresh work, among other practices.[16] It is therefore not surprising that art writing here is thoroughly politicized.

Intellectuals and the Los Angeles Times

In the *Life & Style* section of the *Los Angeles Times* (August 7, 1998), Susan Saltor Reynolds previewed the publication (coming attractions?) of Mike Davis's *Ecology of Fear*. The August 16, 1998, edition published an opinion page excerpt from Davis's book, as well as a review of it by Tom Hines, a UCLA architectural historian. Davis's excerpt bemoaned the depiction of Los Angeles as "a new glamour of decay," said to be not just rampant in film and literature, but all too common with editorial writers such as the *Times'* Neil Gabler, "decay" a "condition" of at least cultural existence here.[17] "Disaster," Davis writes, "saturates almost everything now written about Southern California." He then goes on to offer the "real" disaster affecting life here, a "white fear of [the] dark races," revealed in the "secret meaning of L.A. disaster fiction." Let us leave aside how the truth of fiction is the truth of nonfiction; without a trace of conceptual subtlety, nonwhites are placed beyond analysis. Worse, "white fear" in Southern California is said to mirror the "nervous breakdown of American exceptionalism itself." Because American exceptionalism has collapsed, taking with it the ideological underpinnings of liberalism and conservatism, whites having lost their screen against others, "anxiety" over race supplants competition—class—within and between each group as the basic social problem. Davis seems not to notice that invoking politically correct racial divisions—white versus everyone else—is misfiguring, a polemic that can justify—and has—further divisions of the political spoils that affect Los Angeles. The nearly inchoate contention over this book, *Ecology of Fear,* which the *Los Angeles Times* subjected to a front-page reading of its research foibles, raises the kind of boundary issues writers concerned with intellectual property and public/private ask about, in particular disputes over scholarly and critical work that hover between "gift" and "commodity." The editorial and review wavers between a moral responsibility to "speak" in the interests of citizens (reviewing a gift to the public), and its need to have Los Angeles a consumable commodity for readers.[18] L.A.—our contemporary Moby Dick, an empty slot, a void, a lack to be filled. Promoting and disparaging Davis's work is a strong symptom of what is at stake.

Now consider the *Times'* figuring forth images of intellectual work, as to what society can expect from its intellectuals by way of formulating problems, solutions, and giving images of such endeavors. This is a question of the contemporary newspaper's attempt to attract an audience to those views believed to be essential for the "common good." The *Book Review* section of the *Times,* in other words, affords an opportunity to sort out the pressure to have intellectuals "matter" in terms of the judgments they deliver on issues "of the day." Prose judgment crosses the territories of opinion, evaluation, verdicts, confirming ideas and refuting others. As Renato Barilli has suggested in his survey of the history of rhetoric, the contemporary newspaper may well now stand as mostly an extension of commercial persuasion, since the review (and editorial) directs "our attention to products," even if such products are beliefs and ideas, where such a belief or idea "is not something requested by the public but rather fills up 'dead' space and time and is situated in almost subliminal zones."[19]

Inaugurating its revamped *Book Review,* the lead editor insisted that "Los Angeles is fast becoming America's cultural capital," this because it is the

United States' number one market for books. "Number one" means quantity of books sold. Los Angeles is said to be, in 1998, where New York was in 1886, "making real a vision" of its own cultural imperium; the *Times'* inauguration of a book review manages to turn 1998 into 1886, a historiographic marvel. Embedding a new book review in such mythic history is of course pure self-capitalization: "We aim to become the most trusted guide to the most important books being published in America today, giving news of the knowledge needed to survive—and thrive—in the city of the future." Idealism and Darwinism fuse in this "in the name of history." But history does not much matter once 1998 and 1886 are so convertible, especially in the face of the premise "It's L.A.'s turn" to become what New York once was. A mixture of assertion, idealism, and possessiveness that sometimes results in astounding wish—"We should now be able to imagine our great grandchildren gathering 100 years from today at the L.A. Public Library"—one cannot be optimistic that book reviewing is determined by anything less than its telos or end, to make Los Angeles a "cultural capital."[20] *You* will *have* L.A. in your "cultural" life is a suitable paraphrase for the politics/desire involved.

The image of the intellectual can be inferred from the reviews themselves. Let us begin with a review of two books on the sixties. The *sixties* is a name often torqued between nostalgia and an *ominatio* of it, a retrospective prophecy of evil toward it. Our lead editor starts with an historiographic cliché: "People never find it easy to confront the past; they generally prefer to consign it to oblivion." That is a truism that refers to the ubiquity of repression *and* a figure of preparation for enlightenment-to-come, the claim that today's citizen is "without memory." History as a whole, but especially the name *sixties,* has been reduced to "exorcism and kitsch." The editor immediately calls into question his own judgment when he matter of factly states that the sixties were "over-oxygenated years."[21] It is no mean feat to denounce the reduction of history to kitsch in the very sentence that "kitsches."

But the sixties have now received a correct historicization provided by the two books under review. One of them, by Arthur Marwick, is approvingly quoted, the sixties rendered intelligible by reference to the "'measured judgment' of a malleable establishment that both blunted the period's excesses and absorbed its sensibility," the sixties a "multicultural" society that showed what the future must look like. Multiculturalism had a future and Marwick's book "dispels the fog" that the sixties were narrowly political. What the name *sixties* synthesizes then is the "inchoate yearnings of a generation . . . that spent its youth acting as midwife to hopes that continue to haunt the imagination."

What undid such hopes, according to the editor, now breaking off from Marwick's text, was the dissolve of Marxist class analysis to explain the "upheavals of the twentieth-century," suicidal in the face of capitalism's "intelligence" at absorbing critique. The Frankfurt School style of analysis associated with Adorno, and now Habermas, got it right. Through the vehicle of American groups, such as those at Port Huron, some "'regretted the decline' in utopia and hope, acknowledging its cause in the gas ovens." The authentic or "true" intellectuals of the sixties knew that "utopia and hope" are essential to any social transformation. Was the Nazi gas chamber the consequence of a *lack* of utopia and hope? American capitalism integrated the wrong kind of utopia—consumerism. If the sixties failed vis-à-vis their own radical claims, its "early phase" did very good things, its critique of power said here to give calls for justice a moral footing. Because the U.S. government succeeded in limiting the New Left's dissent, it is "utopia and hope" that was the real victim of the government versus the "people" in the sixties.

That utopia and hope might themselves be considered agencies of victimization is, of course, unthinkable here. The *Los Angeles Times Book Review* gives us a progressivism critical of capitalism only for the latter's immorality, eliminating far stronger views that capitalism might, say, signify nihilisms of all sorts. By comparison to the hope/utopia legacy, the editor demonizes sixties drugs and "messianic eschatology," which replaced "virtues of patience and reflection and nonviolence embraced by the early New Left." This New Left, historiographically, repeats "early = truth" (one can fill in the lack or blank, but "early Marx" fits); and what came later = "Lunacy was the result."[22] The New Left's mission canceled by false utopian thought gave way to "ahistorical wandering." The "New Left's mission" cut off from the language of Marxism resulted in a "theoretical shallowness that would prove to be its undoing." The New Left was "unable to muster the tenacity required by its ambition," a sentence that is itself a model of impossibility, of joining politics and morality in something other than hope and utopia. The long historical lens of Enlightenment used here denounces the "political process [which] remains one in which discourse is sacrificed to spectacle," a phrase right out of Frankfurt School emphasis upon historical consciousness as the necessary form of social understanding. The editor closes his review/editorial with a warning: current ideas of authenticity mixed with a demand for politics "as a total art form" leads to a "dialectic of defeat." Only lives filtered through the Ideals of hope and utopia are worth striving for in this fusion of Frankfurt School and myth.[23] Only a certain type or mode of historical consciousness offers us a way to the past and the capacity to use the past for a better future.

So between the editor's call for the *Times* as a guide to the best writing and the extreme politicization—Enlightenment only—one can judge that the *Book Review* performs an invaluable function: to provide the right kind of "consciousness" for readers who are deemed to lack Enlightenment, since it is unthinkable, isn't it, that the *Times* is preaching to the converted?

Trotting out Adorno to denounce existentialists' "abuse of language"[24] goes hand in hand in the *Book Review* with its willful misrepresentation of everything that goes under the name of deconstruction. David Lehman's 1993 review of Alice Kaplan's *French Lessons* lauds the book because, among other things, it polemicized against "cutting-edge critical theories," Lehman reducing deconstruction, more than once, to the belief that "language always lies," which simply cannot be found in the writings of any deconstructionist.[25] Does it mean something that the *Los Angeles Times*' sole review of a book on deconstruction performs such politicization? In a review called "Danger: Historians at Work," another historian insisted on noticing conflict between "experts" (historians and curators) and groups such as veterans, whose experiences make up the content of historical commemorations. The "fidelity and comprehensiveness" of scholars is set against the "indifference of the public" (true enough). The "distinguished record of sober analysis" by experts is set against Congress's control of the monies for displays of public history. The experts are set against "historical revisionism and elite deconstructionists [who] trivialize the serious issues involved here," it being insisted that history in a democratic society is finally left (pun intended) to the experts who "will probably have the last word—mainly because they have so many good ones." As an expert historian, surely this professor knows that to connect "revisionists," of whom the most notorious is Faurisson with his denial of the Holocaust, with deconstructionists, as she does, is a malicious smear? It is a professional kiss of death for historians in America to welcome the methods and analysis offered by deconstructionists. Thus, *expert* operates here as a code word for professional self-protection and anti-intellectualism encoded by directly linking idiots like Faurisson with deconstructionists.[26] Perhaps the historians get the last word as this professor insists, but public language and thought is not about last words, but words that matter. Herodotus, after all, was not just the father of history, but, among his peers, also the father of lies.

Commemorating the one hundred and fiftieth anniversary of the *Commu-*

nist Manifesto in a 1998 super-review entitled "Why Read Marx?" the lead editor notes that "apart from Darwin's *Origin of Species* [*The Communist Manifesto*] is arguably the most important work of nonfiction written in the 19th century."[27]

The job of assigning this importance is left to Eric Hobsbawm, whose new introduction on the *Manifesto* is republished here. Asserting that the *Manifesto* is an "astonishing masterpiece," Hobsbawm lays out for *Times* readers a very strange image of Marxism. This image is predicated on the fact that the *Manifesto* in 1998 has become great literature, political rhetoric with "an almost biblical force." This rhetorical force/status establishes its power to diagnose and sustain continuity between 1848 and 1998—the *Manifesto*'s "unrealistic optimism . . . has proved to be the 'Manifesto's' most lasting strength," this because what is of inestimable value is its "vision" that capitalism "was not permanent . . . but a temporary phase in the history of humanity." Capitalism is destined to "pass." That is what *to vision* visions, infinitive mode, and this knowledge of capitalism's end protects utopia from obsolescence and presentism. Thus, it is really the *Manifesto*'s *predictive* power that makes it relevant today, for us, so it is merely a question of acknowledging that the *Communist Manifesto* has come true in 1998. Hobsbawm's rhetoric updates the *Manifesto* as a consumable cultural product: if we reckon temporality according to the clock provided by the *Manifesto,* we will surely realize not only that 1848 is 1998, but Marx and Engels were only "wrong" about the conclusions they drew from their vision: the fact that the proletariat did not conquer the bourgeoisie is not intrinsic to the importance of the *Manifesto.* "Social management," it is insisted, must still "necessarily" replace "private appropriation," a proposition that refuses to understand capitalism as potentially unlimited, or that social democracy, as is now happening in Europe, often self-reduces to sorting out the claimants to fewer and fewer resources.

Politics over determinism or utopian vision over presentism: this is, for Hobsbawm, the singular message of the *Manifesto,* and in what is surely a phrase of sheer arrogance, historical inevitability preserved, Hobsbawm demands that for history to happen, for utopia to matter, "the graves have to be dug by or through human action." The historian wants the right to legislate over who lives, who dies, the *Manifesto*'s vision seeing as far as the binary of "socialism or barbarism." In these hallucinogenics, can 1998 = 1933? This review/editorial mix insists that the *Manifesto* has nothing to do with the "killing fields" of the twentieth century, only with the Enlightenment, these "bookish socialists" really good utopians. But, unsaid here, the *Manifesto*

Hegelianized the proletariat, baptizing it in spirit such that the *Manifesto* could claim the proletariat's "mission is to destroy all previous securities for, and insurances of, individual property," and that once proletarians captured the State, they would have to make "despotic inroads" on society, even including "confiscation of the property of all emigrants *and rebels.*"[28] As anyone remotely familiar with the actual history of Marxism's relations to the *rest of the left* understands, the kind of vision featured by the *Los Angeles Times* has always waged war against its "internal enemies," as Marx and Engels called for in the *Manifesto.*

So what does it mean when the *Los Angeles Times Book Review* promotes a text stripped of many of its most interesting theses, refusing to actually historicize it as it sells the *Communist Manifesto* as a "vision thing"? In this sense, doesn't the book review show rigid command utterances, appealing to a "model reader" who is subject to the "inflexible project" of the review, the latter "potentially speaking to everyone" and which "presupposes an average reader resulting from . . . intuitive sociological speculation" in the same way an advertisement chooses its possible audience?[29] Isn't this the Mandarinism the left ordinarily denounces?

Hobsbawm returned to the pages of the *Los Angeles Times Book Review* a few weeks later in a review of David Landes's *Wealth and Poverty of Nations,* the kind of "big" book that purports to inform and give this average reader a sense of depth and adequation to the conceivably impossible mountains of facts and events of the past. Hobsbawm praises the book by insisting that "the ideas may not always be easy, but for a serious book the reading is."[30] Hobsbawm's own prose is eloquent and systematically misleading: immediately after praising Landes's style, ex cathedra takes over: "When all the world was poorer, it was also less unequal." The good historian does not even need to understand how numbers work or can be misused. Citing 400 to 1 wealth extremes today versus 3 to 1 a hundred and fifty years ago—without any sense of the method used—Hobsbawm seems not to notice that the very comparison presumes continuity between then and now, hardly an historical attitude (like many historians, he does not notice that the rigorous application of historical method, or sensitivity to context, might obliterate the very basis for comparing differences in time—epistemology never stands in the way of politics). What does "less unequal" actually refer to or mean? Since we cannot go back in time, what are we to do with differences that cannot be experienced or even compared,[31] that cannot be anything but asserted as important *now*? Criticizing Landes for inadequate attention to the "catastrophes" of the twentieth century, even worse is Landes's focus on the absurdities of "political correctness" in recent history. Hobsbawm dismisses the subject: "living amid the culture wars of *fin de siècle* America, he [Landes] spends much time on controverting [political correctness], though unfortunately not on controverting the even more dangerous fashion for the new Darwinian reduction of history to . . . sociobiology."[32] Good historical consciousness just means resistance to "the right" (sociobiology) instead of asking after the left's use of "right ideas," here the assumption of a *humanism* that is unassailably threaded to thinking historically.

This defense of humanism is not surprising, but it definitely smacks of the archaic if not anachronistic idea that intellectuals can pose issues that are universal. Adding its own commemorations of the death of Isaiah Berlin, his death elicits from one review that his achievement was to support pluralism over monism, a pluralism that testified to "a common core of humanity . . . beneath the enormous differences bequeathed to us by history," this "common core" set against theory or excessive analysis. Even the death notice of Berlin elicits some antideconstruction out of the *Times*.

The *Book Review* offered Michael Ignatieff's commentary on a book written by Stephen Toulmin, who insists that as the "Best of Oxford," Berlin warrants the superlative because he was the luckiest intellectual *courtier* England had between 1940 and 1960 or so. In another review, Berlin's real achievement had nothing to do with criticism and ideas, but with his Jewishness having opened England itself to "the art of conversation" and "weekends in intellectual chat." Indeed, Toulmin offers that Berlin's "distinctive position was to criticize most liberal theory for ignoring the inevitability of tragic choice."[33] Affirmation of tragedy makes one a humanist, and tragedy complements hope and utopia, stick-figure thoughts. It is simply amazing that historians can so neatly synthesize human feelings in such "poetic" forms. Eugene Genovese, a distinguished historian, is called upon in another review to pronounce that "great religious and intellectual movements" have given way to "performance" and cultural studies, the latter movements part of the unfortunate elimination of "breadth," "drama," and "most dangerously," "tragedy," which historical knowledge used to render, what used to give history "its abiding hold over the public imagination."[34] It does not occur to this distinguished historian that such a "hold over the public imagination" is itself a dangerous idea, or that it is not such a disaster when public imagination frees itself from an all-pervasive sense of tragedy, the latter almost always used to insinuate a sense of limit and futility, namely, any particular present's resistance to change. Indeed, to use "tragedy" here is to presume a sense of modernism as cultural universal, precisely the kind of presupposition that should be ruthlessly examined according to more than one critical model.

A few more instances of "historical Enlightenment." Lawrence Levine reviews historiographic issues raised by other historians (Hobsbawm's book one of them), concluding that historical knowledge is about a "conversation" essential to American self-understanding. *Conversation* is not a contentious term and idea, or a problem in itself. In a review of recent Holocaust books, Neal Ascherson demands more affirmation of Enlightenment: the "central, simple, human question—'How could they' [Nazis kill so many]—remains without a satisfactory answer."[35] Ascherson cannot imagine that the question may be the wrong question, or if any question could be the right one, not exactly the same thing. After pointing out how the Goldhagen "thesis" has polarized contemporary Germans, and going silent as to how American readers are involved in the book industry of the Holocaust (we in fact keep it going), Ascherson treats Goldhagen's thesis by praising another book and declares Goldhagen incorrect that "almost nobody thought in terms of mass murder" in Germany before the Final Solution was in progress. Ascherson then damns Goldhagen's "semantic tricks," how he shifts the terms from "elimination" to "extermination" as the connective tissue for what happened after 1933. Ascherson promotes a thesis far more "fair and carefully balanced," found in Klaus Fischer's *The History of an Obsession,* that the murder of the Jews "had little to do with ideology and much to do with the darkest and most disgusting mechanisms of the human psyche."[36] In the name of historical propriety history itself is undone by this appeal to "human psyche," as we are now enlightened about these "mechanisms"—the basic one is "gratuitous cruelty," so we understand that the Germans of 1943 mesh with exterminators in "Latin America or Rwanda or Bosnia," which undercuts any such notion as culturally based "exterminist" beliefs urged on us by the Goldhagen types. Since "dehumanization" is universal, German history is not the key to German history: the human psyche is the key, so that like many other reviews "in the name of history," it actually is not history that is at stake, historical consciousness reduced to moral pleading and big themes that install Enlightenment as a boundary for criticism's self-protection.

The *Los Angeles Times Book Review* section is politically driven by Enlightenment-based judgments about the value and virtue of historicization: the reviews are in effect editorials that preserve hope and utopia as necessary, a reactive scouring of dissidence directed at the wrong left. That the historian as

public intellectual is believed to render judgments necessary for social understanding is sustained by discursive modes that actually appeal to a reader's "safe
intuitions," i.e., affirmation of tragedy. That historians are actually serving the
Book Review's own agenda as politically correct connoisseurs of the destruc-
tions of modern life is also outside the realm of discussability, which is to say
that one is to affirm historical consciousness with no sense at all of the *stakes*
or necessities involved in the knowledge we are supposed to desire.

Art Criticism and Language

By comparison to the Frankfurt School–type model, which uses historical
consciousness to sort out claimants and deliver telling judgments about present uses of the past—giving us a "good" sixties—the writings discussed below
are interested in opening a market for new things, objects of all sorts, to borrow a phrase from the estimable writings of Vincent Descombes. The collective problem of this group is how to "free" artworks from critical discourses of
all sorts.

In recent years, the *Los Angeles Times* has consistently displayed a policy of
rejection of critical discourse brought to bear on works of art: the notion that
works of art do not "take" *critical* language of the types associated with Marxism (e.g., Bourdieu) or Foucauldian readings. This dovetails with artistic and
institutional formations offering financial and symbolic recognition that are
not interested in the exposure of techniques of how aesthetics is positioned.
Each formation is progressive—but how progressivism is put together is also
off the table, or relegated to discussion at a conference of fifty scholars/stu-
dents at one of the schools.

It requires a lot of protection to sustain the intricate networks that inform
much of the current art world, everywhere. The cultural ethnographer George
Marcus has offered some reasons for this. After enjoying a Getty Museum research fellowship, Marcus went on to analyze the museum as predicated on
middlebrow culture "earnestly pursuing objects of high culture," an aggressive
middle-class demand for high culture, instead of the supposed forced domination of high against low.[37] Cynical high groups lose nothing by receiving the
desire and interests of those who want in. Consequently, each group formation
in the arts here pursues an agenda not exactly self-flattering when analyzed,
whether it is the Getty deciding how to select worthy scholars or an off-the-
street "marginal" group concerned with making linkages, it needs to continue.

For the art writers in Los Angeles, there is a consensus that works of art are not subject to categorical relations such as commodification. A recurring premise of this anticritical criticism is that evaluative language and economics are relations that a work of art *refutes* in its very "objectness." The result is that the critic's job is drastically simplified: passing to readers ideas that sustain an art object's nonverbal significance. The job of elimination can even accommodate the desire for art-as-ambiguity, an uncertainty that is still "certain," i.e., the surprise of nonrecognition as an object's "impact," at times a highly prized epithet. *To see,* infinitive mode, has become the catchword of this formation, language and economics, declared to interfere with the consideration of the art object. What is said to be "really given" by the object itself, if only we could pay heed to what it "does" instead of what we want it to say, is not its relation to language, economics, history, or network, but its purge of language, the "best" objects those that are "bad" for language. There is a tradition that offers art-as-resistance to precoded interpretations, Duchampian modernism, but that is not the argument synthesized by the *Times* and related authors. The synthetic unity to this formation may be found in the juncture of the language of enthusiasm and anti-intellectualism, or the return of a certain kind of philosophical *naturalism,* "naturalism" standing in here for rejection of language whenever it complicates and interferes with affective states said to be fundamental to art's impact. A commentator on naturalism in American philosophy has emphasized this as an experience of "rapt attention which involves the intransitive apprehension of an object's immanent meanings in their full presentational immediacy."[38] Rapt attention is a good thing—but as an end in itself?

The philosophical premises of using language to reject language are not difficult to describe, since the critics discussed below are active in this endeavor. Let us start with a show originating at the Otis College of Art and Design, Los Angeles, in 1994, *Plane/Structures.* David Pagel's essay, "Looking into Seeing," insists that our "corporeal organs" all by themselves make coherence "out of intangible visual phenomena," which does not mean matching or fitting visual signals to a viewer's experiences, but the viewer submitting to objects, to the point where "we cannot distinguish our beliefs about it from our beliefs about our own experience." The objects in *Plane/Structures* are linked by their attempt to "elicit experiences from us prior to trying to get us to believe anything," a "hedonism" and "optimism" to be had from objects, encoded into them, that embraces the "hypnotic force" of an object, the viewer defined as a subject who wills being "captive to" an object's "capacity to test us." The language models the object as a probe of one's openness to the enticing, the viewer required to submit to the experience of being "awestruck" in front of such works. Such experiences are without language: "a piece either works or it doesn't," and when it does "work," they result in "mesmeric intensity" that somehow, it is insisted, is said to result in "gracefulness" as a primary affect within the intransitive experience. "Awestruck" does not mean sublime, as there is no hint of a contest between the faculties of the viewer, but the viewer made "dumb." According to Pagel, unlike the earlier L.A. generation of Light-and-Space artists, the works in *Plane/Structures* are not illusionistic, but *naturalistic:* "we see things before consciousness locates them in sensible, consistent pictures," which is what happens "when late-afternoon Southern California sunlight strikes the facades . . . bright planes that appear to be discontinuous with the substantial volumes we know they circumscribe." Art is one with nature in being against the will, "by pointing out . . . what's already there,"[39] or art is affirmed as continuous with preconscious experience. It would have been interesting had Pagel brought these contrasts to a description of why there is any need for criticism at all.

A second writer in the catalogue here is Dave Hickey, who has, for more than twenty years, taken the critic to task, recently intoning that "there is no money in criticism; no power accrues to its practice; and, sadly enough, hardly anyone wants to have sex with a critic."[40] Now a university professor and MacArthur Fellow, Hickey has managed to retread clichéd typologies along the way, worth raising here for their faux-populist effect, before moving to his catalogue essay.

1. *National Character.* Europeans are "ironic" when sharp enough to be so, but Americans at their artistic best are "cool": "Washington . . . Peirce, Henry James, Gertrude Stein, Andy Warhol, and Alex Katz are cool. Presuming to embody their beliefs, they decline to plead them—yet wish to be seen embodying them . . . one's own embodied authority as a citizen, without deigning to invest it with fancy justifications, personal explanations, or expressive urgency. One simply paints the soup can."[41] Cool is cool and style is the thing, a tautology modeled on narcissism.

2. *Friendly Art.* In a comparison of Titian and the painter David Reed, we are told that the continuity of "the body in the box" which links these artists is a matter of "warm corporeality and cool geometry," this conjunction the positive version of much art's "anxiety and instability." "Exciting" is opposed to "painful" experiences of critical art. Art should be "sexy as hell."[42]

3. *The Cave of Innocence.* Art should be considered "bad, silly, frivolous.

Imagine the lightness we would feel if this burden of hypocrisy [art = moral good] were lifted from our shoulders." Art should strive to have "good effects" rather than "dramatizing good intentions." Art belongs to the agora, like sports; it belongs to democratic "competition and cooperation" where we "vote" on the art we "get" and hence get the art we deserve. This is innocence as opposed to the "caregivers" all over the art world. Hickey seems not to notice the "care-giving" rendered in comparing Titian and Reed, or the sense of "warm and cool," which is nothing if not caregiving in the mode of a perfect art hot tub.[43]

4. *Direct Identification with "the People."* In a book review, Hickey unloads on intellectually informed criticism as he becomes "one" in pure conversation with Andy Warhol, replete with recited sounds of "the moment."[44] He has it that chromophobia or maintenance of distinction between color and figure is "in its final redoubt as a vehicle of institutionalized loathing and disdain for proletarian taste and commercial culture." The love of "colors" is proletarian, which legitimizes this piece of pure *ressentiment* against scholars; anyone identified with an institution (which is clearly Hickey's repressive blindness, for he is a professor—or is this canceled by the reception of democratic "prizes"?) falls under the ban of a reading: "Batchelor's book [*Chromophobia*] . . . a joy . . . the rare pleasure of vicarious revenge, of seeing the biter bit, the table turned, the bully unmasked and made to look foolish. Thirty years of annoyance at creepy, sneering, semi-educated chromophobes in nice-ish suits melted away."[45]

To return to the *Plane/Structures* show: Hickey insists that "once past Jeremy Gilbert-Rolfe's yellow [painting] (or more accurately, *Yellow!*) . . . words start slipping off the wall and we find ourselves poised between the undeniable visibility of the color we see before our eyes and the demonstrable inadequacy of our English color-vocabulary to describe it."[46] Hickey does not notice that calling out *Yellow!*—a scream—might produce the very "inadequacy of . . . vocabulary" asserted, gripped as the language is by getting rid of language. Wanting to find a nondiscursive and bodily response to an object, Hickey offers that such connections to an object are found in eloquence, in an object's capacity to force its viewer to go *"through* language to some bodily inference of the 'full world' of phenomenal reality." The object's rhetoric matters. But imputing rhetorical trope and figure to the object is weird, as there is no concept of rhetoric that reduces rhetoric to "body" and its inferences, whatever they might be. No, language interferes with the ability to experience art, and we must assume the body "itself" involuntarily "speaks" a truth in the presence of art, an exceedingly strange idea unless one believes the body never lies (or always tells the truth, not the same thing). Suppressing the idea that art might be here modeled, by analogy, on non-art (e.g., an act of violence often produces the indescribable), Hickey restricts his discussion of works to those that give an indescribable pleasure; not unlike the upsurge today in apocalyptic discourse, it is the *effect* that matters, and here is where politics takes over.

The effect of an object's eloquence can never, Hickey insists, be "counterfeited."[47] An object possesses intrinsic identity, end of story. Cryptic and mystical, the kind of language naturalism favors, an object's eloquence emerges by "involuntary, bodily consent and approval," an artwork's *"political power."*[48] Tying the eloquent to the involuntary to the political leads to the public, the latter coming into existence when "eloquence elicits our involuntary consent." The chain of associations does not make anything but assertive or enthymemic (illogical) sense, and, as said above, this "Ciceronian imperative" utterly mangles the history and theory of rhetoric, especially by assuming an object is already rhetoric, or language, and then denying the logic.

But—and it is a big but—rhetoric *is* inseparable from the epistemic and the grammatical, or logic and grammar in Paul de Man's terms. Since rhetoric is language, even if language does not reduce to rhetoric, how could rhetoric ever be determined by "involuntary consent"? For Cicero, eloquence was modeled on literature, whereas Hickey insists that works of art share with music an antipathy toward literature's encoding of the visible world.[49] Why such misreading and reduction of rhetoric to sensory or bodily effect? Because in the end, Hickey wants to privilege a certain kind of work: those that allow for "seeing the world," language silenced in a "democracy of rhetorical advocacy," an equality between work/audience. The *wrong language prevents the body's involuntary enjoyment of an object. To see* is not *to look:* the former is positive, the latter is to submit an object to scrutiny; to look encodes vision by language and is a disaster. The only remedy or medicine is to get the eye to see; this alone can affirm "the full positive, uniform reality that we hope . . . is."[50] Rhetoric is modeled as natural thought—of course with one good and one bad side—a truly illiterate idea of rhetoric or an idea of rhetoric fit for illiterates, since it cuts rhetoric off from the social and intellectual, or language's life with thought and others. Art based on rhetoric is art that equals affirmation, or the social world returned to a naturalism that does not contain negation. Or, if you like, negation is associated with critical language. In short, the naturalism insisted upon here wants to achieve a rescue of sensibility against overcoded language. While the project is understandable insofar as many artists have been precisely *reduced* to giving us objects that often only feed what we already "know," the anti-intellectualism above systematically cleanses art and language of language, dreading an audience that is critical, skeptical, and generally suspicious about the claims any particular object makes on us.[51] It does, however, historicize the new, attached to making *authenticity* of the present attractive.

The September–October 1998 issue of *Art Issues,* a privately financed magazine now defunct, featured a diatribe by *Times* staff writer David Pagel[52] entitled "Designer Marxism: The Rise of White-Market Art." "White" means bloodless art, or critical-conceptual art, or the art shown at university galleries. Pagel has taught in several Los Angeles colleges, and is an independent curator, as well as a writer for the *Los Angeles Times.* With only one reference to an artist or critic, "Designer Marxism" is without notes and without a single reference to a work of art. Cast in the literary mode of parody, using the *Communist Manifesto* to excoriate Marxism (= criticism), Pagel even anticipates objections to his diatribe by asserting that "Designer Marxists commonly reinforce their authority by labeling anyone who criticizes them as an anti-intellectual—if not a McCarthyite."[53] So Designer Marxists must be McCarthyites by virtue of their misuse of authority—their use of criticism so as to reject criticism of themselves, a charge that has enough credibility to make it malicious when *not* attached to precise names and texts. It would have been helpful if Pagel had been able to introduce a division or distinction within the category "Designer Marxism," for his claim tends to say artists and critics are implicitly carrying out the tactics of Designer Marxism unless they are avowedly anti-Marxist.[54] It would have been helpful if Pagel noted that nearly all of the important university posts in Los Angeles that concern art are led by those on the left.

Be that as it may, here are the claims made by Pagel: (1) Designer Marxism disdains "ordinary commerce," such disdain a "fashion" peculiar to the left. It rejects "ordinary commercial exchange," the "common market" as well as the open "calculation" of the "black [private] market." It is not specified why "ordinary commercial exchange" should be thought in color terms at all (an interpretation of capitalism in painterly terms?). This Designer Marxism practices a hypocrisy of criticism, where the "normal consumer" is usually, if not always, reduced to "dim-wittedness."[55] (2) Accompanying that series of assertions, Designer Marxism is castigated for embodying all or part of the following qualities and attributes: it is said to be engaged in hypocrisy for selling "good works" as it puts "ordinary commerce" down; it is "cynical and naive" at once, this for devaluing art as social transaction; it is Orwellian "double speak" for being nothing but itself another style, obsessed with "technical innovations" while it denounces art as fetish; its scientific or critical pretensions are just that; it overvalues the circulation of "institutional" structures instead of accepting any given "single work of art . . . as interesting or potent"; and it is academic, connoisseur-obsessed, a "mandarin activism" that "ignores the actual, low-level, give-and-take interactions by which 99% of contemporary art changes hands."[56] (3) These attributes and qualities are, in turn, given a sociological denunciation: Designer Marxism is an "aberration [that] goes back to the sixties" and has turned the "brash, colorful objects" of Pop and its "constituency" into an "ironic" relationship, instead of Pop works being objects whose constituency knew "what they were getting."[57] In denial over its own market connections being exposed (Designer Marxism = academic art), Designer Marxism's real market is the *white* one, "an insular world" filled with "esoteric innovations." In a word, Designer Marxism comes to stand for everything that inhibits the transactions of the "common market" where, like *Forrest Gump,* everyone is already in on the irony of being ironic in the present, hence there is no room or space for irony since the latter is self-canceling in normal art transactions. Using parody to undermine irony, Pagel calls for artists and, if there are any critics left standing, to submit to the enthusiasm of this common market. As conservatives have tended to insist, "real people" always somehow "know" what they are doing and reviewers must follow their lead—no discussion of production or consumption of art can even be taken up once "real people" are invoked and the critic is modeled as an interference machine with "real life."[58]

"Designer Marxism" synthesizes the Los Angeles strand of hysterical anti-criticism or delirium, in Deleuze and Guattari's terms. Economics and language are to be put to death in a language that wants a certain kind of submission (= idealization) to the object. Fear of language marks the language. Needless to say, putting language to death is transpolitical (the left's version subjects language to notions of historical significance). It is, again, not just a question that the critic protests too much in the creation of a larger share of a fractured art market, a power play in eliminating a rival position; it is, rather, and here are the mean words, a question of politics and epistemics—why is critical discourse considered so threatening and unfortunately not restricted to art writing?[59] For there is an arguable national trend to anti-intellectualism, signaled not just in L.A. writing, but in venues such as the *New York Times* (e.g., Bernard Holland's diatribe against music that requires understanding instead of immersion in feeling). Decrying the "intimidation of listeners" Holland, in the same assertive anti-intellectualism as Pagel and Hickey, insists that "in art, one decides what one likes."[60] Well, yes, but how is "one decides" *decided,* since viewers already have language at their disposal? Can't critics consider alienating their audience? Why not?

"Designer Marxism's" assertions against language have become a regularity in Los Angeles, complementary to the discourse of Davis-style apocalypse and Enlightenment ideals. Hickey is tireless in reiterating the discourse of antidiscourse, views laid out in *Art Issues* and, through the conduit of Christopher Knight (on whom, more below), the *Los Angeles Times'* senior art critic, these views are proclaimed as rational, ordinary, natural.[61]

Hickey's writings are an astounding and lugubrious mix of aggression cast in the faux-pop idiom of just being one of the little people ill served by our main institutions. "Art is a bad, silly, frivolous thing to do"—so defined, no one in their right mind would subject art to language since the tags of "bad, silly, frivolous" leave no space for critical tentacles, nor would one want to invoke economics since "bad" takes care of that by making art a poor exchange. Fleshed out, the implicit presupposition is that any art object, found in museum, gallery, classroom, office, or bedroom, is there because of an undifferentiated "love" for said object—and for no other reason. Where Pagel asserts that "ritualistic religiosity" continues to infuse art of the left,[62] Hickey claims that art-as-bad eliminates the pretenses of art as religion.[63] Love of art requires that we cleanse ourselves of irony so as to return to naïveté, Schiller over Marx, return to the naïve by sheer fiat. Whatever else this is, it is a purge and cleansing, but it prepares the way to historicize *authentic* beautiful things offered by those artists praised by these critics. It does not want to address what Baudrillard called prestation or sign-value: that a gallery shows artist Y's work because it wants to create a *future market* for that work; that a catalogue essay establishes a work's dubious superiority; that curators put together shows in the hope of acquiring more funds for bigger and better shows—these ideas are removed in favor of "communities of desire." Art *is* feeling: "a confluence of simple hearts, a community united not in what they [artworks] are—not in any cult of class, race, region or ideology—but in the collective mystery of what they are *not* and now find embodied before them."[64] This affirmation of religion in objects is just as ridiculous as any sense that an art object comes before us as commodity. The mysticism of a tribal community pushes language out of the way, religion now recoded as community. In Pagel's overheated and even childish rhetoric, familiar to readers of the *Times,* a valued effect of seeing is the "gorgeous" object, "breathtakingly beautiful," or "ravishing," "eye-popping," and "juicy," terms that make any discourse but its own irrelevant. Again, rendered devoid of use and exchange value by the assertion of mysteries, it is a category mistake to confuse art with anything other than "interest, enthusiasm and volunteer commitment," that is, protection of a common market (or better, the myth thereof). Calling out *Yellow!* in front of a yellow painting—is this anything but a verbal equivalent of a sports metonym, a slam dunk?

In this magicscape, artworks are really about the public's "referendum on how things should look and the way we should look at things," which means that once something is built, say, thousands of McDonald's restaurants, we should accept the given reality as a judgment of the fact of acceptance of such objects. Democracy and pop culture are embodied in their common "involuntary desire," the dumbness of the masses affirmed (on which, more below). Because McDonald's is there, the public has already implicitly judged such buildings to be part of its negotiation with public space, a fact on the ground. Denouncing any such doubts about these assertions, calling anyone who does so a caregiver, the only *kind* of art Hickey actually tolerates is that which *"catches our eye,"* where hearts and minds will follow.[65] This faux-populist rhetoric is an update of bucolic sentimentalism, or the idealization of the pastoral. Calling for an art that is "wrong thinking" and in that way making "things look right" (the Michael Douglas character in *Falling Down* become art enthusiast?), we must learn to be dumb again. The audience will be silent in the face of things that overwhelm; the critic will protect this experience; the audience will not be disturbed in its enjoyment of the spectacle of things, even intimacies. When Pagel writes in November 2002 that "at 71, John Baldessari is making the best work of his career," the main reviewing or evaluating term is "deliciously puzzling pictures," objects not described but the discourse of a vassal enthralled, part of the larger, no doubt, urban / art world discourse of wonder and amazement. The fealty comes out again, for example, in a March 2000 review where the Getty exhibition of eleven L.A. artists gives "electrifying energy . . . You can *feel* the power that positively crackles," terms that kill off too many other experiences.[66]

Pagel's lumping together of Designer Marxism with any kind of criticism and Hickey's celebration of a desire for "wrong thinking" come together in the remarks and assertions by Jeremy Gilbert-Rolfe in his *Beyond Piety* (1995). A veteran of the L.A. art wars of the 1980s, unfairly pushed out of CalArts in 1986 in one of CalArts' periodic turns to left-hysteria (Pagel is not completely wrong about the element of in-house clubness, only blind to his own), and a key member in Art Center, College of Design's (Pasadena) revival in the early nineties, Gilbert-Rolfe offers a much more controlled discourse of antidiscourse and rejection of Foucauldian type analysis. Indeed, where Pagel and Hickey rail against irony and embrace the naïve, Gilbert-Rolfe embraces the ironic so as to achieve a new state of the naïve. If journalistic situations drive the writings previously considered, here it is more of a question of what to make of the use and abuse of theory, Baudrillard in particular. Gilbert-Rolfe's work spans academic discourse and a local institution's impact in the art market. Specifically, Baudrillard has claimed that art, like politics, ethics, and history, is bound to "infinite retrospective analyses of what happened before," nearly a culture of autopsy, where art is part of the "fossilized irony" of every social relation. This is another version of the death of art. In the May 7, 1997, issue of *Liberation,* Baudrillard joined "the total worthlessness of contemporary art" to the "impotence" of French political life in the face of Le Pen's reactionary challenge and, in another place, insists on art's reduction to the "irony of repentance and resentment against our own culture."[67] Interestingly, Gilbert-Rolfe omits Baudrillard's treatment of art in his own model of invoking Baudrillard to salvage art, projecting Baudrillard's social theses (implosion, simulation) onto art while removing Baudrillard's theses *on* art. *Historicization involves radical selective reading.* In a paper given at a conference in New York in November of 1997, Gilbert-Rolfe insisted that Foucault's notions of power have the same function as the Frankfurt School texts, both of which reduce art to a space "filled with objects, installations and non-objects of other sorts that can have a socio-anthropological function" that is social and discursive. Amalgamating Foucault to Peter Berger's *Theory of the Avant-Garde,* without any supporting analysis, Gilbert-Rolfe asserts that any interest in "social contradictions" is by definition anti-art, or anti-"the art object's form," or hostility toward an art object's own recursive self-production.[68]

Declaring on nearly every page wrath against Conceptualism for its overall procedure of "illustrating" ideas, Gilbert-Rolfe asserts that the works of John Baldessari—certainly a respected teaching artist in the L.A. art world (pace Arthur Danto)—are the most interesting Conceptualist objects to have come out of Los Angeles, this *because* Baldessari takes a "bad idea" (Hickey's "wrong thinking") and displays its "dumbness."[69] Where "good ideas" are "complete," tending to a moralistic holism/identity, bad ideas can allow for "supplementation," that is, using Derridean notions grafted to Baudrillard's idea of art as irresponsible, one should embrace bad ideas because they make for an art that is humorous or ironic. This move issues in a pronouncement—that works made from bad ideas and a dumb premise are said to "proceed from a reduction. A reduction which turns into a refusal. The refusal of singularity, the refusal of wrongness."[70] The opacity of that statement resounds with the intellectual and emotional space of the cryptic. Continuing, Baldessari's valorization of the bad, the dumb, is said to belong to the "uncontrollability of color," whose work shows the layering of "indeterminate meaning [that] reinforces the indeterminacy of another system of indeterminate meaning."[71] The language here is icy and sharp instead of pop, but its sharpness is devoted to ensuring that the art object refutes all discourse but the one that is capable of penetrating the object's intention to not-mean anything determinate. *Indeterminacy simply replaces determinacy as the choice of effect.* Indeed, Baldessari's main interest for Gilbert-Rolfe is that his work has systematically been preoccupied with the "irresponsibility of the sign," parsed as "its endless deferring from one reference to the other," famous in, say, Olitski's ambiguous use of color. While one can appreciate Gilbert-Rolfe's vigorous defense of difficult art—even if the categories of the "irresponsible" and Derridean indeterminacy co-imply the other is just asserted—how a moral feeling, the irresponsible, is joined to the technical effect of indeterminate meaning and "deferred" seems a wish about painting, even a demand for a kind of artist subjectivity. Baldessari's own statement that his work has been about creating a market for visual play is swept aside.[72]

Beyond Piety finds a natural rejection of critique and language in nearly every phenomenon said to be irresponsible. For instance, in fashion, language and discourse on it hover between the complete and the incomplete. But the swimsuit is lodged in the visual, said to be mute and antidiscursive, the swimsuit "clothing which doesn't clothe . . . the cruel truth that if you are not attractive then a swimsuit will not help."[73] Paintings, restaurant/bars, swimsuits—the writing *insists* on the upsurge of nonresponsibility or the distancing of writing and language. Amalgamating Baldessari's work to that of Jean Baudrillard, giving it the gloss of theoretical sophistication—"The world is aestheticized by becoming an image of an image"—Gilbert-Rolfe's discourse insists that such art is at the same time a critique of critique, accomplished "by works which, whether they make sense or not, can only make sense, because they are so completely composed, which is itself a kind of sense." In a crescendo of forcing language to say what Baldessari's art means, it comes down to art that "allows us to see complication in entirely aesthetic terms . . . that any purely discursive approach to complication is a simplification *of* it."[74] What makes for an important work is the aesthetic over the discursive, which hardly seems anything but traditional. As with the other writers considered above, discourse kills art: as you stand before a Baldessari piece, no language is adequate (a truism about any potent event), but the stronger claim is paradoxically defensive. It takes writing *to say what cannot be said,* why discourse fails in the face of (some) objects. So, after all, the critic's job is to give the right language to an object. Isn't this another way of smuggling identity back in, where nonidentity of the visual is in fact the purest form of identity?

Baudrillard is invoked as providing a discourse that eliminates art's immersion in "social conditions," the "conditions of its production," which Gilbert-Rolfe certainly theorizes in a more exacting way than the enthusiastic suppressions offered by Pagel or Hickey. Nonetheless, it is the discourse of exorcism and insistence that makes social conditions evaporate. Art is asserted as nonproduction (Hickey's "love," or translation), as it stems from *Homo otiosis* instead of *Homo faber,* art objects being nothing but signs "indifferent to the real." This assertion radically *mis-takes* Baudrillard's provocative *social* hypothesis for a fact on the ground *about art.* A "real art object" is always something "out of control . . . it cannot be seen . . . as a negation."[75] Negation has nothing to do with art. Here, political artwork is given a theoretical gloss, which Pagel seems to have cribbed from;[76] where Pagel says Designer Marxism is "double speak" and hypocritical, Gilbert-Rolfe casts this in significations that condemn political art to "self-congratulation . . . an elite object exhibiting . . . the superiority of the consciousness which it seeks to articulate." And since consciousness of language is part of the destructive tendencies of criticism, consciousness must go the way of language: accepted only when it offers no interference to the valorization of the "uncontrollable" object.[77]

This uncontrollable object is said to "manufacture ambiguity," but how plausible is this concept once it is transformed into the counternorm of art making? As its "own pure simulacrum," the art object is said not to participate in the self-deception of political artwork, but again, how plausible is this once the actual art market, or segment of it, is driven by the demand for ambiguity? It strains credibility to believe that overt political work is the only kind of work to employ use-value: *anti-use-value* just completes the very concept of use-value. If left-wing critiques complement and even require what they are opposed to, how does the inversion of the inversion not complement the complement? It would seem that invoking Baudrillard to alienate belief in Hegelian categories reproduces a Hegelianism of Baudrillard.[78] For once you say that the "manipulation of difference" is opposed to the "predictable mirroring of opposition [= left-wing]," haven't you in fact still reproduced the very same conditions that are denounced? Gilbert-Rolfe insists that Warhol has turned the ready-made into a "cosmetic device" and subverts the subversion of Brecht and Duchamp, but the next question is squelched: what accounts for the monumentalization of the Warhol effect? To insist, without complication, that advertising "can let thought run free because the pleasure principle is already wholly incorporated into an ideology whose form is aesthetic" and to equate this with works of art said to *possess* "inherent irresponsibility," is to precisely make a discursive code (the amoral, the nonmoral) into the conditions of a better morality.[79] One can only agree with Gilbert-Rolfe that any object made warrants our interest insofar as such objects do not give us the grounds of confirmation; but once you make not-giving such grounds the basis of judgment, you have reproduced the same problem set. In short, the proof of the pudding for Gilbert-Rolfe's argument would lie in the *social* uncontrollability of art, when people no longer used terms at all like *best, better, great art,* and hundreds of other such terms and one no longer cared where art was "looked at." That he and Pagel and Hickey want to exploit the existing institutions through a discourse of antidiscursivity is simply power politics—an affirmation that is just as aggressive as the negations of Frankfurt-style historical consciousness, which predominates in the *Book Review* section of the *Times.*

While Pagel does not name names of those Designer Marxists he finds so destructive, Gilbert-Rolfe cannot resist denouncing "the Presbyterian rectitude of Tom Lawson, the Episcopalian certainty of Hal Foster, or the Lutheran conscience of Benjamin Buchloh."[80] Good for him that he says such things: his language has the merit of pointing to the actuality of local and nonlocal subject/institution mixes, i.e., why *October* has an effect on art making and the *Los Angeles Times* tries to. However, that does not settle his own position, which is to reject any discourse that joins conditions of production and aesthetic effects; it ends up insisting on art that is irresponsible, but this is actually another Good (*the goods*), perhaps the only Good. At one point Gilbert-Rolfe defines the interestedness of the work of art in its eroticism—"The erotic involves a relationship of nonrelationship between two incompletenesses."[81] Gilbert-Rolfe is probably the best working critic of things aesthetic-social in Los Angeles, but his own position reinforces the mystery of art, which has been appropriated by the faux-populist anti-intellectualism discussed above.

In a discussion of vision and language, language is said to ruin the visual. "Naming the visual robs it of its visuality and lodges it in language. The object of vision is thereby detached from the world of things and inserted . . . into . . . discourse."[82] Only nonrepresentational painting can try to present "the unnameable . . . its mute and antidiscursive power . . . surprise rather than recognition."[83] In this version of philosophical naturalism, the visual is made the equivalent of those events that produce effects that cannot be withdrawn, like gunshots and violence—which no work of art could ever do anything but simulate. It is important to note that such propositions are another way of re-installing a more perfected sense of the connoisseur: the latter does not deliver judgments from outside or on high as much as enter the object and provide it with a discourse that blocks anything but Derridean mixed with Baudrillar-dian "play." In other words, connoisseurship has been reestablished, this time to return as mastery, in being transferred from language to the object itself. Only those aware of this displacement can make any judgments at all. The art object conceived as image gives way to the object made *enargheic*—the object cannot be interpreted, only experienced, or experienced only with a language that follows the object into the realm of play and, undoubtedly, spirit. Vivid-ness, like Davis's use of apocalyptic rhetoric, comes first. In any future history of the culture of Los Angeles, someone will have to account for the discursive connections between school, review, and recognition in explaining the *kind of impact* achieved, which seems, overall, as predicated on a strange sense of putting discourse out of the way.

No writer working out of Los Angeles with the intent to historicize local art production has been as consistently politicizing as the *Times'* senior critic, Christopher Knight. Over the years, his writings have chastised the Los Ange-les County Museum for failing local artists, for LACMA's failure to offer new artists as historically significant. He has ranged directly into the pedagogical while denouncing, like Hickey, contemporary criticism. In one of dozens of metaphysically Philistine concoctions—as in describing the ascendancy of technology as a "galloping triumph"—Knight roams, as senior editors some-times do, over Philistine Historiography.[84] Thus, in a discussion of the art schools in Los Angeles and their role in moving from school to public exhibi-tion, the schools are graded as "the Good, the Bad and the Ugly," the latter where technique is emphasized, the Good where art practice "is immersion in a calling or vocation," the Bad where theory is privileged but presented here as something "easy."[85] Philistine Historiography offers stunning presuppositions as to why artists make things in the first place: artists "have an acute awareness of their own invisibility. They look at the world around them, don't find them-selves included anywhere . . . and so make art to invent a habitable realm."[86] A retrospective of Gerhard Richter's work shown in Los Angeles is critiqued because the way the work was presented turns Richter into a Conceptualist, when he was actually—who knew—a Pop artist because he never renounced painting.[87] Denouncing LACMA again for a sculpture exhibit that fused Conceptualism and celebrities in potentially complex angles, Knight writes that, in this exhibit, "an artist's muse is indistinguishable from a teenager's wet dream."[88]

Roaming as senior critic means when it comes to historicizing from the "ground up," it is acceptable to applaud celebrity shows when the narcissistic and institutional blend. The same LACMA retrospective of Lari Pittman's work "is easily the most important mid-career survey mounted in the U.S. in recent years," a judgment *all too possible* given the history left out. In his version of denouncing Marxist criticism, this in the context of reviewing a Warhol show at Cal State–Long Beach, Thomas Crow was taken to task for neglecting to understand that Warhol "actually helped change the world." The success of Warhol the artist meant "Perennial social outcasts suddenly found a way in." This is a strange consequence for a critic who claims that causes in art are irrelevant to its consequences: through Warhol in his very person (hagiography) Pop told the truth of the marginal, now a truth so safe *it* requires the caretaking denounced as Conceptual art. In a review of a Danish show, "Sunshine and Noir," a catalogue writer is slammed for making entries about L.A. artists that are "vapid," the writer having lived "in Los Angeles only since 1994." That is extreme territorialization. None of these judgments are ever argued: as with Pagel and Hickey, assertion dissolves argument, or assertion is one of the standard forms of evoking "primary historicization."[89] Recently, Knight denounced two shows at a museum in San Diego as edutainment and worse because sponsored by Clear Channel, no doubt an obnoxious corporation; but within a day, a review of over one hundred artists' work—all students from the local graduate schools—was applauded because it "puts new artists in the limelight." Unmentioned is that the *showcasing* of artists also required lots of corporate funding, some of it recycled from student tuition.[90]

I have argued that one can describe historicization as it happens: the review function is part of historiography. Given that reviewing is subject to all sorts of tugs and pushes, if not stronger and more violent relations, the materials above suggest the repetition of business as usual *and* a newly perverse moment in Los Angeles art writing and book reviewing. The business as usual is the relentless aggression of publicity that threads artist, institution, and the pursuit of a public, and the perversity lies in legitimizing L.A. artists and theory in the antidiscursive moves of naturalism, which is not separate from Enlightenment.

From a critical perspective, or adding more ideas to the mix, the book reviews discussed ensure that deconstruction and other dissident ideas are misrepresented. There are many more writers engaged in the politics of misfiguration than the ones discussed above. It should be emphasized that the anti-intellectualism involved is, again, transpolitical: no group is free of trying to impose an agenda on the ranking of art objects or the circulation of historical consciousness. It should be obvious, but it is not, that scholarly "hope" (from on high) and art critique can be turned into political-cultural commodities just as easily as anything in a gallery or museum. Institutionalization of ideas and school programs and academicism are not isolated problems in Los Angeles; in fact, I would suggest that there is hardly any outside to artistic/intellectual life in Los Angeles, as the "connoisseurships" of antidiscourse form a block. One can join the existing divisions in hopes of receiving a share of their surplus. To the writer's "publish while teaching," there is the artist's "show or [and] disappear," and both are part of historicization, which, as discussed "from the bottom up," is itself included in the overall *homogenization* of intellect and art.

It is notable that the artists invoked by the L.A. writers rarely write about their work, how many are but a few years out of school. This is a global process now: artists are subject to and voluntarily join the networks of representation in the chance that their work will last long enough to acquire institutional recognition, more words, more chances to make more work. In this sense, and stepping from history to a small prophecy, there will be a further collapse of reviewing into promotion, a further taming of the intellectual and artist reduced to saying those things that are safe—smothering an entire city in the discourses of social apocalypse and cultural enthusiasm, endless rants about the necessity of Pop affirmations, more historical consciousness that imposes the Same.[91] The materials discussed above suggest that having a future on the basis of being given a history is inseparable from commodity-life.

Finally, dread over language parallels the refusal of irony (Pagel, Hickey) and an appeal to ambiguity (Gilbert-Rolfe), these tactics employed to dislodge academics, intellectuals, and curators who might be suspicious about the affirmations given by these critics. The anti-intellectualism or semantic despotism by writers such as Hobsbawm featured in the *Book Review* is distressing to those fed up with the Mandarinism of "high culture," as the art writers say they are; but in reading the writing on art, it becomes perfectly clear that Mandarinism is not something restricted. Now we have a generalized spread of Mandarin discourse, an unlimited fetishism of objects crossed with competition over who and what is represented as history.

The art writers assume that art compensates for the failures of the social as such, or the social's failure entails the success of art that is presocial. No doubt left-wing, socially driven art is just as problematic: its tendency to monumentalize the moral and discursive around theories of lack is disturbing, just as is its relentless sexual policing. In both cases, history is created by elimination of complex language, for in the end, the art critics want to drive the academics back into school (which they themselves are part of), and the historians want to ensure that the phantom general public is protected from the wrong thoughts such as deconstruction without apologies. For the artists trying to make work and a life in Los Angeles, the art discourse ensures that their work "translates" fast and easily, which may explain why so much of the language discussed above "heads" into the body and, in terms of book reviewing, why "good minds" are required to think about all the bodies of history.

Future historians: what is the difference between what can be called a right-wing body that always looks good, confusing the moral and the aesthetic, with a left-wing body that confuses the same categories, under a different injunction?

4

Figuring Forth the Historian Today
On Images and Goals

The discussion of the *Los Angeles Times* materials indicates an historiography of restriction, evaluations and reviews that sort claims for narrative inclusion. This chapter moves to a larger arena: what to make of the image of historians and the roles they play in contemporary life? Who is the historian today? The discipline of Western historiography is twenty-four hundred years going—are historians to be thought of in terms of that continuity, so archaic and ever modern at once? How can such continuity be imaged in what are incomparable contexts? Have historians changed their role in relation to contemporary thought, using and not using methods from other disciplines, and has this affected the ways in which processes are imagined? For instance, has contemporary psychological knowledge produced a narrative of American history about an increase of indifference conceived as a psychomaterial force, historians drawing from, borrowing, adapting, transforming, theories of mass, notions of the multiple, the stresses of "advanced" societies? The classical roles—judge, prosecutor and defender, connoisseur, lover of the past (Michelet)—do these hold up with globalization?

"Who is the historian today?" can mean asking as to whether the historian is a friend of dominant processes or whether historians are able, today, to play the role of, say, judge, if processes are underway that challenge modern criteria of judgment. If, say, technological applications are more invasive in the upheaval in the American labor market since the early seventies, how do the historians of this "invasion" stay within the structures of "balanced" judgments toward processes that may be "unbalanced"? "Who" asks as to how historian's accommodate the continuity of historiographic operations—synthesis, narrative inclusion, the use of literary devices, the making of political-moral judgments—as such operations are pressured by contemporary forces working against modern representation. In this chapter then, the objective is to make a subject: how are images and roles *for* historians established, given the ubiquitous discussion of ruptures and breaks today (e.g., the withdrawal of the "literary tradition")? How can historians trust in the sense of continuity of plot if their readers are increasingly pre- and postliterary? Here is an example (image-process) of what might be at stake in all these questions.

Peter Sloterdijk recently declared as fact the dissolution of liberal humanism in Germany: the conjunction between reading and socialization has evaporated, he claims; beneath its own social and cultural ideals of education, liberal humanism's reliance on radio, TV, and Internet has undercut socialization. He takes this to mean that education has been severed from "deep" reading. The various dimensions of social life do not translate as commensurable worlds, mediated by common literary and intellectual structures. Cultural incommensurables (reading/screening) index social disjunction, and Sloterdijk's text indexes the withdrawal of reading as an element of future historical improvement. Literature, science, art, and philosophy are mere islands surrounded by the void of serious reading. The upper social levels are floating in a Philistinism driven by technology and fashion, setting the pace for a new conformity, manifested in curriculum changes favoring design as an end in itself.[1] (I might add that Sloterdijk's construal of design and antireading fits with similar changes in contemporary Los Angeles, where design is often promoted as the new model of humanistics.)

Yet the role Sloterdijk performs is not new—it is quite close to the argument Hannah Arendt made in her essay "The Concept of Culture" (1961). Old analysis forgotten and revived? For many progressives, Sloterdijk's discourse falls into the image-stock of the nihilist. He is accused of exploiting the declining influence of progressive intellectuals, while he counters that such intellectuals prepared the ground for his critique by their promotion of reading's promise and denial of reading's social actualities, that literary models disappeared long ago as connective social tissue, linking classes and smaller groups by virtue of the "same" referents, including formal ones (like plot structures shared). Because of this rivalry—images of rupture tied to nihilism (the progressive's dread) and images of the same rupture tied to myth-breaking (Sloterdijk is saying wake up!)—distinctive images and roles are shown in treatments of the representation of social processes. The process of reading's "break" tilts the historian's job to salvage (with nostalgia?) over reading's demise, in rivalry with the prophet, announcing the future. In this chapter, the subject the writing is "looking for" is how contemporary historiography connects with images and roles attached to transformed social processes, and what this suggests about historiography's outfitting of new ways of grappling with those futures moving toward us.

Nihilist and progressive are far too easy as images/roles concerning historians. The profession long ago shed an overt hostile image of making judgments from a disenchanted present (presentism) and settled into progressive relations (from at least Michelet on out, as friend of the people). One cannot assume that images and roles for historians follow from their prosaic entanglements; hence what follows must attend to the use of data in engaging such images/roles of historiography today. A concern here is to assemble materials so as to suggest new problems about historical consciousness, problems often delicately elided in the very pursuit of research. The earlier example of German intellectuals is meant to draw attention to the idea that changes in process—reading not intrinsic to socialization, at least not in the way it must be presented in public life—involves changes on other levels, cultural and political. Further, the data used are entered from a sense that in American society, the historian has withdrawn from earlier roles of providing *inclusive* cultural functions, to that of making rationalizations for *exclusion;* the pressure of *to historicize* is so great that giving existing relations of all kinds a future has rattled the normative conjunction of images of historical knowledge and ideas of process and goal. When the norm of historiography shows images and roles that gate-keep the future, or increasingly do so, sorting and ranking claimants in the here and now not as to how they descended from the past, but as to what they deserve as a future, then historiography as such can be said to have been pulled into cultural politics. In short, historians might be out of joint with their earlier incarnations—*to historicize* is what happens when historiography cannot offer normative *synthesis and proper distance,* for understanding, when the very idea of synthesis as providing useful social distance is thoroughly unsettled.

These matters will be taken up in the following sequence: I start with a discussion of the ambiguity of both the historian's image in public life and the goals of historical knowledge, what can be called the currency or cultural value/exchange of historical representation. This is followed by a discussion about image and goal in Roland Barthes's seminal essay "Historical Discourse"

(1967). I discuss what Barthes called a schizophrenic aspect of historical writing, its suppression of the author and vividness of the referent (narrated), which was classically aestheticized when historical writing could presume literary and cultural links with a general audience. Historians could rely on synthesis as the very point of historical representation, and the reader could lean on shared literary and social knowledge of the narrative as told. No one was much concerned with what was left out; schizophrenia comes into historiography when one actively notices the restrictions placed on what can count as a narrative subject. Further, I ask if this form of use and abuse of history is becoming dominant in American society—the more historical knowledge of all kinds is used to secure various futures, does the more *exclusive* such historiography become? Have the critiques of metanarrative unsettled historical synthesis as such? This is not the decline of "general history" and its replacement by fractured or narrowly construed narratives ("weak" big books, "strong" narrow ones), but *having a future* has affected historiography. I conclude with analysis of the obituaries on Isaiah Berlin, read as an index of giving historians an image/role that can withstand the possible schizophrenia of historiography.

Some words, however, are also needed for the methodological aspects of this chapter, given such contentious and truculent material. How does one select data to discuss, to make representative? The procedure here draws on *contemplative historiography.* "Contemplative" is drawn from Gilles Deleuze's 1968 *Difference and Repetition.* For Deleuze, contemplation is *sign-work*—a sign being a contraction, retention, and expectation of other signs, other events or "cuttings" from them, an incessant construal of time-sense. A sign emits valences of passive and active synthesis, which every present accommodates, where such syntheses, say, habit in one domain of experience, are linked to a "move" in another, opening and closing a myriad number of possible and actual relations with other signs. "To contemplate is to draw something from," writes Deleuze, the sense of which is strongly rendered in this remark: "A scar is the sign not of a past wound but of 'the present fact of having been wounded': we can say that it is the contemplation of the wound, that it contracts all the instants which separate us from it into a living present . . . 'What difference is there . . . ?' This is the question the contemplative soul puts to repetition."[2] Deleuze's equation of contemplation with inquiry—asking what difference does difference make—is best considered a *procedure.* As an interpretive practice, contemplation resists stupefaction in the face of the "big" past and the obscure future; we contemplate a "living present" through its signs, what stands out, even in obscurity, subject to our estimations and evaluations, our constructions, especially of socially sanctioned passive syntheses or habits. Why, for example, does the public seem to need the figure of the "celebrity-scientist" in order to stay interested in science? Or, when one senses, from many different sources, that this is a living present of economic and cultural "bubbles," what does "bubble" give to contemplation to think of in the construction of a real world in which we use bubbles to create and dissolve social relations? Deleuze's attention to signs, linked to the most diverse modes of temporal arrangement, is not unlike what Jean-Jacques Lecercle proposed about basic linguistic *interpellation,* in which signs are acts of subjection as well as acts of "unexpected rejoinder."[3] The data analyzed below were selected precisely for their sign-value—as synthetic congealings that suggest processes momentarily available when contemplated as complex signs. Historiographically, sign-value means thinking through the *cultural sense* of "how it goes" with historical sensibility, as it circulates in various domains of public life, where the historian comes forward with a role to play, such role(s) leading to the epistemology, the politics, and the credibility historians give to social formations. If a form of thought and sensibility called historical consciousness makes a difference in social relations because such consciousness and sensibility are able to span or traverse many dimensions of social life (legal, media, social acts); if history is everywhere—from helping German and other corporations come to terms with the past (reparations, settlements) to disputes over land use, to textbook production—then anywhere history is called upon to legitimize and delegitimize becomes "data" as to historical sensibility, or group sensitivity to time and transition. Given the vastness of such material and modes of experience, "contemplation" here refers to the methodology of reading signs in relation to processes that are murky. It is a risky practice, and contrary to those aspects of historical criticism that read signs for answers, the signs read below are threaded to the murk.

History and Its Currency

Physical remains are so actively pursued today that archeology may well re-monumentalize ancient history—the city of Megeddon restored will be known as Armeggedon, its historical as opposed to its geographic or place name; other practices stemming from technology threaten to privatize—who are the ancestors of Jesse James, now that his DNA is "recovered"? A small family legend has it that the Cohens of San Francisco, descended from European peasant stock via Absoroka, Colorado, had a relative known in Los Angeles as Mickey Cohen, mobster, friend of Bugsy Siegel—science will tell us if family image succumbs to the invisibility of DNA, which can ferociously deliver effects of exposure of past-in-present. How fantastic: the big past, ancientness, joined to intimacies of all sorts in the present. New exposures; new mechanisms to protect images and secrets—surely one is safe in remarking that historiography is changing, if for no other reason than techniques of representation have changed, dissolving some previous limits to representations.

At the same time, a sense of melancholy accompanies the history of, say, lighthouses and the vanishing of "sailors" from contemporary images of labor. More than ever, all of historiography is under pressure to adapt, to survive, in the face of pressures on writing and representation—the concept of *relevance* is in dispute at the same time that it is one of the primary "stakes" of the historical profession. The temporal beatings of the present are *recoded* (i.e., new enthusiasms emerge). Notice of a conference circulating in Los Angeles begins by insisting that "1989 . . . has replaced 1968 as the defining moment for contemporary theory . . . the electronic, networked, market-oriented culture that emerged from the events of '89," which actually means the removal of one wall in Berlin is taken as the sign of a "starting-point" for dismissal of sixties politics.[4] From all directions, such statements make the active present and the coming of the future into an object of possession by using the past—and it is an open question whether this desire to possess is anything but a generalized (misused) Darwinian excuse to say again, "It's our turn, we're giving the orders." Is the *context of doing history* in some implosion as new claims of representation compete for the prize, public recognition?[5] Better: there are diverse prizes and diverse stakes—and what counts as a distinctive achievement in one area of historical representation hardly enters the discursive ambience of another. What do the archeologists of Armageddon have to do with the contemporary writing of, say, the history of rock and roll? What does cyberhype have to do with the historical representation of the sixties as dead?

Further, the shrinking of the historical profession in the United States paradoxically accompanies extensions of historiography into the general culture, a reach into a culture that is more at odds than ever with professional historiography. What counts in the historical profession is a decisive evaluation, or introduction of a method, that changes research problems; what counts for PBS representation is another thing, entirely; what counts in areas such as the history of pop music has to do with yet other social relations, giving it narrative cohesion. All in all, don't we actually live in a Lyotardian world of "narrative clouds," islands of stories circulated amidst social and intellectual processes that perhaps annul the social bonds of storytelling? How valuable are Benjaminian notions of story—of historical *salvage*—or those of literary theorists such as Genette in which the "best" narratives are those that are the most ironic? And next to reconstructions of archaic pasts like Megeddon, we have distressing, ongoing news: only a small percent of Los Angeles Unified School District graduates can read the professional narratives about their own institution. For some, historiography threatens to dissolve into pockets of little more than cultural despotism, competing centers for the focus of research and problem-setting; for others, professional historiography is irrelevant to the social act of making identifications and judgments with the past, as many millions of people scramble to create all kinds of social relations "broken" by contemporary life. Where should one look for continuity of historical—anything?

A first place to examine this comes from a model of *necessary* history, here the public intellectual raising the question why social bonds are historical ones. The *New York Review of Books* (October 22, 1998) featured Ronald Dworkin's essay "Affirming Affirmative Action," a book-review essay on *The Shape of the River,* written by two former university presidents, William Bowen and Derek Bok. These authors have now rendered, according to Dworkin, the key "standard of argument" for any "respectable discussion" of affirmative action and its history/narratives, their use of statistical indices said to be irrefutable (so far).[6] Dworkin's writing gives signs of menace—if affirmative action is rolled back, it will "cripple" the need for "race-sensitive" policies at our "best" institutions, the ones that provide a model of leadership for the rest of America's universities and colleges. The defense of affirmative action laid out by Bowen and Bok is a defense of the "best" by the "best." Of course, repetition of the superlative establishes fear: if we do not identify with what Harvard and thirty similar institutions do to remedy the consequences of racism in America, then we are all doomed to decline. Citing Bowen and Bok, it is insisted that "the most selective colleges and universities" have been "highly successful in using race-sensitive admissions policies to advance educational goals important to everyone."[7] The narrative of affirmative action is secure—this remedy of the past-present entails a better future.

Is it a stunning piece of research that African-Americans do "best" in the "better" schools or is it a confirmation of a rigid social rule, the better one's contacts, the better one's chances of success? Calling any piece of contradictory evidence either "shoddy scholarship" or "anecdote," in effect castrating rival theories and concepts, cutting them off by sheer cursing,[8] Dworkin insists that we acknowledge that even rejected white applicants to the best schools do not evince any high rate of resentment toward affirmative action. To the even more incendiary argument by blacks that affirmative action harms their self-image or self-esteem, Dworkin calls that "an undoubted and regrettable cost of the policy [of affirmative action]," for the "cost" is worth it. Nineteen eighty-nine's total of 2,171 African-Americans who entered the "best" schools (thirty in all) is enough: "How could we think ourselves better off if . . . racial stratification were even more absolute than it is, and if we saw no or fewer signs of its lessening?"[9]

The goal, "better off" (less segregation by and of elite institutions), is justified with this invocation of history to sort out what "counts as a qualification" for admission:

> In some competitions, like a beauty contest or a quiz show, qualification is a matter of only some physical or intellectual quality: the winner should be the most beautiful or knowledgeable candidate. In others, like a book prize or awarding a medal for bravery, qualification is a matter of prior achievement: the winner should be the candidate who has produced the best work or product, or shown special character in some way, in the past. In still other competitions, however, qualification is a matter of forward-looking promise rather than backward-looking achievement or natural property: a rational person . . . choose[s] . . . the doctor that he expects will do best for him in the future. . . .
>
> Competitions for university places are, *of course,* competitions of the last sort. Admissions officers should not award places or prizes for past achievements or effort, or as medals for inherent talents or virtues; their duty is to try to choose a student body that, as a whole, will make the greatest future contribution to the legitimate goals their institution has defined. Elite higher education is a valuable and scarce resource, and though it is available only to very few students, it is paid for by the community generally, even in the case of "private" universities that are partly financed by public grants and whose "private" donors benefit from tax deductions.[10]

Four concepts serve to control Dworkin's model—"quality," "prior achievement," "forward-looking," and "of course"—and which congeal into something like this proposition: *what has been done is not qualification: what the future is to look like must be the only qualification.* Notions of competing goals are reduced to sheer institutional and random power—to reproduce the institution, a "better" future for the arbitrarily chosen. In such instances, as Klaus Theweleit offered in his study, *Male Fantasies,* the "collective life of the community" is asserted as impervious to criticism; here, affirmative action at the best universities is the way those institutions can command the future, the way they can set their own goals, as Dworkin insists, and clinch their own enhancement. History is not, to use a phrase of Avital Ronell, allowed to "mess with" goals, and present lives, with their multiple points of contact with pasts not past, are effaced. *Future-control* is what matters, survival in the name of a final goal, an eschatology, dependent on what Kenneth Burke once referred to as "eulogistic coverings" that mask "material interests," "best" and "better" running interference for these future outcomes.[11] Even more radical than on issues of qualification, the discourse exposes a rigidity about history and goals in the name of diversity and social justice, where "no student has a right to a university place in virtue of past achievements or innate virtues, talents, or other qualities: students must be judged only by asking how likely each is . . . to contribute to the various goals that the institution has legitimately chosen."[12] "Diversity," social justice, and stability matter,[13] but no thought is given to the possibility that diversity and stability may not fit with each other too well, or are otherwise unstable categories.

Does the writing announce, for the present, a restriction of "historical" to institutional determinations? Disseminated through the *New York Review of Books* and threaded to active discussions, public and academic, legal and cultural, what to make of the way that history is restricted—for an outcome in the name of one past that is set against another? Further, the discourse *syntactically* veers toward the *obsessional*—it sutures "best" to "elite" to "small" (numbers) to "model" to "whole," in which a key temporal element—a student's "contribution"—is refused legitimation. The charged phrase—evaluation by institutions that are "forward-looking"—evidences a narrative *mood* that is restrictive instead of inclusive. This tiny amount of text—is it not a sign in the sense offered by Deleuze, above, because so many layered powers are given? Of course many historians would be critical of Dworkin's restriction/reduction of history to a social function that is as much a mode of social ranking as it is a piece of social improvement, inappropriate neoliberal pragmatism that has all but lost sight of the complexity of history.

But I think more is at work in Dworkin's text. I think it does announce a "given," a shift where *important* uses of history are defensive and aggressive at the same time, in this case a social elite abandoning its own Enlightenment ideal of inclusion in favor of a restricted cultural economy of institutions. Historicization by restriction lets institutions play for the future—so does everyone desirous of more chances, more moves. Are we in the vicinity of a new *episteme* for historiography? This capture of the future is predicated, in

Dworkin's text, on the binarism of present-future as progress and decline, hardly new; what is new is the *disqualification* of past achievements in the name of settling a problem not created by present subjects; the rhetoric here relies on dissuasion about the implications of networking; it uses the rhetoric of menace and curse, moralized as "how could we not . . ."—a *destruction of history* in the name of negating a negative past, which suggests that the *stakes of invoking history* require a lot of force. Dworkin's discourse legitimizes—but its discourse is selective, political, restrictive, and exclusive. The image of the historian, speaking out of the discipline of law, is not that of mediator but judge of the future, the future in the present, a seizure of the present by the present.

A conceptual take on such discourse can be gained from a consideration of Roland Barthes's work on the shift from narrative to "intelligible" history, that is, historical writing after the collapse of the idea that "the historian shares with his audience general notions of the forms that significant human situations must take."[14] The pluralism of contemporary readers does not cohere with the training of historians—they do not share rhetorical presuppositions, for instance, as Hayden White insisted in his *Metahistory* (1973). This shift to the intelligible, which has affected competitions between historians over the intelligible, with moves toward microhistory, history from the "bottom," and the history of mentalities, also brings with it a shift as to what *counts* as historical.

Roland Barthes's essay "Historical Discourse," first published in 1967, asked: who does the historian "resemble" in terms of a cultural figure able to represent what untold numbers of humans believe, think, and will in regard to history? That is a tough question. In alignment with the structuralist impulses of the times, Barthes asked if there is such a thing as a "deep" cultural basis to historians' representations, whether the historian is bound to classical or traditional roles associated with politics, the historian as judge. Barthes proposed that the classical historians, such as Machiavelli, Michelet, or Thiers, shared a sense of cultural inseparability with their audience, of *meaning and referent:* to narrate was to *incorporate* both at once. When historical discourse was assumed to *mean its referents,* a successful narrative obtained when a reader shared in the narrative's construction, especially its description. Of course we know that this narrative cohesion assumed epistemologies, plots, and politics shared—and contested. Description had come to mean *vividness,* and one of its consequences was that historical narrative was located in one version or another of realism.[15] A shift to intelligibility would imply new cognitive tasks. Believing that the times had changed sufficiently to call into doubt this conjunction of meaning and referent, Barthes argued for a "linguistics of discourse" to study the "reality-effects" of historical discourse.

Barthes argued that any such "linguistics" must question whether or not the distinction between prose and poetry or fact and fiction was warranted on the basis of linguistic evidence "beyond the sentence."[16] He extended the query about distinctions between poetics and prose to include questions as to how prose, fact, fiction, *and* politics, *and* psychology are distinguished in the first place. "At what point in the language-act," he wrote, does language *index* the difference between "factual and imaginary discourse"? In Barthes's classification, there are language-acts that separate historical discourse from its shared elements with "the epic, novel, and drama." First, historical discourse indexes the *shifter.* Here, there are *monitorial* subcodes, or any reference by the author/historian to the *evidence,* and signaled in asides to the reader ("as far as can be ascertained"); this code is said to be "common in conversation." From this, an image can be formed of the historian as judicious, someone who weighs and measures things, congealed as something like a fair judge (= a good listener). A second, the *organization-shifter,* includes any displacement of the discourse, when the narrator immobilizes the telling, a "paragrammatism in historical statement."[17] This function uses text devices as different as anecdote and logical forms (e.g., enthymemes), connecting different strata of descriptions (e.g., narrative embedding). Further, both subcodes pertain to the author-function, the author as usually presented in deliberative and judicial rhetoric. This was signaled by such effects as the "performative onset," narration "in the name of" (God, people) or in a preface's metastatement or announced self-origin. Here the author-function is endowed with cultural certification so as to claim legitimacy to intervene *on the referent.* Overall, the shifters merge "sui-referential metastatement[s]" that "braid" the chronology of the content narrated with the "language-act which reports it." Hence the author-function makes indirect appearances.

Historical discourse radically displaces the author vis-à-vis *overt* appearances. Because direct address or signals to readers are notoriously absent in history writing, "history seems to write itself," a *referential illusion: absence of clues to the narrator involves the fiction* that "the referent is speaking for itself."[18] The classical narrator-function is the connoisseur-as-author, implicit in Barthes's technical disentanglement. The conjunction of language shifters, the referential illusion, and implied connoisseur are co-coded. Moreover, Barthes argued that analysis of the *significata,* or referent "named and intelligible," also implies certain roles. Historians use *collections,* or lists of "existents" and "occurrences" in subdividing referents into entities subject to narration; each collection implies acts of *selection,* possibly the author's obsessions (Barthes's term), examples of which are Machiavelli's focus on actions that maintain and ruin a State, or Tacitus's use of "fame" to organize his narrative, or the figures that warn about relativism, prominent today. These roles imply images of who historians-imagine-they-are as well as of the audience they address. In any case, historical discourse registers the author-as and reader-of at the same time, and emerges via the syntactic curve of a text, precisely at those junctions where repetition of figure indicates solidity of selection, where textual cohesion is revealing.

Working on these notions, Barthes's strong proposal was that it is the act of *nominalization* by which historians *condense* situations and actions, incidents, and events, multiplicities of temporal rhythm, and which makes selection political—"single-noun short hand notations" are highly discrete rankings that claim to give *right word for thing,* words that belong to things, words that things require. "Classical" historiography could submerge most problems of nominalization in metanarrative structures when origin and end were in tacit reference to the other, but that is precisely what has fallen apart. ("The goals are missing" from modernity, wrote Nietzsche.) To return, for a moment, to Dworkin's narrative. It nominates affirmative action as progress but diminishes consideration of its construal of such restricted progress in relation to *other processes;* its obsession with restricting history not only gives it a genealogy of spell, Gorgias's and Nietzsche's *warnings* about the wizardry of prose, but also codes its own proper subject. For Barthes, mythification starts with discursive nomination *by* condensation on certain names. Dworkin's use of selection—fear of racial apocalypse and progress dizzily connected in linking affirmative action to "best," "best" to "progress" to a necessary "decline" imagined as "unthinkable" ("How could we . . .")—can certainly be interpreted as obsession. Is it not then somewhat "schizo" for readers of Dworkin if they ask how the narrative of affirmative action depends on fiction and fact mixed with fear of future? Isn't this, to continue the argument of chapters 2 and 3, in the area of desperate historical narration?

Finally, all historiographical processes, according to Barthes, are subject to the historian's use of statements that are *assertive.*[19] "What happened" trumps what "didn't happen" and assertive discourse shares a quality with "psychotic" discourse: neither can directly voice the "negative." In both *there is a radical censorship of the utterance . . . massive reversion of discourse away from any form of sui-reference . . . reversion towards the level of pure referent—the utterance for which no one is responsible.*"[20] Dworkin's restriction of competition to future contribution *censors* the past as it severs past from future; the act of selection shows in the stress on the narrative outcome, the syntactic curve implied by "the legitimate goals their institution has defined." This rationale makes up the equivalent to "the utterance for which no one is responsible." In this, *historical meaning* sutures the notable to the assertive, history used for a specific design. Is this not the intelligibility Barthes postulated about historical discourse in a period that experiences competition over each aspect of historical representation?[21] Again, if one conceives our present as a period with a restricted economy of historical representation, signaled or indexed by public intellectuals withdrawing history-as-inclusion in favor of history-as-resource-for-exclusion, then one has some grounds to suppose that historical representation is part of schizo exchange, means and ends at the same time, which suggests their confusion.

Currency, Image, and Role

In 1943 Simone Weil wrote a book later published as *The Need for Roots* in which she equated ancient Israel and Rome with Hitler—murderous States, monoliths, instances of run-amok monotheisms. Weil's history of Europe made the Romans the centerpiece of the repetitions of historical "disaster," just as Weil's moving tribute to Carthage places it "outside history," as she located Carthage in the realm of love, a poetic people who tell us some truth about Rome's own brutal existential choices. Somewhat later, Hannah Arendt, in the essay "The Concept of Culture" linked Rome, through Cicero, to Kant and the celebration of judgments of "quality" and "taste." Rome and Kant are linked by an Idea of Culture—the cultivation of taste in judgments of quality. For Arendt, art and politics historically share the possibility of making judgments where "quality is beyond dispute," Arendt desperately trying to salvage a European tradition of inestimable values.[22] Despite their differences, both were tethered to European Idealism, and they model the historian in a moment of utter cultural crisis—as the one who can provide value and continuity (positive and negative), activist notions rather than exclusionary.

Weil and Arendt rendered experiences of *historical crisis*—where history in general was assumed to be a condition of existential possibility. If Dworkin's text is a *sign of a transition* out of existentialism, as well as a *technique for effecting transition,* then, following the recommendation of Deleuze's notion of contemplation, one could argue that Dworkin's restriction of history to functions of management operates as a mechanism that reduces history to a routine of sorting out, a job for intellectuals set against intellectuals. Does the *transition* from crisis to management imply a rise or fall or something else in terms of our estimations of historians / historical knowledge? More difficult problems.

Of course historians have never been "one" representable persona; nineteenth-century literature and twentieth-century philosophy commented on historians in different registers, only similar in that each group used decidedly mixed terms in grappling with historians—the historian as seductivist in Ibsen, the historian as folk psychologist to those identified with philosophy of science. But conflict over image survives.

Consider, in the face of the above remarks, the social image of the historian in contemporary society. According to the critic and film historian Dana Polan, historians have an image problem. Historians suffer by comparison to their companions in the sciences and humanities.[23] Somehow, when the media gets hold of a scientist able to energize some segment of the public, a little bit of the madness of scientific work comes through as charm. Stephen Hawking's image seems "made" to speak of the mysteries of the universe, discussions of esoteric nature from the human, all too human: what could match this from an historian? In Polan's recounting, one of the most striking cultural and psychological, historical portrayals of the historian can be found in Sartre's novel *Nausea,* a characterization rejected by most historians, since the historian of *Nausea,* the ever ambivalent Roquentin, torn between fiction and fact, is not just an historian *manqué,* but a neurotic more like Woody Allen than not. The image of the historian, in the film *Jonah Will Be 25 in the Year Two Thousand* (1975), slicing off chunks of sausage in front of his high school class to "illustrate" the subject of history—cut and slice (writing as scissors and paste?)—is a continuation of Roquentin's irony toward narrative. Certainly, in terms of contemporary image-values, the scientist is often portrayed as a doer, while the humanist of, say, the typical English department is rendered in images of self-help (e.g., self-improvement, the vast hermeneutics of coming-to-terms-with).[24] For Polan, historians are nearly "non-figurable" today, the historian "neither hard enough to be [part of] real science nor soft enough to be a real branch of the humanities." We could quibble with Polan's categorization or use of "hard" and "soft," but he does have a point: historians are more cultural ciphers today than some of their kin in the other knowledges (a kind of bon vivant discourse-energy sustains some of Bruno Latour's writing in science studies).

But notice: even in Polan's workup, historians are figured in their nonfigurability—they are between scientific truth and self-development, synonyms for objective/subjective. Historians are "like" the knowledge they make: mediative. Neither dead nor alive, but "un-dead," or even "un-alive"?[25] Polan figures this potential unfigurability as an image that, in "popular thought," amounts to a knowledge/image-of-the-historian "derivative, second-degree, a mere reportage both of historical events that are old and of the historical facts or truths that precedent figures have produced . . . a skilled lecturer, at worst an irrelevant antiquarian."[26] A lecturer and an antiquarian? Polan does not consider that historians might very much welcome these figurations, which at least have the merit of lodging the historian in images of work and achievement, and which do not invite any active critique on the public's side. One rarely hears from the side of the public, colloquially, "Hey, what's up with the historians?" although one often hears challenges to curators and others more directly involved in cultural circulation.[27] Indeed, Polan affirms that if there is a public sense of the historian / historical enterprise, it comes down to "being an historian has no bearing on one's fundamental existential identity," where over and over popular literature gives us "history as profession . . . incidental to the real existential work of historical reflection a man must engage in to figure out his place in the cosmos." Historians have been decisively exorcised from anything resembling an existential crisis.[28] There is no "burden of history" concerning historians (pace Hayden White), since the public does not expect historians to plunge us into existential crisis. The present is a time of an "indefinability and insubstantiality of the historical vocation within popular representation." It says something that historians are not even portrayable as political/cultural "seducers," a venerable, if negative, image (e.g., Remarque's sinister historian in *All Quiet on the Western Front*). Again, while "conceptions of the historical past are rampant in popular culture . . . conceptions of the historian are few and far between," the profession having "no real identity or significant purpose within public imagery." This seems to dovetail with statistics distributed by the U.S. Department of Education where fewer than one thousand PhDs were awarded in the "discipline" of history in 2000, a far smaller ratio to the general population than twenty or even ten years ago, let alone further back.[29]

But Polan misses the force in this "lack of image," what one could call the functionalization of lack: to say that historians are imaged to provide mediation between science and art is not the absence of an image, but a very precise one; the historian is a straddler, joining differences, a cultural operator of *re-lay,* with emphasis on *re.* In terms of knowledge functions, the historian is thus as close to therapists as to scientists and artists—whose "cultural spaces" are in dispute. To scientists and artists belong zones of experimentation, big failures and bigger mistakes, part of their job, but failures of therapy, like those of his-torical representation, are usually located further out of sight. One could sug-gest that the historian *repairs,* is a patcher, not a *bricoleur,* for whom invention is vastly more important than the correction function of historians-as-repre-sentors. But, artifactually considered, the *disjunction between the smoothness of the narrative text with functions of exclusion* locates historical discourse in a schizo zone, as Barthes noted concerning the linguistic register of historical writing. Exclusion is tricky: it does not mean just what is left out (politics by omission), but the illusion of noncontestable knowledge, discourse turned into a monument. Contemporary historiographic literature is swarming with competitors for this psychosynthetic function, which, since Hegel, has rotated on the idea of a nonfictional mediator and mediation—the historian that third party who gives perspective that first and second parties deny to each other. Is this possible with restrictions à la Dworkin's text, or notions of straddling, or of repair? The historian should be a social agent capable of giving place and judgment to what is separated or out of place, according to Jacques Rancière, social "excess" made familiar.[30]

But as with therapists, literature professors, and some lawyers, the writings of historians can shift between giving mediation and *despotic and fashionable judgments:* despotic because the historian assumes the right to have the last word on facts (render a determined perspective, not just a coherent one) and fashionable because this last word is constantly shifting according to political and cultural demands, even those of a market. One could say that the in-credulity toward metanarrative, which Jean-François Lyotard introduced in his *Postmodern Condition* (1979), has helped float away the image of the historian as belonging to a third party, or exposed (deposed?) the fiction of a side that has no side to take—narration with secure goals framed by consensus on the mediator. Set in the context of a capitalization that ceaselessly deterritorializes names, customs, habits, forms—financial debt is bad, unless not having debt is worse—throwing up a boundless cynicism of recoding, the historian must provide reterritorializations—nominalizations, more right names and processes given. Yet what distinguishes between historical representation and the man-agement of the present through restrictive uses of the past?

Might the historian's contemporary function(s) be compared to that of a psychoanalyst: "to ensure that beliefs survive, even after they have been repudiated. And to instill a belief in something into those who no longer believe in anything"?[31] Kenneth Starr, historian laureate of California, insists that historians must narrate the reality-consequences of what people first "dreamed" as their goals and objectives, assuming that dreams are the real stuff of narrative. Or could what Polan calls lack of image be the *impossibility* of function, even if culturally and discursively ubiquitous—to make history matter, if it can, in a time out of joint—offering "gregarious identifications" for lost souls, installing the language of necessity and repression (the ubiquity of testing), protecting psychic investments, with many quasi-private cults of writing that lay claim to the public? Who is the historian when each individual and group is crisscrossed by new connections: in and out of delirium (e.g., a singular date that cannot be withdrawn), depression (acceptance of your lot in life)? Sometimes, when historians do step forward to embrace a public image, an image for the public, it can get bizarre. A piece in the *Wall Street Journal* playfully noted that historians have "come back" to life a bit in the public's imagination because of Nazi history: the lawsuits over various non-Nazi corporations (IBM in Germany) doing business with Nazism has spawned a corporate need for historical research, truth-sorting (a rhetorician might use the term *sorites* or truth-heaping). One historian, asked by Ford Motors to investigate its relations with German manufacturers during World War II, gave the following explanation for his involvement: "I live in Pittsburgh, the home of Andy Warhol, so I'm perfectly aware that everyone gets their 15 minutes of fame . . . So I'm just determined to enjoy mine."[32] Is a synthetic or mediative role possible if historiography as such is swallowed by Pop?

Deleuze and Guattari have argued that historical writing belongs to the genealogy of despotism, part of "the deliberate creation of lack as a function . . . the art of the dominant class." This lack can be seen in the performative onset of the *Peloponnesian Wars,* where Thucydides says that he wrote this history as a witness of the living and their various claims, to place readers in the scene of violence and destruction, giving his readers a warning—the future will resemble the past—so we must not lack the past. Rejecting the poets and the chroniclers, he offered his history as "an everlasting possession, not a prize composition that is heard and forgotten." Does the "everlasting" still hang over historiography? Lack and everlasting: allied in obligation, a cultural debt, grafted to the memory of those who support and receive the text that is vivid and everlasting? Of course different groups use such constructed or artifactual memory for diverse purposes, but in opposition to "nocturnal intensities" (i.e., thoughts of skepticism, of withdrawal from the social), submerging the latter in the social world, marked by a conjunction of narrative, debt, and memory. Transculturally, Greek democrats, tyrants, and aristocrats, like Ford Motors today, engineer lack by devices Deleuze and Guattari called intellectual resonance, conceptual retention, fuzzy criteria of selection and psychological detachment—the written word set forth to dissolve evidence of the eyes and experiences of all sorts. Deleuze and Guattari make historiography the sole *cultural activity* necessary to despotism: "Legislation, bureaucracy, accounting, the collection of taxes, the State monopoly, imperial justice, the functionaries' activity, historiography: everything is written in the despot's procession."[33] In her essay "The Concept of History," Hannah Arendt argued that borrowing by historians of the scientific method of the seventeenth century required self-delusion: the shift to the "referent that seems to tell itself" was an appropriation from scientific practices that soon surpassed its own methods, historians blind to their own historicity. A falsely objectified history surrounds every attempt to think historically. Deleuze and Guattari believed that historical writing, like writing itself, survives under capitalism as an "archaism" co-coded with scientificity—an inherently schizo mode of writing, where historical texts survive in a nonhistorical society as a writing that "indicates what is going to be done, something that the shrewd or the competent are able to decode," a combination of "archaism and futurism, neoarchaism and ex-futurism, paranoia and schizophrenia."[34] It is very difficult for historians to come forward and embrace an image of *that*.

In sum, to Polan's sense of the nonfigurability or lack of image attending to contemporary historians, we could say: the shift from classical to intelligible history opens discourse and images to contention. If we asked, text by text, what historians perform on their readers, we might be flabbergasted at the answers.

Images of Goal-Talk: Currency and "Master Historians"

To go further into transformations of *to historicize,* I would like to conclude by beginning again, as it were, with an instance that probes image and role, the materials that came forward on the death of Isaiah Berlin.

By nearly unanimous agreement in the Western press, the writings of Isaiah Berlin are said to represent precisely what Polan says cannot be represented: an *image* of the historian who can enunciate clear goals, said to be universal in their legitimacy or validity. A year or so before his death in 1997, an

Isaiah Berlin at home, Oxford, 1976. Photograph by Dominique Nabokov. Reproduced by permission of Dominique Nabokov.

article in the *Times Literary Supplement* discussed Berlin's *Proper Study of Mankind,* in which his intellectual effect was said to stem from his writing's very *breath*—the image of the historian as pure voice, writing that manages to speak directly to the reader's mind.[35] Before and shortly after his death, there appeared a number of encomiums, two each from the *New York Times Book Review,* the *Times Literary Supplement,* and the *New York Review of Books,* dating from August 1997 until December 1998. Of the six encomiums, it is significant that each of them gives a photographic or drawn image, a picture, of Berlin—there is a photograph of him from around 1917, in Russia, three drawings or paintings (one made by Lucien Freud), and two photographs, both taken in Berlin's sixties or seventies, the latter divided into "hard" with a direct "look" to the camera, the other "soft," of a thoughtful man in chair with pipe.

The drawings and paintings index not just the likeness of the person but the friend of ideas, grave but with a light touch, the scholarly-dreamy and the serious. Apollonian in Nietzsche's sense of a beautiful soul. The body of a man who embodies the historian's duty and responsibility, hence an iconography: the image of concern with weighty thoughts, thoughts of an intellectual. To this iconography some of the texts cite anecdotes and details that confirm these icons. Avishai Margalit notes that Berlin himself confessed to his chief fault, of "anxiousness to please" the upper orders of England and America, and immediately qualifies this by insisting that "this was not a coy confession about a cute character flaw, designed to extract denials, or to fish for double compliments," as it was always only the "immigrant Jewish child" in the adult Berlin who understood "lack of home" that drove such "anxiousness."[36] The discourse indexes *the historian who has a "feel for lack."* This anxiousness to please, subject to all sorts of possible scorn, is placed beyond judgment, for who would dare to challenge the broken childhood of Isaiah Berlin? Indeed, another reviewer goes into the very act of Berlin's birth, noting that "an incompetent doctor pulled Isaiah into the world so violently that his left arm was permanently damaged."[37] The anecdotal in the service of immortalizing is rare in contemporary society.

The six texts are astonishing in their resemblance to each other, and in their fidelity to the word-spells of idealism, so often co-coded with icons. Berlin's essays on modern European intellectual history—the history of ideas, history of movements correlated with ideas, history of sensibility and culture—are said, by all the reviewers, to embody the "chief voice of liberalism," essays said to be "joyful, free of illusion, and vitally alive," not only because of the gravitas of the ideas, but because of the "moral quality of his voice." More: Berlin's writings are the result of the "cadence" of this "speaking voice," a voice "impossible to separate the speaker from the text," someone who "enjoyed" letting people "into his thoughts." The iconic dimension is bolstered by these references to the visuality of a "master's voice."[38] Taken together, the iconic and the textual compose a *personification* of the intellectual.

Prepared for monumentalization, to join the very immortals of history with whom he belongs, the reviews give to their readers nothing less than an institutionalization of voice/text. One of the writers says, without hesitation, that when the English establishment wanted "judgment about intellectual quality, its reflex was to 'ask Isaiah.'"[39] The judgments are sure that Berlin, text and person, can only be ranked as peerless, as the very someone whose delivery of judgments of rank are transcendent to any first- or second-party judgments.

Indeed, the connoisseur's sure touch is so sure that in matters of taste, Berlin's writings are said to evidence the "scholarly equivalent of the novelist's free indirect style," this style familiar and expository and lending itself to the right kind of distance, where ideas and movements can be judged by "an almost complete absence of the kind of close critical engagement with verbal details that one associates with a certain style of literary-critical essay," or judgment utterly severed from legalism, the juridical, all the better to signify the pure taste of the connoisseur.[40] Berlin, speaker and writer at once, did not have to prove anything, which is exactly what all the embedding of voice means. For example, by sheer discernment through criteria unavailable to others, Berlin's sense that inadequate ideas from the past simply perish while "'the great illuminating models' still stir us either to adherence or to criticism"[41] registers the putting down of skepticism about the very dualism of adherence/criticism, and obviously linearizes the present as the continuation of a goal/telos. Through Berlin, writer and speaker, the present is competent to "buttonhole the immortal dead in a transhistorical conversation."[42] We are enabled, through the monumentalizing and personification of the indistinguishable Berlin text/image, to ourselves have transportation to the "best" and the "better" and the "great." Here indeed is an historiography of influence, an unwithdrawable legacy, perhaps a fever dream of historians when they come to contemplate their legacy.

All the reviews applaud Berlin's liberalism, each finding its own way of saying that Berlin's arguments within intellectual history frustrated both left and right. The rank given to Berlin's writings stems not just from Berlin's judgments of connoisseurship and taste, but from a "rank" intrinsic to liberalism. First, it is a question of liberalism's humanistic and scholarly genealogy: Isaiah Berlin was one of the champions of Giambattista Vico, historiographer extraordinaire (Vico deserves, rightly, every acclaim). Berlin's appropriation of Vico gives liberalism a solid anchor in sensibility, imagination. Liberalism has cultural value, and this cultural value is of inestimable worth in creating the kinds of subjectivities liberalism can favor. This cultural basis is said to be derived from Vico's special love for and deployment of *fantasy:* "Berlin wrote at length about Vico's concept of *fantasia,* a term that no paraphrase quite captures, but that embraces among other things the capacity for an empathetic entering into the minds of others that the historian needs and the physicist does not . . . almost to reexperience the lives and thoughts of the persons and cultures we study . . . like the knowledge we claim of a friend, of his character . . . the intuitive sense of the nuances of personality or feelings or ideas."[43] This is a remarkable statement, and it prompts an immediate question: what precisely connects "entering into the minds" of others—a definition of connoisseurship—and liberalism? Are the two key terms—"empathetic" and "intuitive"—inherently part of a specific liberal sensibility for others?

Fantasia is completely severed from acts of interpretation and is said here to be reducible to the textual personification of Alexander Herzen as performed by Berlin's writings, the life of Herzen an imprint of Berlin's liberalism: "values . . . binding upon those who lived in their light; that suffering was inescapable, and infallible knowledge neither attainable nor needed."[44] Derived from connoisseurship and its correlates ("empathy," "intuition"), the liberal historiography promoted here makes dismissal of radicalism attractive. The overall image is that of the connoisseur-historian inexplicably capable of rendering sure judgments on any subject. Better: image and goal are joined in the ideal historian, the textualization and imaging of Berlin using the concept of legacy to idealize and monumentalize at once.

To historicize, as argued above, is as much now a tactic placed in the service of making a future as it is recuperation of any lost and forgotten past. It is not possible to prove that this shift is as potent as has been argued, but it is worth thinking that the audience presupposed by the texts analyzed above is not the one presupposed by historiographers such as Hayden White, writers and readers who *share* literary sensibility. The materials presented do not lead us to notions of text and audience common being, but to restrictions and idealizations.

Is it then a mistake to try and offer historical synthesis in a society more and more shattered by its divisions of labor, by its divisions of wealth, by its divisions of sign/prestation? How could historical representation that plays for the future of its reader be epistemically responsible to the actual intersubjective relations of contemporary society? I think it is an open question as to whether the kinds of synthetic history we are told that we need can offer more than a sanitized past. The long historiography of "coming-to-terms-with" is not contradictory to a historiography that scours the present, to select for the future (of representation). In another register, how does a sense of historical danger come alive if the past is another way of securing identity (including anti-identity) which then becomes a device to have a not-yet future reach into the present? In sum, *to historicize* goes schizo. Coming-to-terms with the past threatens to become infinitive while popular usages of history expand, a mixture of caregiving and scouting for the future?

Is it time to relegate the assumption of shared culture to some dustbin of history, relax in the shadow of a lack of concern for history? In a society that is as luxurious as ours is in providing to audiences popular veneration and connoisseurship of nearly anything, scholarly or not, new subjects of narrative coherence are also embedded in new schizo relations. I think that the language of goals is at odds with the discourses of selection; the social *episteme* (Foucault) has shifted. What could be more socially vital than what, as a society, happens to and with affirmative action—goal and selection in conflict? To return to Deleuze's sense of contemplation and signs: I am tempted to say here that narrative synthesis is impossible because synthesis is not attached to new goals, but to the survival of old ones.

Image and goals in contemporary society are overcoded. The distribution, allocation, and circulation of image feeds the requirement for the timely, endlessly collapsed and reconstituted on the spot, while goals are more nebulous, subject to capital in its triumphal mode, which means extending the life span of the "winners." That is the only goal that can be said to be quasi-transcendent; it is capitalism that kills history by ensuring fragmentation and ceaseless recoding by syntheses that are more and more local in their meaning and significance. *To historicize:* modern historical knowledge emerged with one mode of capitalist society, when integration was demanded by each collective group strong enough to press claims over public knowledge and their own sense of telos. Now such groups either do not exist or are already integrated in the capitalized systems of sign and other values, hence using history to historicize their future(s). *We are overhistoricized and undercritical* in relation to the schizo conditions outlined in this essay. This disjunction is stupid.

5 | *A Critical Analysis of the Historiographic Anecdote*

> *In extreme cases, the tellable takes precedence over the current topic in almost any speech situation. The appearance of an escaped elephant would be grounds for an exclamatory interruption no matter who is talking or what the subject is.*
> Mary Louise Pratt, *Toward a Speech Act Theory of Literary Discourse*

Procedurally, this chapter analyzes a brilliant essay by the late Joel Fineman on the indispensability of the anecdote in any mode of writing that lays claim to historical representation. Fineman's essay is one of the most incisive attempts to think about historiography at its conceptual nucleus, the place where language and referent might join necessarily, and his essay performs this by linking Lacanian notions of subjectivity, language theory, and narratology to a reading of modern philosophy and ancient historical writings (Thucydides). Is the anecdote despised in the historical profession because it shows/tells *itself* a device at once literary/realist and a pleasurable disruption, without which there could be no historical representation at all? The ceaseless put-down of the anecdote is proof enough that the anecdote signifies representation at some extreme from the credible knowledge claims of historical narration, the anecdote a threat to claims of objectivity made in the name of historical writing.

While the philosophical and cultural ideas Fineman brought to this task are, I believe, highly politicized, his transformation of the "map" of historiography—the theory of history writing—is striking. That is, Fineman unmistakably *sexualized* theory of historical representation, and I offer some comments on that job, since it is a unique essay in that regard. After trying to give the scope of Fineman's work, I then turn to an analysis or close reading in the political use of anecdotes in narrative writing. The argument is that "normal" historiographic usage of an anecdote can be highly politicized and so raise issues of historical knowledge. So the two dimensions of use and abuse meet as use in the case of Fineman's enterprise, and abuse in an actualized historian's narrative. Compared are two levels of the anecdote, concept and application. Again: one text treats ideas of history as having a basis in literary form and is said to give historical thought a foundation; the other uses the anecdote in a way that directly politicizes its data/interpretation, unleashing a narrative that trashes recent debates over questions of identity, or, worse, reduces many years of contentious issues to the safety of conventional historiography.

In comparing a discourse on the anecdote to one that uses them, I hope to evoke an excess of discourse on all aspects and functions of the historiographic *devices* that rivet us to history. This critical excess challenges the belief that historical writing has any necessary *phenomenal* form, either intralinguistic, like the literary form of the anecdote, or extralinguistic, when we say an anecdote registers reality more or less directly in language. In his recent *Figural Realism: Studies in the Mimesis Effect,* Hayden White has it that the "principal problem for any theory of historical writing . . . is . . . that of explaining the persistence of narrative in historiography."[1] An answer to White's implicit question about persistence is that narrative persists because of the politics of control carried out in acts of narrativization—history can be a powerful resource to include and eliminate cultural and political differences, spanning claims of memory to those of social reproduction. Narrative discourse is a relatively easy device by which to privilege one concept or value or process over another.

White's most recent series of essays examine the phenomenal basis of historiography in terms of existential phenomenology. In the introduction to *Figural Realism,* he offers that historical discourse, of whatever version, reads as indistinguishable between content and form, its discourse "a discursive 'thing' that interferes with our perception of its putative referent even while fixing our attention on and illuminating it."[2] That is, historical discourse is *not* its referent, yet no referent eludes our discourse, even to where this discourse can stand as perceptual experience for a reader. Yet a few pages later White claims that the convergence in historical discourse of trope and fiction "has nothing to say about perception." Setting forth perception as the historian's articulation of a "verbal image" and then denying its effect strikes me as exactly the kind of tangle to be expected from the historical. White goes on to say that the value of historical narratives, because they are figural and tropological, is to serve as a means, a test, hence a form of our very own Western practical reason, where Westerners "imagine the different kinds of meaning (tragic, comic, epic, farcical, etc.) which a distinctively human form of life *might have* are tested against the information and knowledge that specific forms of human life *have had* in the past. In the process, not only are past forms of life endowed with the kinds of meaning met with in the forms of fiction produced by a given culture, but the degrees of truthfulness and realism of these forms of fiction to the facts of historical reality and our knowledge of it can be measured."[3] Clearly, "had" and "might" are the operative terms—but what operates "can be measured," this nonfigural reference to the phenomenal basis of history? Is this concept not then a magical signifier—which cannot be explained as trope, discursive, fictional, theoretical, precisely because it is a political construct—any text's actual amalgam of trope, discourse, fiction, and so forth?

In this chapter, then, I want to keep historical representation suspended as to how narrative form is sufficient to the phenomena so narrated. I also intend to raise doubts, as said above, as to *which terms* are appropriate to the analysis of historical discourse, as the latter makes an anecdote swing between metaphysics and politics.

Conceiving the Anecdote

The citation from Pratt at the beginning of this chapter opens to a number of associations, including comparing the "tellable" to an "escaped elephant" where both can be experienced as "interruption" of a speaker's mastery. Interruption can be interpreted as one of the effects of an anecdote's force. Say you are sitting in a sun-drenched café in Trastevere, Rome, one of many great neighborhoods in a great city, and suddenly, over your glass of wine and pizza (tomato and tuna only, please) an "escaped elephant" jumps out from behind a wall—in the form of a hand delivering a subpoena from the States, from one's colleagues who do not want you to come back—is this not the occurrence of an elephant/anecdote that interrupts and starts another event, another story? Apart from the causal links that could be set off here, from disruption of the meal so that the wine goes to the wrong pipe, to instantaneous escape/revenge plans vis-à-vis a subpoena, isn't the conceptual value of the experience of an escaped elephant the anecdote in person? An anecdote opens up the telling of the told of one story to introduce the past and future of other stories, and what narrative, which kind of narrative, could be immune to its power? And isn't such consciousness of disruption part of the legends of historical thought, as in Pascal's witticism that if (conditional) Cleopatra had looked differently, history itself would have been changed? In a great book,

The History of History (1939), James Shotwell offered that any serious, that is "scientific," treatment of historiography would have to consider all the "incidental mention[s]" of past narratives, including those cast in the modes of legend and the annal, ransacking the historical writings of the past for their anecdotal suggestibility. In a general way, Shotwell offered, the anecdote made it possible for peoples and groups of all sorts to render "laudatory" and "originary" judgments at once, on themselves and others, through their evocations of anecdotal mentions.[4]

Nonetheless, the anecdote is a kind of embarrassed family member within the discourses of historiography. It is not possible for a research-based historian to offer an affirmation of the anecdote as anything but the literary superstructure that comes into being once research has to be made tellable, narratable. The anecdote has been a perfect object to negate in the name of professional history writing, it has a bad name. No doubt this stems from the denotations of anecdote that we have made ourselves accustomed to: the *Oxford English Dictionary* has it that *anecdote* means "things unpublished," including "tales of the private life of the court," with the more neutral sense of "details of history" also mentioned. "Things unpublished" refers to, one supposes, the representation of experiences more closely allied with the private than not. Historians have often referred to the anecdote as a kind of dirty laundry, where things unpublished are anecdotal to the degree that they add nothing to the main story. Further, the OED also has it that an anecdote is inclusive of those designations that open onto a "narrative of a detached incident . . . in itself interesting or striking," which correlates anecdote with the figure of *enargheia,* the vivid thing/telling of something. In turning over such designations, even the OED is unable to render a coherent, unified sense of anecdote—does this already allude to the extreme derision of anecdotes in certain modes of historical writing, as well as a certain reliance on the anecdote in even those writings that dismiss its very use?

From another perspective, Gérard Genette put forth a notion of rhetorical classification in which trope, diction, construction, elocution, style, and thought are the main zones of rhetoric, and it is unclear where to "put" anecdotes.[5] Is an anecdote manifested in a specific mode, a textual mention, intense and abrupt? Should it be classified as *paraliterary* and *quasi-existential,* since an anecdote might affect a reader's connection to the intratextual and the extratextual at once? In Ducrot and Todorov's great *Encyclopedic Dictionary of the Sciences of Language,* it would appear that anecdotes can work as syntagmatic rules, more specifically part of the class of context-sensitive rules, where substitution of one name for another is predicated on rewriting.[6] Emile Benveniste, whose work is endlessly rereadable on account of his having anticipated ongoing problems of methods pursued in the humanities, described deictic expressions as an irruption of contrary sense within sense, so should one think of anecdotes as the condensed *expressed* of syntactic forms? Some writers imply that an anecdote has the effective force of rhetorical hyperbole, or that anecdotes belong to the very practice of dissociative thinking.[7] Finally, to cite Hayden White once again: in his commentary on New Historicism (on which, more below), White discusses this movement's use of cultural poetics to analyze past instances where dominant codes of representation were lessened—"whence their interest in what appears to be the emergent, episodic, anecdotal, contingent, exotic, abjected or simply uncanny aspects of the historical record."[8] Clearly, the anecdote belongs to more than one armature of discourse and thought in which its movements and functions are unsettled.

In an interesting passage on the anecdotal, Kenneth Burke showed just how confounding the anecdote can be when we have to conceive it affirmatively, and not just as a literary device exhausted in our using it. An anecdote, Burke averred, runs across acts of thought such as reflection on one's use of references; it shows up in the act of selection in which some privilege is granted to the framing of thoughts; and it is common in the use of figures to displace others' thoughts. An anecdote can disturb understanding, show us what we have focused on (and omitted), and it allows for a necessary spacing in the use and abuse of thoughts of all sorts. Burke went on to argue that anecdotes are a *movement* of language in relation to both states of mind and to the qualities and entities they refer to, a movement that is at once strange and familiar. Burke describes the scientist-type who has come to a conclusion about behavior in general, but who is unable to cast the conclusions in an appropriate anecdote, for the anecdote cannot, in narrative, convey the energy and dynamics of the anecdote that triggered the research project to begin with, its "point of departure."[9] Anecdote and insight make for another link deeply under suspicion in the humanities. Haven't I just used Burke's text as an example anecdotally, in that I started to tell a little story about the slipperiness of anecdote? If anecdotes can be identified in discourse as having such obviously complex operations as representing—by way of summarizing an issue, of serving as a paradigm for branchings, for linking to more interesting narratives that are virtual to the one told at X moment, and even make prototype thoughts for subsequent classifications—then it seems to me that historiography's contemporary use and abuse of anecdotes are worth considering.

Like many images, the elephant anecdote is self-limiting. Hayden White has another interesting passage on the anecdote and its range. Where historians once coded accidents (anecdotes) as events "that yielded to the imperatives of storytelling and followed the rules of narrativization," it is now more difficult to decide on events/accidents that are less beautiful and/or ugly than they are sublime/disgusting.[10] Social life changes narrative and anecdotal forms and functions. Can an anecdote actually *import the real* into narrative? Considered more fully below, "imports the real" is a metonym for practices intrinsic to the philosophy of reference, from Plato to Goodman to Deleuze, as to how we can transpose, with continuity and assurance, sensations into a discourse at once adequate to the sensations and, where, for an instant, something happens in the telling that introduces events-as-differences into narration. In Nietzsche's terms: the anecdote can be conceived as beyond epistemology and aesthetics. To paraphrase a comment of Arthur Danto, the anecdote, prior to its transformation into a set description, can be compared to a resistance within thought/language to the notion of destiny, due to the latter's submeanings of determination and outcome.[11] Again, the concept of the anecdote—*detached* and *striking* as the OED also put it—might clinch for some readers of a particular narrative a sense of the real as it also figures forth another derealization of a competing story.

In sum, crucial in establishing the particularity of a discourse, the narrative singularity that has to be given of any object or complex that can be narrated, the anecdote is also put down so frequently in the name of reason that one is dealing with something strange and familiar, and something else besides. It is not enough to know that research historians are openly contemptuous of anecdotes except when they nod to an audience and the need to make a narrative readable, the anecdote a necessary pill (medicine) to the uninitiated. If the anecdote is at the hinge between the sensory and the tellable, its reach is disturbing.

Formulated as an intellectual problem: *why* does the anecdote have the cultural life of being simultaneously elevated and despised? Does the anecdote take historical theory to "the real" in a way more vital than other techniques of (re)presentation? As if these questions are not enough, there are more: is the anecdote a condition of historicity, as one of the essays analyzed below insists, just because concepts of the tellable, the particular and time-interruptions meet as anecdote? And if so, what are we to make of the anecdote used as a political weapon—the work of discrediting—as another essay, also analyzed below, shows when evaluated for the way it uses anecdotes?

Joel Fineman's Historiographic Theory

Given the real profusion of discourses concerning the anecdotal, now consider some renderings of historical *meanings* drawn from quite distinctive anecdotal fields, or areas of application. (1) An editorial writer in the *New York Times* insists, incorrectly, that given the "simple economics" of university publishing, writing and tenure are now "determined" by Barnes and Noble customers, who want books on "women's studies, African-American studies, gay and lesbian studies, Asian-American studies, studies of popular culture and literary biographies, to say nothing of that inevitable publishing troika, Nazis, dogs, and the Civil War."[12] Barnes and Noble sales reach into the quite contested zone of confidential and private academic meetings; this is amusing and scary, but true? In which senses? Here, the anecdotal sounds exceedingly dramatic, the world of scholarly significance reduced to the instance of Barnes and Noble consumers. Traditional, critical scholarship is "ending" in the face of a commercially driven academia. The idea of simple economics is the anecdotal effect of assuming there is a real existence of something called simple economics. (2) Consider that in evaluating the term *postmodernism,* Fredric Jameson describes it, in one and the same paragraph, as a "momentous cultural mutation" and as a repetition from the Freudian catalogue of symptoms of denial.[13] Postmodernism can be dated by application of the concept of dialectic—as mutation, postmodernism indexes an interruption of smooth historical time. If the first example gave us a periodization *that is happening,* this second renders a sense of today as a crossroads, an intersection, a presentistic sense more open to transformation. One could multiply, with the randomness or rigor as required, that the "now" of publishing and Jameson's concatenation of "momentous" and "repetition" are instances of thinking the historical, each relying on facts and data that could easily be dismissed as anecdotal. It would seem that quite a lot of what is called historical significance actually does turn on anecdotes that are regularly derided. In the example from the *New York Times,* the concept of the end of "normal scholarly publishing" *must presume* not just that "end" is the name of the right fact, but also that this "determination" is the right concept. Jameson's text, if it is to be believed, must *not* make the contradiction between "momentous" and "repetition" explicit for his text to have extralinguistic or cognitive force. How does an anecdote join significance and datability, whether phenomenologically driven as in microhistory, or dilatory as with macronarratives, a century rendered in a page?

The first text is an essay that appeared in the volume *The New Historicism,* "The History of the Anecdote: Fiction and Fiction," written by Joel Fineman. Historiographers and critics have written on this intellectual movement, but the strategy here is to engage this New Historicism mostly through Fineman's text, representative of the *strongest* intellectual claims that New Historicism has made. In this regard, White, in his analysis of the claims made by New Historicism, has emphasized its transformation of what counts as the sensibility of *historical sequence.* New Historicism juxtaposed creative resistance—what we now call Shakespeare—to then dominant codes of writing and civic life.[14] White sees in New Historicism methods of description, connection, analysis, and so on that legitimately probed the humanities' ability to engage the past without importing our sense of its future into our interpretations of its "thingness."[15] The weaker claims made by New Historicists can be seen in its practitioners who outfit the New Historicist as a late-coming Baudelairean *flâneur* of theory, the new narrator who affirms the anecdotal, the marginal, the neglected. For example, in the same volume with Fineman's essay, consideration of Shakespeare "sets his plays in the context of the social drama out of which theatre in Elizabethan England arose." "Context" and "social drama" remain in aesthesis, however, as these terms actually presume a unity to that time that may be altogether spurious. The New Historicist author-narrator slips from such unities to praising the power people in those times had to make "riffs," using tonality, a "tuning" or the importation of musical theme into historical method/research. "Riff" gives a figure at once ineffable and sensuous, giving New Historicism the currency of cultural connoisseurship.[16]

Now Fineman's essay is an extraordinary piece of analysis of theory of history. In effect, his essay gives a theorization, construal, to the logic of sequence, storytelling, and the method is structural—bringing to bear on theory of history questions that probe its internal cohesion, its field of force, its effects.

Fineman jumps right in: a form that is literary, the anecdote, is grafted to a text written by Thucydides. The "formal operation of the anecdote, understood as a specific literary genre, with peculiar literary properties," can give a "determination" to the "practice of historiography."[17] Fineman has a rather complicated sense of today's New Historicism, and sees it as a renewal of, or radically continuous with, Thucydides' *History of the Peloponnesian War,* that text "the first example of a New Historicist" (50). Of course that makes today's

New Historicism part of repetition, and immediately raises a question: if Fineman's New Historicism is correct about the *fact* that actual continuity in historiography belongs to the persistence of the anecdotal *relation,* language's continuity with the real, then why such resistance to it?

The anecdote, to employ a Wittgensteinian phrase, "shows" what it has in common with extralinguistic realities, and therefore must itself be already, in some part, not of language. Hence its "peculiar" literary form. Historiography is always "refound" in a literary genre itself more than literary, at once potentially too real and not-real enough. Fineman does not take up the somewhat eerie reasons for why the Greek tradition of "emphatic criticism of historical sources" was the work of *logographers,* whose motto was "Hecataeus of Miletus thus speaks: I write what I deem true." What were, in other words, some of the reasons for Greek narrativists to turn to the anecdote, given the fact that in the Greek world there were many contests over the representations of the past?

Moving between Thucydides and New Historicism, Fineman defines the latter as a methodological and interdisciplinary approach whose main technique or procedure is the embedding of artifacts and social context in the other, each referred to the metaphor of constructing a weave of past events. "Weaving" is archaic—a premodern image of historical representation—even if endlessly *re*performed in the humanities. More so than the anecdote, *to weave,* infinitive mode, is one of the defining conceptual conditions of representing anything in Western culture, from ideas of empathy with others, to the differentiation of the humanities from the sciences. In using the image of weaving, Fineman equates it with the "historical as such," set within a discipline (postwar literary criticism) that did not have any consistent use for such ideas. That is to say, the now old New Criticism and formalism from the 1920s on out were so random in the ways they historicized literature that they canceled out the singularity of the historical. Hence, New Historicism called for "an historiographic consciousness and conscience . . . materialized primarily in the study of the Renaissance" (51). Polemically, New Historicism called for practices of contextualization "against the formalism," the "mere formalism," which "was thought to be apolitical, sexist, hermetic, elitist, etc." (51). These "meres" of formalism are the objects of Fineman's New Historicist imaginary of what it opposed, and also include "close reading" (his phrase), all serving aims that were "scientistic, agentless, essentialist, Structuralis[t] . . . to . . . deconstructive, but still mandarin . . . textual" practices (51). Fineman lumps together these movements, which bind his own commitment to New Historicism, these barriers to historical comprehension. Is New Historicism here also coded as a resistance to contemporary forms of *enlightened historiography*? He acknowledges that New Historicism is also "one merchandisable rubric amongst others in the not so free marketplace of academic ideas," but sets this anecdotal ("merchandise") notion aside.

At this point, Fineman's own self-styled method of genealogy locates New Historicism as different from both practical literalism and theoretical literalism, the first associated with U.K. materialist readings (i.e., what does a text "do" in life), the second with deconstruction. Opposed to any mode of literalism, New Historicism is compared to a ramble, "undirected . . . [an] idle through the historical archives," and within academic life, shows itself to be an "impulse towards the historical," whose exemplary manifestation can be found, again, in Thucydides (52). It is an audacious move on Fineman's part, linking, through nothing more than impulse, New Historicism to the archaic, making Thucydides the hero of the critical (scientific?) dimension of historiography. Why Thucydides? He posed "laws of historical causation" ("nomological historical succession"), where episode (part) and narrative (totality) cohere. Thucydides' *History* displays the skeletal bones of a "recurrent pattern," giving historiography a "usefulness," an "absence of the fabulous," and is certainly "less pleasing to the ear" than, say, adulation.

In this genealogy, which mixes contemporary historiographic disputes with ancient texts, the genius of Thucydides' historiography was to shear literariness from "probabilities," codified as interest in what will "happen again in the same or a similar way" (52). Fineman parses this to mean that events have an intrinsic "generic logic of succession," seen in Thucydides' *modulation* of "moments" within the narrative serving to give historiography the particularity of a "this" ("*touto*") inseparable from a "generic, representative urgency of the logic of the *meta* [which] reciprocally will call each other up." This conjunction of sequence and event constitutes historical significance, a *collation* of "structure and genesis" (53). As Fineman puts it in an endnote, Thucydides located the moment of the Plague after Pericles' "Funeral Oration": "so that the plague appears as the diagetic surprise that determines, by inexorable chance, the history and the 'History' of the Peloponnesian War. The inevitability of this accident corresponds to the equivocal prediction and retrospection with which Thucydides codes the plague" (69). Surprise and inexorable chance, an "inevitable" accident: the anecdote is that literary form or discursive event that allows for reciprocity between discourse and event. The anecdote brings to the narration *what did not have to happen;* it brings a possible otherness to any specific telling, which none of the agents of the story could have predicted. The anecdote is simultaneously the connective tissue between literature and not-literature as well as a principle of uncontrollability, without which no narrative could be read. For without anecdote, narrative would figure forth as pure determination, pure successivity, plot without chance, nothing more significant than a story that read as sheer dictate and fiat, a judgment of finality, in Kantian terms, where cognition and aesthetics can fuse, a true nightmare of reason. Because of the anecdote, readers of Thucydides find the narrated past given both determination and accident. What a reader judges concerning the determination of the story is based upon a narrative's multiple use of anecdotes.

All of this, Fineman argues, allows us to think to an "historiseme." Narratives considered to be epistemologically responsible rely on the "aporetic structure of the anecdote" (69), called here an "equivoceme," the anecdote that has no "essence" but nonetheless gives any particular narrative pattern the patina of necessity and chance. Again, Fineman's point is that an anecdote is both epistemologically *responsible* to reality, the outside, events, and necessary in holding determinism at bay. Judged from the perspective of its effects, a "successful" historical narrative is distilled in a reader's synthetic judgment that "it had to have happened like that" precisely because it did not have to happen *only like that.* Perhaps an instance of this relation is the citation from White, above, about "might" and "have had." A successful historical narration gives something for a reader to imagine, to compare.

An endnote cryptically encodes this paradoxical continuity of historiography, narrative inexorability and event-accident, the anecdote at once empty and real. This set of terms allows Fineman to open his discourse to contemporary notions of subjectivity, from Hegel to Lacan, or through Lacan, to Hegel and questions as to which human faculty sustains a sense, if not need, for history felt to be a necessary form of understanding. How are we to grasp the anecdote not just as literary artifact/form but as an aesthetic, a psychology, a mode of perception even? If historiography is partly if importantly based on the anecdote, then a "subjective burden of history" is presumed to exist—but how are anecdotes selected? How did this subjective burden of history arise— to tell a true story processed by fiction? Importantly, how could such a faculty *come and go,* since historiography has frequently been evicted from interference in social understanding? Wouldn't the sense of *modulation,* previously mentioned, signify something permanent? How do we account for the fact that it is a long time between Thucydides and modern realism, where historical consciousness is said to have mushroomed, especially by reference to so many wars far more horrific than the Peloponnesian? Or has Fineman actually depicted a theory of *ricorso,* in Vico's sense of a return, so that Thucydides' Greece and the Renaissance lived that point of cultural poetics, an exhaustion with prose, and so a proliferation of anecdotes helped to breach the dominant codes of those times?

In short, we have arrived at a question: what does it take for historical consciousness to be activated, since its creation is not an issue? We have Thucydides and much else besides. Is historical consciousness, as consciousness and not trope, if that distinction holds, to be conceived as always there, like a faculty, yet switched off, its activity blocked by the dominant modes of thought that surround it? Was historical narration too dangerous from the Renaissance until reactivated in the nineteenth century? In the wars of historiography over the last century, was the anecdote suppressed because of the requirement for the scientization of historical writing, scientization a domestication, overall, of the humanities?

Sliding into a discourse that owes much to Kant, Fineman writes that narrative patterns give a "logic of events" and are based upon a "faculty psychology" that was revivified in the Renaissance, a sense of "the historically significant occasion." Fineman opens his discourse to the unknown content of a subjective burden of history, including such issues as sorting out what the later interpretation of events has to say that past agents did not—the famous problem, worked over by everyone, of whether and to what degree the present historian has an obligation to *complete the past's incompleteness.* Was grief after Genghis Khan's army literally annihilated Samarkand the same grief elicited in the bombings of Dresden in World War II?[18] Faculty psychology assumes that subjects *must* ask why things turned out the way they did, where history (passage, transition) melds with psychology. More questions than answers: does this make the Renaissance reinvention of powerfully oppositional concepts— structure and genesis, metaphor/metonymy, system/process, and related terms—*metahistorical* to future generations? What does it require for historicity to not always happen, or to activate it, for it to intervene? To be historical, in Fineman's terms, means that one is always aware of the shift between structures and emergences, new starts, event-lines, bizarre connections, dead ends, and so on, and this implies a faculty that is superhistorical—the ability to turn off an excess of historical sense, to place such a sensibility in pause mode, and so on. In sum, historical consciousness, its relation to notions of subjective lack, evokes a subjective competence to use history, which opens an excruciating mess. If our lives are calibrated with the variations of narrative(s) to the point where we cannot know the difference between action and reaction to events and their telling, when the telling precedes the event, the event thereafter ambiguous (the modern event par excellence, according to White), then should we think a constructed subjective condition of historicity has become both habitual and impossible?[19] History out of joint?

In fact, Fineman does specify this faculty psychology—he calls it the Greek elaboration of medical semiotics. This intellectual discipline or set of practices joined symptom/sign and analysis, diagnosis and prognosis, curiosity and autopsy. In medicine an initial symptom may lead in many directions, of which death is only one outcome. But not with narrativity: narrations render stories that locate its referents in the sequence, even if highly variable. What supports both Thucydides' scientization of logography and New Historicism is the "medical model," events following disease patterns in the sense that, like the doctor, the historian interprets "for the sake of diagnosis and prognosis." The subjectivity that turned to medical semiotics to create scientific narrative made a cognitive pattern that defines historiography: the latter employs a "compressed and stressedly antithetical prose style and the noticeably aphoristic manner of the Hippocrates corpus," these formal modes joining the "medical case history" and the "generic frame of Thucydides' events" (55). Antithetic understanding—descriptions that use contraries to highlight a contest—is itself a *verbal image of synthesis,* and aphorisms the literary kernel of the anecdote; as joined, historiography is a generic activity continuous with the organicism of medical semiotics, itself a knowledge from embodiment: "items noticed as well as those ignored, acquire their specifically medical significance insofar as they are understood to articulate in their appearance or omission what are coherently segmented moments in the fluid and continuous unfolding of the internal logic of the disease—[Thucydides'] nomological narrative or *meta*" (55). This "medical case history of the aphoristic, Hippocratic corpus, coincides with the logic of event and context" (56), and the specific mechanism that allows the medical to be transposed to the narrative of any event believed to warrant historical significance is the literary form of the *anecdote,* conceived now as integrative of event and context; anecdote allows the "narration of a singular event" that "uniquely refers to the real" (56). The anecdote is not alone in such referring (direct description also refers), but there is "something about the anecdote that exceeds its literary status," a "something more" than its effects of representation (modulations of time).

In a crucial passage, Fineman insists that "however literary" an anecdote, it nonetheless is "directly pointed towards or [is] rooted in the real," a conflation that is, so to speak, telling as to Fineman's criteria of selection. If experiences of deixis, reference, metonymy are similar to anecdotal presence, we have subjective recording of real experience. As a subjective condition, these terms are a redescription of the "autarchy of will" that Kant made the important engine in his version of a regulative Idea of history.[20] The anecdote, as literary device, is turned into a cognitive anchor, a condition of narrative truth and credibility—someone tells experience modulating both truth and the effects of narration. As interruption, the anecdote is conceived as a sensory connection to an "outside" (other, difference), Fineman's use of "towards" and "rooted" overlapping in the sense of a primordial trope: where intralinguistic and extralinguistic are already mixed with the other. This is not a Cratylism of language, an illusory motivation of signs, giving them magical and analogical force.[21] Again, all this is to say that the anecdote is clearly active in the register of opening narratives to singular experiences and subjectivity, but "rooted" makes this organic, natural. The anecdote is given the cognitive power to disrupt any continuous narrative so long as its disruption is immediately recuperated into the "modulation" of a narrative, so that its readers can experience the simultaneity of "it did and did not have to happen—that way." In this sense, the anecdote spans catachresis and prosopopoeia—it gives a name to the nameless, the latter understood as the real that moves toward the narrative, calling out, as it were, for inclusion. Anecdotes move *toward* the real as surely as the real moves toward anecdote, anecdote a linguistic modality that visualizes or concretizes temporality and sensibility at once—hence faculty psychology. The subjective burden of history is an ever present possibility of allowing anecdote to *dynamize* what one previously believed to be "the real story." Anecdotes can be dangerous. The return to the figure of Thucydides' plague is decisive in Fineman's workup since "plague" gives the "face" of a disruption that had to occur, whether or not *as plague.* Such a decisive textual moment suggests that the anecdote also schematizes the place of the vivid—an event not easily forgotten because so readily schematized or fitted into languages' representative capacities. That linkage goes to a reader—when someone says an historical narrative got it "just right." Historiography and danger: historical narration believed to be a continuation of the referent, the historian not creating truth but only realizing it. Truth as created in language becomes the truth of things that can be placed back, as it were, in things.

Fineman considers the various announcements of the collapse of the *grand recit,* or master/super narratives. They are part of the modern plague befalling historiography. He notes the objections made to "teleological unfolding" by critics such as Jean-François Lyotard, but he is no friend of a philosophy of history that is only riven by paradoxes. It is somewhat unsettling that Fineman does not make more of paradox intrinsic to historiography, offering philosophy of history compared to narrative modulation—of what turned out to be subjective and group senses of fate, how different subjects/groups modulate their decisions and understanding through narration.

Now one can certainly agree with Fineman that modern critics of metanarrative paid little attention to the literary and cognitive fusions of the anecdotal, continuing the nineteenth-century emphasis on scientific history, giving anecdotes only enough attention to be "passing moments in a story whose conclusion is already written" (57). Think of the American historians who borrowed psychoanalysis beginning in the 1920s, and subsumed subjective experiences of temporality to the overarching revelation of the truth-of-the-subject, culminating in a book like Erik Erikson's *Young Man Luther,* which made Luther's coming-to-terms-with-Oedipus the driving force of the narrative, everything else controlled by that story.

We can, Fineman thinks, experience today the "self-completing self-reflecting of Hegelian historicity . . . turned over on itself, turned over and turned inside-out, so as to open up in space a space for space to take its place." Fineman's essay raises the stakes in any consideration of historiography's structure and genesis, the back and forth of language and referent, the strategies used by historians so as to calibrate determination and events. He introduces Lacan's notion of the Real, a "genuinely historical opening." He writes that "Lacan's formulation of an unimaginable and unspeakable 'real' accounts for my use of the word 'anecdote,' which, at least etymologically, means that which is 'unpublished'" (67). In this highly charged, highly aphoristic or condensed rendering of Lacan, why is the real unspeakable? In the peculiar metaphysics of Lacan—and "peculiar" is the right word, as Elizabeth Roudinescu has so completely demonstrated[22]—to enter the zone of the symbolic (language) is to be cut off from one's instincts, the subject severed from its own "presence" to immediate self-experience. The most perspicuous critics of Lacan have stressed how subjectivity in the Lacanian system is predicated on nothingness, the metafiction of a trauma of separation.[23]

Lodged in an endnote, marginalized within the essay form Fineman claims has been marginalized by the dominant tradition, tucked away, one confronts Fineman's insistence on a Lacanian determination: the anecdote subjectifies as such, historical narration the medium where the subject-as-anecdote-making makes itself visible (publishable), the unspeakable and the unpublishable in movement, the anecdote that *instant* in which subjectivity assumes lack. Fineman does not notice that his affirmation of the anecdote is stamped by the verbal forge of Lacanian metaphysics, which to repeat, depends upon the concept of lack as its concept-driver. With Lacan and his crew, the concept of lack explains almost anything about subjectivity.[24] Historical narration only really makes sense when it can provide a synthesis the reading of which varies the path of confirming and disconfirming previous identifications and differentiations. At their strongest, anecdotes not only modulate narratives, they shift subjectivity from its imaginary identifications with ends, to a consideration of the unpublished, a thinking and a saying of what has not been yet said or thought. Fineman insists this structure finds its confirmation in the anecdote treated as unpublishable, the anecdote revealing the void of the *grand recit* precisely because the anecdote shows telos to be the "revelation of a void, the presence of an absence of reality."[25] The bigger the story, the emptier it is of the real.

As mentioned, the problem with the *grand recit,* and what this version of New Historicism comes to correct/replace, is that the "big stories" we tell are predicated on what we cannot tell, not what did not happen, but the unpublishable. The anecdote shows that something did happen and thus challenges the very sense of the *grand recit* within which it appears. Without subjectively selected anecdotes that undo the rigidity of a narrative's always false *coherence,* its finality and determination, we simply could not read any work of history. We would be forced to nod with it as it carries us to an end; the anecdote performs the labor of the unpublishable because it requires of its readers to think the contingent, disturbing the body of historicism. Fineman's New Historicism makes a "cut" in the overcoded reality of historicism, this cut "witness to or earnest of an impulse to discover or to disclose some wrinkling and historicizing interruption, a breaking and a *realizing* interjection, within the encyclopaedically enclosed circle of Hegelian self-reflection" (60). Fineman believes this sense of New Historicism thus warrants a "provisional definition of history," set forth as: "History is what happens when it happens—but as it only sometimes, in particular cases, happens—that something happens when you combine Being and Time" (61). He then synthesizes anecdote and historicity in a strangely powerful, yet troubling way, worth quoting in full:

> the anecdote is the literary form that uniquely *lets history happen* by virtue of the way it introduces an opening into the teleological, and therefore timeless, narration of beginning, middle and end ["timeless" means in the face of a plot that renders closure to a past event]. The anecdote produces

> the effect of the real, the occurrence of contingency, by establishing an event as an event within and yet without the framing context of historical succes- sivity, i.e., it does so only in so far as its narration both comprises and re- fracts the narration it reports. Further . . . that the opening of history that is effected by the anecdote, the hole and rim—using psychoanalytic language, the orifice—traced out by the anecdote . . . is something that is characteris- tically and ahistorically plugged up by a teleological narration. (61)

Teleology is anal. The inhumanity of the "big stories" is that they carry us away from subjective consciousness of choice; against this inhuman force, the anecdote *tells time* because it is a "prescriptive opening that forever forecloses any finalizing or finitizing closure" (61). In one sense the anecdote is that tex- tual marker that allows a reader to recognize the specificity and singularity of any given account and allows for any given narrative to be *rewritten:* instead of the successivity of the story as told, the anecdote opens in the virtuality of every direction, allowing the unpublishable its time/space.

But what does Fineman's sexualization of the anecdote—"hole and rim," body orifices—transform his own anecdote of disruption into? Is this an- tiphallocentrism, antinormative, as it makes phallus imagery absolute? This is contestable stuff, a great merit of Fineman's essay. Should we read his text as not merely a Lacanian defense of New Historicism, but as a remarkable sexu- alization of historiography, "hole" for "whole," by pure metonymic substitu- tion, the subjective burden of history *named* as desire to open and close holes, instead of identification with ends, the whole?

Yet, and this is critical, the subjective burden of history is built on the pre- supposition of identity—of a subject always in lack and so making anecdotes to ward off the bad (falsely essentializing, over inclusive) stories that mark themselves as inauthentic because they are falsely coherent. In a world where every action is shadowed both by the anecdotal escaped elephants of others' and everyone's subjective desire to impress into existence anecdotes that open up experience to alternative tellings/showings, who could argue with this de- fense of New Historicism?

To summarize: the major claims, as I understand them, propose to affirm *dis- continuity* as the condition of historicity, figured forth as the "seductive open- ing of anecdotal form" (61). Fineman's strongest claim is that historiography, as founded on the anecdote, can render the discontinuous visible. As men- tioned above, historiography would remain frozen, in ceaseless and pointless disputes about direction and telos without the literary-subjectifications performed by anecdotal disruptions. We have many histories of the Vietnam War told from the perspective of tragedy; but each narrative achieves meaning via the openings its precise anecdotes offer—historical meaning is predicated on variability, not truth as totality (completeness), variability giving retroactive significance to a narrative's events. In this sense, Fineman's theoretical account calls for *perpetual* recoding/recording of history, insofar as any given narrative has a blind spot in relation to the anecdotes it does and does not cite, each invocation of an anecdote calling out to another, each pertaining to a holistic (intended) narrative that can be, and must be, reworked. Fineman has given us an extraordinary account of historiographic *rewriting*, based on a reading of Thucydides and a sexualized reworking of his New Historicist education. The anecdote separates from its literary form as *it forecloses on the closure* of narrative, and merges with reference where descriptions and definitions "do not call up the narration of beginning, middle and end," the anecdote making a "dilation of narrative successivity" and so an "effect of the real" (61). Yet again: "the formal play of anecdotal hole and whole," the "dilation and contraction of the entrance into history through the opening" of anecdote thus accounts for the history of historiography understood as a "traceable, genealogical progression from the medical case history of the aphoristic Hippocrates, through Thucydides, through collections . . . in late antiquity and in the middle ages . . . chronicles, lives of saints . . . parables . . . dictionaries, riddles, jest-books, etc." We should then affirm what was baptized by the Berkeley group associated with the journal *Representations* as the Grand Tradition of Erudition, "a penchant for the arresting detail, trace, clue, sign, shard and so on," or "effects of 'presence.'"[26] They should have added "anecdote."

Two further comments. Fineman at times writes of the "aporetic anecdote," or "historicizing chance," an element of contingency (62), which, as we have seen above, opens a narrative to as much of the outside as can possibly occur with writing. Moreover, Fineman insists that a new "universal history of historiography" organized around the aporetic and the anecdote would be comic. In bringing together aporia and the comic or chance, the connection draws out their mutual alienation from totalizing or falsely coherent narratives. But isn't the conjunction of the comic and the aporetic (chance) similar to what it opposes, a totality? Further, a comic history of historiography would have to be a history of the *failure of historiography*, its *periodic collapse* due to its own suppression of anecdotal proliferation, where the subjective experiences of agents come to "tell time" in their own manner. The comic could only dissolve the objectivist illusions of omniscient narratives. Unfortunately, these issues are sidetracked. Fineman's narrative returns to his frame or discipline, the Renaissance. The Renaissance created a "thematic historical consciousness—the subject as a subject *of* history" (62). The Renaissance represents "when the language of science . . . grows so formal that the sedimented meanings embedded within it grow too faint to recall," when a *technicist historicism* "carries as its cost its unspoken sense of estranged distance from the anecdotal" (63). The anecdote was revived in the Renaissance as a response to an overwhelming scientism of the real, the late Renaissance treated "as a baby born *as* an abortion, i.e., as the issue of the 'invention' of secondariness" (72). Because "historiography gave over to science the *experience* of history, when the force of the anecdote was rewritten as experiment" (e.g., the triumph of Boyle and Hobbes and the "constitution" of science and politics) (63), the *anomalies* treated by science disgorged their anecdotal shell, emptying historiography of the very thing that made it possible, the discontinuous or anomalous event. New Historicism, on this account, has it that "the Renaissance is both a period and a period term, like the period and period term of the New Historicism, haunted by its failure to sustain the historical aspirations of its self-pronounced and new historicizing name" (63). The conjunction of comic/failure postulates that a well-placed anecdote could unravel totalizing narratives. New Historicism announces here its solidarity with defeat—it theorizes what Reinhart Koselleck has called "history . . . made in the short run by the victors, historical gains in knowledge stem in the long run from the vanquished."[27] The story of this story of the anecdote is of course itself a success of failure, an oxymoron, and insofar as it lends itself to erudition and not narration, Fineman's superhistorical encoding ends up affirming the armature of anecdotal historiography as support for continuing a subjective burden of history.

"The History of the Anecdote" concludes by insisting that "it is the prosaic and considerable achievement of the New Historicism to have reinvented for our time the essay form" (64). But is such a reflection on the anecdote actually, then, a reflection on historiography or on the anecdote linked to the essay, the essay linked in turn to affirmation of the poetics of experience, as such? Let us be very clear about this: is it conceivable that Fineman's project of displacing the *grand recit* and opening historiography to the chance, modulation, and contingency of anecdote is also a deeply conservative attempt to salvage the very subjective burden of history, which is itself threatened with extinction? For where, and on whom, in the West, does this subjective burden now weigh? Urgently: if Thucydides, the Renaissance, and our own times resemble each other by means of the threat of scientism rendering experience more and more irrelevant, which accounts for New Historicism and the revival of the essay, as testimony to and of lived experience, at what point is the repetition of this behavior historical as opposed to, say, defensive? What was Thucydides defending in his narrative? What is the New Historicist here holding on to? The brilliance of Fineman's essay gives me no sure answer.

A Political Use of the Anecdote

Rather than read Thucydides or a contemporary New Historicist so as to evaluate the force of Fineman's model of the anecdote, to compare its theorization with other dimensions of textual practice, I shall take as my example a recent essay in intellectual history that appeared in a special issue on the history of the American academy since 1945, in *Daedalus*. It concerns boundary wars in the humanities. The essay is "The Disciplines and the Identity Debates, 1945–1970," by David Hollinger.[28] This narrative shares with Thucydides an interest in contemporary history, an immediate and ongoing past rendered visible for an audience who may well also be contemporaries of the telling.

Hollinger's account tells the story of contemporary American identity debates by signaling 1992 as a watershed year. Nineteen ninety-two inaugurated narratives about the sixties critiques of humanities and social science, "high knowledge," publication in transdisciplinary journals of special issues that year on "the identity question." The emergence and articulation of contemporary identity questions is taken as an emblem of change, a mark of an interruption, the coming together of discourse on identity and academic journals to "institutionalize this discourse across the lines separating the . . . disciplines."[29] How to historicize the contemporary conflicts concerning identity? Given the materials to contend with, the historian engages the subjects of discipline and identity by restarting the story to be told from 1970, the emergence of a "striking blend of *wissenschafliche* and essayistic styles." Hollinger distinguishes between disciplinary journals (e.g., the *Journal of Philosophy*) and journalism (e.g., the *Nation*), and encodes the new transdisciplinary publications as offering "oodles of opportunities," combining "something . . . of the 'rigorism' of the academic culture of the fifties while addressing the normative dimensions of life that 'rigorists' in the various disciplines were felt to have slighted" (336). The division between specialized professional knowledge and its neglect of "normative" issues (race, gender, multiculturalism) frames the historical context. Identity debates are traced to the arguments in the 1960s in which the experts had ignored their own enclosures, assuming "universalist, rationalist and individualist biases," which made it all but impossible to discuss "the enabling function of groups," especially those of ethnicity and race. In other words, the humanities had failed—and were called on it in the 1960s—to address the new audiences of modern life, who wanted issues discussed that were seen as blocked *within the specialization of knowledge.* Hollinger narrates the 1960s, already shorthand for a disruption of traditional narratives of American history, by stressing its sense of critical intellection and determinism, its near obsession with showing that "knowledge . . . needed to be 'situated'" (336). Those who raised the identity question were targeting the comfort and security of those who wrote (tenured professors), the said obsession with "situated" standing in for those critiques that challenged the position of the speaker, the junction of institution, subjectivity, and the power to represent. In this sense, the discourse here reduces the sixties to Althusser's analysis of the Ideological State Apparatus (ISA), *positionality* the question of questions. Marx and Freud can stand in as models used by sixties writers to dislodge the American ideologies of free will and unsituated knowledge.

Thus, the emergence of identity questions and transdisciplinary journals are narrated here as expressions of a much more inclusive story, the story of the sixties generation *demand* to enter the production of knowledge. Not only are the sixties reduced to the demand of *to situate,* infinitive mode, but identity is reduced to demand, the congruence severe in its simultaneous synthesis/reduction. Hollinger's narrative tactic is to totalize. The sixties critics of situated knowledge misunderstood that the experts' objectivity was neither relativistic nor exclusive. The story told of the sixties critique is the story of their illusion, their misunderstanding of concepts like objectivity and relativism, *excessively* analyzed by the proponents of identity. In fine, the *grand recit* here is the comic story of unnecessary conflict, between the expert's rigor and the dissident's demands, which need never have occurred but for the illusions of the young, a political story told from the expert's presumption of the very "position" of knowledge production.

Hence the blind spots of the previous generation were challenged by promoters of situated knowledge in the early and mid-1970s, "often in a spirit of great confidence and conviction"(337). That is, the transdisciplinary journals took up the slack, the openings in Fineman's terms, and filled them with knowledges that were continuous with demands, drawing in the pull of the larger, referential world. From demand to conviction, these identity-obsessed critics, with their self-proclaimed sense of historical appreciation (i.e., sensitivity to context) ran up "against the Enlightenment conscience," or scholars "unwilling to renounce altogether the old vision of the epistemic and moral unity of a humankind consisting of intrinsically valuable individual selves" (337). Quickly cutting to the 1990s, the telling of "The Disciplines and the Identity Debates" notes a flurry of "neo-Enlightenment" counterattacks against the situating of knowledge, and instead of allowing any identity theorist to speak—exactly what constitutes identity theory remains undefined here—Hollinger cites one text. That text—a representative anecdote in the terms of Kenneth Burke—bemoans identity questions having ushered in a rejection of "Eurocentric models," this anecdote turning nasty: the identity theorists descended into organicism, trying to grave-dig in "the Enlightenment's demise" (337). By this point in the narrative, one is reading the story of identity questions as error, cultural mistake, political ineptness, figures of *cataplexis,* or threat to the tenured elder's sanity.

At this point in the telling the narrator of Hollinger's story gives a synthetic judgment by citing another historian named David Hollinger, this on multiculturalism's misguided attempt to assign "cultural identity to individuals on the basis of the physical marks of descent" (338), now encoding "identity and its discontents" as the determined result of "the drive to come to grips with previously ignored or undervalued enclosures [and which] came up against residual universalist, rationalist, and individualistic values" (338). Those who put forward a critique of scholarship's enclosures (e.g., membrane, protective gear, a.k.a. departments of . . .) are written off as hopelessly anecdotal in their demands. The identity critics played out their hand, producing in the contested enclosures (disciplines with firm borders, like history departments) a sense of "frustration with a discourse in which the 'context' for just about everything has turned out to be the salient ethnoracial and gender identities" (338). The specific demon is "ethnoracial and gender identities," but the epithet directed their way is wider, directed at any discourse or identity theory/criticism plagued, to borrow from Thucydides, with the error of excessive specification, with going too far, with the error of excessive criticism. Reduced to a drive, given no context at all, the sixties extremists confronted the propriety of that neo-Enlightenment *position* that was sure of its belief in the "agency of individuals, epistemic authority actually earned by scientific communities, the emancipatory potential of intersubjective reason" (337). Each of these superconcepts, unstable yet politicized, are the devices by which this narrative of error crosses out the story of *neo-Enlightenment's difficulties* (its truths perceived as myths, and worse), this to maintain the *inevitable* failure of extremism. "The Disciplines and the Identity Debates" reads, in short, as the story of correcting the illusions of sixties excess, the flip side of neo-Enlightenment revivification, whose opponents—68ers—were asking the wrong questions.[30]

It continues. The narrator bemoans that by 1973 the sixties became an historiographic monster *now* (in 1973) called "the 60's," and has received too much emphasis as a time of interruptions. The narrator resolutely insists on the frustration felt by his group of neo-Enlightenment scholars by the demands for situating knowledge. After all, the "epistemic authority actually earned by scientific communities," cited above to disqualify identity questions, should have made scholars immune to the claims made against them. The narrator then lists some conditions in this story of extremists, Enlighteners, and frustration: the oil-caused inflation of 1973; the end of the Vietnam War, "in that same year," although the war did not end until 1975 (for Americans); the environmental movement signed into law; the abortion changes; the American Psychiatric Association dropping homosexuality from its list of mental disorders; the dearth of scholarly positions; the emergence of concepts of metahistory (history as construction, the discourses of *posthistoire*); the recent intellectual turn to "culture"; the publication of *Gravity's Rainbow;* the emergence of postmodernism (339). Nineteen seventy-three marks the point at which the list congealed into four factors: Kuhn's analysis of paradigms, antiracism, feminism, and Foucault, all of this further synthesized as "the salient result of their far-from-harmonious commingling was an imperative to 'situate' ideas and to recognize the 'identity' of people" (339). These four conditions "created an intellectual setting" (Fineman's holism) for the dynamics of the present. In this telling, Kuhn's historicization of knowledge has proved useful and habitual to scholarly work, but antiracism's success, through laws pertaining to affirmative action or in shows such as *Roots* (1976), has created a public life of "ethnoracial distinctions," called here an "essentialism" of color, this social/cultural dimension "made a function of biology," an "ethnoracial pentagon" overseeing this disaster. The narrator, after having discredited identity now draws the enthymatic conclusion—he feels *oppressed* by the gender and racial police within and without the academy. The historian's sense of Enlightenment and scholarship's "scientific community" is threatened with too many subjective burden's of history clamoring for attention. The telling has shrunk questions of *representation to questions of identity,* since identity fractures the very institution in charge of synthesis and unity (e.g., the academy understood as an Enlightened / historically justified institution), issues of the politics of representation thus removed.

This synthesis of race and gender's multicomplicated relations to neo-Enlightenment enclosures ends with a theorist of gender, who is made to call for a critique of "presumptive heterosexuality" and who speaks "self-consciously in the idiom of Michel Foucault." Foucault comes to the story at the right moment: in and as an anecdote, standing in for "poststructuralist ideas," judged as "less vital" than neo-Enlightenment, a "peculiar Frenchness" even attributed to their ideas. This *anecdote,* of the prosopopoeia of national character, marks the story's transition "from 'objectivist' to 'constructivist' theories of knowledge" (344). Foucault's texts are reduced to the stereotype of a French obsession with "power/knowledge," the narrative claiming that Foucault reduced knowledge to the function of "cutting," shifting truth-claims to "epistemic regimes," culminating in "poststructuralists [who] studied the naturalist subject, the lesbian subject, the Chicano subject, and a host of other subject identities." Again, the story becomes "the exploration of identity that 'problematized' (as it was often put, to the horror of those valuing 'good English')" (345) a story of failed insurrections against *Enlightened identity,* a narrative that makes no distinction between those in favor of installing identifications (e.g., markers of the oppressed) and those for whom identity is the longest-running European form of capture of differences (e.g., Deleuze's text, *Difference and Repetition,* 1968). In short, there is no epistemic responsibility anywhere near this narrative; it is political through and through, to the point of its self-destruction as historical knowledge.

Finally, repeating twice that it was "professors of English" who promoted "transdisciplinarity" (codeword for poststructuralism) (346), "more engulfed by the tensions within American society" than any other discipline, these literary critics' most notable trait was their very commitment to the politics of discourse: "What enabled literary critics to talk 'professionally' about almost anything they pleased—to be 'real intellectuals' while colleagues in other disciplines risked becoming 'mere technicians'—was the textualization of the world" (346), or no recognizable discipline. In a final anecdote, or proof through the very subjectivity that Fineman believed so necessary for any *historiographic opening,* the narrator insists that "the culmination of this development was the inclusion of science in literature . . . an embarrassment for literary studies in 1996 when a physicist managed to place in *Social Text* a killing parody of the literary theorist's analysis of physical theory" (346). Thus the *time of poststructuralism* is told: through the Sokol fiasco-anecdote, so that while "literature and science" has achieved "some rigorous work, " the "social text fiasco called widespread attention . . . to ask what professional training or specialized knowledge would be required" for cultural studies as such. *The defense of Enlightenment community/scientificity/universality* has now become "cultural studies" *lack of specialization,* i.e., absence of disciplinary boundaries. "Fiasco" is the face of an anecdote grafted to an admonition: only "discipline-honed clarity" will prevent the errors and excesses of poststructuralism, that the "virtues to enclosures . . . subject to critical revision . . . was the soundest of the claims made in the name of 'identity.' Those of us who are living 'after identity' would do well to remember its modest vision" (350).

This narration of the identity question and "situated knowledge" is not a narrative that gives sense as to what would constitute evidence for its judgments; it allows no other perspective to emerge, its citations from the literature are entirely anecdotal or, in Fineman's sense, "burdened by subjectivity," blind spots that also burden historical narration.

What are the right questions given the materials analyzed above? The two discourses presented here are radically incommensurable in relation to the concept of the anecdote. Fineman's essay makes a strong case for the subjective or faculty basis of historical representation as dependent upon the much-scorned anecdote, while Hollinger's narrative uses anecdotes in the name of a political discrediting of critiques held to be extreme in their demands and convictions. No doubt anecdotes give a narrative textually recognizable effects, but in what way do anecdotes also convey cognitive reliability? Could it be asked whether the very concept of the anecdote is a chimera of thinking? A philosophical text such as Fineman's wants the anecdote to serve as an *affirmative condition* of historical significance; Hollinger's narrative uses anecdotes to write off subjects whose story is deemed unworthy. What to think of the anecdote as an historiographic form that can both radically open narrative and eliminate other contentious ideas at the same time? The ambiguation of the anecdote seems more confirmed than ever, and, in this sense, perhaps it is better to suggest what remains glued to historiography, whether metahistorical in the case of Fineman or narrative in the instance of Hollinger's story: a confluence between literary and political categories. What is intra- and extralinguistic about historiography is inseparable from rhetoric, politics, and epistemology. Yet historiography has no "epistemically responsible" moment that would make it scientific because it must rely on anecdotes; it *is* embedded in the politics of writing, competition, selection, and restriction. In which case, Fineman's epistemic desire and Hollinger's political desire indeed testify to the nearly unbearable, and unknown, subjective condition of historiography.

PART TWO

Affirmation and the Philosophy of History

6 ■ Derrida's "New Scholar"
Between Philosophy and History

The argument thus far allows for a tentative synthesis. Chapters 2 and 3 offered instances of desperate narration, or present evaluations of culture-politics performed in the name of history-for-the-future. Historiography turned to the future competes with other narratologic styles and *epistemes,* and against other representors—to rank and sort things that will-have-a-future. *To historicize* is then less about present-past and more about intellectual and political energies, including rhetoric, shifted to futurity, to ensure that the future has a future, if that is the right way of putting it. At the same time, this turn allows that historiography's exclusions and restrictions show themselves as representation, the materials from the newspaper giving excessive—in this case, progressive—coherence and solidity to such contentious things as art objects and books, a sign of desperation. Chapters 3 and 4 indicated the fuzziness of images and goals concerning historians, as should be clear through the discussion of the anecdote, the historiographic theorist's discourse wrecked, so to speak, by the historian working against a past, figured forth here as beyond a judge, becoming executioner in the name of to-have-a-future. Together, the materials discussed open to some upheaval about basic functions of historiography. In a sense, the materials suggest the appropriateness of Lévi-Strauss's remark that history is never actually "history-of" or representation about, but always "history-for"—very much restricted today, as a coding device, in the sense of removing claimants. A bigger past than ever set to work armed with claims on the future: perhaps this is close to a new *episteme,* in Foucault's sense, historiography's (ever?) strange relations to contemporary life?[1]

The larger issue concerns the politicization of historiography, set in present and ongoing cultural-political rivalries and competitions. The materials in chapters 2 through 5 suggest that even if chronology is an "inescapable means of orienting ourselves," it does not follow that "the past is always earlier than the present and the future," nor "the present is always earlier than the future and later than the past; the future is always later than the past and the present."[2] Chronology does not hold if the future, as argued, comes first and last, and now.

In this chapter, consonant with the discussion of excluding claims and claimants and the role/image of the historian, I propose to switch levels, to philosophy proper. I intend to discuss Jacques Derrida's singular contribution to historiography, *Specters of Marx,* as it introduces a philosophical mode of thinking that also practices exclusions as a philosophy of history. Of especial interest here is how *Specters* offers a "new scholar" for its historiographic project. I should say that I am not going to discuss every concept that Derrida has created in his deconstruction of the metaphysics of temporalization, such as arche-trace, *différance,* supplementarity, iterability, and re-mark, "infrastructures" of temporality. Some of these notions do come up with the focus here, strictly on *Specters of Marx,* but emphasis is more on what David Krell has called Derrida's affirmation of the promises of memory.[3] While it is true that Derrida's sense of history does not give "one main river of being from which tributaries flow; not one core element which is carried forward through a history. There is only process . . . of substitution and dissemination," these latter concepts do not account for the swerve that characterizes *Specters of Marx.*[4]

A few general remarks: I read *Specters* as an instance of the middle voice, a discourse and story mixture, in some sense continuous with its origin as lectures, here the written marks of a scholar's voice. The story it tells belongs to the genre of the scholar, in particular the story of the scholar's dislocation and dislocating relations to the general culture.[5] Yet *Specters of Marx* is nonetheless a deeply problematical text in theory of history and politics. Not least because of certain "spells" of language that inform even this most reflexive of texts (which does not mean free of blindness). Linking historiography to the role of a new scholar is to play for rather large stakes, yet both are hardly matters of urgency for, say, the public. How is the scholar to register a productive social difference? Is it possible—foreswearing agreement with Derrida that it is possible because already impossible. I am going to argue that *Specters of Marx* joins philosophical work and politics through a model historiographer, a new scholar, a someone who announces, opens, against ordinary historical writing and thinking, *new needs. Specters,* however, flirts with, if not goes over to, an historiography of the "chosen," which in Derrida's idiom means self-selecting, self-reflexive, on-the-edge-of-thought intellectuals and artists. As we will see, it is a question here of a discourse that has the nerve to demand an ideal, of a communion with "ghosts" available only to a special faculty of a scholar properly attuned. In this sense, *Specters of Marx* may well be continuous with lines of writing that mistake the idealized *subjectivity of a scholar-ideal* for the subjectivity of any subject whatsoever, an ideal hard pressed today, which gives *Specters* great persuasive force for some artists and intellectuals.[6] The focus here is also on a strain of anticriticism registered in *Specters,* which may serve as a guide to the book's very smart commitment to European Idealist philosophy. My reading is at odds with Derrida's project. I think criticism should make cultural satisfaction, of every sort, harder; and *Specters of Marx* is nothing if not resolute in its anticriticism. While it calls for intellectual openness and conceptual stretching, its writing *re*turns to a discourse that is unsettling in its modulation (pace Fineman) of radicalism and conservatism. In short, *Specters* threatens to leap out of language altogether, an extremely forceful move, but it risks making a transcendence of contestation, settling in with concepts that should remain more than contestatory, including the whole of academic life. I will come back, more carefully, to this subject.[7]

A Derrida-Effect?

It is not possible to write about Derrida's work without considering some of the vast literature on it already. So, by way of more delay, pause, opening, trying to connect with material extremely difficult to arrange, before turning to *Specters of Marx,* I would like to elaborate on three senses of the intellectual context appropriate to *Specters.* The first two, by Hayden White and Paul de Man, respectively, concern prior readings of Derrida that isolated general intellectual problems in his work, use and abuse of history, in particular, while the third sense involves the application of Derrida's conceptual effect in philosophy of history in a specific academic practice.

In 1976 Hayden White published an essay entitled "The Absurdist Moment in Contemporary Literary Theory." He asked about a certain antiexistentialist strain in Derrida's work: was writing to the "unthinkable" (or impossible, in more recent texts) another version of intellectual mana? White asked if the textual-conceptual effects of "oracularness" and "sterility" indicated a certain "blindness," which turned on privileging writing over speech, this in the name of a war against speech.[8] To White, Derrida's writing, style/voice, was a mimesis of speech, questions implying conversation set amidst more impossible-to-answer questions; speech and writing may not be more fundamental than a constantly contested opposition. For White, Derrida's stratagems in war against dualism was something *farcical* because Derrida made writing and speech textually and conceptually intertwined with paradox and metonymy, resulting in the absurdity of affirming existence as metonymic (part to part, fragment to fragment, etc.), the only identity left a paradox that ground itself out. Writing and speech did not elude the figural. For White, Derrida privileged the tropes of Mandarin discourse, a generalized suspension of ordinary meaning, part of White's own existential equipment at the time. With this, White judged that Derrida's enterprise, however offensive to all sorts of normative criticism in the humanities, was another push-reaction of academic Mandarins, this because raising the stakes on what counts as reflection, saying the "ghost thinks us" as *Specters* will do, may be a way of challenging calcified philosophy, but it is also a move in the politics of the intellect nervous at intellectual confrontation with actual social forces. William Spanos put this in a different way: deconstruction with Derrida avoided issues of "historical specification."[9] Derrida offered enigmas of meaning in which undecidable boundaries between speech and writing (or any other conceptual pair) operate against conceptual identification, but cannot obscure its own performance, the intellectual's disidentification-with. White called this "absurdist," a gnosticism of scholarship itself.[10] In terms, then, of embedding *Specters of Marx* within contemporary historiographic theory, I will try to specify how this work moves out of the farcical to something else, as *Specters of Marx* is neither farcical nor absurd, even if in some ways still both.

The historiographer White emphasized the rhetorical politics of Derrida's work. But it was the rhetorician de Man who brought out an historicist premise of Derrida's writing. According to de Man, Derrida interpreted Rousseau's ambivalence about the significance of writing by misreading or not interpreting Rousseau's texts. Because of Derrida's reduction of Rousseau's work to the name *modern*, Rousseau's textual or syntactic disturbance of self-presence and self-consciousness was historicized, given a period turn by Derrida, Rousseau the good precursor, but obscuring the thought-proposal by Rousseau challenging how we make *any* judgment of time and memory. For de Man, Rousseau's theory of the sign as already disidentical to itself and world—a sign to be interpreted must be substituted by another sign, hence each sign is subject to making changes interpretation can easily miss—indicated that meaning is no more identical to itself or to anything else, not a stable presence always subject to rules of substitution. For Rousseau, as de Man noted, musical signs were devoid of substance, without identity, bound up in "the future of their repetition," and the musical sign was carried over to Rousseau's consideration of language as such: "The structural characteristics of language [for Rousseau] are exactly the same as those attributed to music: the misleading synchronism of the visual perception which creates a false illusion of presence has to be replaced by a succession of discontinuous moments that create the fiction of a repetitive temporality."[11] Melody and allegory have precedence over painting and mimesis because these forms indicate "chronology is the structural correlative of the necessarily figural nature of literary language," which does not privilege the literal over the metaphorical, as Derrida insisted, but rather acknowledges that *all modes of temporal representation are partly fictional.* What Derrida was actually doing, then, was misrepresenting a *precursor* whose work was historicized (around the name *modern*)—killing a "father" (brother, etc.) in the old game of opening another cleared space of cultural work (here, criticism). Rousseau's "best modern interpreter had to go out of his way *not* to understand him."[12] The issue of historicization is crucial. Derrida insisted that Rousseau's work marked the birth of a "modern" form of logocentrism; and because Rousseau's work left few if any disciples, because his writing does not particularly invite readers to identify with the text, and who thought that, as writing, language contains undeniable *re*gressive effects, it is Derrida who finds himself confronted with a writer on whom the tag "logocentric" does not work. De Man's argument was that in Rousseau, Derrida confronted an example of the *ahistoricity of effects,* texts that radically dehistoricize present and future readers, which is to say, they invite more complex readings. Derrida's program of deconstruction reveals its own obsession with chronicity in the very denial of Rousseauist achronicity.

Contextually, then, White's analysis refers us to the persistence of a mode of radical Mandarin rhetoric and de Man's analysis opens toward questions of periodicity and precursors. With this in mind, I want to specify more closely why I am reading Derrida *today* in terms of philosophy of history and its political implications. For in addition to the problems offered by de Man and White, there is the question as to the "Derrida-effect": the transference of Derridean discourse into issues concerning the philosophy of history and the politics of scholarship, the ease with which notions of Derrida's version of deconstruction's promise to *re*model long-standing cultural-political issues. There is nothing strange about this—historiography can be understood as *recoding*, e.g., the replacement of legal models of history (dominant in the 1920s) with psychological models, in turn giving way to other formations. Foucault's idea of epistemic cohesion seems apposite—recoding offers a kind of intellectual safety, where concepts are brought to historiography in the name of "opening" it but actually have the effect of a further *control* of it. Let me give a somewhat detailed example of what is involved here, drawn from the application of Derrida's concepts to set up a small piece of doing history of science.

In a recent essay, Hans-Jorg Rheinberger urges that the concept of historiality should replace the couple history/historicity. The former concept does not invoke "origins" and "grounds" as the latter couple does with its commitment to a "foregoing past" moving to a determinate future. Historiality, said to have an affinity with processes and not goals (telos), offers a way for historians to examine "a past that is the product of a past deferred, if not of a presence." To do this, to alienate the equation that every past *was* present unto itself, the historial "not only has to accept and even postulate a kind of recurrence inherent in any hindsight—hence interpretation or hermeneutic action. It has to assume that recurrence works in the differential activity of the system that is itself at stake, and in its time structure. What is called its history is 'deferred' in a rather constitutive sense: the recent . . . is the result of something that did not happen. And the past is the trace of something that will not have occurred. Such is the temporal structure of the production of a trace."[13] As postulated, "recurrence" upends the linking together of origin and outcome: what recurs is deferral. No event begins or ends—what comes again is already a part of the future of what is deferred. What is deferred, the trace (here, processes of research and thought, written notes), is soaked in the rhetoric of paradox, the nonorigin of an origin, the existence of the nonexistent. Are we dealing here with time-structures or literary figures? Or the literariness of temporality? Rheinberger insists that emphasis on deferral, where origins are always nonorigins, undercuts both the revolutionary time-model of science (rupture) and that of accumulative growth (evolution), because the time-relations of the historial emphasize the "microdynamics of scientific activity," or the localization of differential times within scientific practices. Research time yields a different sense of temporality than its presentations to the public, just as the time it takes for a scientist to digest new contradictions is incomparable to reception-times of newly offered knowledge to readers of, say, newspapers. All human sense that can be said to effectuate temporality—enact, conjure, invoke, and dissolve it—thereby produces its own temporality. If we are still reading, say, Aristotle in order to discuss the ethics of emotional distance, this is because there is an ongoing production of an "Aristotle-ethics-time-code." Historiality is offered so as to bring out this differential element in all systems of sense. Historiality, or history-in-the-making, seems guaranteed to drive a little crazy historians obsessed with narrative continuity and periodization.

Yet it is impossible not to notice recurrence/deferral are given a *behavioral co-coding* in Rheinberger's text. Systems of action, like scientific research, are said to be characterized by a differential reproduction, where the generation of the unknown becomes the reproductive driving force of the whole machinery.[14] Systems can only survive when they produce their own *age,* the "youth" of a system indicated by the degree to which it elucidates the unknown, hence sclerosis is the telos of a system when it only *re*iterates the known. Research capable of replicating itself has effected the chance/cause of its own survival in competition with other systems. Rheinberger's text insists that the production and differentiation of time eliminates the possibility of any mode of power, society, or model of context from "pervading and coordinating this universe of meaning."[15] The point is unobjectionable: procedures of knowledge, including those of subjective agency, produce what counts as temporal significance. But this can also mean that *internal organization is so "tight"* that so-called outside agencies are ineffectual a priori, especially given, here, recourse to behaviorism: "reproductive series retain their own internal times as long as they replicate as such, and the epistemic field can no longer be seen as dominated by a general theme, or paradigm."[16] "Replicate as such"—is this anything other than a recoding of Lyotard's critical assessment of the postmodern: "be operational or disappear!"? Recurrence and replication: are these concepts new or are they a reworking of another code, that of the power of performativity in its all pervasive generality? Causation, influence, dominance, and singularities are effects of replication, but if the latter is already *inclusive* of historiality, then this makes power and determination so internal that they need not be raised as such. In this sense, Rheinberger's trading with Derridean constructs replaces historicity with historiality by *re*peating a *survivalist* model: Rheinberger calls it "an ecological reticulum," or a "patchwork of precocious and deferred actions with its extinctions and reinforcements, interferences and intercalations," terms that suggest that political issues are *withdrawn* from explicit discussion.

Derrida's notion of "blind tactics," or the suggestion of a wild-card effect such that within any system there is always an outcome that exceeds its coding and function, is invoked to substantiate the value of historiality. Such a tactic, be it an uncontrollable word, an audacious game move, a political bluff, surpasses causality in that it opens onto a grafting operation: dependent on a system/source, the wild card defines its effect by separation from that system/source. Historiality implies impurity and transplantation (continuous with paradox and mutation). But even in Rheinberger's narrative domain, that of the history of viral pathology, impurity and transplantation allow for historiality to only confirm that recurrence and deferral allow us to understand that "viruses should be considered viruses because viruses are viruses."[17] The scientist working in an experimental system provides the model for historiality: to *tinker* with facts and remove them from one order of representation to another, a practice of repetitive dislocation: viruses are not what scientists thought they were but are nonetheless viruses after all. Rheinberger's essay, written with verve and wit, remains blind to the tropological dimension of its own writing: that it might figure forth a larger behaviorism, co-coded with paradox and performative models.

Specters of Marx: *Suspending Philosophy and History*

Some of the most interesting pages written on Marx, Marxism, commodification, and fetishism are found in Derrida's *Specters of Marx.* Interesting for insights on how the commodity-effect is not contained in the commodity-thing, on how labor is incessantly stifled as productive labor, and how concerns with this commodity-relation and destruction of labor offer an opportunity to think again about philosophy, politics, and history. These aspects of *Specters* are a significant addition to the literature on Marx. If nothing else, *Specters of Marx* gives a Marx/Marxism that opens the possibility of a necessary separation between Marxism and its political premises, requiring its readers to disturb equations between Marxism and its own "normal" politics. Samuel Weber characterizes this political aspect in *Specters:* Derrida's main conceptual device of *différance* involves both repeatability and nonpresence as indispensable moments in concept work, and *Specters* carries *différance* into politics—Marxism will not be about setting things right in any simple way, and *Specters* will not construe neo-Marxism in the frames of its own latent exclusions, subordinations, or dominations of others. In short, *Specters of Marx* offers Marxism another "chance" to show its differences from politics as most of us ordinarily use the term *politics.*[18]

The dedication to *Specters* insists on an "infinite responsibility" belonging to intellectual work. The text cites the "historic violence of Apartheid" as an instance of this responsibility. But why say "historic" instead of just "violence"? The dedication is given over to the memory of Chris Hani, assassinated in South Africa just before Derrida's lectures at UC-Irvine, the basis for the writing of *Specters*. The name *communist* is invoked—the murder of Hani is figured forth as a conjunction of minorities, for Hani had returned to the Communist Party shortly before his murder, a return that Derrida insists ties together the names *minority* and *communist*. The writing bypasses the *majoritarianism* of the name *communist*, e.g., the Soviet Union, China, North Korea, or the fate of East German communists now caught up in the vicissitudes of German unity. Do *communist* and *minority* already load the scholar's discourse?

A second opening, called "exordium," is outright gnostic: "Someone, you or me, comes forward and says: *I would like to learn to live finally.*" This urgent question or second inauguration allows the writing to proceed with insistencies: the exordium's question is a "magisterial locution," it "would always say something about violence," it is an expression of "ethics itself," and "to learn to live finally" is such that it "cannot be *just* unless it comes to terms with death."[19] The writing arrives at the destination of a synthetic command utterance: "If it—learning to live—remains to be done, it can happen only between life and death. Neither in life nor in death alone. What happens between two, and between all the two's one likes, such as between life and death, can only maintain itself with some ghost, can only *talk with or about* some ghost. So it would be necessary to learn spirits" (xviii). In the space of a few sentences, language is yoked to the grammar of insistence, to an urgency concerning the ethics of a need to acknowledge ghosts/spirits. The rigor of Derrida's version of deconstruction, that binaries are simulacra of limits within language, is reiterated, but the sentences above now mime the idea of *différance;* the sentences just cited read as ghostlike meanings. There *are* ghosts, it says, and it does not say: language is spectral and ghostly in its ability to figure forth senses of the unnameable.

Hence *Specters of Marx* makes enormous claims: to learn to live, or to become, requires that one learn to live with ghosts, to learn that capitalized History has always been a matter of ghosts. The concept of history is subject to a reiteration that eclipses its traditional functions: "The time of the 'learning to live,' a time without tutelary present, would amount to this, to which the exordium is leading: to learn to live *with* ghosts, in the upkeep, the conversation, the company, or the companionship, in the commerce without commerce of ghosts" (xviii). What does this give to mean? That there are no present models for life/learning, that there has never been a time where such models were truly enabling? This "never has been" is delivered out of the infinitive mode: "with ghosts" is what has not happened, and in their absence, there can be no conversation *to come.* Lack and future belong together. The phrase "commerce without commerce" means no reciprocity "with ghosts": we need to "be" with them, but we can make no expectation of reciprocity—they can do as they please. Ghosts, perhaps like deconstructive wild cards or even like God, may or may not care about us. But philosophy and politics can have no sense unless one follows their demand: "no *socius* without this *with* that makes *being-with* in general more enigmatic than ever for us . . . And this being-with-*Specters* would also be, not only but also, a politics of memory, of inheritance, and of generations" (xviii, xix). Is the history of historiography then the story of assigning the wrong names to things so that history remains obscured, because being-with-specters has not happened? This is a much more interesting version than, say, Pierre Nora's insistence on an underived psychology where "memory installs remembrance within the sacred," set against the relativizing tendencies of an unlimited historical consciousness, memory signifying "warmth," "silence of custom," "repetition of the ancestral."[20] History is not invoked here to offer comfort, even a melancholic one.

Thus responsibility and respect for justice concerning "those who *are not there*" (absence) makes possible the condition for comportment with future/past. We are in that conceptual/mystical territory in which Benjamin, after Lotze, after Goethe, after many Europeans, outlined a kind of priestcraft, a deepening of a special kind of memory, one available only to a certain kind of inscriber: "to be just: beyond the living present in general—and beyond its simple negative reversal. A spectral moment, a moment that no longer belongs to time" (xx). This "spectral moment" is a clear recoding of *différance,* as "beyond reversal" and "out of time" lift intellectual work to the realm of "to differ and to defer." *Différance* can now mean "spectral" and both terms here belong to the Same by virtue of their identical function at least by comparison to what they are "beyond"—opposition and criticism, these concepts entombed in time and reversal (on which, more below). Derrida calls this special attunement of the intellectual an axiom, a dignity (from Kant), and this attunement is not answerable to any living present. *Specters* registers an objection to this, but insists that in the face of present life, empirical or ontological actuality, there is something beyond: "a *living-on* [sur-vie] . . . a survival . . . to disjoin or dis-adjust the identity to itself of the living present . . . There is then *some* spirit" (xx). As in all of Derrida's efforts, intellectual work is directed against presencing, but this against is *presented* as a command utterance: "Spirits. And *one must* reckon with them. One cannot not have to" (xx). Let one be clear about this: the negation of presence is accomplished by a greater presencing—of what is not present (spirit, ghost). The syntax of paradox and negation dominates here, and it is not unfair to say that even the gesture of writing with disjunction *functions* as another mode of conjunction. What White called absurd can be considered schizophrenic—the writing affirms what it denies, in the name of a specific mode of intellectual practice, a tactic in the spiritualization of cultural warfare(s). The *survival* of disjunction, in short, carries with it a stronger injunction: the Ghosts of History matter. In this sense, it is textually clear—as such things can be—that insistence on disjunction in present life relies on a transcendental injunction, no disavowal of ghosts. Werner Hamacher gives a friendly and elegant gloss to this opening to ghosts and specters when he writes that *Specters of Marx* shows "what *must* be opposed is the death of the promise in theoretical certainty and practical complacency—of the promise that precedes both."[21] But is this also a move toward the threshold of a connoisseurship of the netherworld?

The Historiography of Being-Haunted

From Pascal, who insisted that there must be no sleeping while Jesus is in agony, to Benjamin, with the delirium of the straight-gate, which might usher in a messianic irruption shattering present negative forces, intellectuals have set up communication with the nonliving as their own form of transcoding religious precepts. There is nothing strange about this practice until it is made a stake in the ability of intellectuals to work, once such demands are normalized and institutionalized as work/writing permits. Hardly anyone can publish on Benjamin today without demonstrating their commitment to "spirit." *Specters of Marx* will circulate as a raising of the ante of historical discourse on account of its dramatistic (in Kenneth Burke's sense) and opaque phrases taken as signs and signals of a "higher reflection" in the scholarly endeavor to install a taste for spirit. In fact, "haunted by history" is already a social trope, circulating between the academy and places where the academy touches the public, as in *New York Times* book reviewing; a review of W. G. Sebald approves his engagement with the history of Nazism, "nightmares that haunt those who, as survivors, descendents and even precursors, escaped the great nightmare of history—except that they didn't."[22]

"Haunting," *Specters* insists, "would mark the very existence of Europe. It would open the space and the relation to self of what is called by this name"

(4). Is this another way of *reinstating a centrism of Europe,* freeing Europe from one register of history, too ambiguous, to give it another, better history? No discussion of European venality in the Opium Wars, the French treatment of Algeria in the twentieth century, or the current role of the Euro-Americanized IMF in Asia intrudes on spirit. This insistence on haunting issues an equation: philosophy of history and haunting are one and the same. Haunting stands in for the uncanny and irrepressible past of Europe. The text offers unknowns to be said and written about the history of Europe, problems not yet asked, raised, provoked. Even if no decisive historical judgments can be rendered at the level of the "significance of Europe," it does not follow that there are any outstanding problems to be addressed. A "haunted existence" attributed to Europe could be seen as something else: a way for a European intellectual to maintain the openness of the European past, a way of *giving historicity back to Europe,* or at least *re*claiming a historicity never settled. Another rereading of European history is thus made possible. But this recoding, which claims to upset the chronicity of names, also makes for a more inclusive successivity. For the specter-relation can be figured forth not just as a way to dislodge the dominance of presence, but also as a device for hypercontinuity: to-be-haunted "interrupts here all specularity . . . it recalls us to anachrony . . . we do not see who looks at us" (7). Anachrony does not mean just out of time or the untimely or disjunction, as Derrida insists; it also means what is *invisibly continuous,* a supercontinuity such that history is subject to a new law: "all semanticization is given over to *mourning,* to the voice, and to the work of the 'spirit.' The question 'Whither Marxism' whispers to us to *follow* a ghost" (10). Philosophically, then, the function of the ghost is to return a historicity to Europe, stripped of the semantics of invested group conflicts, where none of the narrative models available to ordinary historiography are of use. The new terms of continuity—openness to ghosts and mourning—are posed by *hauntology.*

This hauntology is to function similarly to the concept/nonconcept of *différance,* and replaces ontology and the metaphysics of historiography. For this hauntology already "harbors within itself . . . eschatology and teleology themselves" (10). The discursive aspect of historiography, its incessant return, recalling, and recoding of the past, all the work of *re,* finds itself absorbed by this model. Yet *Specters* is adamant that this absorption is the labor of an ethics of justice, not discourse. Hauntology would "comprehend them [eschatology and teleology], but incomprehensibly," for the ghost has been deferred, and repetition is such that the specter *"begins by coming back"* (11). The presence/nonpresence of ghosts and specters starts from the present, with the scholar who calls for the creation of such return/repetition, for "there has never been a scholar who really, and as scholar, deals with ghosts" (11). The history of philosophy is full of scholars who have been unable to listen to return/repetition. But there is another voice from afar who calls the scholar, Shakespeare's Marcellus, who anticipated "the coming, one day, one night, several centuries later, of another 'scholar.' The latter would finally be capable, beyond the opposition between presence and non-presence, actuality and inactuality, life and non-life, of thinking the possibility of the specter, the specter as possibility. Better (or worse) he would know how to address himself to spirits. He would know that such an address is not only possible, but that it will have at all times conditioned, as such, address in general" (12). A certain scholar can "address himself to spirits." Who or what is the *ancestry* of this special power? Nothing other than the specter itself, which has always "at all times conditioned" such address—a metahistorical axiom, an urgency of unrecognized continuism. Contrary to the argument de Man made about Shelley's understanding that he, Shelley, had no right to try to complete a past's incompleteness, the insistence here is that the past is incomplete and waiting for a modality of completion. Marx's texts are absorbed into this new ethical responsibility, which, as we will see in a moment, jettisons oppositionality: "a specter, this first paternal character, as powerful as it is unreal . . . more actual than what is so blithely called a living presence"(13). The historiographic notions of diagnosis and prognosis, intertwined since antiquity, are overthrown by the rhetoric of obligation.[23] To call this an offering of the *aformative,* as Hamacher does, "the future-oriented structure of the promise," a play on the sense of openness to the future is one thing; but why hold the future as open when we know it is actively constructed in every now?[24]

Specters of Marx thus disconnects historicity understood as continuity in favor of continuity understood as a metahistorical identity of the repression/repetition of specters and ghosts. The scholar/intellectual is turned from opposition (criticism, disruption) to confront the specters internal to scholarship, the scholar turned into an actant, who can find the words to grasp the *secrets* of Marx, which says, "Read me, will you ever be able to do so." This is a scholar pledged to the word of "deferring just so as to affirm, to affirm *justly,* so as to have the power . . . to affirm the coming of the event, its future-to-come itself" (17). Affirmation in this time that is "out of joint," in this "time without certain joining or determinate conjunction," makes opposition a practice detrimental to intellectual work. Opposition means the wrong repetitions (fair enough). But is it so that today is a time without determinate conjunctions—

this said in the face of nearly universal extreme concentrations of wealth, authority, and value? Negated by the affirmations is any sense of a philosophy of history that takes up opposition and disjunction and works these concepts into criticism of existing authorities. Indeed, the modern warnings about intellectuals rushing to promote affirmations are brushed aside: the scholar's time is transcendental to opposition/disjunction. If Marx cannot be *outwritten,* as insisted here, the affirmation of a disadjusted time must not lead back to critique of injustice, a "mere" ontological relation, a relation of chronicity. If intellectuals emphasize injustice, this is an affirmation of the *wrong time,* a time of vengeance, of righting wrongs, and, compared to this, intellectuals must sever connection with critique/opposition. *Différance* into specter also then is offered as negation of criticism.[25]

The disjunction of injustice and the infinite asymmetry of the "place of the other" are the terms of a temporality out of joint. The space opened by *Specters of Marx* does not call for "calculable and distributive justice. Not for law, for the calculation of restitution, the economy of vengeance or punishment . . . Not for calculable equality . . . [or] accountability or imputability of subjects and objects, not for a *rendering* justice that would be limited to sanctioning, to restituting, and to doing right but for a justice as incalculability of the gift and singularity of the an-economic ex-position to others" (23). Urgently, the language tags calls for justice with the direct predicate of "vengeance." And notice how rapidly the text moves to the incalculable of the gift. "Incalculable" suggests the transcendence of what humans may long for but have no right to ask for. Of this "gift," the text associates it with "a musical or poetic work" (26) and the messianic: "the coming of the other, the absolute and unpredictable singularity of the *arrivant as justice.* We believe that this messianic remains an *ineffaceable mark* . . . of Marx's legacy, and doubtless of inheriting" (28). The scholar of this gift enters the plane of *revelation* and *grace.* The scholar is modeled as the medium for a passage to the transcendent. Would noting that one-third of the world's actual population has no daily, reliable source of potable water involve regress to the level of "calculable justice," or is this unfair? There must be "alliance of a rejoining without conjoined mate, without organization, without party, without nation, without State, without property" (29). The intellectual must not be caught speaking for an interest that can be *returned* to actualities fraught with political interests. Philosophy of history must sever its ties with reciprocity. The question then turns on what kind of Marxism can be said to elude even its own best (historicizing) interpretations?

Marx's texts give us "irreducible heterogeneity, an internal untranslatability"

(33). Something was said there that is far more important than a dated message or longer-lived code, and this *Specters of Marx* isolates as the "testamentary dimension." This sense of the testamentary is called the true historiographic legacy of Marx, as it beckons to the contemporary scholar to follow this legacy by surrendering to Marx's injunction (to change the world), immediately put onto the tracks of absolute identity: "*There must be* disjunction, interruption, the heterogeneous if at least *there must be,* if there *must be* a chance given to any 'there must be' whatsoever, be it beyond duty" (35). The desperation signaled in the repetition of so many "there must be's" are lines to the impossible: the testamentary is beyond history, it is "a matter of linking an *affirmation* (in particular a political one) *if there is any,* to the experience of the impossible, which can only be a radical experience of the *perhaps*" (35). Does this approach a ground zero of intellectual life today, the inheritance of Marx's writings now the desert of "perhaps"? Is this "perhaps" a recoding of the famous historiographical notion of necessity, which cannot be addressed now except as the impossible? Actual determinations, how the social is put together, its rules and mechanisms, are squeezed out by the "perhaps" of metahistory.

At which point, questions pertaining to the language of telos are set aside in favor of the language of eschatology: "Is there not a messianic extremity, an *eskhaton* whose ultimate event (immediate rupture, unheard of interruption, untimeliness of the infinite surprise, heterogeneity without accomplishment) can exceed, *at each moment,* the final term of a physis, such as work, the production, and the *telos* of any history?" (37). "Messianic extremity" evokes the idea of an informed *historiographic avant-garde,* here set against philosophy of history whenever it invokes any final term. But the question form—"Is there not"—is highly aggressive, as it demands the question be refuted instead of moving toward answering its own request. The *eskhaton* has explicit bases in religious desires and needs, which might carry over to the modern question "how shall we go ahead?" ("What Shall Be Done?"), a topic as much of prophetism as prognosis. But Karl Löwith reminds us that the idea of the *eskhaton* is inseparable from the related notion of telos, inasmuch as it "also articulates and fulfills a . . . process of history . . . by a definite goal."[26] Unlike much of contemporary French philosophy's rejection of teleology,[27] it is fair to ask why eschatology is favored as the medium of a deconstruction of Marx and Marxism? How can the *eskhaton* be considered if there are no examples of it that are not also instances of teleology?

Haunting and Meta-metahistory

To see how eschatology is privileged, we should note that historical continuity is always provisioned with categories, from Foucault's *epistemes* to such staples as that one and the same "common sense" of the American people, from the Revolution to now (according to Gordon Wood). Or better: two kinds of continuity, one for the things that pass and become, one for the historian. There is great contention over expression of the mechanisms and forms responsible for experiences of the Same and the Identical, historical continuity as such. The concept of ideological hegemony, for example, has played its part in ensuring that intellectuals can focus on, in the case of the power of ideas overriding material contradictions, a negative model of continuity. Hegemony makes for a clear mechanism (as did class conflict, Oedipal conflict, and so on). For *Specters of Marx,* haunting is set forth to replace ideas of the order of hegemony; that is, instead of the repression and suppression involved in classical notions of hegemony, haunting opens a supercontinuity.

Reconstructed, Derrida's argument is that communism "presents itself only as that which could come or could come back" if it *pledges* to not slip into the dualisms that partly account for its own self-suffocation. If between 1848 and today the cultural spectral-form of letting haunting "haunt" was treated as a threat, we should now ask, "What is the time and what is the history of a specter?" (39). If concepts such as hegemony kept us focused on successivity and substitutions (replacement of equivalent forms, as in Marcuse's notion that repression became repressive toleration) in which negation was paramount, the "spectrality effect" or hauntology in operation is meant to undo "this opposition, or even this dialectic, between actual, effective presence and its other" (40). Haunting and spectering are to clear a space for their own senses of continuism. The specter conjures (a ghost) by putting "to work and to produce, without any possible re-appropriation, a forever errant surplus value" (40). These are, again, the syntactic terms that formed the concept/nonconcept called *différance,* as "forever errant surplus value" repeats and supplements *différance* (to differ and to defer), nonidentity the rule. Here, *différance* has become an ideal errancy, not of language, but of surplus value. What is gained by the substitution/fulfillment? To put this directly in historiographic terms: if *metahistory* refers to the conditions of possibility in the writing of a narrative (the use of criteria to select things to narrate), then isn't haunting meta-metahistorical, because it not only controls the field of representations but is always there, timeless, i.e., the condition of conditions? If one believes in history as haunted, then one must believe in meta-metahistory as that which *opens* to what the new scholar can achieve by way of discursive and political mediation, which itself becomes metamediation, an opening that is not reducible to metahistory or the use of narrative forms, whether such forms are literary structures (tragedy) or existential structures, as with the "middle voice."[28]

And what does all this have to do with Marx? That Marx, following the literary exemplum of Shakespeare's Timon of Athens, conjured money and religion as a social disaster, spectropoetic even if critical and historical. Marx conjured a model of the State that showed that the State employs magic when it makes paper into value, just as religion does in making another world valuable, or when language conjures definitions that are mixtures of blindness and insight (pace Paul de Man). And while Marx does not want "to believe in them," in specters and ghosts, he "thinks of nothing else" (47). Marx, like his adversaries, "will have tried to conjure (away) the ghosts *like* the conspirators [*conjurés*] of old Europe on whom the *Manifesto* declares war. However inexpiable this war remains . . . it conspires *with them* in order to *exorc-analyze* the spectrality of the specter. And this is, today, as perhaps it will be tomorrow, our problem" (47). Because of the spectrality of the specter, Marx and Marxism are given to us as *repetition;* Marx cannot eliminate what he contests, and we, inheritors, cannot do without a contest with Marx's writings. These writings must not be returned to the merely historical. It is not just that Marx's texts are a necessary starting point for some discussions about framing neocapitalism; no, the new scholar's reading of Marx has to affirm the *failure* of Marx, that his language was bound over to the logic of negation and opposition, to the use of conjuring and exorcising "formulae," which resulted in a "putting to death" of his rival's positions, hence texts that "phantomalized" in a demand for effectivity or political success. The "heterological tauto-ontology" of Marx's texts, with their demand for presence of the revolution is not just subject to historicization, but to metamediation by the new scholar.

"The time is out of joint": this is not the highlighting of differences on either side of the "joint." *Specters of Marx* does not posit any such time when time was not out of joint, but it does evoke "time is out of joint" as a condition of *timeless ahistoricity.* For the writing glides into eternalizations: "The time is out of joint" evokes "to be present" and this presence "is not a *mot d'esprit* but *le mot d'esprit,* the word of the spirit, it *is* its first verbal body" (50). This is hard to understand, since *Specters* spends so much time eliminating presence. What is affirmed is that "the time is out of joint" is always true, hence every present is always nonpresent to itself, yet present to itself in exactly that way, therefore always related to spirits and specters, which are indices of our avoidance of what haunts us. The present is to be imagined as an always nonpresent present in its own nonpresence. Of course this relation (understanding Derrida) is also then meta-metahistorical, since it affirms that no reading of Marx or of the present can take place without the "first" verbal body of spirit always with us. Hypercontinuity: spirit and specters run on a timeless timing.

Derrida is certainly correct that the Marxism of Marx is often conjured away by bad readings; to call for a "new international" also sounds politically necessary(?). He insists that the media has displaced politics with its own forms of "spectralization," but the question not asked is: when did the modern media not do this?[29] What is gained by insisting that the media mediatizes? He offers that politics, media, and academic discourse have merged, "as it has never done before" and this "conditions and endangers any democracy" (54). Derrida wants the present to be seen through this new combination, but certainly Western society long ago merged knowledge, opinion, and authority in written texts and social institutions, so it is difficult here to understand registering the contemporary in this warning. Convinced that the ongoing repression of specters and ghosts is the most vital intellectual project, that spectral powers, apparitions, simulations, and prosthetic images are rampant and repressed, Marxism will survive only if it places on the drawing board—the new scholar traced from ubiquitous architectural superdiscourse today—what is called here "life-death beyond the opposition between life and death" (54).

"Beyond opposition" means "We are in mourning" for the *to be* of Marxism. If no mourning, then no receptivity to that which haunts and comes as specter, no movement toward spirit. The mourning for Marx and Marxism is for what Marxism did not accomplish, as well as mourning the condition of propriety of inheriting it. No inheritance without mourning. At which point the *testamentary* makes its return: "the being of what we are is first of all inheritance, whether we like it or know it or not . . . we can only *bear witness* to it." As witness and testament, the "critical inheritance" affirmed has its own restriction: domination and conflict must be witnessed and spoken to, but "without necessarily subscribing to the concept of social class" (55). What is it then that transcends the edginess of class conflict, which at least indicates a high degree of social control and differentiation, hence opportunities for criticism? Class and other modes of social conflict must give way to the "irreducible genesis of the spectral." Taking apart Fukuyama's book on the "end of history," Derrida gives as his chief example of the spectral the "worldwide historical stakes" of the Middle East conflicts. Here, three messianic ideologies mobilize "all the forces of the world," such forces said to be archaic and futural. "The war for the 'appropriation of Jerusalem' is today the total war," a proposition numbing in its synecdochic *certainty.* Note the constative form—no disagreement allowed, absolute agreement assumed, that is, no one must say, and the writing will not hear, that the religious zealots of the Middle East are all equally pretenders to the messianic as they invoke history as a tactic of destroying the other. Are such Middle Eastern ideologies messianic or telic in their mutual urge for domination? The text falls silent about doubts as to this "singular figure" of "time out of joint." Marxism, it insists, will have a future only if it accepts such "religious ghosts" (58) and, presumably, views all social relations as if they were the Middle East.

The historiography and philosophy of haunting creates its own affirmation of messianic eschatology, common to religion and to Marxism, that must not renounce "a certain experience of the emancipatory promise; it is perhaps even the formality of a structural messianism, a messianism without religion, even a messianic without messianism, an idea of justice—which we distinguish from its current concept and from its determined predicates today" (59). How can "an idea of justice" be more important than "human rights"? For whom does the impossible matter more than actuality or even virtuality? To the mediatized prosthetics of the three orders of politics, media, academia, to the false "good news" of neoliberalism, Derrida has found the true matter of philosophy of history: a "democracy *to come,* not a *future* democracy in the future present," which would still be enmeshed in conflict over means, ends.

Philosophy as concept and history as process would then be recast according to the multiple logics involved in the three words *différance, messianism,* and *specters* (or *ghosts*). We can glimpse this, *Specters of Marx* insists, only by affirming "the absolutely undetermined messianic hope . . . [an] eschatological relation to the to-come of an event and of a singularity, of an alterity that cannot be anticipated" (65). Doesn't the example of the Middle East undercut the "undetermined" of the messianic hope? Derrida's language keeps raising the ante by using command utterances, here the arrival of the messianic "from which one will not ask anything in return and who or which will not be asked to commit to the domestic contracts of any welcoming power (family, State, nation, territory, native soil or blood, language, culture in general, even humanity)." At this threshold of discursive "learning to live," meta-metahistory dissolves ordinary historical representation. It dissolves all but the transcendence of its concepts as it opens a path for the new scholar. This new scholar enacts the first time of *différance,* time as postponement, or pause; the new scholar is not figured deconstructively, but as bringing into existence the end of reciprocity.[30] Is the messianic hope of this continuous with what White called absurdity?

Historiography without History

Specters of Marx certainly raises the ante on what historical consciousness could look like! It gives us nonidentification with the conventions of historical understanding in its literary, political, and philosophical modes, and works against the proprieties of existing historical discourse. In other words, *hauntology* will be used to uproot historical identities of all sorts. It will, of course, be reduced to a familiar psychologic-seme, as is clear in the spread today of the word *haunted,* which is everywhere.

But the larger problem is that *Specters of Marx* sabotages its own nonidentification in favor of another identification, convergence between *différance,* messianism, specters, and nonreciprocity. This identification is given textual solidity when *Specters* fills in what connects these relations. The new scholar must participate, perform, a *"just* opening . . . a hospitality without reserve, which is . . . the condition . . . of history" (65). Through this opening, certainly a new role for historians, history must be thought through the sense of the "strange concept of messianism without content, of the messianic without messianism, that guides us here like the blind" (65). But as the messianic has already been placed under the injunction against the expectation of reciprocity, how is it possible to even speak of a messianic eschatology "as the unrealized promise of justice and democracy," as Derrida's supporters do?[31] The phrase, "like the blind," is a substitution for the Western religious tradition of *grace* and, further, as Karl Löwith remarks, grace is where the Cross and Resurrection were joined to make the very pattern of "the transformation of the realm of necessity into a realm of freedom," the very medium of the "messianic vocation." If *Specters of Marx* embraces Jewish prophetism as it leaves Greek tragedy behind, where the messianic now dissolves even the play of metaphoricity, the messianic stitched to the nonreciprocal, would it be fair to say that *Specters of Marx* is also an instance of *desperate interpretation*?[32] The messianic as excessive to normal historical thinking is not, however, an excess that opens onto supplementarity or play, because nonreciprocity is its hallmark. Messianic hope, the to-come, "in memory of the hope," what are such terms but nonreciprocals, thought-stoppers?[33]

Normative historical thinking emphasizes the successivity of events, no matter how ambiguous, gathered together as proper names (French Revolution), which at once serve as periodization and event-markers. Let us grant Derrida, without hesitation, that *Specters of Marx* is posthistorical. Nonetheless, this "messianic without messianism," is also embedded in an historiographic category as dubious as anything he critiques. *Specters of Marx* has it— insists—that we should activate the concept of a *latency period* to think time out of joint. "Latency" here means what happened between an event "heralded" (before) and its result, this "temporal medium" that allows for a "mutation" that "perturbs the onto-theological schemas" (70). The idea of a latency period can accommodate biologistic and logical implications and is a substitute for the concept of a *period of transition,* an historiographic concept long contested for its antiphenomenological bias (making some people's lived experience canceled out by dwelling so much on beginnings and ends), but widely used. For whom is there always a transition if not the narrators? "Latency period," as we will soon see, reintroduces the idea of events and occurrences that "happened" without continuous intent or consciousness, where (or when) suddenly, an effect becomes "obvious."

This intellectual machine that dissolves reciprocity and makes messianism return gives it the sense of what I shall call a historiography without history. This is indicated in the text's invocation of the writings of Kojève, who conceived an historicity said to be beyond "the metaphysical concept of history." *Specters* recalls Kojève's interpretation of the United States as a nearly completed calcified social system, and if the United States was the then (feared) future of Europe, Kojève was even more correct in rendering a "task and a duty for the *future* of post-historical man . . . Post-historical man *doit* . . . for eternities of interpretation, there is an 'it is necessary' for the future" (73). We must affirm the indeterminacy of the future for there to be any necessity to link to it. Historiography without history: time emptied of all but spectering. Kojève's *mana* word—there is a "must"—is offered in language frightening in its simplicity, for *Specters* has it that what Kojève has given us is nothing less than "*this 'it is necessary' is necessary, and that is the law*" and "it is this law that dislodges any present out of contemporaneity with itself." Each of these sentences installs the grammar of insistence and is disturbing to that degree. Again, meta-metahistory or historiography without history is not just about temporal disorder—time is out of joint. Not at all: it brings "the law" to its reign over obligations without any sense of reciprocity. "*It is necessary*" repeats the continuism of the word as pure portent, an utterance that comes from the divine, a "magic power" of words, "mysterious, fatal, and decisive."[34] *Gorgias's wizardry?* Here, it seems to me, *Specters of Marx* goes far beyond what White, cited earlier, called the language of mana—it reduces the divine, which is not absurd, to the grammar of demand, in the name of affirming "some promise" that there is a future. This is not about facing the negative sublime, the possible meaninglessness of history.

Specters of Marx can then move out from Kojève's "doit" to an insistence that the "historicity of history [now] begins." How? Now latency returns—*to herald* and *to promise,* affirmed as the necessary frames of any posthistorical thinking. *To herald* and *to promise* also announce the scholar's new task: the acceptance of the impossible as the "infinite responsibility" of this new "historicity of history."

As we have seen, the concept of telos was terminated, so to speak, with the arrival of the messianic. Telos did not work: "the world has more than one age . . . Neither maturation, nor crisis, nor even agony. Something else" (77). *Specters of Marx* rejects any "unfolding of a normal, normative, or normed process" (78), yet accepts that the world is "going badly . . . almost black." While the equation between "badly" and "black" is an unfortunate conjunction, this "blackboard picture" makes use of the phrase "wearing down beyond wear" to characterize the collective narrative process of the world. How is this not telic? The writing acknowledges the "new unemployment" and the social inactivity of our "new era," but is the "ruthless economic war," which is said to "control everything," not utterly continuous with the persistence of an ever operative neocapitalism? Omitting to analyze such disturbing new solidities such as middle-class hatred for politics, or the withering away of criticism, *Specters of Marx* leaves out any structural modulation that might implicate its own writing in inextricable social problematics. Focusing on the dramatics of "inter-ethnic wars" with their "primitive conceptual phantasm[s]," as are said to inform the structure of conflict in the Middle East, is of a piece with the superdramatization of posthistorical necessity, of the divinity of "doit": "For above all, above all . . . international law and its institutions . . . [with their] fortunate perfectibility, despite an undeniable progress," offer a valid and exemplary filling-in of Kojève's "to come": "Justice demands . . . that one pay tribute to certain of those who are working with [international institutions] in the direction of the perfectibility and emancipation of institutions that must never be renounced . . . We should salute what is heralded today in the reflection on the right of interference or intervention in the name of what is . . . called the *humanitarian,* thereby limiting the sovereignty of the State in certain conditions" (84). One has to ask about the extreme idealization here: on the one hand, *Specters* acknowledges the obvious horrors of the world, but, on the other hand, moves to a *celebratory* discourse on the management of the *least negative*—when the U.N. finally intervened in Bosnia, it was only after continued slaughter there would harm its own survival and threaten the image/power of some member nations. Where *Specters of Marx* thus denigrates "mere" law and rights and elevates an institution that makes internationalism look necessary, it lapses into the politics of the European Idealist–liberalism it has tried to radicalize. To say again that international law is a positive "link of affinity, suffering, and hope, a still discreet, almost secret link, as it was around 1848," means that *Specters* supposes historical continuity, even historical identity: a "new international . . . calls to the friendship of an alliance without institution" (86). How is such internationalism, so vital to scientific and intellectual and artistic life, nonetheless not still part of the self-same "media-tele-visibility" syndrome denounced by *Specters of Marx?*

Historiography without history involves that Marxism will be allowed to *re*turn insofar as it accepts its task, to "reduce the gap as much as possible" between the ideal and the actual. But this pales by comparison to the program of *différance* and the messianic, whose task is to raise questions so as "to sort out, critique, keep close by, and allow to come back" the spectrality of specters, a "watch [that] itself will engender new ghosts." Calling for the impossible while accepting the inevitable impossibility of the impossible is a figure that nearly defies rhetoric, but the concept of numbness might apply. So much energy is devoted by Derrida to resisting intellectual work as production within immanence, as if to say, no more fragments.[35] Indeed, to call the logic of the messianic something insensible is not a harsh judgment, but a move *Specters* affirms: since there are no actual historical determinations that matter by comparison to keeping watch for the specter's return, the intellectual or new scholar is *re*turned to the job of to "bear witness, at least, to the justice which is demanded." As witnesses of the real protected by the ideal, the new scholar will of course continue as before to occupy a position akin to the infamous third party of representation, the one who can discuss criteria and ratios for sorting out good and bad measures to evaluate the ideal and the actual.[36] A tautology? The messianic depends on the "pure formality" of the messianic spirit, rendered a "gesture of fidelity," an "imperative," a "priority," all this for "a new Enlightenment for the century to come." Thus telos is *re*stored by *Specters of Marx* as it denounces the very idea of the telic.

Historiography offers many instances of the nonliving conjured so as to serve or provide a present with something exemplary. There is a very large traffic in images and literary figures of the exemplary. Much of modern social history, with its emphasis upon the neglected and anonymous subjects of vast historical processes, whose traces are studied in, say, diaries of crossing the American plains, or Carlo Ginzburg's insistence that ancient peasant messianism was "echoed" in the words of a fifteenth-century miller, has tried to make the nonliving relevant in the form of *ekphrasis,* or vivid retellings and accounts. Vivid in the minds of present readers is a highly prized effect; the novelist James Ellroy engaged the murder of his mother to motivate restoring his severed life. Historiography has never been separable from *ekphrasis.* Yet what *Specters of Marx* brings to this table is a prosopopoeia that has forgotten itself: "we know better than ever today that the dead must be able to work. And to cause to work, perhaps more than ever. There is also a mode of production of the phantom, itself a phantomatic mode of production. As in the work of mourning, after a trauma" (97). "The dead must be able to work"—the textual sense is not figural and imaginative, but just about literal, and when we ask after this intense insistence, we return to mourning, now called "work in general" (97) because the engulfing processes of life continue to inflict trauma. But is there no difference between mourning, or responses to trauma, and, say, positive forgetting, using memory for critical projects? The fracturing, the deconstruction, of the concept of mourning is prevented because *Specters* is concerned with "the ghost in general": "In a word, the whole history of European politics at least, and at least since Marx, would be that of a ruthless war between solidary camps that are equally terrorized by the ghost, the ghost of the other, and its own ghost as the ghost of the other." Were the liberals of 1870 haunted by the ghost of Marxism? Are the neoconservatives of the American Republican Party haunted by the ghosts of Roosevelt? Is Chirac sometimes haunted by the specter of de Gaulle? Ghosts, remember, are not reciprocal, so the questions are preposterous: is active politics a matter of politicians not able to face their ghosts or, worse, who turn lethal in the generalized repression of the ghostly, as if politics had nothing of material interests, social choices, the chance to choose existential possibles? Historiography without history comes to mean: the ghosts and ghostly relations already with us have absolute precedence. Even the "density of death" is not, for *Specters of Marx,* a powerful reaction determined by convention, language, inertia, repetition; it is one with a debt: *"to answer for the dead, to respond to the dead"* (109). And such debt is the greatest of all presences: "nothing is more serious and nothing is more true, nothing is more exact [*juste*] than this phantasmagoria" (109). Historiography without history would then *bridge* historiography and the nonliving, an identity conceived as "itself within the very inside of life," so that life must justify itself to the demands of spectral-history.

As if one thought it safe to stay in these waters of reading, Derrida still raises the ante on his readers (poker over water). This is now an *historiospectography*, which determines, as presence, "rights of succession" or fills in the form of inheritance: if one does not agree to engage with the specters inside and out, one cannot participate in this new "law of the fiduciary" (109). What I am calling Derrida's historiospectography is the unlimited awareness of being-haunted, "as general as it is irreducible," where all temporal convolutions go the way of an impossible temporality, a "disadjustment which will no doubt ever end," since relations with specters, once grasped as the "it is necessary," are interminable. What kind of historical consciousness is that? Again, *Specters of Marx* is not recoding historiography through psychoanalysis or the idea of the return of the repressed, even if at times it overlaps with those discourses; *Specters* insists that "the figure of the ghost is not just one figure among others. It is perhaps the hidden figure of all figures" (120). In a stunning piece of writing, haunting is so transcendental that it even eliminates a relation with language: "There would be no metarhetoric of the ghost" (120). Thus, spiritualized historiography realizes the secret or enigma to the workings of the telos of history, for "no metarhetoric of the ghost" means that no theory or hypothesis or signification figured in language matters by comparison to the ghosts within life. Why? As one commentator has noted, spiritualized historiography is about the goal of *awakening.*[37]

Historiospectography

Specters of Marx notices that the masterpieces of historiography can be read in the framework of a "eucharistic Narcissus," where readers of Marx will find that Marx's self-deception with specters and ghosts was of a piece with a writing that tried to capture the real presence of the proletariat. Marx and, say, his adversary Max Stirner, used techniques to make their thoughts "seen by ghosts," for each conjured phantoms for consciousness to support their criticisms of the phantoms they sought to negate. Stirner's delirious evocation of the isolation of self-consciousness to ward off the bourgeois Other was a conflict of phantom and phantom. But to say, as *Specters* does, that "*The ghost, always, is looking at me,*" that "the phenomenal form of the world itself is spectral [and that] the *phainesthai* itself . . . is the very possibility of the specter, it brings death, it gives death, it works at mourning," pushes death into language. Or better—it announces the replacement of philosophy of history by historiospectography. What matters is our rising to the occasion of acknowledging the temporalities of ghosts and specters, their now time. *Specters of Marx* is not shy about insisting what will replace historiography: "Humanity is but a collection or series of ghosts . . . since everyone reads, acts, writes with *his or her* ghosts, even when one goes after the ghosts of the other" (138–39). And this historiospectography belongs to a structure itself "before" history: "words always cause to come back, they convoke the *revenant* that they conjure away. Come so that I may chase you! You hear! I chase you. I pursue you. I run after you to chase you away from here. I will not leave you alone. And the ghost does not leave its prey, namely, its hunter. It has understood instantly that one is hunting it just to hunt it, chasing it away only so as to chase after it. Specular circle . . . The *long time* is here the time of this distance *hunt . . .* lure and prey" (140). It is no stretch to say that with this passage, *Specters of Marx* has closed on its own hunt, issuing an identity between *to haunt* and *to hunt,* which English registers through the presence and absence of the *a.* The operative phrases are "always" and "only so as to." *To hunt* and *to haunt* come before history, before social determinations, before language, before . . . : haunting is the before of before, hunt and prey already inside haunting, their mixtures making for a "long time," the interminability of their crossings, all life "ghosted" (my term) by the "invincible force and the original power" of the ghost (148). Historiospectography would be the name of our connections with the eternal presence of this force and original power. In a different idiom, was a phrase like "original power" what Gorgias heard in Sicily so long ago and sent him spinning?

From history to historiography to historiospectography—such is the trajectory of the new scholar, as *Specters of Marx* moves away from issues of successivity—what to do with Marx and Marxism—to nonsuccessivity, as it carves out an intellectual project for scholarly writing. For the new scholar *must survive,* here, where the impact of Kojève comes back. *To survive* and *to return* are the binding terms of *to hunt* and *to haunt,* and this "double socius binds *on the one hand* men to each other. It associates them insofar as they have for all times been interested in time . . . the time of the duration of labor, and this in all cultures and at all stages of techno-economic development . . . which itself would not be possible without surviving and returning" (154). Are *to survive* and *to return* concepts that Western historiography has presupposed, thus revived here? Derrida continues with the presupposition of *to survive* and *to return:* "one would have to say that the phantasmagoria began before the said exchange-value, at the threshold of the value of value in general, or that the commodity—form began before the commodity-form, itself before itself . . . A culture began before culture—and humanity. Capitalization also. Which is as much to say that, for this very reason, it is destined to survive them" (160). The raft of concepts discussed here are meta-meta—is all this an ungraspable ever present past? "To haunt does not mean to be present, and it is necessary to introduce haunting into the very construction of a concept" (161). Historiospectography: how does the mode of thinking that must be available to the new scholar transmit instruction on all this? How does the new scholar "receive"? "Everything begins before it begins"—the hunter "knows" what is required, what to do (161). Deep transmission: repetition is history, history is repetition, but timeless and before. The new scholar must break with philosophy and politics as we know them, since both domains of experience and concept are wedded to illusions of resolvability. The hunter knows it can be hunted. The new scholar of historiography has a feel for "began before."

Specters of Marx is an astounding defense of European history played out on the territory of philosophy of history—this text offers serious terms by which to affirm some continuity, or relations of continuity. But despite the heroics of the project, it unfortunately makes ghosts and specters come before every "before." The truly archaic or "fabulous" search for the logic of relation to the past that would satisfy a present philosophy and politics is settled by *Specters of Marx.* It hollows out, first, the cultural space of language with phantoms, specters, and ghosts, and second, idealizes a new scholar who can speak to absences of all kinds. Setting aside the privilege of philosophy of history to articulate one telic aim or another, *Specters of Marx* makes a near tyranny of the ghosts who are waiting for us to elicit them. The new scholar as outlined above is hardly a *bricoleur,* but more a spirit engineer—a master of impossibles and incalculables. Is the new scholar continuous with Fineman's Thucydides, here giving a superphilosophy of history that can awaken us? This new scholar is to offer sure play instead of opting for the risks of criticism.[38] White's critique fretted over the Mandarinism of Derrida's style and tone. That is resolved here in the mode of rhetorical *exergasa*: *différance* has now become recast as specter that "began before," and by prosopopoeia, giving name to the invisible now insisted as nonimaginary. Interestingly, what de Man noticed in Derrida's reduction of Rousseau to a modernist precursor gives way to the textual destruction of any sense of periodization—but without this leading to any existential charging of the present, except for the openings given to the new scholar. In demanding that "phantasmorization" alone is without limit, the deconstruction of *Specters of Marx* opts for the satisfactions of gnosis: to say that "one has to realize that the ghost is there" is to severely constrict what *différance* has supposedly been all about. *Specters of Marx* moves from contestations of discourse to an insistence on presence.

The single most disturbing sentence of *Specters of Marx* comes precisely at the end of this text: "we are wagering here that thinking never has done with the conjuring impulse. It would instead be born of that impulse" (165). Modern philosophy of language has taught us that this enunciation is in fact a statement performing itself, and the part "born of that impulse" indicates another *re*treat to idealism—to an implicit biologism and psychologism of what "impulse" suggests. Is it not fair to ask here about desperate historiography?

Finally, there is the issue of why desire for the messianic comes today, now. Is the messianic compelling because of a sense of historical impasse? "The messianic, including its revolutionary forms . . . would be urgency, imminence, but irreducible paradox, a waiting without horizon expectation" (168). An attentive reader could say, instead, that there is no paradox here—there is Derrida's writing that insists on urgency for the messianic, not the messanic's urgency, which is canceled in each move that the logic of *Specters of Marx* has made toward the eternal. In refusing to think through the messianic, that it is a specific discourse with specific textual and social effects, *Specters of Marx* shows a high degree of intellectual fear that the messianic will go the way of the telic, into unlimited social disagreements. Because of this soft textual hysteria that, once more, the messianic might become registered in our intellectual economy as an *obsolete* term of relation, we should listen when Derrida tells us that Marx could not grasp the "it ghosts," the truth of which is here figured forth in Freud, who said: "Marx—*das Unheimliche*"? What does it say that we must affirm Marx's texts as uncanny through Freud?

Messianic haunting, "before life *as such*, before death *as such*," is given a commanding *continuism*, and *Specters of Marx* closes with the injunction that "if he loves justice at least, the 'scholar' of the future, the 'intellectual' of tomorrow should learn it and from the ghost" (176). The scholar of this historiospectography is then the figure of *Specters of Marx* who survives to relate to us future connections with the ghosts; *Specters of Marx* has already decided that this is an "it is necessary." In this regard, I should like to close with a mention of Deleuze and Guattari's discussion of psychosocial types and "conceptual personae." For these authors, a philosophy of existence, which *Specters* announced on its first page, presupposes elements of prephilosophy (immanence), the persona invented (an insistence for an idea and role), and philosophical concepts that link to each other (consistency), further specified as "laying out, inventing, and creating [which] constitute the philosophical trinity—diagrammatic, personalistic, and intensive features." They would write a history of philosophy from the perspective of its transformations of the very "image of thought."[39] Is it stretching things to say that the uncanny, invoked by Derrida to form the internal structure of the spectral, belongs to the past, not to the future, so that the new scholar offered by *Specters of Marx*—under the injunction of so many "musts"—informs us of what is passing away? That is, the uncanny comes too late?

7

The Use and Abuse of History according to Jean-François Lyotard

The purposiveness that the 20th century has witnessed has not consisted, as Kant had hoped, of securing fragile passages above abysses. Rather, it has consisted of filling up those abysses at the cost of the destruction of whole worlds of names.
The precursor arrives too late.

Jean-François Lyotard

The Lyotard-Effect

In this chapter, the writings of Jean-François Lyotard serve as a transition to a critical theory of history—to concepts that sharpen the problematic of "use and abuse of history." Here, Lyotard's work is contrasted, among other discussions, to the new scholar of the messianic by virtue of its commitment to criticism, where Lyotard takes criticism of historiography to a nearly unbearable cultural and political tension.

Lyotard's work in historiography has elicited the scorn of the historical profession, at its institutionally most important thresholds—denounced by a president of the American Historical Association—with accusations of nihilism because Lyotard dared to use the concept of a cultural-social psychosis to discuss Western history. His work probed the discourse of ends and goals, specifically why the closer we get to the present, the more an event seems to slip out of Western modes of life, as if an event could lose its existence. Very extreme and thoughtful.[1] At what moment did historiography, philosophy, politics, and rhetoric join to make "speakers" whose stories bring belief and authority—the tangle of first, second, and third parties?[2] Lyotard dared to ask, openly, persistently, and thoroughly, what to think if historical representation, principally narrative, was a little psychotic from the perspective of how its word-forms or sanctified language-games connect with its readers. If narrative answers pressing, open problems, giving synthesis after synthesis, its form locking up the referent in its discourse, the writing giving aesthetic satisfaction that nudges out epistemic issues, then how to insist on making the referent the true event, the real thing, when in fact the referent is turned into art as often as not? Who can separate truth and the arts of truth from truth as disclosure and truth as opinion? Jean-François Lyotard had the nerve to write up such problems that the humanities, overall, cannot seem to resolve. (Has the last reader become a social type?) At any rate, I intend to discuss here Lyotard's arguments about historical representation and alternatives to it, which he also carefully argued for.

The apothegms from Lyotard stress conjunctions between violence and what Westerners call historical sense, consciousness, and knowledge. Is there a concept more used and abused in Western historiography than violence, especially its justifications "in the name of history"? The first apothegm reminds us of the violence of actualities, whichever processes and mechanisms are named as causal, however responsibility is parceled out; the second apothegm suggests that when we believe we have historically grasped something, even ourselves, such possession is irremediably asymmetrical with itself. Periodization is at best a singular psychological experience until socially organized. That much of deconstruction Lyotard agrees with, intellectual pressure brought to bear on identity and its temporal forms. The key phrase is "destruction of whole worlds of names." This is not a phrase of mourning for those wiped out, unnecessarily, in any past, but the more frightful, because possibly transformative experience, of what could actually come now if we activated prior names and the ones we invented for ourselves and use—this might introduce resistance to the discipline and control that comes with *naming* (*narrating*). Running through Lyotard's writing is an affirmation to always name, to say more.

The historians had every right to fear actually reading Lyotard on historiography. How far is historical *extinction* from ordinary historical *processes* if past names are so thoroughly obliterated? A name is a world, isn't it, or at least some names? In this, Lyotard brought the concept of *incommensurability* into historiography. In this, the violence of actualities carries over into the violence of historical writing, its own aggressions, often an aestheticizing of mayhem and the logical justification of it as well. Aestheticized art and historical narration are violence done against the complete understanding of an event, which always shows something we prefer to rationalize. An event "is alien to the language or structure of understanding to which it occurs."[3] If incommensurability affects knowledge, art, and politics in different ways, discourses that install history are then less representations *of* a past than commands for how to use a past in the present. In short, the intersections and slippages of historical representation with language and its social effects were theorized by Lyotard, who brought its political-epistemic distortions to consideration. While the materials here might seem a long way from the prior analysis of the *Los Angeles Times,* I will try to show how reflection on Lyotard's apothegms, as well as a more general contemplation on Lyotard's writings, the use and abuse of history, after Nietzsche, raises conceptual problems that underlie the most ordinary of historical representations.

Lyotard's Genealogy of Historiography

Lyotard agrees with Deleuze and Guattari when they say that the concept of history comes into its own with the State, the concept of history having adjusted its relations with archaic narratives (the epic) and magic, the State having dislocated all sorts of local forms of life. The advent of "history" brought the destruction of names and genealogies—what was discredited or placed outside lines of succession and points or moments of concentration. History—as discourse—was always pragmatic, political, moral, worked up from a fusion of logical and aesthetic elements, or what Joel Fineman, discussed in chapter 5, believed constituted the moment of Thucydides. Lyotard asks if narrative "coherence" can even separate into one part that is logical, another that is aesthetic. Why? Here is Lyotard's somewhat condensed proposition: "Historicity is a product of the Jewish West. This historicity presupposes foreclosure, and the renunciation of compromise, myth and figure, the exclusion of female . . . mediation, a face to face encounter with a faceless other. The immobility of the matrix form in which evil is expiated disappears when historicity arises."[4] By comparison to the Greek synthesis in which reality and pleasure were reconciled, that dissolved with their invention of discursive, political knowledge, opening themselves to endless political contests, the Judeo-Christian line activated foreclosure—an inaccessible God and humans subject to the word of the moment, political law. An intellectual historian offers a sense of the context when historicity and foreclosure touched: "The great god Pan lay long a-dying, and everywhere men grasped at the straws of whatever faith would solace them most. Mystery religions appeared, coalesced, and dissolved apart again, all trying frantically to improve man's sorry lot by repudiating the world . . . If man could not save himself and slough off his sense of sin, he might enjoy vicarious salvation . . . The quest of Justin Martyr is symbolic: he sought comfort from a Stoic, then from an Aristotelian, then a

Pythagorean, then a Platonist—only to fall at last gracefully into the bosom of the Christian church."[5] Foreclosure occurred in such a way that the past never disappears and can never be mastered—history happens to those who do not understand one is an "allocator" before the "discourse of an absent one."[6]

Judeo-Christianity passed violence to thought as through a religious caesura—the present does not absorb the rhythm of experiences, there is a breaking off from reconciliation or synthesis of life and spirit. Judaism produced time as point-in-time, a disavowal of the possibility of a life in which neither action nor remembrance dominated the other. As a "point" discourse, only much later called referential, after the codifications of discourse begin, the insertion of "before and after" into everything it narrates, historical discourse has been remarkably consistent. Considered strictly as a language/cultural operation, the discourse of history has something about it that feels like a "temporalized *house of correction* for morality," in Reinhart Koselleck's phrase, borrowed from Kant.[7]

Since Thucydides, that touchstone of historiography, who was actually a substantial "local" narrator turned into the "creator" of a successful political and pragmatic epic "father" of realistic narrative, there is no lack of evidence of this coming-forward of history as a quasi-transcendental fusion of foreclosure, absence, and words/things. As a discourse of/on "point," it has the function of making other words/things "in" and "out" to other points and lines of succession. Everyone has an anecdote to signal this relation. In the film *Uncommon Valor* (1982) a man is dropped to his death from a helicopter to the accompaniment of the words, "You're history." In the academic domain, Mario Biagioli has convincingly argued that a discipline as specific as "science studies" gained ground as a scholarly practice by attacking grand narratives, yet at times *reinstalling* them on a local level.[8] With and after foreclosure, any genealogy of historiography, by any fair account, demonstrates such mixed origins that the very concept of history descends as much from cultural *naming absences* as it does from any of the various "objective" regulative ideals (e.g., "get your facts straight") that have replaced each other, almost regularly. Recent accusations of plagiarism against well-known historians elicited some sharp legal maneuvering, including the argument that if plagiarists get people to read, where is the harm? Is plagiarism to be counted as part of historical representation, its "bad" genealogy?[9] Lyotard poses questions: is there any *sense of history* that does not strive to insert its moral point—judgment, survival for the future—into words/things, an insertion that is suspect given the "mixed" genealogies of historical writing? A second question: given the *mixtures* of history as actuality and historical writing—the thing itself and its representations—how are these junctions organized?

No writer went further than Lyotard in raising unpleasant aspects of historiography. I am not referring to his withering criticism of the "grand narratives," taken up below. More immediately, these unpleasant aspects are shown in the *rivalries* between "official" versions of historical sense, self-baptized as realism. Historians are in competition for the "public mind," for "audience share" of all sorts, and the act of foreclosure, negation of reconciliation, carries into narrative—think of what each version on the "same" events *eliminates.* Or think of how the ideal narrative takes the violence it recounts and gives a reconciliation—casting out the larger discord. If there are always presuppositions in any act of representation, why aren't such presuppositions affirmations of discordance instead of stabilizing concepts? For example, in his 1941 book, *History as the Story of Liberty,* Benedetto Croce cudgeled the rival claims of Marxists, Gentilian idealists, the emerging psychohistory, and Diltheyian empathy, among other concepts of historical method, proclaiming that "the practical requirements which underlie every historical judgment give to all history the character of 'contemporary history,'" which Croce took to mean that historical thought "is the act of comprehending and understanding induced by the requirements of practical life."[10] At the threshold of what could be called a more rigid presupposition, neither good, true, nor beautiful but *practical,* every present must come to terms with its laws of life, which would then undercut ideological projections on the past. The more the historian knew of life's practicalities, the better. That, in turn, presupposes that the past itself is not connected to us by goals, as Croce's rivals thought. Indeed, for Croce "historical accounts were *nothing but* sets of existential statements," as much primitive and sophisticated identification as narration.[11] At some point, historical representation had to accept things as they are.[12] Arthur Danto thinks historical representation presupposes a sense of time-relevance, the same thing as a feel for irrelevance.[13] There is no historical writing that does not exist without rival presuppositions. Lyotard will register that historical consciousness is a form of practical reason, "of being obliged."[14]

In Lyotard's reconstruction, the creation of hierarchies as well as types of simplification are coextensive with the reach of historical thought. In the genealogy of *Anti-Oedipus* as well as much of what can be called French Theory (here, Lévi-Strauss's *Tristes Tropiques* is one of a number of ur-texts), history, Statist thought, and *transcendental illusions* were fused in the mixed genealogy of history. How did the concept of history, a word-thing, install a form of despotism in which "history" became "*of* history," a singular universal that could claim to represent the place from which judgment and evaluation can consider actions, past and future? Was this transcendental illusion a deprivation of the polyvocity and diversity of experience? Experiences that had to be signified from on high, from history's height, rendered in images and senses of lines of succession threaded to hierarchical rankings? Odo Marquand has an acute evaluation of this despotism—history results in *everyone* required to become competent to narrate what is, for them, some *sole story* grafted to some existing "sole power."[15] Woe to those who do not know they belong "in history," as teller and told. The singular universal of history ushered in a "you must" attached to "now." Obligation and time, irreversibility and necessity, history and Statist writing, history and memorialization, history and sanitized names—such are some of the connections, volatilized, thickened, thinned, negated, and replaced, that ensure subjectivity will merge with the categories of *already* and *to come,* images and social markers (class, position, function), blended with identity, language brought to coherence with time-points, including breaks and, in short, representation secured and anchored to a time outside of time, the despotic moment of an obligation that can be neither rejected nor satisfied. Gottfried Benn, poet and doctor, expressed an aspect of this "of history," especially the subject who is "restricted to suffer or observe" the *has happened* (an "ideal reader" of despotic signification): "Five hoplites [armored infantry] armed with machine-guns attack a boy they had promised not to harm; then they march in somewhere—: history. Mahomet began as a robber of caravans . . . poisoned the wells in the desert . . . an unimaginable crime, but now ennobled by divine and racial needs: first theft, then religion, finally history. Under Nero, in 67 A.D., private correspondence in Rome had ceased entirely, since all letters were opened; the postmen came to the houses in the mornings bringing news by word of mouth about the latest executions: world history." Most Westerners cringe at Benn's brutal satire of historical knowledge—ceaseless mayhem and chaos turned into aestheticized stories, site of both "exoticism and criticism," as Michel de Certeau put it, its historiography oscillating between conservatism and utopianism, "beginnings" and "endings" *for us,* for survivors and spectators.[16]

Lyotard reminds us that *to historicize,* infinitive mode, is to subject the innumerable happenings of life to functions of time-management and social regulation—the famous phrase "coming-to-terms-with-the past" marks one of contemporary humanism's ideal regimes of signification. As a didactic discourse that turns already overcoded metaphor into enthymeme, narrative representations construct a past by eroding others—no, it wasn't the Luther-effect that caused German passivity; yes, it was the hatred toward the industrial that blueprinted such passivity; or Hitlerism promised a way out. The "historiographical operation"[17] turns on this filling of a void or process that cannot be ended, so ceaselessly filled that filling the void becomes the only meaning. Lyotard noted that a key temporal operation of historiography was to *insert time-points* so as to diminish a society's confrontation with the time-voids it actually created. The American Civil War voided segments of society, the war now a time-point for countless narratives on what was created and destroyed. The German people created Nazism, but where are the people "after Nazism" who can account for who "they were" when the Germans created Nazis? A recipe for schizophrenia? As a socializing discourse, historiography has then to offer time-points that can be attached to a transcendental illusion: an ideal that organizes action and representation in the hopes of a satisfaction that arrives, which of course it doesn't. That it does not keeps open the very troubles that called for history in the first place. To narrate or write history is itself a duplication, a ditto machine, of the violence (voids) that writers such as Gottfried Benn returned for consideration to the philosophy of history. Benn wrote when history was not severed from dangerous genealogies; and now?

There are so many contributions to the concept of *posthistoire* that one hesitates to make any statement that unnecessarily reduces the contention around this particular name to just a few main ones. *Posthistoire* runs through French Theory since the 1920s, and there is hardly any unified position. Lyotard's writings on historiography pertain to "French Nietzscheanism," upheaval brought into models of cultural processes, resistance to the temporalities of political order, or now the use of history in a consumer social order. As he argued in *Advantage and Disadvantage of History,* Nietzsche emphasized that history is of especial concern to artists and writers. For them, history is often given as antiproduction, a "brakeshoe" on present intensity and critique. Artists are encouraged to make their effects within narration, the preferred form of cultural identification. As we have seen, historical narration gives to subjects notification of acceptable differences, or "salvation in evolution," as Nietzsche put it.[18] Historical narration is one of the best forms in which to present the worst things, as it also works against experimentation—experience habitually *foreclosed* by telling stories. It can hardly be intellectually accidental that years of conflict in Bosnia resulted in political, social disaster with dozens of historical narratives justifying images of impasse and impossibility instead of radical experimentation—a Bosnian local experiment with their history and politics could not escape from the factions armed with their own "sole" story and "sole" power rivalries, to cite Marquand, above. So narrative historiography reduces the present to something like a switching station, making it as smooth and consistent as possible in reducing the virtual and the futural to points of continuity with the dominant formations of the present. Upheaval toward historiography, then, could only mean scathing intellectual analysis toward narration and the construction of better intellectual problems than those posed by historians. How and what does historical narration foreclose? Lyotard speaks of present experimentations with narrative that would weaken the sense of the future's continuity with the present, instead of offering big, medium, and small stories that *re*establish continuity that satisfy present political and *mythic* requirements.[19]

Lyotard's contribution to *posthistoire* is radically different from the arguments raised by writers such as Alexander Kojève when the latter insisted that *la fin de l'histoire* involved the triumph of insipid happiness and the cessation of action. Kojève held that homogeneity trumped adversity, or that the alienations of the modern would simply dissipate. Or, history will put (has put, is putting) an end to history, the result of action coming to a termination in the success of inaction, this inaction itself nothing but the triumph of a particular kind of action, that of reconciliation between oppositions. For Kojève, *posthistoire* was located in "idleness" and "aimlessness," or, according to Bataille, the "unemployment" of the dialectic and the negative.[20]

Lyotard takes up these issues in the context of "what is postmodern?" He emphasizes that "postmodern" is derived from a shift in the field of architectural practice and discipline away from visions like the Bauhaus (1919–33) rebuilding of the human environment. These modernist visions are, today (1979), incredulous because they were sustained by the monomyths, the integrative myths, of that very modernity—the myths of the emancipation of humanity, the liberation of the subject, or the victory of knowledge. Lyotard relates incredulity toward metanarrative to widely shared current feelings, such as "there is a sort of sorrow in the Zeitgeist," or, affirmatively, there is "toleration for incommensurables." In social terms, as the avant-garde is assimilated—an assimilation unfortunately exemplary for nearly everything coming under the name *culture*—so, too, capital forms greater social tangles and complications toward strategies of resistance and opposition. Unlike Kojève, it is not *posthistoire* as victory over conflict, but *posthistoire* as critique of assimilation and integration that Lyotard celebrates; postmodern is not *posthistoire* as the dismantling or reassembling of modernism, popularized by, for example, the *October* group in the United States, where art history according to Lacan replaces that of Freud and Marx. The postmodern is understood as a "condition of possibility" that requires strategies of thought, where "thousands of uncomfortable little stories"[21] in a "constant state" of aesthetic experimentation add to "finality without end," instead of further bloating the great histories.[22] Postmodernism is continuous with modernism insofar as the latter is about the destruction of universalist claims,[23] but postmodernism has a stronger sense, that of challenging any existing mode of representation, or representation in itself. The modernist intellectual—"having reproduced power put . . . [stories] into circulation . . . at the same time using them to curse power"[24]— gives way to the intellectual as *faber*, not representor, if that is even possible.

The arguments are continuous with those of Barthes where, from *Mythologies*, sarcasm toward society's so-called revealed truths "fills [the myth-reader's] task to the brim," or Godard's insistence that "in every image we must ask who speaks." Criticism toward genetic patterns is complementary with *posthistoire* as experimentation. Lyotard emphasized movements such as Pop or Op art when (if) they intensified strategies of representation, or distanced viewers from everyday aesthetic and political judgments, norms, or lent themselves to small bursts in the liquidization of identities, of dislocating cultural intuitions of sense and direction transmitted by the grand narratives.

If incredulity toward metanarratives became the elementary condition of criticism, then it is *satire* that is sarcasm's complement: "Don't [the arts] form both a satire through the immense diversity of the genres, and at the same time a field where the whole point is always to try out whether that situation, that event, that hole in the ground, that wrapping of a building, those pebbles placed on the ground, that cut made on a body, that illustrated diary of a schizophrenic, those *trompe l'oeil* sculptures, and all the rest . . . of sensing and phrasing are being probed on the limits of what is possible . . . This is our postmodernity's entire vocation."[25]

So postmodernity involves experimentation *and* terror. Under the general conditions of postmodernity, mainstream imagistic systems organize the exchange of unrealities rather than directly exploiting people, as occurred with industrial models; social relations are more plasticized (e.g., over half of all professors in the United States are now part-time, *adjunctive*), and perhaps

Western social systems no longer require metanarrative integration; ends are vague and more sinister, and, with Nietzsche, it may well be that the goals are missing in every sense but that of accumulation/survival. Artists and intellectuals who choose to add to the cultural endowment of a "unitary end of history and of a subject" are simply recapitalized.[26] It should be noted that Lyotard does not dismiss out of hand the use of categories such as negation, alienation, and nonidentity championed by Adorno and others. Lyotard maintains such practices but put to the task of intensifying a *dispossession* of the rules offered by negation. Lyotard urges dispossession of rules, of identities, of simple opposition, of blind affirmation, a generalized undoing of the politics of the signified—any group's use of a transcendental illusion. In short, the artist and intellectual are urged to "investigate what makes . . . an art object and whether it will be able to find an audience,"[27] this in the face of rampant and incessant rehistoricizaton. For example, contemporary art movements have been so monumentalized (Minimalism is less the name of an object-effect and more the name of a canon) that an artist has to ask how it is even possible to "humble and disqualify reality," to "flush out artifices of representation" and what can it mean to "assay" an "increase of being" without furthering existing group historicizations?[28] There is no new scholar here—only a restless probe of temporal possibles in relation to capital and the political groups it has spawned.

Conflict between Historiography and Philosophies of an Event

Lyotard's contribution to *posthistoire,* like Nietzsche's, is to conceive an event as unpresentable, this to expand and make uncomfortable acts of speaking and thinking. The notion of the unpresentable has a similar status to Nietzsche's sense of eternal return and can also be compared with Deleuze and Guattari's sense of "nonthought," which is different from negation and "no." Nonthought constitutes experiences not-yet placed in historical language and representation, and may not be able to be so placed—requiring a thought-experiment without a determinate origin and end.[29] The unpresentable is not another version of what is lacking and missing from representation, but rather those experiences unable to be fully *historicized.* If the point, variously articulated, of historical culture was to ensure people are as little affected as possible by their own experiences, who become "careless and accommodating in external matters . . . if only their memories are kept continually titillated and there flows a constant stream of new things to be known that can be neatly packed up in the cupboards of their memory,"[30] then the unpresentable is not riveted to nostalgia for masterpieces, for holistic works. Here Lyotard lines up with authors like Joyce or Woolf when they made works the rules of which those very same works did not possess. Art making, like speech or language, is itself an event, an organized action before it is a representation. Unlike the historicist versions of Habermas, where a clear goal is maintained for art (social consensus) or Jameson, where *transition* to a better future is to be historically imagined by sifting positive and negative for progressive purposes, Lyotard hews to strategies and tactics of experimentation. This experimentation flourishes only by a forgetting, one that cannot affirm injustice "to what is behind . . . [but] only recognizes one law—the law of that which is to come."[31] Despite the ominous possibilities of the latter part of that formulation, the unpresentable dances with forgetting, among other connections, and makes life all middle, all between, no founding negation attached to either end, the unpresentable an orphan from parentage and heirs. Perhaps the unpresentable, in being materialized in representation, suspends the great game of pessimism and optimism, which artists, scientists, and intellectuals know all too well, pessimism and optimism uttered in that "strange voice . . . under the scholar's hood"?[32]

History always means unity, simplicity, and communicability, past and future made into clear roads and linearities that render truth as before and after, or completion of an event and story in the mode of an *exhibited* absence. The "end of fascism," the "end of the Soviet Union"—time periodized with a date—now begins, now starts, making the now full. In the essay "Judiciousness in Dispute, or Kant after Marx," Lyotard argued that narrative continuity succeeds because it suppresses a "convulsion in which 'before' and 'after' lose their co-presence in . . . discourse."[33] If we could not make clear separations between before and after, or, in Arthur Danto's terms, separate "relevance and irrelevance," then what? Despite the accounts of turmoil and carnage, waste and unnecessity entered into historical narration, historical thought only knows how to present its results in a beautiful way, by good forms, by incorporating "convulsion" into time-lines, time-insertions: the high road in the writing of German history as tragedy, the satisfactions of the apocalypse in writings about Los Angeles.[34] Even when it admits irony as undeniable, historical thought is unable to sever its ties with the beautiful. Its magical term is *synthesis.*[35]

In Lyotard's view, the postmodern, less a period in time as it is a provocation, leaves off from the institutionalized games of pleasure derived from pain.

A better question is how to suspend the beautiful and the exquisite gravitas of the negative? We are enjoined to instead make new presentations; *posthistoire* is a test, whether we can thicken the unpresentability of the unpresentable, where difference becomes more urgent. In this, the State, humanity, and the university can be conceived today as language-particles set in a more violent scene of fractured social bonds. Has the very idea of a core social bond—usually believed to operate both as a macroexplanation and microdescription, as when there is said to be trust *gluing* subjects together—slipped as a way of legitimizing narration? Has historical writing spooned itself inside the implicit terror of "be operational or disappear," that inclusive set of *performative-motions,* whose direction is every direction at once (a fork in the intellectual road that lead to Jean Baudrillard's antihistoricism, history as more orgylike than not)? Indeed, the very concept of subjective performance grafted to objective history wavers, insofar as capitalist "input/output equation[s]" and "context control" have replaced history as the medium of social bonds.[36] In this sense, history is another of those constructs of the social bond that died long ago, the news of which also died long ago. If the *Los Angeles Times* materials offered in chapters 2 and 3 are relevant, narrative history has become a restricted ticket.

Today, as art and other types of culture have seen the partial bursting of their own names, a generalized Duchampianism of culture, new concepts of sensory experience and their transformation into conceptual notions come forward. Cultural endeavors, particularly from university-based art and criticism, legitimize their objectness by addressing and becoming "masters" of recognition— now satisfying the public by reviews that give the public dialogue with itself and its representors. In the contentious stream of competing claims for painting, one has no choice but to accept the existence of new norms whose audience (interlocutors) give legitimation. All high culture, and increasingly every other layer as well, is saturated with mediations that can transform an object into quasi-insider chitchat, criticism a form of "fan-work," the proliferation of new taste. The near infinity of objects that could constitute and could be considered as constituting works of art is so immeasurably big that judgments of reason on these objects sounds increasingly desperate and terroristic, reducing this manifold by exclusions unsaid or by more direct acts. The edifice, as in *necessary edification,* where *to historicize* = legitimation, has gone a bit haywire—but does not disappear. Lyotard blasted connoisseurship exactly as high-cultural senses of connoisseurship were extended to the general culture— the Elvis literature, rock and roll turned into another canon war. Artists and writers were enjoined by Lyotard's texts to start with the actually existing plurality of games and moves that can be *exploited,* to make new games hard to exploit by system-performativity and history-synthesis. Lyotard was constantly asking about the "we" of art and writing, its relations to "us," "them," "they." He brought linguistic and discursive theories to bear on these matters. Any object/text that gave an opportunity for some dissension and contestation was welcomed. To welcome experience in art and criticism might sound, well, utopian today; but that could also be the result of a failure to challenge writing and institutions in a more interesting way.

Instead of return and recoding, fright in the face of metanarrative dissolve and reconstitution, Lyotard's writings evoked the motions of concepts, approximating the sense of an *event.* He argued that the strong sense of a critical/cultural event went hand in hand with a sense of cultural enigmatics: "I believe that it is important that there be no addressee, [that someone] no longer knows for whom he writes, since there is no longer any taste; there is no longer any internalized system of rules that would permit a sorting out . . . We are without interlocutors."[37] Who actually speaks to and listens to whom? Lyotard's "without interlocutors" is an historical judgment that events disturb one. That is the kind of statement that has made many American commentators on Lyotard apoplectic, or a critic such as Bruno Latour decry Lyotard as mad, as he did in *We Have Never Been Modern.* How many histories of modernism are expended on narrating some monomyth of loss instead of antagonizing one's contemporaries! Lyotard affirmed "without" interlocutors not as *absence*—lack for him a grotesque epistemic error—but as a call for "new effects" and connections. In *Just Gaming,* Lyotard noted that effects (of text, of painting) can always be sent to the bin marked "failed" and psychotic because they went too far. Here is how Lyotard put the problem: "one cannot work telling oneself that, yes, there are values that arranged in a specific way form a subject. This is the subject to whom I speak: I communicate what I have to say in its name. To presuppose such an addressee or tutor, is to admit that all the actions that form history . . . find their ultimate meaning in the accomplishments of a universal subject. It is the idea of such a subject that modern artists refuse."[38]

Constantly moving between the concerns of contemporary criticism, philosophy of language, and the already discussed issues of *to historicize,* Lyotard sought out the links between these domains. To represent actualities or situate a present as something historical, certain modes of representation have to be easily available, part of a specific moment's equipment. With fixed time-inserts such as modern, postmodern, or large periodizations, comes a taste for aesthetic returns and revivals, new senses of obsolescence, some events institutionalized and others marginalized in discourse/institution mixtures. Lyotard never tired of emphasizing what was at stake when claims, time, and discourse join: "No matter what its regimen, every phrase is in principle . . . in a differend between genres of discourse . . . genres of discourse . . . fill the void between phrases."[39] The concept of a differend was introduced so as to account for the *incommensurability* between genres of discourse, of disjunctions between inherited, temporalized language, and experiences that do not fit with inheritance, with continuity. "The differend is the unstable state and instant of language wherein something which must be able to be put into phrases cannot yet be . . . what remains to be phrased exceeds what they can presently phrase . . . to institute idioms which do not yet exist."[40] Aestheticized narrative history gives way to *naming*, with and without history—a "we" can try to reconcile claims between, say, a victim and a perpetrator, but their differend can persist despite legal and moral arrangements. Existentialism is sharpened in real time as it is dulled in narrative time. Incredulity toward metanarrative does not mean there is not furious competition in and of the present over use and abuse of history. The sense of a differend or a possible incommensurable between evaluation and description, between an order and a request, between an ameliorative act and one that provokes, pries apart the fusions in which "to declare the world to be historical, is to assume that it can be treated in narrative terms."[41] We could ask: are there processes that culminate in our social system that make it nonhistorical today? Lyotard never stopped asking about the social question and historiography.

Once we stop using historical discourse in its ordinary way, as common and good sense, one is under the obligation to signify differently. Once the tacit acceptance between the genre of a speculative regime and, say, the Idea of emancipation is disconnected, no longer inherently the good form of narrative history, then the linking concepts are deposed: redemption, knowledge, and dialectic cease representing necessity and obligation, and become contested concepts. This is another place where the genealogies of prose surface. In this, Lyotard's arguments are consonant with those of de Man, who argued that "genetic models"—an intent oriented towards an end—are predicated on *confusion* between rhetoric and reference. For de Man, such confusions require the deception of believing in an end without deception.[42]

Lyotard did not speak from *posthistoire* but rather out of a differend between *history and context,* not the same thing at all. Because of the weakening or *defaillancy* of the modern project of emancipation, the incredulity toward the great narratives carries its own potential self-deception: "it is therefore tempting to lend credence to the great narrative of the decline of great narratives."[43] In Lyotard's version of incommensurability and history, belief in decline completely restores history, switched from incredulity to a loss that must or can be made good. This type of discourse simply repeats the implicit terror of narrative history (to be historicized), since the "history of loss" is as self-serving as any other temporal or genetic pattern. Domination and loss are a nice married couple. Like Nietzsche's "On Truth and Lies in a Nonmoral Sense," which asked about language's *value*—since it can engender truth, lie, beautiful error, and necessary illusions at the same time, in the same phrase— Lyotard gestured toward "little stories," where names mean proper names and units of value, and transmit local realities and new patterns of connection. Because little stories have the advantage of signifying to other senders and receivers the tempo or *beat* of experience, these stories are one way in which a community or society, no matter its scale, "reactivates names and nominal relations . . . [and] reassures itself as to the permanence and legitimacy of its world of names." There is a strong message in that quote about history and name-destiny, which goes to the apothegm at the beginning of this chapter. So even little stories can convey an inexpungeable sense of tautology—many stories are ultimately about identity preservation, even if anti-identitarian; primary narcissism (e.g., idealization of an origin) may well be unavoidable in narrative worlds. But these fuzzy logics—what actual people believe in terms of their narrations—span temporal differences and are more important than before/after.

With *posthistoire,* or societies that have passed through the *agonistics* of Western modernization, *universal* civic identities have turned spongy in relation to metanarratives; identities are cosmopolitical—the types called scientist, artist, global intellectual, nongovernment official—and contemporary narratives from accredited domains (e.g., the university) must still beat back the question "whether or not there is a human history."[44] Universal history may be discredited by deconstructionists and other dissident types, but that does not stop the universal being invoked to discredit groups, big and small, said to lack the universal. The game of giving and withdrawing historical significance might be a *local Western language game,* but the West has moved its "local" to the universal, into nearly all socioeconomic functions. In this, how is it possible to believe in the *innocence* of history? Or what do we do with history's innocence as constantly recoded in schemes of disqualifying the un-innocent?

These questions are more urgent than ever. Is there *danger* that arrives with the many "we's" and claims to history? Can artists and intellectuals evade choosing politics or choose to experiment—alienate the narratives that wish to appropriate artistic energies? Little stories, because they are closer as language to facts on the ground, may be less or more misleading, and every narration is potentially an affirmation of a cliché as well as a joyously *illegitimate idea,* since our stories are always those of particular groups, there being no "we" that can be found to measure the very stories we tell. For Lyotard, when narration, obligation, and subjectivity join, they often cohere as a subservience to a particular story. But in the aftermath of the West's actual violence, which provoked skepticism toward its own metanarrative ideals, historical representation can be contested by a *posthistoire* that sketches only an opening, a way of working representation in suspension from the claims of universal and local history. Truth, lie, poetics, and skepticism—Lyotard chooses the artist/intellectual who affirms without the protection of narrative.

Auschwitz is a name that destroys speculative history, or history as positive genetic reconciliation. Auschwitz exposed the inanity of one great synthesis that linked Hegelians to Marxists to conservatives and liberals, the easy pragmatism of "the real is rational and the rational real." But did it take an Auschwitz to show this, to expose historical writing as part of the slaughters of history, prose/poetics with teeth? Gorgias with gas masks? Lyotard asks us to consider current modes of political and cultural violence, and not subject them to metanarrative. For instance, the ongoing, well-documented privatization of science in America, adds to the difficulty of maintaining the university as an Ideal community, torn as it is between financial, social, and political rivalries: why put this in the form of a story we already know? What form is required to bring out the *unpresentability* of the things evoked? If historical narration presupposes certain rules—of coherence, of synthesis, of the appropriateness of anecdotes—then *posthistoire* is an opportunity: the invention of temporary criteria.[45] Such temporary criteria, double-edged because new, yet interest-driven, emerge once one thinks that "reason is not sufficient to make links in accordance with an aim."[46]

Lyotard, as said in the introduction, kept going. He goes into the destruction of historiography. *Posthistoire* means that instead of chronology or "before and after" treated as sure criterion, one has only signs, deprived of the criterion of intuitive certainty. This is one of the strongest senses of *posthistoire.* Historians insist that *something happened* and link this something to preexistent rules of interpretation. For example, Auschwitz is like/unlike other barbarities, its madness linked to industrialization and social regression—but that is not the end of it. Is madness the right name? Is the process of the industrialization of death the actual process? Whose sensations *span* these dimensions, whose are diminished? How can such ethicocognitive puzzles be settled? Historical narration brings programs of sign-management, to ensure readers will be clarified. But that does not release historians or readers from petitio principii. For example, Lyotard carefully argued that judgment, surely a structure of historical representation, concerns the ability to make cases: "in cognitive phrases under the rule of the schema, in dialectical argumentative phrases under that of the *symbol,* and in prescriptive phrases (in evaluation of responsibility and morality) under that of the *type.*"[47] Insofar as historical thought or historiography as such wishes to make such judgments—cognitive (action), dialectical (thought-about), and prescriptive (rank what happens)—the faculty of judgment becomes a *milieu* of knowledge. But schemas, symbols, and types do not work without the presupposition of identity; is it a *demand* that makes Auschwitz "first" in disasters? Doesn't Thucydides belong to Holocaust representation, since the Peloponnesian Wars were so barbaric? In another domain: it is a presupposition that capitalism is rational or has a "proper goal" (satisfaction, security, order). But how does one judge—historicize—capitalism to be rational if our phrase-regimes are themselves rationalizations? *Posthistoire* asks for verbal performance to suspend such phrases, whether they lessen especially the force of past events or socialize the future that has not happened yet. A discussion here of the essay, "The Sign of History" will elucidate the stakes involved for historiography.

"The Sign of History" has it that attunement to historical experience has been based on a misuse of the phrase "common being," made subject to cognitive rules and a rule of telos, or finality. Acceptance of such common being, say toleration for capitalism's ordinary violence, that of the workplace, is signaled in subjective-teleological phrases, of the type in which the present is judged adequate or inadequate, acceptable or unacceptable. For example, one can say that capitalism does not mistreat one too badly, but what is the "I" that says so worth? What does "too" mean? What is compared there? "I" and "too" are signs, already connected to and closed off from other signs. If names dissolve into the more fluid ambiguities of dense and opaque signs, if all one has in making the present historical are signs, then the historian's *research* is no guarantee of objective sense, of common being, but only another *medium* of cultural filtering. Signs require an assay, an assessment, or strong reflection, and *refer*, at best, to "an event, a deal (in the card-playing sense) . . . which would only indicate and not prove that humanity is capable of being not only the cause but also the author of its progress."[48] There are worlds of contestation in that phrase: is it progress or the extension of medical techniques that accelerates the further extension of such techniques? The *afterness of historical representation* turns event/sign into a genetic or telic pattern, precisely what "sign" resists. In this sense, *posthistoire* is itself the name and sign of the risks and dangers of interpretation and analysis of a present not yet historicized.

The pragmatic and moral dimensions of historical writing need Ideas of continuity and discontinuity, progress and decline; pragmatic morality requires an *undetermined cause* so as to allow humanity or any cognitive subject to schematize history as freedom (i.e., not mechanical, or reducible to mechanistic causation). Historians need to make what happened appear necessary but not determined by, say, human nature, social laws, or any other explanation that installs "history is." That is what Fineman's analysis showed—law and anecdote are not incompatible. But, Lyotard asked, what type of event now indexes the Idea of free causality?[49] As subject to power, force, domination, authority, institutions, and codes, signs mark a fissure between mechanism and liberty, allowing for an affirmation, which may not arrive, that the historical world exemplifies an Idea of progress and/or decline, so that there is an index as to a "moral disposition within the human race." As Lyotard points out, Kant set out to synthesize deeds and misdeeds with spectators disinterested enough—only enough—to arrive at criteria for assessing progress and decline. "Sublime feeling" can become a phrase spectators give themselves: Kant's ideal subject of history seeks to make and to participate in signs of events that will satisfy Ideas. In failing to do so, if the Terror of 1791 is not affirmed, negative judgment is made; but with positive sublime feelings, the imagination must make a presentation that allows for synthesis of the type whereby an Idea of humanity is conserved *that* the Terror is necessary. The Idea of humanity, or humanity's progress, of history as the medium of human realization, is secured on the sublime feeling of an incommensurability between Ideas and their presentation, a failure that acts as subjective and group cause "of having to supply a presentation for the unpresentable." Signs are what we have. Enthusiasm is such a sign-feeling: it requires a presentation that cannot be directly proved but drives itself further into the mediums of signification, continuously affecting its possessors. There is no denying that in moving toward Kant's discursive arrangements about history and signs, Lyotard theorized history as closer to pathology. Although a sign, enthusiasm is also an affection where a possible "nothingness" of experience is experienced, "an energetical *sign,* a tensor." At the time, the French Revolution was both attracted and repulsed, an "agitation on the spot"; its many signs required a subjective wager on them.[50]

As Lyotard reads Kant, historical connection as such is thus established on the basis of sublime feelings. The formlessness and potential unfigurability of events and actions, their indeterminacy, presupposes a capacity of the subject to experience history as *sense and confusion,* inseparable from sign-interpretation. While the form of narrative is also inseparable from an obvious practical rationality, say the ability to join, or not, movements of different kinds, narrative form is also part of self-deception. One makes mistakes in choosing and interpreting signs. Insofar as feelings are both constructed but not just constructed, they are amenable to inclusion in what Lyotard called the *dialectical, cognitive,* and *moral* genres. These genres have classically addressed the *claims of history,* but in good forms that annul the experience of the sublime. Consequence: *new experiences are turned into historical experience;* enthusiasm, or any equivalent feeling, can contest historical narration, not confirm it. An ever-presence of sense and confusion. The genres of historiography (e.g., epic history, lyrical, etc.) are dependent upon a condition of representability—subjective feelings—which they cannot account for, not without potentially unraveling. Written history can then be conceived as sometimes the *destruction of events, elimination of events* that fall outside the protocols of recognized feelings. Even more strongly, *signs* indicate that things have happened that require phrases that have not been said, and may not be sayable: one has a feeling that the American middle class has voluntarily chosen formal democracy as a means of preserving economic self-interest, sacrificing Ideas of critique to subjective narcissism; could narrating such feelings *prove* their historical validity?

In "The Sign of History," and other writings, Lyotard worked back to that territory ploughed by Nietzsche, especially picking up the idea that historians must not have the last word(s) on anything of intellectual dispute. An event transmits an excess and surplus that might sabotage the historian's carefully chosen criteria of judgment, so long as we let ourselves be affected by signs. What is frequently called the subject of modernity and postmodernity may be a split subject, in trauma, schizo, obsessively practical, and surely more all at once, but when such conditions do not lead to more uncomfortable, discordant affects, or people are affected morally and aesthetically, *and not cognitively,* as Nietzsche put it, the feeling of the sublime gives way to historicization: "the man who has once learned to crook the knee and bow the head before the power of history nods 'yes' at last, like a Chinese doll, to every power, whether it be a government or a public opinion or a numerical majority; and his limbs move correctly as the power pulls the string. If each success has come by a 'rational necessity' and every event shows the victory of logic or the Idea, then—down on your knees quickly, and let every step in the ladder of success have its reverence!"[51] More hard words from our hard case.

Thus, if normal historical writing continues to reduce past-future to the dominance of present actualities—consider the number of books on empire—other writing must let "signs" fulminate, where they might "push philosophy and politics into a reflexive, critical mode, to defer indefinitely the imposition of an end on the historical-political process."[52] Endless—this is one of the results of Lyotard carrying analytic criticism into contemporary historicism. This sense of without-end, in all of its ramifications, is a disavowal of historicism and its ever-present aestheticism—the finality of narrative-form set against recalcitrant events. In this sense, Lyotard's discourse on these matters is intended to *neutralize* our use of the past and the future—in the name of a disruption of the present's lines of access to past and future. His work makes alliance with resistance to historiography, but does not offer a new role for the scholar. The sublime sense or feel for the unpresentable is not another intellectual hunting license for the imposition of temporal cleansing, but a perpetual suspension of any Idea, aesthetic, political, or moral, that tries to "correct existence," as Nietzsche put it in *The Birth of Tragedy*. After all is said and done (how easy to slide into historicizing), isn't it the job of the historian to provide such corrections? Isn't this why such reverence for historians like Isaiah Berlin was shown?

Lyotard's reflections on historiography turned the latter into a zone of such intense contestation that his work has simply befuddled the vast majority of historians—but they prefer it that way. Always insisting on some mode of transcendence—the transcendence of facts; the naturalness of narrative; the demand for closure; the need for the soul to have resolution of its temporal fate—the historical profession continues to believe in its own essential ground or mode of deployment—"telling the truth" is the most often heard phrase. Let us recall Nietzsche's arguments, in their mixture of literary and philosophical discourse attached to the dangers of rhetoric, which is so singular of his writing: what is wrong with historical discourse or historical culture is that it serves to give the actual the form of an apology; it turns narrative into aesthetic pleasure, the most destructive things wrapped in discourse, narrating a passing-away more powerful than a passage-to. A typical historical narrative has the effect, Nietzsche and Lyotard as one on this, of installing the "blind power of the actual."

"After" Lyotard, historiography might be discussed as that kind of writing that does not really want readers as much as it craves admirers, aestheticism affirming itself through political-moral significations. The authors of a recent work on the historian's practice acknowledge that narration is often fictitious or mythical, but the need for identity is greater than the hazards: "narrative is essential both to individual and social identity. It is consequently a defining element in history-writing, and the historiographical tradition . . . is an important element in identity, both for historians in a profession and for citizens in modern societies."[53] Identity before narration, identity after narration; the withdrawal of the sublime—is it really difficult to understand that investment in this transcendence of identity is the actual discursive subject of a typical historical text? Lyotard also gives us writing that is an on-the-spot resistance to the rehistoricization of the sixties and after. He stayed in the breach—of writing's flight from the rationalization of the negative.

The commitment to a different criticism, notably theorized by Roland Barthes as the possibility of all sorts of middle voices, remains open. Consonant with experimentation and middles, there bolts through Lyotard's texts Nietzschean joys and exhilarations toward the welcoming of events without *to historicize,* infinitive mode. "Not to drag their generation to the grave" was the injunction of Nietzsche's unhistorical and superhistorical, self-experimental quasi-subject, manifested in Lyotard's writings, among other phrases, as experimentation with subjectivity, this to the point where one might "invent allusions to the conceivable which cannot be presented."[54] Of this, contemporary historiography knows almost nothing.

8 | *The Genealogy of History according to Deleuze and Guattari*

The genealogy of historical knowledge remains a tentative project. It invites speculation. The linguistic, social, and cognitive workup of historical knowledge suggested by Barthes and Lyotard focused on contact between acts of selection and the determined—a determined narration, thoroughly aestheticized, often structured with shaky epistemic assumptions, takes the place of the referent. Between text and reader, the reader has to implicitly say, "I will not confuse word and thing," but they are thoroughly saturated in the other, already. Readers are not asked to separate aesthetics and epistemology, an interesting thing to do, but highly political, since that separation is required for a text to be considered knowledge and not merely interpretation. What historians write is at odds with senses of knowledge, which might be why Polan, as we saw in chapter 4, was so perplexed by the image of historians.

Historiography invites speculation as to its formation. One of the most well-known essays on the subject is Foucault's, from the late sixties, "Nietzsche, Genealogy, History." Foucault's sense of genealogy is an approach to known and unknown materials that maintains aporia toward historians and historical knowledge—toward the form of story. Genealogy, Foucault writes, acknowledges that "the world of speech and desires has known invasions, struggles, plundering, disguises, ploys . . . from these elements . . . genealogy retrieves . . . the singularity of events outside of any monotonous finality . . . it rejects the metahistorical deployment of ideal significations and indefinite teleologies."[1] Genealogy asks if *history* is the right name for the complex we call past/present use and abuse, and historical narration appropriate to the dissemination of temporal continuities and anomalies? What serves as boundary between the historian and other narrators, and what should we study to glean the effects of historical knowledge in society? Why endless histories of the "founding fathers" instead of monstrous histories of Los Angeles or New York building and safety departments, which might show us better how things work? The genealogical pressure is to ask whether history, inclusively, is a cultural and intellectual complex of not fully known social value. It pursues issues of writing history without losing sight of social bonds implied. Speculation is inevitable on a form of writing life that itself seems to have no clear boundary.

For example, each of the following propositions concerning historical knowledge is "true," of course not in the same way: historical knowledge has never happened, only the circulation of hypotheses about the past, thus historical knowledge can never but begin; historical knowledge cannot give us the truth of end, but ends are offered anyway; historical knowledge is myth for moderns; historical knowledge—as record—is all there is. Each of these propositions, and many more besides, compete in claims that smuggle *some* degree of speculation into even the most resistant empirical reflections, descriptions, and narrations that claim to deploy historical knowledge. These speculations tie beginnings to ends, ends to ends, beginnings to beginnings, ends to beginnings. "Substantive philosophy of history," Arthur Danto has written, always tells a story "before the story can properly be told," but there can be no "story of history as a whole," this because "philosophy of history is an intellectual monster." Yet such "monstrousness" cannot be prevented from invading syntax, even if it has no place in description and textual organization.[2] A genealogy of telos would show how the concept, not its assumed identity, is put to various functions, historical knowledge only one of its adventures and coherences. For example, the professional historian's presumption that post–World War I skepticism and relativism led to Nazism, that in modernized societies like Germany or the United States, right-wing solutions follow from social and cultural upheaval, is a proposition shared by many different political groups, and is anything but a speculation at the level of practical thought, where it serves as warning, as a curse on skepticism, a badge of faith separating historians from skeptics.[3] Speculation is transdiscursive and, in the broadest way, concerns then the metaphysics of historical thought—which senses of being and becoming it offers. The German critic of posthistory, referred to in the introduction to this book, dismisses it, calling it a "negative utopia peculiar to the loss of perspectives in the advanced industrialized societies." The historian can still be a good helper, a good provider, a mediator, if he or she makes historical knowledge something "to support the subjectivity of individuals in their historical perception of themselves . . . [instead of] the truth of great systems." Against so-called postmodern doubts, each individual can obtain through "historical groundwork" a way of "opening" the "apparent certainties . . . of experience," a speculation that supposes we are still to be historicized and are not already overhistorical.[4] Any cogent genealogy of historians / historical knowledge would definitely have to consider why we are constantly called "to history" after we have received so much history already.

So how can one say with certainty what the components are, of necessity, in making a genealogy of historical knowledge that does not violate "fact" and is not too speculative? Better: how are certain speculations legitimized by historians / historical knowledge? After all, the sense of historical groundwork for present decisions is fraught with possible misreadings, overestimations of agents and agencies and much more. A genealogy would have to focus on the training of the historian, but exactly what makes such training different from other humanistic professions (it is widely believed literature is part of self-help while history is part of a bigger realism) and how does it show itself? A genealogy might try to measure the impact of university-based readings of history on the formation of students after they leave university, examining such constructs as "breadth" and "depth" of education. Or consider textual materials. There are many genealogies of narrative, of course, but are narrative modes such as the enthymeme, *ekphrasis* (vividness), or plot-coherence always connected to the good faith of historians, when such forms are often used for distortion? A genealogy would have a lot to say about use and abuse of facts (Ian Hacking's work is valuable on this), but with which distinctions introduced into the concept—when should one apply the distinction between "hard" and "soft" facts? Might a present genealogy of historical knowledge consider what happened with American Sovietology which, after half a century of support from the American State, claims it had no idea of the collapse immanent in the events of 1989? Joel Fineman, as discussed in chapter 5, thinks historical knowledge has a genealogy traceable to the anecdotal form, interruptions of narration. In this view, history, requoting Jacques Rancière from chapter 4, is a form of thought "because there is speech in excess, words that cut into life, wars of writing. And there is a historical science because there is something written that quells these wars and scars these wounds." While that is true of language as much as history, Rancière's words evoke Michelet—the historian is connected to the positive "will of the people"—while "quells" evokes Der-

rida's *Specters of Marx,* with its demand for a new scholar of historical ghosts, genealogy here offering the historian as perpetrator of "vision" (Rancière) and representor of past phenomenological insights recorded by past agents (Fineman).[5]

Still speculating, genealogy seems close to connoisseurship, where it
fetishizes the rare, the exemplar, the "only once," but genealogy prefers to operate out of mixtures of curious skepticism and some humor toward all things
cultural, especially seizing upon origins overvalued and made icons of delirious identifications in the present.[6] The American historian Gordon Wood tells
us that it was not so much "constitutional inventions" that generated the
founders of America, but their "Englishness," which continued into American
society, and represents "the common sense of the American people throughout
our entire history," the doubling of "throughout" and "entire" markers of resistance to genealogical impurities.[7] Genealogy brought to cultural analysis
serves as a wild card, allergic to the impositions of what is demanded as timely.
Why does genealogy pressure historiography? It asks what credibility should
be given to historical writings when they depend upon identification structures transmitted by "ordinary" discourse. Genealogy awakens the humor of
skepticism analytically applied to ideals of culture, whereas historiography installs verbal monuments, concepts of a subject and necessity engineered to
bolster narrative models—as in the Cartesian subject, the technological subject, or even the new and so timely subject, the "hybrid" we "all" are now. Historiography can be evaluated as language's use of time so as to assign *finality*
and *last words,* but genealogy says historiography partially comes out of suppressive aspects of law, from forms of cultural evaluation, as in the phantasm
of neutral third parties who mix judging and connoisseurship; genealogically,
historians derive from despotic survivals of political terror, sentimentalisms
forgotten but nonetheless lethal, and other modes of passive nihilism. Historians may be "grey" cultural operators, as Dana Polan thought, but their genealogy should not come second to their own historical self-legitimation. Foucault insisted that genealogic readings undo any sense of identity suggested by
historical knowledge, preferring to "isolate the different scenes . . . [and] different roles" of action.[8] Michel de Certeau has suggested one think of the contemporary genealogy of historical knowledge as schizoid: the historian is
stretched between such functions as making explanations that "nag" at their
readers and offering "exceptions" and "particularities" that involve a ceaseless
ridiculing of overcoherent "theory."[9]

In this chapter, I focus on the specific genealogy of history as raised in
Gilles Deleuze and Félix Guattari's *Anti-Oedipus,* drawing as well on other

writings by Deleuze. In addition to specifying the uniqueness of *Anti-Oedipus*'s metahistorical or speculative transformation of the concept of history, it is a question of accounting for historiography's resistance to genealogy. Ordinary historical writing, Isaiah Berlin told us, has no genealogy—it is just common sense narrativized. Frank Ankersmit insists, strangely, that the genuine assignment of the historian is to occupy a place between truth and life, "beyond truth but where life is not yet," taking the measure "when the past and a former identity define ourselves in terms of what we are no longer."[10] The surety here to historiography as consciousness of periodization is itself an antigenealogical premise—how did periodization become so fixed, so rigid?

From *Nietzsche and Philosophy* (1962) to *What Is Philosophy?* (1991), Deleuze and Guattari wrote no "critique of pure history." Nonetheless, I would now like to bring together many of the arguments that arise from their genealogy of history. In chapter 2, I discussed the People's Republic of China's insistence that Taiwan has always been part of China, where "always" and "part" operate as false continuity in the service of unification, or discursive terror against Taiwan. Two questions then: what does a conceptual genealogy of history imply for criticism of misleading narratives? And, in favor of a complex sense of historical transformation, what is the force of the enigmatic idea that "Becoming does not belong to history"?[11]

Speculative Philosophy of History

Anti-Oedipus (1972) continues the Nietzschean account of the concept of history. First of all, how should we interpret the conjunction of Statist or despotic writing and historiography? One historiographer has it that this conjunction shows "the prose in history came by way of city chroniclers . . . busied in the Ionian cities . . . in carrying back [their] story to Homer's heroes . . . they took material from temple and civic records . . . broke away from verse and put their 'sayings' into prose. This in itself was a real liberation . . . One must recall the whole situation—the vague chronology, the involved calendar, the unreliable genealogies, the comparative absence of even bad material concerning the past."[12] Is the basic issue how time was brought under the control of language, bureaucratization mixed with commemoration? This is a thicket of contention among many researchers, across the disciplines today. But it was no accident that the State and historiography summoned each other, even with a lot of variability. For example, by the death of Alexander the Great, at least three kinds of historical writing were recognized from surviving texts, the majority of them for "excitement and entertainment," pleasure and reality not yet separated, suggesting despotic regimes flexible toward culture.[13]

Anti-Oedipus develops notions of production and antiproduction by asking as to the processes of group and subjective "desiring-machines," whose most infamous actualization is the notorious Body without Organs, a process and story at once of intensity and failure.[14] *Anti-Oedipus* argues that we can speak to senses of history by speculating on metahistorical patterns—the Body without Organs, like the egg it is patterned after, is both a structure of existence (states of existence, names, brains, minds, body parts) yet comes at the *non-end* of capital, even if built-in as one the outcomes or ends of capital. At the very least, *Anti-Oedipus* begins in paradox: schizophrenia as both cause and effect. Obviously, the idea of any first form of history will be partly fictional and speculative, and *Anti-Oedipus* dramatizes the emergence of history and subjectivity together in three phases: savage, barbaric, and capital.

Genealogically, this emergence of a subject of history belongs to the convergence of narrative structures with political authority, a cultural-political fusion. This is seen in the idea of the "juridic person," detached from the earth, or where division of labor has segmented socially necessary tasks. Or was it the formation of ancient "single reigns," "in which the royal scribe had every incentive to tell a striking story, dress it up in the details of actuality" that gives an origin to historical writing?[15] Much of *Anti-Oedipus* is structured as a nearly classically modulated narrative of development (consonant with Fineman's discussion of Thucydides), but with a twist: the notion of a first or unique subject required overcoming savage paranoia—groups that held fast to the idea that they had something worth losing—initiation rites, attachment to the earth, animisms, obsession with evil. For these groups, "it is in being marked . . . tattooed . . . the original subject of obligation is not the persona, the subject as autonomous . . . it is my . . . productive body parts which have been incorporated into the social code by being marked, inscribed, incised . . . couplings of organs." Such societies were *inscriptive,* not literary or narrative. They were not based on contracts, legislation, or exchange, but on the coupling of organs to the *socius.*[16] Ritual and ecstasy are not conceived as forms of exchange, but as the power of celebrants: "The Dionysiac frenzy thus induced *enthusiasmos,* by which the god entered into and possessed the celebrant."[17] What we still call narrative cohesion makes a "miracle" of social unity because the *socius* was disrupted by the *disinvestment* of group relations that were "always partial, following the compact, agglutinated series of ancestors, and the fragmented series of companions and cousins."[18] Savage societies code their existence, but in such a way as to rely on the "use of scission to exorcize fusion, and impedes the concentration of power . . . primitive societies are not outside history; rather it is capitalism that is at the end of history" (*AO,* 153). A savage *socius* uses *ambiguous* signs, which are not felt to be exclusively positive or negative, and which are not yet attached to signs that belong to "an extensive somatic memory, created from filiations that have become extended and from the alliances that they imply." It is only when "'either / or else' replaces the intense 'either . . . or . . . or'" that we arrive at fixed names, whose "appellations no longer designate intensive states, but discernible persons. Discernability settles on . . . persons" (*AO,* 160). Of course these same savage societies also invented conjunctions between *cruelty and memory* (*AO,* 185), the topic of Nietzsche's *Genealogy of Morals* and many other commentaries.

A second phase, despotic succession or absorption of the savage, brings with it repression and destruction of an affirmation of "biocosmic memory." Separated from the earth as a *socius,* this second mode ushers in "a collective memory of the spoken word and of alliances . . . that endows . . . faculties of resonance and retention, of selection and detachment . . . a memory straining toward the future" (*AO,* 190). Borrowing from Nietzsche that this second movement is based on debtor-creditor relations, it creates an internalized structuring of memory, obligation, promise, and mourning. Language incorporates the actions and passions of bodies, and relies on mental deliriums, formed by "recording the process of production," writing absorbing inscription, giving a "true consciousness of a false movement." Narrative discourse requires that contentious significations disappear below established thresholds of recognition—to protect the more dependent social bonds of obligation and subjective personification. Telos makes itself known in direct alliances between a subject and that which gives transcendence to the vicissitudes of subjectivity, a group/subject's fragility as it moves toward political solidity.[19] Here too enters the alliance or synthesis between aesthesis, narrative, and politics: each works to install in the other form the deterritorialized signs from which their unity wards off disunity or difference, a reterritorialization. Well-told, sequenced hierarchy: the first Western historical narratives, like the ones we continue to make, are "miracles" of continuity between language and things. Most of all, narrative aesthesis creates a subject riveted to the invisible, to nonpresence: prose is superb at generating hierarchies as its form threads its readers to the invisible, mentalistic sense, and significance. God wills it, your ancestors desire it, to be true to yourself, you must do . . . , "miraculations" not just of sense and continuity, as all narratives are, but removal of self and groups from a life that should not be lived, placed now in the past. This historiographic "operation" (de Certeau) had much to do with the removal from language of the virtual, or intellectual turbulence brought under the smoothness of syntax and semantic determination, narrative itself "furnishing or realizing surplus value." Vico thought this code-switch could be seen in the Roman Twelve Tables, which still echoed primitive society, but which gave way to the legal act of testamentary succession, or law arising out of domestic authority.[20]

Despotism secures the "recording rights" necessary for state functions or, in fact, any relation based on narrative identity—agreement precedes disagreement. The paranoia associated with a first, savage phase was read as the persistence of nonidentitarian actions, once historiography became an attraction machine, an "enchanted recording or inscribing surface that arrogates to itself all the productive forces and all the organs of production, and that acts as a quasi cause by communicating the apparent movement (the fetish) to them." The historian Gordon Wood's "founding fathers," discussed earlier, is in fact a good example of this historiographic arrogation and fetishism. This "recording surface" generates narratives of succession and filiation and the reduction of events to continuous lines of force. Historical narratives are one with the bureaucratization of culture, as we understand the term, requiring a prose discourse that can regulate concepts as to their combinations with other signs so as to effect the protection of hierarchies.[21] Historiography becomes for Westerners the narrative form that appears as "the absence of deliberate partisan purpose," what we now call the narrative that seems to tell itself (Barthes), which displaced the "biocosmic memory" not yet immersed in debtor-creditor relations. These tangles are suggested in the lost historiography of Posidonius, who "thought in terms of imperial cycles" informed by magic, not yet in political commitments to a power center based on royal names stamped as monograms on hard surfaces.[22]

Historical thinking is impossible in savage societies where the mode of social inscription, the signified or the represented of a representation, "has not yet taken the place of the representative" (*AO*, 165). In savage or paranoid (not a pejorative) societies, people do not think in terms that one sign actually includes the sense of other signs. Dynamic savage thinking disputes representation when it gives itself an autonomous function, someone speaking for some "no-thing." In such societies, interpretation is still *assessment* of forces to contend with instead of affirming an alliance with emerging powers. Lyotard summed this up by saying that savages think and speak in the suspension of "one" true story, true outcome or true political filiation, a commitment to disrupt narrative politics.[23]

Savage inscription reached its limits through intercourse with power centers. The chieftain is usurped by barbarian despots who claim direct filiation with a god and who bring "a memory of words" to bear on an entire group. Deleuze and Guattari's genealogy asks about the costs paid to make historiography a medium co-coded with retrieval, with blocking its rivals, stressing its new projections, screens, filters, and all the devices by which societies approve and disapprove the *recounted*. Repressed in this attachment of memory to words-in-debt was "the great mute, intense filiative memory, the germinal flux as the representative of the noncoded flows of desire capable of submerging everything." If one likes, they are trying to unfold a conceptual moment of historical narrative, a mode of telling severely political—the elimination of rivals, or intolerance toward difference. Once language is hitched to memory it closes off subversive connections of desire, memory reduced to and co-coded with the timings of debt, language given over to a recalling, retention, and protention. At the close of the savage phase, there was an already large accumulation of alliance-debt, nurtured by sacerdotalists urging their audiences to commit to political filiations, to abandon their own modes of conflict. The steles of Xian to this day testify to administrators and bureaucrats cutting and carving their ancestry/prestige into their present, addressing the inducements of "a fictitious voice" (*AO*, 188), that of the emperor, or their family, as well as the gods. The same words might let one pay a debt to one's ancestors as one proved one's fidelity to political authorities. By the time of Hesiod (700 BCE), "the past had acquired not only something akin to continuity but also a direction." The "datelessness" of Homer's *Iliad* gave way to concerns over rise, fall, decline, and all the related terms of telos and end we are more than familiar with.[24] Interestingly, the Greeks produced "no real history . . . until in the climax of its civilization," its oblique relations between inquirer, truth-seeker, and arbitrator unsettled; interest in hard facts comes *late*, but was still so fluid that "histor" could apply to Polybius as well as to the actions of a painter.[25]

Against the oral and vocal richness as well as graphisms of the savage, a graphics independent of a central voice, prose subordinated distinctive voices. Nietzsche tells us in *The Birth of Tragedy* about art that voices or speaks into the abyss to ask if it would have been better not to have lived, a horrific but necessary test of becoming. But the abyss of prosaic representation catches and pulls toward itself or appropriates what it writes against, and folds what it opposes into incorporated synthesis. The earliest historical narratives make future events conform to existing powers as much as possible. In place of the pagan organization of bodies by voice-audition, hand-graphics, and eye-pain (realized in cruelty or torture), subjects incorporate direct filiations, a time of the Cities and Deserts: "no longer the bush paranoiac and the encampment or village perverts, but the desert paranoiac and the town perverts" (*AO*, 193), which applies to Roswell, New Mexico, and Los Angeles, as these latter cities have as much to do with Ulan Bator in the thirteenth century as they do with the history of California in the twentieth, genealogically considered (centers of politics, centers of culture, nomads on the prowl, hunters and thieves all over the place, as "genealogy" here means types).

As despotism flourished, the Body without Organs "organizes" itself into military and religious hierarchies, each of these hierarchical groups deployed against other territorial inscriptions, territorial systems, a double movement of centralization and local independence. At the same time, the despot and his representations detach themselves, or jump out of the social chain, erecting a social machine, a megamachine, a pyramid, a despotic apex, an immobile motor, an extensive "bureaucratic apparatus at its lateral surface and its transmission gear, and the villagers at its base, serving as its working parts." A synecdoche for these processes is alphabetic writing, which overwhelmed other signifying regimes. Before Thucydides there were mixed narratives (e.g., of firstborn, of euphemisms) (*AO*, 196), which, interestingly, puts *Anti-Oedipus* in a contrary position to Derrida's insistence on the suppression of writing. For Deleuze and Guattari, despotic writing, the grafting of a text to the name of a power and to the perpetuation of writing the future, goes so far back as to call into question exactly what kind of liberation it is *to write*, infinitive mode. (Suspicion toward language-as-rationalization accompanies every text Deleuze and Guattari wrote; indeed, some of the most hostile writing ever directed against metaphor can be seen in chapter 4 of their *Thousand Plateaus*).

It was the need for taxes and servicing a widening debt that was the tipping factor of intellectual/cultural frictions over the future: obligations coming from the past belonged to "the infinite creditor and infinite credit, this to linearize and discipline" (*AO*, 197). Language and guilt were co-coded because internal states of feeling and signs are co-coded. The multiple functions of the prefix *re* were reduced in the language-matrix so as to privilege negative repetitions—the discipline of obedience. Imperial discourse, the long period of codification of law was not separable from prisons, walls, barriers, schools included. There was no doubt great pleasure in this, for many to identify with religious-political masters, a school master, or *Socrates,* if one takes Nietzsche's *Birth of Tragedy* as appropriate. The cities have walls, towers, and alleys: since each is predicated on a disjunctive synthesis (exclusion), historiography is intrinsic to such overcoded places and machines, as well as burgeoning anonymities. Into this mix, *Anti-Oedipus* makes the decisive cultural/literary moment the synthesis of historiography and bureaucratic functions, and gives historical writing a genealogy that is *extractive and reactive:* "Legislation, bureaucracy, accounting, the collection of taxes, the State monopoly, imperial justice, the functionaries' activity, historiography: everything is written in the despot's procession" (*AO,* 202). So historiography is "first" in writing's extension of passive nihilism, its promotion of centers of subservience, for it is now the eye "that . . . sees the word" (*AO,* 204), the eye reduced to reading orders instead of appraising, which, as late as Kant's flirtation with distant savage thoughts, was considered a source of aesthetic distinction. No more does the eye move within the field of its coexistence, in which this "origin" of historiography is hardly about the exquisite continuity between writing and world than it is the successful incorporation of the dangers of suspicion and resistance to despotic functions, big and small. Perhaps all historical texts have something of life and death, as the historiographer Ankersmit thinks, but that is a generality that could be said of any cultural type (literature, art).

Anti-Oedipus focuses on historiography in the moment when its form indicates that social contention is transformed into the "most minute permutations . . . a response to the new situation or a reply to the indiscreet questioner" (*AO,* 12). Historiography is a way of reading the events of the world because the world has been reduced to history, i.e., places from which alliances are made and broken, power centered. Historiography even anticipates opposition to its own power, for it survives by outflanking other narratives, by inventing a reduction—*injunctive inscription*—to linearize temporality as an initial move in controlling it, temporal disjunctions disappearing into the line-by-line concoction of narrative continuities so severe that reading is barely able to offer much of a disruption. In some stories, Greeks considered the "histor" the wise man who knew the tribal customs and who could make inquiry and story cohere. Before/after, philosophically and critically considered, became part of the madhouse of the world, a *political* standard of measuring and hence obstructing the production of time.

It is in this second mode, again, coded as despotic, miraculating and incorporative, where the real is turned into signs held to be continuous with necessities and obligations and true to things signified. This is also then the politics of the "miracle" of centralization and hierarchy: the historian has a genealogy with sacerdotal and military aims, an inscriptor who finds inside other inscriptions yet further hidden inscriptions, like a priest or seer and, like the politician and lawyer, who gives the "miracle" of verbal proof and symbolic incarnation congealed through a story. Not magic, but mythmaking of settled names and lineage is what mattered. Facts and symptoms, part of Greek medical thought, were subsumed by causal thought, itself reduced to the pragmatics of linearity, presupposing an interest in *outcomes,* just as language was reduced to a *peace treaty* (Nietzsche) between terms of disagreement. A name for this is the triumph of the vicarious. In things cultural/political, a continuous delirium of historiography runs from Thucydides to the present: the narration one reads takes the place of one's experience of the real. It will be possible and then mandatory to compare a life to a story. Later, much later, that ambiguous celibate, Roquentin (*Nausea*), will try to stop incorporating the deliriums of inquiry and fact. Roquentin will *re*treat to literature.

That is not all there is to this synthesis of historiography—State, incorporation, and language shunted into the proprieties of prose. *Anti-Oedipus* insists that historiography's cultural/political interests are entirely destructive of the virtual in the name of supporting the actual: historical representation bears "witness for a vanquished despot who still functions" (AO, 207). The historian operates two levers, one active/reactive and one passive/reactive. In the first mode, historians strive to give a synthesis of previously inassimilable materials, offering new "gregarious identifications" for lost souls, giving new enthusiasms and new repulsions. We can see this today in the recent public presentations over Germans who "suffered" from the Allied bombing runs of 1940–45, who have not had their story told till now—those who claim we now wish to be heard before we die, for we are victims, too. Historiography legislates over these names. "Give us our historical due"—as if that were different from "give us our psychological comfort." In the second mode, the historian reimparts the significations of culturally necessary truths so as to rank and thus protect preexisting libidinal or other investments in institutions. We can see this at work in the surplus of books on recent American art history, where Warhol is the "true precursor" of postmodernism set against Rauschenberg's art strategies, Warhol "smarter" than his rival because Warhol "knew" Rauschenberg's tactics to be outmoded.[26] Contemporary art is full of hyper, hysterical, and historicist mixtures over recognition and memory, just as American literature still shifts between cosmopolitanism and regionalism and their precursors.[27]

As rendered in *Anti-Oedipus,* historiography codifies infinitive forms of identification that are also forms of avoiding narrative complication, and makes inevitable the logic of the least worst: what has happened and happens now is the devil one has to live with. Every individual and group is organized by this pressure, especially once historiography is embedded in narratives of learning, manuals, symbolized everywhere (coins, paintings, etc.). In the first paragraph of his *History,* Thucydides says that he wrote his work because the Athenians and Peloponnesians went to war and "it might even be said to affect the world at large," Thucydides giving us *an historic war,* and therefore his own text was to be read, as he put it, as an "everlasting possession, not a prize composition that is heard and forgotten." It will be remembered. Thucydides made an alliance and perpetuated a debt: the alliance is to the truth as vivid (*enargheia*), which is a way to stabilize names, and the debt is to memory. But this memory achieves its goal by coding a flux of *surplus desire* in opposition to "nocturnal intensities," now submerged, as it were, in the light of visibility. "Nocturnal intensities" is neither a psychological nor a psychoanalytic category, but "becoming" as it is sliced off into sections of representations that attract attention but avoids inciting public upheaval. Historiography employs the specific devices of mental resonance, retention, selection, and detachment, modalities of the inscription of memory. In this, Thucydides announced membership by historians in a "new perverse group," whose purpose was to spread the "fame and power" of a despot, whether person or institution, ideal or thing. "Wherever a despot and his army pass, doctors, priests, scribes and officials are part of the procession," a system of code, orders, exclusions, not territorial markings, but reterritorializations (*AO,* 192–93).

This genealogy involves historical thinking in an overcoding function, which *Anti-Oedipus* describes as "infinitivization," where "the eye sets itself to reading," a "blindness,"and "loss of vision and of the ability to appraise; it is now the eye that suffers" (*AO,* 205). To see for what purposes after we are detached from *Homo natura*? The biggest of all questions comes: "what does it mean"? People can only ask such a question once "life" is not its own answer, however it happens. "The mouth no longer speaks, it drinks the letter. The eye no longer sees, it reads" (*AO,* 206). Bodies of all kinds are disappearing into sign-bodies, i.e., the subject becomes an object of study. All this occurs in "the shadow of Oriental despotism." Prose narrations utilize codings that linearize deterritorialized signs, past and future reference incorporated in narrative fantasies, sense experience made impotent in terms of thinking the present: even life is not what history is about—once the concept of history is a singular-universal, it becomes a place where subjects deliver themselves to the "empty tomb, the dead father, and the mystery of the name" (*AO*, 209). The opening and closing, appropriately enough, of *Saving Private Ryan* pivots on the question "was it worth it," a pure psychologically driven *historical* question. Created partly to spread terror, partly to enchant or sustain unity, historical thought becomes directly cynical, once overcoding gives way to ceaseless capitalist recoding: the signifier and the signified keep slipping away from each other, rejoined in fresh deliriums. We can see this at work over the last thirty years or so: new trends in social history dissolve patriarchical models, yet immediately turn into another territory to defend. New histories of art urge there is such a thing as a singular "American Art" without challenging incorporative namings. Despotism may or may not have definitely passed as a social force, but narrative lives on through the despotism of historical representation. *Anti-Oedipus* is unsparing.

In a third phase, the "civilized capitalist machine," subjects of alliance and filiation are pressured by decoded flows: feudalism dries up in the face of a specific capitalist "creativity," and so comes the "schizoid time of the new creative break" (*AO*, 224). Time is completely out of joint. Schizophrenic opportunities increase, so to speak, and cultural movements such as psychoanalysis, one of the last sacerdotal systems, are favored because they directly repress experimentation, under the tutelage, let it be said, of progressives. Where savage society operated on *inclusive disjunctions* of production—magic and the reconciliation of different powers—and the despotic on disjunctions of inscription derived from overcoding, capitalism is established on the conjunction of production for production's sake and a deterritorialized full body, that is, any subject whatsoever stripped to abstraction/exchange. The cities gorge. Contradiction becomes the hallowed verbal space of, and for, dialectical thought. In place of the cruelty and terror of the previous phases, civilized capitalism brings with it cynicism and piety. It has broken with the identifications of the first two systems, and in fact has very little identity to lose. Subjects are integrated in the very breakdowns they encounter (*AO*, 230), no exterior limit possible, "but only an interior limit that is capital itself and that it does not encounter but reproduces by always displacing it" (*AO*, 231). New savages, outlaws, and outsiders, are produced. In the face of fascists, Nazis, and, now, managers and consumers (whose type is not settled), the favorite tactic of local despots in charge of the engines of performativity (i.e., schools) is to add cultural axioms: everyone is subject to laws, everyone is subject to arbitrariness, everyone is subject . . . ; the extraordinary proliferation of *to write about* (infinitive mode) supposes illiteracy and ignorance as active-passive modes, as writing increasingly erases (oxymoron in ecstasy?) itself in the demographics of unreadability (e.g., 99 percent of scholarly texts fall below the threshold of citability within five years, according to the experts). *Anti-Oedipus does not flinch:* writing comes under the incorporation of *written "purchasing power,"* an axiom in which lack and stupidity are transformed into products, given to consumers as what they desire, because of what they lack, what they need, because they desire phantoms of absence delivered in the here and now: *read this* (*AO*, 236–48).

The more willfully conformist people there are, the better; the more gradients (books targeted from 1,000- to 40,000-member audiences), the better. Hence full-blown representation takes place. Many historicisms. Capitalism comes to pressure historical writing, as its prior despotic forms of "in the name of . . ." have to be replaced as they compete for prestige and recognition. The idea of a Nobel Prize for one book in history per year—madness desired, institutionalized. With capitalism, representation is tied to illiteracy—dozens of millions of Americans cannot read complex writing, but our most vetted journals, like *Nature,* must ask their authors to pay a share of production costs. From micro- to macrorelations, events cannot be forgotten in creative ways because there are too few consumers for creative forgetting (some professors, some bums). Capitalism and schizophrenia get married under the "mortgage of the signifier" (*AO*, 244). Even historical knowledge starts to disappear in providing despotic unity in the face of incessant recoding and deterritorialization.

History and Cultural Schizophrenia

The macronarrative of *Anti-Oedipus* makes this third temporal pattern, a schizo phase, drastically affect historicity and language. As I have suggested, especially in the first chapter, discursive organization has close affinities with despotism, particularly as concerns standards of representation, its usages. De Landa asks us to consider language and social replication, enforced repetition, discourse giving reference and group membership simultaneously.[28] Historiography, in this third phase "indicates what is going to be done, something that the shrewd or the competent are able to decode." Imagine and plan the future—what's the difference? Within a system of immanent recoding of sur-plus-value, capitalized societies accelerate and restrict negotiation between "ar-chaism and futurism, neoarchaism and ex-futurism, paranoia and schizophre-nia" (*AO,* 260). These names of movement pretty well characterize time out of joint or the attractions and repulsions of historiography in the contemporary art world.

As capitalism incorporates its produced undergrounds, the power to make signification belongs to those who can find an audience, mediators, whether or not recognitions provided by "high culture" still matter, or obtain. Minor despotisms proliferate, traced in advance by employment patterns, as in the shift from 70 percent to 30 percent of regular teaching positions for American academics. New command posts emerge—what adds value to new capital flur-ries of investment and disinvestment requires managerial authority, new law. There is no doubt that *Anti-Oedipus* speaks to issues of telos: "schizophrenia as a process is desiring-production, but it is this production as it functions at the end, as the limit of social production determined by the conditions of capital-ism." And: "The end of history has no other meaning" (*AO,* 130). Speculative and determinative at once? This "end of history" invokes a New Age, the *aco-herence* of many groups that operate at disjunctive angles to each other, medi-ated by intractable recoding. The scholarly, line-by-line restoration of every word written by Mark Twain is where many of the resources of scholarship are brought to bear on making a small segment of the past complete, totalized, at the same time that the application of Twain's texts to the society are largely ir-relevant in terms of informing present cultural entanglements; we cannot let the classics go, but our use of them shows our bad faith, keeping something going that we only *believe in because to do otherwise is too hard.* This is not a "torn to pieces by history" but making events and processes in which we tear because we historicize. We are not prepared to call the present into question through the past, such a gesture itself archaic, and, more critically, current pos-itive functions, as with university entanglements with corporations, finances, student changes, and much more, satisfy the extended reach of *to survive,* which makes resistance immediately part of the scrap heap of "archaisms with a current function." Working the schizophrenia is not an abstract or airy pos-sibility in a culturally schizoid system, it is a fact.

According to Nietzsche, the transition to modernity or relaxation of imperial modes of writing in favor of those suitable for a democratic society reorga-nized the genealogy of the historian. Modern historians, he wrote, overcode everything in delirium, offer a positivism of research, and "wrap themselves in wisdom and look 'objective'; I like not the agitators dressed up as heroes, who hide their dummy-heads behind the stalking horse of an ideal; I like not the ambitious artists who would fain play the ascetic and the priest, and are at bottom nothing but tragic clowns . . . we have in our hands the possibility of idealizing the whole earth."[29]

Ceaselessly trying to provide verbal simulacra of transcendence and continuity to connect with their readers, modern historiographic writing rotates on the function of providing synthesis or a fair nonfictional mediation. The ideal remains. This is still the historian-as-third-party who gives perspective denied to first and second parties, still counting in that mode. Here returns the last reader since historians are placed in the situation of last writers, in the literal sense of offering last words on the past-present, even if this is now pressurized to install various futures as mandatory. Historians are not immune to market-driven issues, either. Set in the framing of a capitalization that ceaselessly deterritorializes names, customs, habits, forms, etc., throwing up cycles of recoding and decoding, historicism yields to psychologization, or reterritorialization, satisfying if it can gregarious identifications. There is more than one return of "states, fatherlands, families," the past offering multiple Derridean specters or new hallucinations and deliriums, the historian providing new audiences with new psychocomplexes of identification. One thinks now of the multiple histories of "places of trauma," truly a global event of representation (*AO*, 23). Notions such as lack, utopia, hope, alternative, etc., breathe and exude the speculative air that "there exists some other place that contains the key to desire (missing in this world)" (*AO*, 26). The historian's participation in lack indicates a moment of subjection of future to past, of past abruptions incorporated within inclusive disjunctions—the Americans "had to" drop the bomb on the Japanese and we must have trauma studies: we must not lack. Does this occur as historiography withdraws as an active cultural mediator (our metanarrative vessels have sprung *leaks*). Joel Fineman worried about this question—what does it take for historical knowledge to actually help generate a sense of social danger?

Developing unevenly over the past centuries, the forces that tear at historical thinking culminate in a Body without Organs, who stands in for the "residuum of a deterritorialized socius" or, in narrative terms, the impossibility of anything but stories of the moment, whether internally disjunctive or not (*AO*, 33). This is where capitalism, in applying the unyielding decoding of money-capital and labor, ceases to provide a code for the *socius*/field, and tends toward making the *socius* itself a Body without Organs. What functions can historical thinking have when the social field is schizzed-out, schizophrenia a product and process of capital, just as "manic-depression and paranoia are the product of the despotic machine, and hysteria the product of the territorial machine" (*AO*, 33)? The very idea of the modern will be, in these terms, considered a triumph of recoding the distribution of lack and negativity, the *socius* passing from "detachable partial objects to the detached complete object, from which global persons derive by an assigning of lack" (*AO*, 73). History is more than pulled to pieces as a singular universal—in its current organization, we learn to fear events.

Our Era as Schizophrenic Labor

Anti-Oedipus asks whether or not the "name that haunts all history [is] . . . simply the paternal name." Does the concept of history as such stand for power? Is it a barrier to the production of events? Historians give us images of the Great, the Exception, the Incomparable, and so on, playing with singularities, probabilities, repetitions. But these recognitions are no longer necessarily paternal, since capital cares more about functions of consumption—and historians continue to make recognitions that segregate actions and events from contamination by the wrong names. It is vitally important that public life receives infusions about Lincoln the Liberator over Lincoln the would-be exiler of blacks from the United States. How much of historiography becomes a protection of prior investments, of all kinds, in names that are linked to groups, institutions, finances, media? In the overall professionalization of the humanities contained (and being undone) by capital formations, historiography is deeply effected. Apart from the distribution of historians in processes of acculturation, among other relations, historiography must provide rules of synthesis, able to offer political and cultural instruction that relies on syntactic forms like "It's a case of . . ." How else to fuse moral and historical modes of treating objects? To nomadic and polyvocal uses of conjunctive syntheses, connections inclusive of different matters and logics from the archaic and futural, the historical and psychological install meanings that return us to fathers or forefathers, even if the forefather is a mother, an ideal, a dreaded ancestor, a . . .

Hence the strangeness of the idea of an event in schizo times. Of course this is complex material, but *Anti-Oedipus* definitely raised the ante on historiography and the social bond. No definition of a significant event can be agreed upon, once actions freely mix with prosopopoeias, renamings, giving a new imaginary charge to narratives.[30] Is an event to be conceived as the transformation of common notions, forged out of differences by joyful passions "necessary in the event"?[31] Historians work very hard to nominate things, but schizo culture extends contradictory forces into palpable oxymorons: perpetuation of racist and nationalist narratives give delirium fresh infusions while, on the other hand, we incessantly name new things and give them placement in various semiotic regimes (center, periphery, post, pre, etc.), cutting off an event's (or action's, or practice's) *own* decoding, how things are put together, as mysterious as ever across the social bond. How to speak of events in a society in which what most people do not know also informs their sense of things? It seems that in things cultural, many roads lead back to despotism through recoding. Too frequently, what happens *outside* the representation apparatus is acknowledged only if such events "are subjected to the alternative of the undifferentiated or exclusion" (*AO*, 120). The example of the painter J. M. Turner is exemplary: in relation to his own historical world, his paintings depict the end of the world, catastrophes, storms; in a second mode, they work up delirious reconstructions, archaisms modernized; finally, the paintings move toward something ageless, an eternal future, "a hole in a lake," a canvas broken, gold and fog, "traversed in depth by what has just sundered its breadth . . . breakthrough . . . not breakdown" (*AO*, 132). But that *we* have institutionalized a "Turner-model" as a way of excluding *other* paintings says something terrible. We have cultural wars over the right to affirm what is to be excluded. In the current forms or modes of cultural despotism(s)—recodings, recenterings, freshening of signification—institutions set timetables, the goal agreed upon so as to beat the competition. A cultural event (e.g., a critical text) resists if it engages an *agon*—embraces the schizo condition through "the absence of style—asyntactic, agrammatical: the moment when language is no longer defined by what it says, even less by what makes it a signifying thing, but by what causes it to move, to flow, and to explode." If capital makes it hard for experimentation, there is no alternative to the differential (*AO*, 133).

The nihilistic processes flow. But nihilism is also subjectivity's own self-evaluation—we allow ourselves to write about loss instead of creating a runaway production of criticism and pleasure. The Greek model of reconciling pleasure and reality remains an extraordinary fact. Yet problems with history give more than enough past and current reactivity to go around, since past negations have a long life. How does historical writing attract new energies and arrangements? Can it share with its readers how the dice were thrown in the past, but not to legitimize the necessity of outcomes? Why can't historical writing know what to do with conceiving events as a "differential element of corresponding values," critical and creative? Or why does historiography still offer an "indifferent element of the valuable in itself or the valuable for all," modes of omniscience and neutralization?[32] If historians have straddled the modern line between judges and novelists so as to maintain their mediative function, an event has a genealogy separate from universality and resemblance (narrations), as an event makes its own pathos of difference, not assimilated to indifference, ordinary repetition, or reaction.

Understood as schizo labor, the present is surely a burden: there are many historicisms that put events to sleep, where the very concept of an event is threatened with extinction, and the capacities to provoke further dislocations of ingrained subjectivity are weakened. *What Is Philosophy?* asked whether or not an event is *livable,* since it is the *reserve* of actuality, the what-can-happen (*WP,* 156). Historicism narrates the what-can-happen as luxury, of what might have been, as with the famous counterfactual history of slavery carried out by Robert Fogel and others. But what to do with connections that are *a*semantic, that do not lend themselves to narrative coherence? Deleuze and Guattari claim that an event that resists indifference subjugates the interpretations that are part of the resistance to it, in order to jump across chance and necessity, to turn chance into a destiny, and make multiple destinies out of different chances (*NP,* 27). This is to ask: What has becoming? An event belongs to affirmation insofar as events are fatal to the Same and to negative repetition: new beings with new attractions and repulsions, new conjunctions and syntheses *dismantle risk and chance,* assemble the dismantled into affects and concepts and functions whose precursor relations are made irrelevant. All of which requires not mourning, as we have today, but production—only runaway production can outproduce the counterproduction of capitalized relations and things. In the (conceptual) end, if there is no other measure but to compare, which the Romantics understood in their critiques of the comparative method, one should try to move toward symptomatology and semiology, readings that resist narrative incorporation of action, events shifted to issues of *coadaptation* instead of opposition and negation. In areas of criticism, coadaptation asks for well-made concepts that less measure (distancing, connoisseurship, control), but allow for "a sort of stimulation," temporal coordinates suspended: "Van Gogh takes yellow to the limitless only by inventing the man-sunflower and by laying out the plane of infinite little commas" (*WP,* 78). Such events affirm "chance and the necessity of chance; because it affirms multiplicity and the unity of multiplicity" (*NP,* 36).

Hence the current fretting about loss of memory, collective brooding about repression of the past, or demands for liberation from various inherited blindnesses are mostly rationalizations that support recoding, not conceptual disorientation, let alone configuration of new arrangements. Under many historicisms, memory remains attached to the negative projection of "fragmenting chance into chances of winning and losing," the pseudoscience of computing one's probabilities, a nihilistic downgrading of the risks of critical or experimental thinking (*NP,* 37). The fact that memory so frequently occurs in a mode of sadness testifies to, is a symptom of, melancholic pleasure: we remember sorrowfully, an echo of the sadness of "open sesame," which *Advantage and Disadvantage of History* used to construe the movement of consciousness toward the nostalgic choices it did not make, did not articulate. Memory still serves conservation, adaptation, and utility, three modes of social regulation, buttressed by habit, nutrition, and reproduction (*NP,* 41). Memory dwells with reactivity, oscillating between mechanistic aspects (automatons, grooved habit) and vitalism (delirium); both obscure the thought that "the only true science is that of activity." Activity is the ability to reach out for power (*NP,* 42), the capacity to appropriate and impose forms, "to create forms by exploiting circumstances" (*NP,* 42). Memory equalizes, reduces inequalities and counterproduces the undifferentiated (e.g., logical identity, mathematical equality, physical equilibrium, and historical continuity), which make memory "part of the nihilism of modern thought," an *adiaphoria* or indifference to the creation of potentially uncontrollable ways of doing that have no clear outcome (*NP,* 45).

Yet, on the other side of memory, there is Nietzsche's eternal return, the thought of the ahistorical: "a thought of synthesis . . . of the reproduction of diversity as such." (In chapter 2, I tried to offer Taiwan as an instance of this.) To the "once, only once" of memory/historicism, eternal return posits an open horizon: "Only action and affirmation return: becoming has being and only becoming has being," which means *reactivities of every sort* may dominate, but they have no future, even if they have a long life (*NP,* xii).

At the end of history in both its classical and contemporary modes, Deleuze and Guattari would rather speak of production. Eternal return is "itself the one which ought to belong to diversity and to that which differs" (*NP,* 46). Of course historians go mad at such utterances, but eternal return is frightening precisely because it is neither terminus nor equilibrium, nor contained by any other metahistorical reflection. In relation to overhistoricization, eternal return shows maximum skepticism toward narrative resolutions and answers. It does not ask "how becoming could have started and why it has not yet finished," as it throws more dice concerning things to be made and interpreted. Becoming may not be presence, but positively considered, "returning is the being of that which becomes" (*NP,* 48). If one's most intimate friends know that they love each other now, with loving that is not reducible to an identity across their differences, then the death of the other cannot remove the dice throws of the hows and ways by which they loved; such affirmations do come back, not as Derridean ghosts and specters leading us to new impossible ideals, but to more chances in making more selections. To revive eternal return in present-day circumstances is considered crucial by Deleuze and Guattari.

"How can the present pass?" is a question Deleuze and Guattari raise in resistance to many historicism(s). The present can pass only if it is made to stay, by coming again to serve another chance, another selection, another affirmation, another new being, another "and." As argued above, historicism(s) are unable to abandon narrative incorporation of present differences, are unable to leave the ideal of rationalizing the negative; historicism(s) must endeavor to make significations that give current audiences present necessities. "How can the present pass?" is a way of asking about an event's status—against periodization. In this, it might be required to affirm it is "returning itself that constitutes being insofar as it is affirmed of becoming and of that which passes . . . returning itself is the one thing which is affirmed of diversity or multiplicity . . . the fact of returning for that which differs." Something is done, made, that invites one to make more connections, in all senses. As capital becomes less historical and more normative, eternal return resists mechanism and related notions of time that invite finalities. Affirmation is part of selection, not automatic; eternal return is not a new cycle of temporality, but the "diversity of co-existing cycles and, above all, the existence of diversity within the cycle." It suspends the modern obsession with periodization. Which is to say that the genealogical element, "differential and genetic," matters in any situation as chances-to-add, it brings new forces into new relations. The current emphasis on trauma studies is one of our historiographic dramatic personae. Such studies—even if wracked by internal dissension over their reach and necessity—must differentiate between the choices of incomparable genocides ("only once") or recurrence (e.g., in history of science today, the death of the Neanderthal has been compared to a genocide). "Trauma studies" assumes the "differential" element of "trauma" can be possessed, that interpretation can *capture its identical movement.* But the issue is how does any notion of history become compelling without ruining the differential elements?

So historicism, positivism, fatalism, and humanism are co-coded by the modern obsession with "recovering human contents" (*NP,* 60). DNA is not safe from such exercises in recovery. Purified notions of memory proliferate, instead of memories that muddy things in an interesting way. Wedded to the identity offered by narration, historians treat narrative and event as one, not incommensurable; historians are uncomfortable with the idea that their generalized synthesis of differential elements is mythic, or that events might call for "plastic and dominating" exertions, a capacity to be affected (*NP,* 62). Art suffers, as the famous appendix to *The Logic of Sense* has it, in its becoming turned into the *timely,* which is the very way in which it self-reduces to the formulas of not offending.

Historiographic schizophrenia culminates in the demand for mediators. As mentioned, an unparalleled *third-party reaction of power against force* requires memory and language to ensure the frame of "the sufferer and the spectator," which organize each other, and requires as well managerial processing, judging contestants as to who is fit to judge all the syntheses of the negative. Genealogically, the priest-type lives on. The difficulties that obstruct events are matched by discourses that scuttle intellectual conflict: language and memory require someone "who considers the action that he does not perform—precisely because of the advantage which he draws or can draw from it. The person who does not act considers that he possesses a natural light over action, that he deserves to derive advantage or profit from it." No public intellectual in Germany can give an interview and matter of factly say, "I don't give a shit about German history, here's what I want to talk about." In this, "critique is destruction as joy, the aggression of the creator. The creator of values cannot be distinguished from a destroyer, from a criminal or from a critic: a critic of established values, reactive values and baseness" (*NP,* 87). To the historian's working in the rationalization of the negative, genealogy is asked to dismantle truth = negation or truth = transcendence—both at once—in order to emphasize the genetic and plastic; to think to the dice throws of combinations so as to weigh selections, not to claim to arbitrate like a legislator, but to investigate established values, like the feigned universality of the idea of the contract; it emphasizes the critical type instead of the reactive man; it is only interested in the past insofar as this can contribute to another sensibility (*NP,* 94).

Is it wrong to say that the connections between historical consciousness, name, memory, and reaction come together as a cultural monster? Being trained, learning to select, obeying the morality of customs, identifying all this with being timely (historicized) are the basic modes of cultural reaction. *Nietzsche and Philosophy* insists that cultural activity is mostly a matter where "the morality of customs" amounts to "the law of obeying laws" (*NP,* 133). If, as practice, culture gives reactive forces "habits and imposes models on them in order to make them suitable for being acted" (*NP,* 134), then historical culture reinforces a subject whose consciousness is "happy" with unequal comparisons, with prestige as it assimilates fugitive excitations, and can render consistency to forgetting ("you are forgetting for a reason!"), demands a memory of will, not one of sensibility (empirical stimulation), requires words that promise commitment to the future, installing a "memory of the future itself" (*NP,* 134). The genetic element of culture is expressed in the selective objects of culture: a promise to be held to in the future, which really makes unmaking the future in advance; historical culture fuses the cohabitation of training, withdrawal from events, rationalization, and debtor-creditor. Reaction is not the basis of culture, but has come to be: so the pleasure of training reactive forces "measures the suitability of reactive forces for being acted" (*NP,* 137), "preserving, organizing and propagating the reactive life" (*NP,* 139). Hence the emergence of overmediated cultures: there is a surplus of training for reactivity.

   Historicism(s) often culminate in postulating a dialectic, perhaps more frequently now a paradox. The name *dialectic* conveys the power of the negative in modes of opposition and contradiction; it gives suffering and sadness value. Often, what passes for the culturally positive is a result of the production of negation. Recall that historicist claims such as Harold Bloom's love of melancholy actually smother laughter toward history as reconciliation. Historicism, whose most perfect model is Hegelianism, inverts the cultural image of difference: it does not affirm difference, but rather affirms "the negation of that which differs; for the affirmation of self it substitutes the negation of the other, and for the affirmation of affirmation it substitutes the famous negation of the negation" (*NP,* 196). Harsh?

Conflict over interpretation manifests a chasm between historical thinking and dissensions from the historical, or genealogy affirmed as an event of interpretive analysis. Historical representation, according to Deleuze and Guattari, is hydralike, always growing another head in order to bite off a dissenting event, word, thing. Separately and together, Deleuze and Guattari always circled back to historiography as a measure of the force of reactive thought. But historiography provoked them to a conception of the production of events that would be hard to narrate. In art, philosophy, science or throughout the social bond(s), they conceived an event as *aternal,* an infinite Now, the untimely, an intensive becoming (*WP,* 112).

Metanarratives eliminate the singularities of experiences, subjective and group amalgamations of reality, deliriums, blown opportunities, extraordinary lucky breaks, strange accidents, and overdetermined economic structures—lived. *Anti-Oedipus* and the related texts discussed here do not defer to present (neo)historicisms over trying to seize the past—let the historians have the past. It does not follow, however, that historians can give adequate names and narrate the actual, which belongs to "becomings [which] pass through us today, which sink back into history but do not arise from it, or rather that arise from it only to leave it" (*WP,* 113). Events pass into becomings and out of representation. The genealogy of history leads to a reconsideration then of an event, its conceptual persona.

9 Nothing Affirmative Ever Dies
Deleuze's Notion of Time and History in *Difference and Repetition*

Gilles Deleuze's *Difference and Repetition,* first published in 1968, is explicated here strictly for its conceptual yield about historical representation including philosophical alienation *from* such representation. *Difference and Repetition* will be treated as a philosophical test of "ordinary" historical thought. It will not be treated as a text we can extract new intellectual smoothness from, although its citational value is today quite high, at least in some academic and art world areas. For example, it is common to now read statements that Deleuze's Idea of the virtual, or the Idea of eternal return give us "passage . . . to the joyful wisdom of difference," or that, in Deleuze's handling, eternal return "dissolves the habit and displaces memory for the sake of the ultimate triumph of difference." These statements make *Difference and Repetition* a bit too user- or culturally friendly.[1] To be clear: drawing on Deleuzian concepts such as multitude and machinic, in *Empire,* Michael Hardt and Antonio Negri go prophetic: "the hybridization of humans and machines is no longer defined by the linear path it followed throughout the modern period. We have reached the moment when the relationship of power that had dominated the hybridizations and machinic metamorphoses can now be overturned."[2] "No longer" and "overturned" are problematic. I propose that *Difference and Repetition* instead raises the ante about the metaphysics of *historicity* and related terms (historiality, historicism, historical representation), that *Difference and Repetition* belongs to a project of "systematic philosophy" and is not particularly useful as pragmatics. "I feel like a pure metaphysician," wrote Deleuze; and it is precisely such commitment to a metaphysics that postpones applications of Deleuze's writings to popularizing, say, a postmodern justification for nomadic or errant thought. I emphasize below that difficulties with Deleuze's philosophical system pivot on how to give the concept of difference its difference, making critical thought reflexive—inadequate word—enough to evade the traps of common and good sense in favor, here, of "opening time" to alternative movements, or the passages and ways by which the sensible becomes nonconventionally thinkable, making "time out of joint" workable for dynamic logics, intellectual and social.[3]

Deleuze's critical metaphysics of history are at work in the affirmation of the "univocity of being," almost an equivalence made among concepts of immanence and virtualization, or even the use of the word *life* "as the adequate name for being." Such statements refer philosophy to problems, not answers, where critical metaphysics is about as unfriendly to good and common sense as language can achieve.[4] Keith Ansell-Pearson, a tireless writer on Deleuze and his philosophical precursors, has it that *Difference and Repetition* is not about memory conceived as a "container" in the mind or brain, but rather with making concepts that might elucidate the "being of memory," asking how it is that memory became something so perplexing, its common notions having little to do with a number of specific and technical discourses on memory.[5] It is not clear there is a being of memory. Deleuze's arrangement of "time is out of joint" and the problems it poses are from texts written *for* the experience of reading and thinking metaphysically, a mode of writing and thinking that especially resists political and cultural extractions, even as they invite such practices that issue in word bites. *Difference and Repetition* is not only a directed critique *of* philosophical concepts such as becoming or duration, but is Conceptualism in action and differentiation in person—as language.[6] My purpose is to provide a nonreductive and minimally paraphrased presentation of those aspects of *Difference and Repetition* that raise problems of historiography, an interpretation, I hope, that will also connect with the materials of the preceding chapters.

Although Deleuze and Guattari are justly famous (or notorious) for their masterwork, *Capitalism and Schizophrenia*, *Difference and Repetition* has not attracted the same attention, no doubt because it is a profoundly undramatic book by comparison to the "hot" theses of *Capitalism and Schizophrenia*. The latter work excoriates psychoanalysis on nearly every page, and even claims that writers are often sellouts, "that is to say, any literature that takes itself as an end or sets ends for itself" panders to an existing audience instead of creating one.[7] Of *Capitalism and Schizophrenia's* analysis of subject and temporality, many commentaries have been critical, to say the least. Luc Ferry and Alain Renaut, in their *French Philosophy of the Sixties,* write that Deleuze and Guattari "contributed greatly to the methodological divestment of the 'I,'" a subject's relations to temporality turned into the "pulverized or disintegrated Ego," a project that Ferry and Renaut make into a "will to annihilation." There must be many thousands of such statements now in circulation claiming that these texts from the sixties are nihilist. They refuse to grant to Deleuze and Guattari's text any affirmative theses or projects.[8] Thomas Pavel, in a 1989 book, *The Feud of Language,* writes that *Capitalism and Schizophrenia* "is hedonistic and violent, often degenerating into intellectual acrobatics . . . theoretical ejaculations devoid of any preparation."[9] In a different tone, Fredric Jameson has called *Capitalism and Schizophrenia* "deeply suspect" for its production of concepts that he took as flawed conceptual "dualisms" that only a properly Marxist philosophy could address. That might be true: but what Jameson did not consider is that a "proper" Marxism must be a dogma, orthodoxy, church, replete with elders and initiates.[10] Better to engage dualism than stay in church?

Such negative reception to *Capitalism and Schizophrenia* is complemented with the silence attending to *Difference and Repetition* within historiography. But careful reading of this text is of utmost interest to anyone working in and around contemporary historiography or theory of history. To be more specific: the concepts discussed below do not lend themselves to a "better" historiography as much as they transform the very basis of what most political groups insist upon as the primary need and satisfaction of historical representation. In this regard, *Difference and Repetition*'s analysis of referential truth, chronology, or successivity, the use of fictional devices in the service of "reality-effects," and the historian's all-too-often acceptance of reality as-it-is indicates degrees to which historical representation has created its own blind alleys, that is, modes of historicity that confirm preexisting intellectual and political categorical relations, or reliance on what rhetoric has called topoi, accepted normative places of thought. "Places" means institutional sites and authorities for those places, such as what Derrida once called the archons or gatekeepers of the archives. This even affects countercultures: writing in *Artforum* about the history of art theory in eighties New York, Sylvère Lotringer notes that *Artforum* placed Baudrillard on the journal's masthead without asking Baudrillard—instant topoi, instant history, instant credibility.[11]

One more comment by way of introduction. No discourse can provide a mastery of time or temporality. There are substantial discourses that use analytic or philosophical rigor and that try to separate, say, tense and aspect (an important distinction). There are many models proposed by evolutionary psychology (sociobiology) that rely on inclusive concepts to account for transitions and leaps. There are existentialist terms such as *being-thrown* into history and time. All such terms add something to temporal relations and connections. For example, in *Capital Times,* Eric Alliez proposes a genealogy of how modernity is the result of a disastrous fusion between what he calls "temporalization, capitalization, and subjectivation," or *conducts* of time in the creation of pervasive social passivity or indifference toward change.[12] Alliez writes in a quasi-scientific idiom, conducts standing in for machinelike actions, functional transmitters of affect and power, even if unleashing passional aspects. On the other hand, as capitalism is felt to mine the future, terms refer to a "global process" that evokes a sense of worry. A small industry of books on such processes (e.g., syncretization) is available. Sentimentality, nostalgia, and fretting about loss are now regular topoi cutting across the human sciences' conjuring of time, as are calls for unity to knowledge in books such as E. O. Wilson's *Consilience.* R. D. Laing once gave a distinctive emphasis to the discourse of temporality: "Concussed. Fragmented scraps of memory. Poor raw, smashed Egg Head . . . groupings, orientations, crumbs, fragments, bits of the jigsaw, a few demented ravings that may help the reconstruction of the lost message."[13] By comparison to these achieved discourses on temporality, history, telos, aims, and ends, *Difference and Repetition* is treated almost as tabula rasa, a text that actually upends the good and common sense about history, one way or the other. Perhaps that is a virtue of philosophical writing, or a thinking so intense that it leaves its readers with little or nothing to go back to.[14] It should not be sufficient for those who reject criticism of historiography to object to discourses the defenders of history claim are too hard.

Repetition (Signs)

Difference and Repetition begins with an economic or quantitative distinction between generalization and repetition: to generalization belong acts of thought that make different things resemble and equal one another. "A cat's a cat" so long as two people agree on cat qualities. But to repetition there belongs "reflections, echoes, doubles and souls," modes of self-affection and comportment with others, cultural, passional, and time-specific in terms of actualization. Unlike "a cat's a cat," one can say to oneself something like, "At that moment, it occurred to me that my wife's new friend, my old friend, was no longer my friend," an address that makes more sense when timed—because it opens and closes multiple times at once, multiple feeling-thoughts, references and associations and multiple causes. With generality there is always exchange. But to repetition belongs "theft and gift," implied by the passive and active "soul-work" (contemplation) of actors and agents, theft and gift no doubt drawn from that Bakhtinian culturescape where culture is always embedded strife, where savage readings of self and others are close by. Here, situations of local individuation are set amidst conflict-ridden State building, which involves mutual obliterations of specific discourses. Think of the conjunction of law and economics in contemporary intellectual property disputes where reputation, gift, and money mix. While the Romans made use of Etruscan rituals, artifacts, and cities, they eradicated all but traces of Etruscan literature. While generalization and exchange are extrinsically linked, repetition creates reciprocity, self-implication.[15] Self-implication is a complex concept (on which more, below). Immersing his readers at the start in textual paradox, Deleuze argues that repetition, strange as it sounds, repeats something unrepeatable, and gives as the example a festival (e.g., Fourth of July) in some here and now that does elicit someone to imagine/remember an earlier event, but *carries* "the first time to the 'nth' power" (1). Perhaps this is a version of Nietzsche's "become what you are," a sense of "again" as sheer intensification, another chance to take an action and event to its limit. Be that as it may, calling repetition the "universality of the singular," the, say, Fall of the Bastille itself "celebrates and repeats in advance" all its commemorations—what comes later in the form of retrospective memory is prefigured not by what something has become *for us* (including earlier generations), but by *how* a past *produced* its own temporality—how events and processes were made. As we will see, concepts such as coexistence, preexistence, contemporary existence mesh and yet are limited in their combinations. There are paradoxes, for instance, in which the eternal is not at all continuous with the permanent.

Because an event is irreplaceable, it can only be repeated and, unlike the law that operates by equivalence and resemblance, repetition offers to consciousness a "transgression," not "a single past that returns in the future."[16] Is repetition paradox in action? Event, transgression, and repetition assemble around a "universality of the singular," a concept some commentators call a concept of the "pure event."[17] Such notions are not a present being "haunted" by a past, but the production of intense time, a transgression in relation to a judged obstacle, a resistance then and there. It is not wrong to say that repetition suggests the force of an event that defies language.

As in *The Logic of Sense* (1969), Deleuze divides repetition in asymmetrical categories. Exact repetition is the dream of exchange, actualized in ideals of precision and equivalence; but "true repetition," the subject of *Difference and Repetition,* pertains to something "singular, unchangeable, and different, without identity," paradoxical qualities, where the singular without identity ("just an idea, not a just idea") transmits actions that do not belong to the power of exchange. An event is not a negation. For example, the by now ubiquitous use of the name "9/11" for the bombing of New York in 2001 is anything but the name of a transgressive singularity. Nine/eleven stands in for traditional topoi all the way through: "don't forget," "not-again," and "self-justification" for foreign policy. "Nine/eleven" as now encoded is a negation (of terror), so it is not the name of event, but the name of something to remember, a monstrous confirmation that serves various interests, from emotional to political. "Transgressive," instead, means that if one makes the interpretation that the Fall of the Bastille brought the Idea of the State to crisis by releasing political prisoners and criminals in which the latter two groups freely mixed for a while, then that event continues to happen every time politics and, say, certain practices of social danger connect. Those acts of thought and creation that dissolve exchangism belong to repetition, and only such acts *authenticate* themselves.[18] That is, an event within the frame of positive affirmation creates its own immanence, or can be said to perform only itself. Repetition signifies "n times as the power of a single time," that is, unlike repetition in law and science, which constantly fight back the "demonic" or the irrational and the "wearisome," or look for repeatable principles, repetition in its positive or affirmative aspect ("kind") is ascent and descent at once, irony and humor, not opposed to generalities, particulars, and universals, indifferent to all but other singularities that are without resemblance or equivalence (5). An event may be provisionally understood as a conjunction of actions and passions, bodies thereof, that generates physical/material linkages that can be used to make more powerful connections, in which both memory and forgetting are simultaneously remembered and forgotten.[19]

When an event is greeted with affirmation, its "again-ness" is also affirmed and human agents *initiate* not a repetition subsumed by generality and equivalence, nor reducible to a particular, but set-off affections, qualities, and thoughts that dissolve the force of analogy and forced senses of equality; an event does not belong to law, to nature, to consciousness, but to the future. As we will see, this previews eternal return, the future imaged as an infinity of affirmed "agains." Of course *Difference and Repetition*'s own historiographical obsession is with the future, not with the past or present. The example of Kant might be instructive. Kant's moral law, the Categorical Imperative, is a transcendental rule, an a priori rule by which subjects bring their own temporal moral patterns and rhythms "into time," that is, by subjection to an invariant law. The time of the law tells the time of the subject who places him- or herself under such law. The way to challenge this is not to write Kant off as an idealist or reject his projection of scientific regularity onto human caprice and will; rather, it is better contested by acts that are nonlaws—an occurrence within the law and beyond it at once, the force of example, instance, case, singularity, affirmations that help to make repetition itself a more interesting "test" for human beings (7). Acts that are affirmed in the mode of *giving themselves their own law* make repetition an "again," which is always a "once" with unknown time implications. The face of a one-year-old smiling in a restaurant into the faces of attentive strangers shows almost all chance, joy-time, even if witnessed by those with an unhappy consciousness of family, a Sartrean family. *Difference and Repetition* thus shifts from the good and common sense of time as container, of time as that within which we find our sense. Indeed, Deleuze assumes that his writing of this is not an answer to a past question, where writing belongs to the *imperative* mode, but a writing that itself makes chances of thought, where "all at once the virtual disparate is condensed and the determination of the actual by means of the virtual begins to unfold." That is not an historical obligation, but more a "deconstruction of the subjective instance."[20] In the most thorough way possible, *Difference and Repetition* grills subjective time as intuitive or belonging to certainty as well as igniting "objective" time for its illusions.

Many specifications. "Difference gives things to be seen and multiplies bodies; but it is repetition which offers things to be spoken, authenticates the multiple, and makes of it a spiritual event." "Spiritual" does not mean mystical or invisible, but the persistence of *affirmations,* the effect of something done capable of drawing us into its "subsistence," "its disquieting power."[21] Repetition is thus separated from its usual containers—habit and memory—as these relations are limited to acts that "recover the particulars dissolved in generality" (7). More: repetition is intrinsic to a "forgetting [that] becomes a positive power" (7), it pertains to those acts of thought and will that maximize their own force—that go to the limit of what can be thought, felt, perceived, of "making movement itself a work" (8). Positively, repetition is more akin to proliferation, the rhizomatic notion of things, events, and words connected in ways that give rise to logics of an inclusive type, where differences are combined that generate new perceptions and new things. As *Anti-Oedipus* put it, repetition counteracts representation: "The theory of proper names should not be conceived of in terms of representation; it refers instead to the class of 'effects': effects that are not a mere dependence on causes, but the occupation of a domain, and the operation of a system of signs . . . the Joule effect, the Seebeck effect, the Kelvin effect. History is like physics: a Joan of Arc effect, a Heliogabulus effect—all the *names* of history."[22] We experience affects with perceptions as we make cuts from semiremembered pasts—why should consciousness not be considered a "theater"—another paradox—that does not just represent, but can perform repetitions irreducible to opposition and mediation (10)? Surely this "terrible power" of making disturbing effects concerning habit and memory would threaten our representations of events that are called historical? In the spate of books about Elvis Presley, for example, where the fate of Elvis comes down to representing the story "success entails failure" in popular culture, e.g., it's downhill after public recognition (overmediation), what would happen if we constantly challenged our criteria about success and failure, forcing ourselves to scramble without such historicist or narrative equations that help to lock popular culture in narrative patterns? If historical representation is unfortunately often a mode of aesthetic satisfaction, particularly in combinations of melancholy and irony, or emphasis on unintended consequences, which makes fools of us, and is at times confused with tragedy,[23] then *Difference and Repetition* just makes such tropes political conventions, mind comforters for the afflicted.

True repetition is not directed to connecting memory and self-consciousness, or causal explanation with antecedent; quite the contrary, repetition belongs to *nonconceptual differences,* that is, what can be said in an actual event or act of thought to escape the indefinite sameness of concepts (13). Sensation is presumed to be the same as yesterday and tomorrow. But for *Difference and Repetition,* repetition is closer to an "unconscious of the free concept" and an "unconscious of representation" rather than sharing metaphysical identities of sense (14). Repetition invites conceptual formation because it has no means of actualization other than to provide for itself masks and disguises "in which terror is closely mingled with movement of selection and freedom" (19). To the historian's specially constituted intuition, a genealogy that runs from Wilhelm Dilthey in the nineteenth century to Carlo Ginzburg's historian as diviner of clues, historical representation judged materially continuous with habit-memory and recollection-memory, almost a "nondeclarative memory," *Difference and Repetition* poses the problem of whether we can think to a *praxial* memory, or the past not adapted to present requirements. If we cannot stop writing the history of Hitlerism in what is surely the genre of negative repetition, horror, never again, is this not due to the fact that we keep on looking for some definitive evil mask that Hitlerism wore, instead of understanding the event called Hitlerism as to what it willed and selected, its mixture of terror and freedom, which necessitated its constant change of masks and disguises? If we cannot settle the roles of intellectuals in mid-1930s fascism and Nazism, from passive to active collaboration, resistance, and so on, isn't this because we are loathe to figure forth the masks and disguises the intellectuals wore and circulated (wrote) so as to sustain themselves, to protect themselves, to . . . ? To do this, to make such a leap, requires engagement with and affirmation of practice, that accepts "each region of the past opens up a continuum made up of unique accents, potentials, and critical moments" that exist independently of our narrative presentations.[24] As a practice of reading signs, "what matters is the possibility of the cause having less symmetry than the effect" (20).

This enigmatic fragment suggests that we treat events as more than tangible things determined by antecedent conditions, as signs ambiguous and volatile, in which their conditions of dynamism are not spent, finished. As with Lyotard, a sign is at once limited, even self-canceling, but provocative of other signs, each serving as a variable of an event and of our connection to it. If we wish to understand what was dynamic in Hitlerism then we must try to understand its *"points of inequality"* in relation to our conceived notions of it, how it created all sorts of signs and gaps within itself so as to render its own movement and motion, working itself with different audiences, that mixed attraction and repulsion, seduction and mayhem. And this holds for every group at the time: what effects did each set in motion to what they thought was the "expressed" of Hitlerism—for some, economic opportunity, for others, restoration of order, for yet others, savage pleasure in unhinging liberalism, or ressentiment on a cosmic scale. What was Hitlerism's activation of "sensory-motivity" instead of its "ideo-motivity" (23)? If "signs are the true elements of theater" and only secondarily of representation, what has power to act generates signs and effects the causes of which disappear into more effects. Signs open onto "powers which act beneath the words, gestures, characters and objects represented . . . repetition as real movement, in opposition to representation which is a false movement of the abstract" (23). In short, what *Difference and Repetition* asks is whether or not we are capable of nonreductively connecting signs to "difference[s] without a concept" and taking the chance that the concepts we come up with will be only tentative, only hypothetical, only themselves transitions to more concepts and more differences, and where events are not necessarily representable as stories.

Here indeed is one of the key critical elements of Deleuze's entire project: to challenge any sense of the finality of language in relation to things that are dynamic and active, things or events that are as frequently misnamed as not. When, for example, Goldhagen argued in *Hitler's Willing Executioners* that Nazism was continuous with a prior generalized German anti-Semitism, the assertion of continuity blocks consideration of what was both intrinsic and dissymetrical about Nazism: the way it *read others* in forming itself, how it made itself by developing "displacements, quickenings, slowdowns, variants or differences" (24) or received the desires and interests of others, turned into "resources" that left nothing untouched, including itself. This is manifestly *not* trying to understand the past in its own terms, what commentators have called "dialogue with the past,"[25] but rather how any such past *produced* its "difference[s] without a concept." *Difference and Repetition* asks us *not* to make ourselves, survivors and historians, sufferers and observers, *satisfied* in our sadness, our melancholia, our sorrow in any historical interpretation. The issue is not "penetrating the in-itself of the past in order to reduce it to the former present it once was or to the current present,"[26] but to jolt ourselves, here, to Nazism-as-difference: think-to those "internal, yet not conceptual . . . differences which dramatize an Idea before representing an object" (26). Repetition welcomes the differences of sensations and nonconceptual difference (openness to sensation, to perception) and asks of us that we nearly wreck our discursive representations so as to be adequate to events we ourselves do not make. This is not some poetic feel for the past.

Difference

As repetition disrupts what we ordinarily think of sense and experience, so too with the sense of difference: thought "makes" difference, but "difference is monstrous. We should not be surprised that difference should appear accursed, that it should be error, sin or the figure of evil for which there must be expiation. There is no sin other than raising the ground and dissolving the form" (29). Does this "difference is monstrous" announce the return of Dionysus, long banished from modernist historiography? While apparently threaded to identity, opposition, analogy, and resemblance by virtue of logical implication, difference poses its own problems for historical thought or historiography as such. Paramount is a problem endemic in any attempt to represent the past: how do we determine a "distinctive concept of difference" for some portion of a past, or not reduce that past to our "inscription[s] of difference within concepts in general," where "the determination of the concept of difference is confused with the inscription of difference in the identity of an undetermined concept" (32)? Which means: bad applications of good and common sense of the present thrust on the past. Presentism = bad objectivism. The emergence of trauma studies is a case in point: so many differences brought under the same concept, the transformation of trauma into concept-trauma comes to annul the very difference articulated as trauma—as in the trauma of genocide, the trauma of the "end of art," the trauma of the breakdown of American exceptionalism. Just as repetition is said to involve nonconceptual differences, difference pertains to nonconcepts or to sensible things, or things without names. Vincent Descombes, in his provocative analysis of modern French philosophy, has posed difference as a problem for historiography by considering the logic of "master and slave": in Marxism, the master is exploitative, with Nietzsche (and Kojève), the master is only an emancipated slave, so when are master and slave actually different?[27] When are we confronting differences that make a difference or are instead in some self-misunderstanding because of reliance on univocal and universal representation, to reduce difference to a "predicate in the comprehension of a concept" (32)? Are we condemned to use, in our treatment of difference, only judgments of good sense and common sense, both to preserve analogy, opposition, resemblance, and identity as markers to sort things out so as to effectively name the emergent, the strange (33)?

Difference and Repetition wants to make of difference a *catastrophe* or "breaks in continuity"(35). Difference does not fill a space between two resemblances or thread a different "before" to the Same that is said to come after, but, actively considered, is a distribution in its own right: unlike analogy that must "relate being to particular existents, but at the same time . . . cannot say what constitutes their individuality" (38), difference unleashes a "plastic, anarchic and nomadic principle . . . [an] individuation that *precedes* matter and form." As catastrophe, things (a belief, a practice) of all sorts excessive in their very inequality transport difference into existence. Deleuze and Guattari's *What Is Philosophy?* puts it this way: "We are not in the world, we become with the world; we become by contemplating it. Everything is vision, becoming. We become universes. Becoming animal, plant, molecular, becoming zero. Kleist . . . wrote with affects, using them like stones or weapons . . . sudden petrification or infinite acceleration . . . This is true of all the arts: what strange becomings . . . What terror haunts van Gogh's head, caught in a becoming-sunflower?"[28]

While I wish Deleuze did not use the name *haunt* in this context, with excess and catastrophe entered as candidates for conceptual use, we can think at least two types of events, but at extremes. On the one hand, as murderers, there is the antiproductive (un)becoming of Nazism, due to its negative repetition of ghoulish ideology; on the other, as in the quote above, a nobility of "energy which is capable of transforming itself," van Gogh's nonconceptual difference of sunflower turned into painted thing (41).[29] Negative repetition evokes some of the worst aspects of "organic representation," where a substance or form is said to be the basis of society, myth-flows thought to be worth killing for, as in nationalism, racism, even versions of cosmopolitanism, unfortunately. Deleuze was ruthless toward left and right versions of organicism. On the other hand, the van Gogh–effect pertains to the "orgiastic," or going to the limit of a contested difference, instead of eliciting a return of the Same (43). There is a phrase in *Anti-Oedipus, sur rabat,* "to fall back," which Deleuze and Guattari use to indicate moments of default to organic form, an extremely dangerous concept, since it implies a turn to acceptable necessity. As concerns presentation or the writing of history, the crucial distinction is between the historian who writes on the assumption that "everyone recognizes that . . ." (good and common sense), and the historian who goes to the boundaries of analysis willing to bear the cost of making representing the past a challenge to the present—why not discuss a past that few in the present can live with?[30] It is a strange relation that the materials discussed in chapter 3—art and book reviewing, their historicizing—can even presuppose a public always relied upon to legitimize—writings that offer no present challenge at all. In this sense, nothing is more destructive of the very ideals of historiography than the books that make us indifferent to the past, an indifference reiterated every time we are given a past that we already know, a past that confirms "we're just like them," "they're just like us," "we're all the same." Or they become exotic creatures, always "more and less" like and unlike us. Lyotard's common being. For instance, what might one think if contemporary art history, since 1960 or so was narrated for its enforced unidirection, artists disciplined toward canonic inclusion, making things because they were easily assimilated to the new institutions? What if contemporary art history was harder to do because it was harder to historicize?

Of course there are risks with all these ideas. One danger of idealizing difference is to relapse to some vague notion of a beautiful soul, the would-be connoisseur of differences, the last reader become complete fussbudget, "who sees differences everywhere . . . while history continues to be made through bloody contradictions" (52). Another risk is to act like the historian who is "concerned to deny that which 'differs' so as to conserve or prolong an established historical order" (53). Both instances make connection with the past hinge on a founding negation—all-difference and no-difference come to the same thing. The worker-in-difference, resistant only to indifference, accepts necessary "burdens of history," a phrase Hayden White introduced so as to say yes to something other than the current "powers of the day" (54). Nietzsche put it well when he emphasized "only he who is building up the future has a right to judge the past." Relations to the past are not a spectator sport. For example, as mentioned in previous chapters, Jacques Rancière argues that "historical science" is "tied by principle to the disturbance of speech," where narrative recounting passes over to the side of difference, to join an "excess of speech" that does not let itself be *redeemed* by future commentators. That way, democracy can *return* (achieve its renovation). By affirming historical excess, we open ourselves to . . . , infinitive form. But when he argues, a few sentences later, that history "needs a poetic regulation of the excess, the substitution of a body of the voice for another," then difference is returned to a good form.[31] In any case, the *being* of difference does not "uncouple consequences from premises" (55); later is not the truth of the earlier, but indicates the persistence, or insistence, of an event—its contractions, retentions, and anticipations in relation to a passing present incessantly working the past.

Representation

Representation, according to *Difference and Repetition,* is that reduction to a graphic (text, voice, inscripted) "center," whether of meaning, value, and evaluation, which "moves nothing," and that knows nothing of "a superposition of perspectives, a tangle of points of view, a coexistence of moments" (56). In this sense, historical representation remains fixated on providing forms of identity—"the prefix RE-in the word representation signifies this conceptual form of the identical which subordinates differences" (56).When Ferry and Renaut, mentioned above, insist that "French philosophy of the sixties" was engaged in genealogical readings, so that no text could "be understood except from the starting point of something other than itself," that the "internal coherence" of scholarly work was thereby disrespected, that such genealogical readings led to "interpretive delirium," then we have representation aggressively in defense of its own center, an identity based on self-possessive coherence.[32] Representation can be defined as resistance to divergence and decentering, or difference understood "as *differing*" (56). How might historiography confederate this sense of difference, this "theater of metamorphoses and permutations . . . A theater where nothing is fixed, a labyrinth without a thread" (56)? Is this where an undoing of historiography occurs, its train wreck because such doubts about representation would make it uncertain that any subject of a narrative is *the* subject? History out of joint? "Founding fathers" disguises the what of selection, cut into and out of which segments of class, prestige, occupation, religion, myth? So it is better to dismiss American exceptionalism from historiography—but which claims are made in doing so, which masks and disguises worn to what ends? It is time for an end—for whom?

To the factism of historical representation *Difference and Repetition* offers a "superior empiricism" capable of being used for participation in a strange "reason," or a reason that gives to language and discourse the "unlimited of the finished itself," a "chao-errancy," the disparate, instead of illusory coherence that serves as the tautological origin of representation. The object of repetition and difference differs in type from that of representation: repetition and difference operate each other in "the formless power of the ground which carries every object to that extreme 'form' in which its representation comes undone," whereas representation's function is to resist the forces of signs, ensuring good and common names are not swept away. Representation belongs to the magic of key terms, like *context, getting it right,* the installation of meaning without humor and irony, sense without attending nonsense (57).

Temporality

After and later are proof for the transcendence of earlier and before, or is it vice versa, according to conventional historiographic practice? What strange concepts, genealogically considered. Is "before the wind" still before the earlier? *Difference and Repetition* tries to dislodge, unbalance, such mustering or gathering of time in the age of "time is out of joint."

Difference and Repetition organizes issues of temporality in almost gnomic terms: "the present alone exists," there is a "living present" and "the present passes" (76). Action and fatigue are said to form the boundaries of any given present (77), "where all our rhythms, our reserves, our reaction times, the thousand intertwinings, the presents and fatigues of which we are composed, are defined on the basis of our contemplations." It would be a mistake to confuse contemplation with conscious reflection. It is that, but contemplation means intensification of thought and feeling, more tension, or tension that is more effective, "the liberty of movement, of a moving-itself of thought within the articulated element of a state of its conditions."[33] First of all, a subject makes *passive syntheses,* or time contracted to our concerns, where memory is not very agitated or dynamic. For instance, "a scar is the sign not of a past wound but of the 'present fact of having been wounded.'" "Having been" is also a clear "now." Given different selections and cuts from experience, there are created orders of memory that intersect in ways that are highly individuated. But this natural synthesis or nonconscious sense of a continuum is offset by artificial synthesis. "Artificial" in the sense that any "present present" contends with previous contractions and fatigues, engagements, and withdrawals, consequences of passion and thought, and further ruminations. "Artificial" includes the most rigorous contemplations that change the sorts of spaces we make for thinking, how we think, as well as the perversions of memory, of which such syndromes as "repressed memory" now seem to be a contemporary example. Where passive synthesis spontaneously and continuously gives to consciousness material and noumenal present objects of contemplation, artificial synthesis ushers in "reflective representation, memory and intelligence" (77). It organizes signs "which refer to the past or the future as distinct dimensions of the present, dimensions on which the present might in turn depend" (77). History is both natural and artificial (as is the schizophrenic of *Anti-Oedipus*). Memory is always contested: the different modalities of how one uses memory testify to the "living present (the urgency of life)," i.e., what can one do, how can one proceed, what will become of someone/them/us? Memory and event are both physical and psychical processes, "points of fusion . . . freezing . . . boiling . . . coagulation . . . crystallization superfusion . . . fragments" (198). While present doing engages the past, which then becomes an *is,* the present becomes an *is not*—the present is not identical to itself at any of its "instants," but divided into "a present that is passing and a past which is preserved."[34] Through habit and memory, we consistently produce many kinds of duration that cannot be reduced to before/after, even if we fall back on chronology.

Succession is not irreversibility, and their confusion is profound. Succession is many things reduced to before/after, and it is just as confusing to mix the wrong sense of "next" with after. All relations of succession are connective tis-

sue of historiography, part of its body. The form of succession and-then enables us to at best assume identity in the mode of a continuous past-present-
future, but is not sufficient. Succession made confirmation of our habitual *intuitions* equals temporality as a container, as a stock of images and ideas that
operate subject and group narratives that occupy a point on a line. Aggressively habitual and formal, succession is less than vibrant, more like what linguists call the transformation of a specific code into a nonconscious norm.[35]
When Isaiah Berlin championed history as an "inexact discipline" but having
the power to represent—because in historical representation we find the
"properties of the language of common sense . . . ordinary judgment"—he was
giving voice to an equation between historical representation and intuition.[36]
Every language has many ways of dividing up temporality. For instance, English associates adverbs of habit that differ from the aspectualism of incomplete
verbs; a habit is assumed to be active over a long time frame, but is often a restricted occurrence.[37] Is it the same succession if someone shops once a year
and selects clothing as an ecstatic event or when someone "lives" to shop? It
matters how temporal combinations are *folded* and assembled into habit and
memory, contemplated and repressed, turned into more images, ideas, concepts, feelings, assays, incessantly and not, and differently connect one to various "worlds." According to Keith Ansell-Pearson, the import of Deleuze's alteration of time-sense is shown in time conceived as "the ground of an *abyss*
and the form of the *formless*," in which an *encounter* matters. How does one
connect with the vastness of the "pure past" and turn it into the past as strictly
recalled? How does one *span* actions and selections—live in and as temporal
stretching, the past ahead, the future as thought?[38] Paradox: all present life
passes, but the past is not inert—there is such a thing as a disjunctive coexistence of temporal slices and their assemblages.[39]

Historiographically, *Difference and Repetition* speaks to such important
questions as *temporal synthesis*. Timothy Murphy has given a clear outline of
what is at stake: Deleuze works with three syntheses of time: (1) passive syntheses, which arise out of a living present and the contraction of past/future,
where time is given to oneself as unidirectional. The iteration of a habit is
predicated on retention and waiting, which are feelings of continuity with
past/future; (2) moving toward a more intense self-affected dimension, there is
active synthesis, or a pure past selected by reminiscence, say of an older past
unclearly mixed with current images, out of which a present-past can fuse, in
preparation for making an action or turning one off; and (3) the conjunction
of future and caesura, or movement that generates difference. Passive and ac-

tive syntheses combine incessantly to allow us to live with our present in some semblance of comfortability and self-affection with the past, with ourselves. These syntheses give us various degrees of straitjacketing: the "naked" repetition of the Same or adherence to specific ends, a general sense of unidirectionality that can be multiply inclusive or exclusive, case by case.[40]

More carefully, we can move with *Difference and Repetition* to the metaphysical texts of Kant, Leibniz, Bergson, and Hegel, where Deleuze fills in the first synthesis, calling it *contraction,* passive, without being pejorative, which plays out as *habit,* a synthesis of the "living present" (97). The act of walking to the store at a set time operates as a transition from writing in the morning, walking a pause in work, a speeding up and slowing down of the other habits in its milieu, adding to and detracting from a sense of future expectation. This "present present" hangs on resemblance and association. Affirming Humeian empiricism, habit is the condition of passive synthesis or a totality of "variable presents," otherwise called here "contractions, contemplations, pretensions, presumptions, satisfactions, fatigues." Paradoxical: these modes "constitute time while passing in the time constituted" (79). Present syntheses render the past available for a passing present, and the past is given passage, so to speak, to the present. Habit both renews and devours itself, inseparable yet different from memory, the latter, *Difference and Repetition* insists, which "constitutes the being of the past (that which causes the present to pass)" (80). With habit, one confronts a "reversibility of energies, the reciprocal mutability of passivity and activity. The continuity or repetition of a change modifies—with respect to that very change—the disposition of the being . . . habit is a reduction in receptivity and an increase in spontaneity."[41] Spontaneity means habit does not just clone itself, but incessantly arranges its connections with other temporal series. Neither habit nor memory is reducible to psychological categories of inner feelings, the self that contemplates its autoaffections already a "dissolved self" (78), not an inner spectator, as said above. "The self does not undergo modifications, it is itself a modification . . . the difference drawn" (79). Present memory coexists with past memories that were/are connected to other memories, habits, etc. Time divides into a passing present and pasts preserved, so that at any moment, a subject-in-action can enlarge and/or diminish just what of the past will be activated in a present, just which "accents, potentials and critical moments" are rendered contingent and necessary for a given action. If in contemporary society many intellectuals and artists bemoan the loss of the past or the speed with which things change (Virilio), and others try to use the past for political agendas, then we are dealing with uses that cannot be reduced to habit or memory.

Which is to say that habit-synthesis is a "foundation" but not the "ground" of time (79); the ground is another synthesis, active, and, as memory, has its own passive synthesis—the difference between a past that has been and the past in general (80). Passive synthesis here is what our useful, immediate recollections are about, or concern.[42] The active synthesis is not *after* passive synthesis, in the sense of succession (or logic, as in following-from), but can be imaged as an act of thought in which an intense present works over and up its contemplations, as it forms the memory of, say, a "former present," memory not restricted to habit, but free and creative in leaping to other times. Active synthesis by memory allows us to consider that memory is not just memory-of, but *memory-for,* something intrasubjectively different from the act of representation that claims to be a memory-of anything whatsoever—like the "memory" of a myth. An historiographic question: what has, in the past, memory been made to do—what are its genealogies—and what can memory do now? Active synthesis moves when a former present has become more than the *past-as;* active is when the whole of the past can be reproduced, reflected, remembered, and whose representation—the four *re*'s—*adds* something to feelings and thoughts that was *not* present in a past's former present. Intensities of experience are manifestly not the same kind of synthesis as, say, passive narrative synthesis, where, for instance, the Founding Fathers are there and here, always behind yet ahead of us. Since each former present was itself a variable conjuncture of passive/active syntheses, individual and group memory is a tangle of images, dates, speeds, and rhythms. A coexistence of nonconceptual times and timings. In this, chronology or succession, before and after, necessarily has a *defensive* purpose, to protect one from truly discomfiting ideas about just, in this case, how past the past is.

Again, with habit, passive synthesis is self-limiting to acts of recognition, or the minimal return of a sign, a trace; but the active synthesis called memory oscillates between subjective *abyss*—can I imagine a past that I can live with, or is it "too big"—and the formless—can I imagine a future for which my actions are adequate?[43] To such metaphysics historians will respond: the only past that matters is the one we can reference, the one we have evidence of and for, and evidence and reference require succession as the form in which we know this evidence and reference(s). "Before and after," they will say, is not a code, but a condition of representing any past. *Difference and Repetition* replies that sometimes one can ask if there are not "more or less close or distant points of view that would make it possible to group different layers over a fairly long period or, on the contrary, to separate layers on what seemed to be a common plane"? That there might even be events without a beginning or end but only a milieu.[44] For example, why think the modern history of the middle classes as anything but a conjunction of profession, interest, self-defense, and the like in which middle class is less a narrated subject, its emergence and tribulations, than it is a geologic plate, which has made its relations with influence, recognition, political power, social services, all of which testify to mechanisms of duration that refute its idealized self-narration?

"No present would ever pass were it not past 'at the same time' as it is present; no past would ever be constituted unless it were first constituted 'at the same time' as it was present" (81). Sheer paradox, this *"ever-increasing coexistence of levels of the past within passive synthesis"* (83). That is a version of what Hayden White once called the burden of history. Hence the past is presupposed by representation in any present act of thought, which Deleuze takes to mean that it is *not* the present that makes the past "past," but the past that *insists,* this insistence a virtuality able to be infused with the present. Most strongly put, there is a past independent of our making of it, which is the sense of an expression like "every present passes." To where? To the past as a whole.

The passive syntheses of habit and memory presuppose a third synthesis, called the "pure past in time," or the contemporaneity of the past with the present that it was, where the past "coexists with the new present in relation to which it is now past" (81). A thirty-year-old has experienced over fifteen million minutes of life—where are they? This synthesis involves that we consider the entire past itself as absolute contraction and available for any present present (82). That is, we lead ourselves to false problems when we say that the "past was" or that it no longer exists—we should rather say that the past "insists, it consists, it *is*" (82). But it is only *available* to us insofar as we transform it, available as contemporaneity, coexistence, and preexistence *at the same time.* To the historiography of periodization, such coexistence provokes us to ask why any story starts where it does—the past now for whom?

Why is this philosophically important for historiography? First, *Difference and Repetition* relocates questions of before/after or history as chronology, as succession, shifting chronology, sequence, and telos into problems of narration. Narration remains the medium of rendering continuity out of discontinuity, but in doing so, historians actually dissolve the force of the paradoxical collision of past and present *disjunctions*. Historical representation, as narrative, makes an aesthetic presentation dominate the cognitive dissonance that belongs to the improprieties and violence of past and present, the past's insistencies and present political selections about that past. Both of course open and close futures. Because continuity and discontinuity have been forced to fit the requirements of narration, to meld the theatrics of our storytelling (the well-timed dramatic rupture) to our habit-driven hurling of ourselves into the future, achronologic relations are quite difficult to sustain. (Derrida's new scholar is not just achronic, but super-so.) Nonetheless, the fracture of any present present does not require restoration of a line broken by distance, by rupture, by superficial notions of differences between past and present, but to shift the question. Better to ask if there are *nonlocalizable connections between successive presents:* how to connect with action at a distance, and all sorts of re-plays, responses, echoes, chances, signs, and signals that make history multiple and temporal experience something more radical than linear connection? As *Anti-Oedipus* put it, at any given moment, affecting every system of sub-jects/subject-groups, there is a *schizophrenic limit to history*, instances of "universal history . . . Fetishes, idols, images, and simulacra . . . territorial fetishes, despotic idols or symbols . . . everything . . . recapitulated in the images of capitalism."[45] We might examine, in and as this schizo time, what is really past, what is real in the modes of virtual and actual, and how these conflict with the other. *Difference and Repetition* asks us to consider how it is that the *archaic and the futural* coexist at once, and not in psychological terms, but rather how it is that subjects and groups are able to make out of the weavings of contemporaneity, coexistence and preexistence any strong sense of *destiny*. This concept opens the historiography of radicalizing an event.

Destiny and Subjectivity

Professional historiography is not exactly friendly to notions of social or historical destiny. Most of the time, destiny remains a concept under historio-graphic suspicion, often used by various conservative and right-wing political historians, although in the past twenty years or so, left-wing notions of destiny as social ideology have made more frequent appearances. The argument so far has been that *Difference and Repetition*'s conceptual applications of repetition, difference, and temporality are usefully conceived as *insistence* and *intensity,* rather than linear succession, which undercuts the force of good and common sense in historiography. Such conceptual deviations affect every subject of narrative, the very transformation of events into narratives. In the recent (2004) presidential elections, George Bush repeats the identity of American history as a fusion of Christian messianism and freedom, while John Kerry repeats assertions that would make Americans live up to a "better" past. Rewrite the history of the American presidency as the history of the American people in their failure to respond to their own powers, a people's unnecessary and extreme deference to political centralization and what will one find? That the history of the presidency turns into the genealogy of default, the genealogy of illusions, the genealogy of the unnecessary?

Many of the concepts deployed by *Difference and Repetition* congeal around destiny, which, as said above, is a name that makes many professional historians nervous. However, *destiny* is a favored term of *Difference and Repetition's* historicity, but stripped of cyclical, circling, and linear senses, as well as separated from laws (of nature) and social restraints (e.g., rules of behavior). Here is a partial case for an affirmation of destiny, whose relations with historiography are more than strained.

Destiny is not determined by some fatal, deterministic, or mechanistic sense of the "earlier" but by what, on individual and group levels, someone/them/us is *becoming*. Consider this on the plateau of an individual. Different levels of many pasts and presents congeal, however quickly, however slowly, and concern how someone/them/us *chooses* to repeat, to initiate, to accept, to reject the data of experience, interpreting and assessing inner and outer relations. There is never a real past that determines the present becoming future, because present habit and memory incessantly weave themselves into degrees of pastness, in the form of powerful memories mixed with obsessions, blended with attempts to self-distract, joined with new projects of forgetting, so that there is no neutral present's relation to the past-as. Recall that the present "is" no more objectively nor subjectively real than the past, as both are embroiled in the other in terms of actualization in any present. Because of this "the sign of the present is a *passage* to the limit, a maximal contraction which comes to sanction the choice of a particular level as such, which is in itself contracted or relaxed among an infinity of other possible levels . . . as if the philosopher and the pig, the criminal and the saint, played out the same past at different levels of a gigantic cone. This is what we call metempsychosis" (83). Destiny to metempsychosis? Deleuze goes there. To the bare, particular, successive, and horizontal aspects of temporality or successivity, which come to be treated as a form of causality itself—narrate enough and soon enough causality is absorbed by narrative ideas—a more complex historicity is both material and noumenal. "Noumenal" refers to a multiplicity, where actions are performed, clothed, in signs and masks (history-as-theater), where agents and agencies of all sorts make partial wholes that dissolve again into more effects and signs. Remember, we are constantly dismantling the past and assembling the present; we are constantly disassembling the present to have a different effect/affect of and with a past. We coexist with fragments from pasts actualized for the strangest of reasons, where we make ourselves virtual to other choices, imagining our subjectivity as verticality, or moving up and down through different levels of existence, where "before and after" is a secondary effect of a sense of historicity. Destiny and metempsychosis are concepts of the noumenal dimension, in the sense that these Ideas indicate actual and virtual connections across the levels of habit and memory and future-projects—destiny is not an outcome, but a selection of which level one makes an event. How and when did Lenin, exactly, jump from revolutionary to murderer? Exactly how and when did Hitler receive the empathy of the German people and leap to the satisfactions of mayhem? Exactly how and when did the American middle class opt out of public school as a place of social amelioration? Exactly how did reviewers of the *Los Angeles Times Book Review* conclude they should warn their readers against excessively cerebral books?[46] *Difference and Repetition* proposes that the contest for historiography is over the difference between narrative history and the past and present reader's becoming—over history as recognition (name) and subjects/groups making new processes. It should be emphasized that this tangle of historicity and destiny does *not* make consciousness the arbiter of historical sense, since consciousness here is merely one element in the ceaseless selection of multiple *destinies,* all of which hover between the actual, the virtual, and the possible, constantly shifting tasks and projects, sometimes a sense of the body predominating, sometimes a sense of ideological purity, sometimes a relaxation to sheer indifference.

Obviously these metaphysical notions brought to historiography distance at once scientistic constructs about history and narrative models, including issues of direction, discussions of processes of development, from phenomenology to objectivism. *Anti-Oedipus* offered the small hope that instead of human endeavor reduced to the psychology of historicism, we should insist on our metaphysics, not to make a purpose of opposing linear succession, but for more effective lives.[47] If most historians understand by habit only versions of common and good sense, a pragmatism of adaptation, and understand by noumenal-history a vague desire for narrative completion and wholeness, then problems like those of destiny cannot be systematically raised. Metempsychosis may be bizarre to our scientistic and narrative strategies of representing, but it does indicate that historiography confronts the strange behavior of incorporeal transformations, transformations where, from one moment to the next, becomings take place.[48] When historians such as Gordon Wood find the continuum of American history in the never broken "common sense of the American people," what kind of event should we then make of current obesity patterns—is the latter metempsychotic, a new leap of "common sense"? Do obesity patterns indicate the continuum of success but so continuous it breaks success, or a hostile and abstract assault on body norms, a judgment about capital?[49] No doubt it is difficult not to locate events/becomings *after the fact,* affirming earlier as the crucial causal antecedent. But to do so is to miss the sense that becomings, as elucidated in *Difference and Repetition,* are more "differenciator[s] of difference" (300) instead of an earlier truth made a future secondariness.

Caesura and Becoming

Granting to Kant's analysis of the types of transcendental a prioris the merit of having posed insoluble problems as to knowledge and subjectivity, Deleuze argues that the strength in Kant's overturning of Descartes is to be found in Kant's insistence that the "I," or subject-as-such, is fractured as an integral whole, except as self-possessive defensiveness. Kant proposes time out of joint as disillusionment toward metaphysics (87), but stops short of pursuing the problem as to where "time itself unfolds . . . ceases to be a circle . . . ceases to be cardinal and becomes ordinal . . . beginning and end no longer coincided" (88–89). This is time extricated from movement, where transcendentals are suspended—no Platonic reminiscence both behind and ahead of oneself, no clear goals, forms, contexts. The American philosopher Josiah Royce put this brilliantly when he argued that the implications of Kant's method were to make "I know" and "I do" potentially incommensurable to each other, held together by an "unstable equilibrium"[50] so that it is subjectivity and its co-occurrence with all sorts of adaptations and adjustments that gives reflection speculative and actual matters, in which the temporal patterns of pause, stop, break, interval, and other experiences of discontinuity become conditions of experience. "Time is out of joint" means new kinds of subjects, monsters, hybrids, mutants, spanning all political filiations, rise up and struggle to go to new limits. Multiplicity and incarnation in strange places become active processes (182, 186). Freed from circles and one-time events, temporality can be conceived as "unequal in the function of a Caesura" (89).

No longer subordinated to movement toward *any* pregiven goal, temporality becomes unmeasurable—as subjectivity is effectively deprived of symmetry between its movements and temporalizing. No wonder the *historic* was invented by barbarians against savages—order, please! One could say that so many clocks are running and the supermeasuring of them—history—becomes a case of poor transcendence, a kind of cultural laziness in middle-class societies, which lives by resistance to combinations of political, economic, social, and cultural intensities.[51] *Difference and Repetition*'s treatment of temporality parallels Deleuze's analysis of Stoic notions of language, where the Stoics had made the conceptual *sense,* the expressed of language, irreducible to pregiven terms, propositions, objects denoted, or concepts. If sense is the expressed of a proposition so that when we say of a green tree that its eventness is something like "the tree greens," can we not say of temporality out of joint that it unleashes timings that our language unfortunately reduces to the main tenses (and tensions) of successivity?[52] If "now" is riddled with effects and forms from many past and futural virtualities, what remains of the historian's "from X to Y," its symmetry or alignment of events, causes, and consequences? For example, the assumption that Western history is positive considered in the long term and negative in the short term is not just a cultural-political working of time, it is an intellectual agenda for rationalization as well. If to every present present the past and the future are synthesized without a telos, where in this present present the past "is too big for me" and the future too much / too little to think-to, then to say that time is out of joint suggests the element of risk around our notions of an event.

On Deleuze's reading of the caesura as a genuine discontinuity of the idea of successivity, it comes forward as part of the struggle against Platonic memory and its recodings. Plato's system used the "circle" of time to incarnate categories of the Same and the Similar, which legislate or give a ready-made movement to before/after (Plato as one genealogic precursor of Marcel Duchamp!), or negative repetition. In the Platonic scaffolding, resemblance to ideal forms is the only "time" that matters (88). But with both Kant and Holderlin where "beginning and end no longer coincided," time itself becomes "the most radical form of change," or time concepts and sensations are pluralized and multiplied. All kinds of cultural experiences in the contemporary world gain new timings, e.g., the complaint now frequently heard in Arthur Danto's sense of the art world, where many viewers and critics feel there is not enough time to experience all the worthy art. Temporality precisely becomes the making of effects unequal to the totality of *timings* and events. In this sense we can then speak of *representation or narration as inferior to the material and noumenal inequalities of time,* "inferior" meaning nothing more than "secondary to."⁵³

Insofar as historical representation brings with it desire for symbolic resolutions, putting up such relations as resemblance and analogy as organizing devices of narration, the modern caesura is rejected in favor of a fictional state of a synthetic unity no longer materially possible; disunity is not an accident but a mode of being. This disunity is what then makes historiography shift to what I called in earlier chapters its restrictions and exclusions. What actually belongs to the "each time" of each "once," what constitutes context within this caesura without limit? To invoke time out of joint is not another way of making temporality whole again, whether as fragment or lost ideal. Fractured, time itself opens to countless pasts, "too big for me," and countless futures, where this bigness is often figured forth as a rejection of inequality in favor of embracing a sense of fictional totality. Which nineteenth- or twentieth-century ideology did not pursue the symbolic reconciliation of "time is out of joint"? Recall that Adorno tried to turn the fragment itself into another mode of proper representation. The great historiographer Reinhart Koselleck thinks that diagnosis and prognosis became standard equipment for the historian's posing of questions, this in the eighteenth century. What do these relations give way to?

In Deleuze's reading, those events in the past that seemed to come out of the blue are what we rewrite. "Rewritten" often means that we foist on the past senses of completion, usually with the aid of another ready-made phrase, the ubiquitous "in the name of history." Use that phrase and its opponents are usually silenced even as one should engage its outrageousness. *Difference and Repetition* challenges any narcissism of the present. Historiography ought to work against any sense of an *equality* of past and present—to activate the differential elements, without the bias that the new and different are in any way already understood. History-for becoming is predicated on inequality: ethically, one might try to become equal to an act, which *Difference and Repetition* calls the "projection of an ideal self in the image of the act (. . . the hero becomes 'capable' . . .)," a recasting of Nietzsche's maxim "become who you are," i.e., maximize power as productive of more assemblages and relations. A feeling-for producing time belongs to an affirmed destiny. Deleuze's affirmation of "time is out of joint" asks how to make an event *for the future,* how to intensify a more productive fracturing of the self, or a self that affirms inequality of past and future (90). Philosophically put, the challenge of historicity as such is always futural and oriented by problems: what can be said, thought, and achieved in any and every medium so that the future is made more difficult and less like the present and our representations of the past? Today, such discourse will be accused of inducing terror toward the future. Be that as it may, caesura here is an existential concept, and belongs less to the subject and more to the creation of events—their destiny of opportunity and destruction, of things and processes. No doubt some would say that Deleuze is actually describing two extremes: works of art and science that produce new challenges or actually change some dimension of social being, and a capitalism that antiproduces the future, where exchange rules everything in advance.

The temporal dimensions that are saturated in habit and memory allow for empirical analogies and resemblances, whether in life or narration, which enable us to retie our narrations and symbols (Paul de Man's remarkable essay, "Shelley Disfigured," offers a critique of this process).[54] Narration and symbol are not at all, however, an excess that is capable of making a future, "the repetition of the future as eternal return" (90). They exhaust themselves in synthesis.

Of course the notion of eternal return is notoriously difficult, there being almost as many versions of it as there are commentators on it. Its version in *Difference and Repetition* is complicated. At any given moment, a present is implicated in a past that was dynamically immediate to itself, the past as its habits, memories, and events synthesized into a past for-us. Its reality is tested and contested by our interpretations and models; a present is always action and intermediary. But belief in the future opens onto the "absolutely new" and is "without a name." Such belief is an opening for the coming into existence of the "independence of the work." That phrase refers to producing effects— artifacts, new specific logics of relation—that silence those noisy "dead gods" (ideals, clichés, stereotypes), or obligations to identities whose sense no longer makes sense, all of this set in the clamor of an occurring "dissolved self." If artists, intellectuals, political dissidents and the like wish to use history, there is no formula: every new "plane of consistency, a creative line of flight, a smooth space of displacement" can easily turn into a new mode of domination (theft and gift are continuous processes).[55] Eternal return names an intensification or multiplication of modes of experience that cannot be anything but "the decentred circle of difference," where memory and resemblance no longer *haunt* the future, or make strong claims on it, or otherwise reduce the future to our pettiness and social demands. In the strongest terms, one can say that the philosophy of history articulated by *Difference and Repetition* is a contemporary response to Nietzsche's challenge for the ahistorical and superhistorical to make their time precisely by means of *dispossession* of the infinitive form *to have*—to "have" history, to possess it through narration. It is a question of distinguishing history as that which one *joins* (in the name of) and becoming or production of events in which one makes something transformative. If history, or to be in history belongs to futuricity, "it is not only the gods who die endlessly and in a variety of ways," but oneself/ourselves as well when we engage with life and thought: "as though there appeared worlds in which the individual was no longer imprisoned in the singular form of the I and the ego, nor the singular imprisoned within the limits of the individual—in short the *insubordinate principle*" (113). Historicity as eternal return is rebellion toward abstract and overcoded social timings, any timing that disrupts habit and memory, no matter how sophisticated and socially integrated.

Difference and Repetition shifts historiography from a discourse anchored in good and common sense to a discourse that would abandon tactics of prose and narrative representation that claim to give us possession of the sense and meaning of continuity and discontinuity. The macroprocesses articulated by *Anti-Oedipus,* the production and antiproduction of political and cultural schizophrenia as conditions of existence, are figured forth in *Difference and Repetition* as affirmation of a positive metaphysics of existence. This request for affirmation is impossible without suspending historical representation as we know it.

For historiography, *Difference and Repetition* offers radical doubts to the question/problem of what "history is for." Historical narration has a double status: it narrates each past, or segment thereof, putting our knowledge of consequences, often little more than present rationalizations, into a story the past did not know belonged to it; it uses that past to legitimize strong, contentious, present interests. We deprive both the past and ourselves from confronting multiple destinies, which is problematic and imperative (284). In an intellectual sense, *Difference and Repetition* asks that we confront "asymmetry *in the cause*" (287). This enigmatic phrase asks that we think of the events we make and the events we interpret as part of "the power of beginning and beginning again . . . forces of thought which are not the forces of recognition, today or tomorrow . . . an unrecognized and unrecognizable *terra incognita*" (136). What dangers can historiography elicit? No doubt such statements make many historians nervous, contextualized as an idealization of experimentation in the destruction of cultural forms. But *Difference and Repetition* is less interested in getting temporality right, by finding its correct mechanism or analogical notion, than it is in a *creative existentialism,* which is worth citing at some length:

The highest test is to understand the eternal return as a selective thought . . . Time must be understood and lived as out of joint, and seen as a straight line which mercilessly eliminates those who embark on it, who come upon the scene but repeat only once and for all. The selection occurs between two repetitions: those who repeat negatively and those who repeat identically will be eliminated. They repeat only once. The eternal return is for the third time . . . after the comic and after the tragic . . . The circle is at the end of the line . . . Eternal return . . . causes those who fail the test to perish. The negative does not return. The identical does not return. The Same and the Similar, the Analogous and the Opposed, do not return. Only affirmation returns—in other words, the Different, the Dissimilar . . . neither the default nor the equal, only the excessive returns. (298–99)

Let us call history as succession the straight line—a point in time, a periodization of . . . To live in habit and memory and subjective self-comfort with obligations posed by ideals that link past and future—that is to "repeat only once and for all." One lived, one died—identity and negation are always satisfied to take charge of one lived, one died. A parallel universe of infinitizing negativity. The Same, Similiar, Analogous, Opposed, connections of connection, ensure straight lines, neither time nor history out of joint. Eternal return asks not that we look to the past for ideals to continue, an obligation to an absence, history for revelation, but that we turn our energies to making events— "The mode of the event is the problematic . . . sensitive crisis points, turning points, boiling points, knots . . . a *tangled tale.*"[56]

The historiographic challenge thus set forth is directly about the social bond and history—how to make an event is of a different kind than turning events into our cultural politics, our institutional appropriations that make the past and present no more than equipment for the future. In a sense, *Difference and Repetition* asks if collectively many of us even know such differences in kind between an event and a narrative-form that drenches actions in stories. Historiographically, *Difference and Repetition* offers no satisfaction at all to a society whose social bonds presume an equation with before, as default, and the passing present a "during," filled with narrations that offer more of the same, only different, so to speak. Making the future makes before and during irrelevant, since only the future is capable of rendering to someone/them/us "no *prior identity*, no *internal resemblance*," or only the future can, paradoxically, effectively allow for "a never attained end" (301). Destiny is anything but end—it manifests not first, second, and third calibrated with before, during, and after (295), but a state of excess.

These are not questions of a historiography that pretends to be torn between the complementary relations of professionalization and political agendas, of university-based history writing internally fractured over conclusive compilations of research and the role of giving useful syntheses to various publics or, now, bearing witness, as Derrida insists, by a new scholar who replaces telos with the messianic.[57] Quite the contrary: *Difference and Repetition* keeps to a philosophical register best dramatized in the closing lines of *Anti-Oedipus.* If history can be of any effective value, a series of conceptual and practical tools, it must be used more abstractly and more nonfiguratively than we have known. Historiography was built to represent continuity, to lend itself to any power-claimant in the singsong of opposition and negation, correction, and so on. The problem now is how to extract from historiography's writings those concepts and temporal forms that are of help in any social disjunction, "completing [a] process and not arresting it, not making it turn about in the void, not assigning it a goal . . . the new earth . . . is no more behind than ahead . . . this process that is always and already complete as it proceeds, and as long as it proceeds."[58]

Conclusion

The alteration of historical representation is a constant, especially in periods when naming and narrating—selection—are intensely charged by disputes over events and processes. But the turn to use and abuse of history for the future is new and radical. At popular and academic levels, historical representation has become a *device to select for the future*. It suggests the eviscerated social bonds of metahistory, postulated universal conditions of historical representation. Are there intact conditions of historical representation? The deep plot-structures offered by Hayden White—shared literary tradition—and notions of subjectivity receptive to temporal experience—openness to history—emphasized by Reinhart Koselleck, are special codes, not cultural universals of historical representation. Doesn't history go out of joint if one cannot affirm shared historical knowledge? Yet how can one affirm such knowledge if narrations rest on dubious, restrictive names of events and processes, as was argued throughout this book? Now, in the face of rampant competition in every cultural and political arena of experience, historical narration removes claimants, and historiography is unable to articulate potentially unshareable disjunctions that, intellectually considered, might further damage narrative credibility. In a sense, history out of joint is about the *unmaking* of historical representation.

The genealogy of prose suggests the constancy of *spells of nominalization*. Here, names serve as monuments that soothe and dominate, that give propriety yet scapegoat at once, and pass into historical representation, strengthening narrative distortion. The lopsided narrative of Taiwan, one of many, many candidates, shows what is at stake. Negative name-spells are thrown at a subject—"tiny" and "troublesome" Taiwan—which complements the myth of One China. Readers are given an up-to-date *function* of historical *misrepresentation*—and history out of joint invites more of this kind of writing. I stressed a genealogy of prose that would unsettle that ordinary language relied upon by historians. Language is strife as much as it is anything else. Hence the critical notion, exploited in this book, that historical narrations might not be adequate to active and dynamic events and processes. For example, how would the prosaic names "founding fathers," "the sixties," or "Taiwaneseness" find support, or otherwise, without the metahistorical presumption that narration builds on the foundation of undisturbed prose? That question implies another: if historical *misrepresentation* is in fact based on the politics of prose, how can social bonds and their outcomes—as opposed to politically driven mythic ones—be claimed as the true subject of historical representation? What would happen, for example, if we consistently attributed Deleuzian improbability to the past and to ourselves, placing historical representation outside of common sense, as we proliferated the naming of events and processes? This is to ask why, at any given moment, there are so *few* names in circulation about events and processes.

With history out of joint, the political organization of prose, tilted to restrictive narratives, can be seen in efforts at neocanonization, discussed in chapters 2 through 4. Neocanonization offers proper names that synthesize and represent events and processes, but under the sway of many kinds of local despotisms. Such narration from the bottom up, through its immediate representors, politicizes from that place. Those materials concern overmediation by story and prose nominalization. The consequences are substantial—an effect, historical representation, becomes a *cause* of what can and cannot have a future. Overall, taking stock of history is less socially dynamic than "stocking" the future. The materials discussed in part I—affirmative action, elimination of aesthetic and cognitive objects (the reviews and editorials of chapters 2 and 3), locating the sixties in the history of error, and establishing canons—are volatile, but were narrated to *select and lessen senses of social danger about history.* The hypothesis that informed my analysis goes to the transformation of historical representation, historical narration, as a writing whose norm was to make a verbal demonstration of social bonds, to a writing that is peculiarly oversocializing, where social distortions are made normal. In chapter 4, Dworkin's construction of affirmative action—certainly a hot name—as vital for how this society looks in the future, necessitated that his story limit itself to black-and-white historical conflict over discrimination. To insist that student experiences—their history—can be selected and deselected by universities as to how *their* future as universities matters, indicates that larger, perhaps unassimilable, patterns (causes, disjunctions) of education remain off the narrative-subject sequence. What would affirmative action read *as* in Dworkin's story if it were embedded in the history of symptoms of class conflict, or as belonging to an educational caste system in the United States, instead of institutional survival? How can historical representation help one to understand contested social relations when narratives are restrictive? The politics of use and abuse of history, from everyday life to its conceptual reflections, or contemplations, is a hypothesis about what *we* have become in relation to history—signaled, in part I, by so much actually desperate narration.

History out of joint comes at a cost—public life is not where one speaks of historical epistemology, what difference it makes—and for whom—as to how and what one knows and learns from historical representation. "Epistemology is useless," writes one theorist of historiography, assimilating it to aesthetics, where the only issue of import for historians is to narrate what past subjects could not know about their future, the historian giving pleasure to current readers and tragedy to past subjects. Pleasure and tragedy are ancient comforts. Should historiography tell what is over and make aestheticization of ends an end in itself? Do only endings matter?[1]

Epistemology has a bad name precisely at the moment when historical representation has shifted to restriction on names that are made to matter—a question of selection. It is no accident that writers such as Barthes, Todorov, Genette, Lyotard, and Deleuze and Guattari made hypotheses about a schizo condition of historical representation. Schizo is no metaphor—it is a complex process of socialization, where capital, cultural authority, and social recognition converge. Restriction on names and narrating was turned by these writers into the historiographic contribution that history and event are definitively changed by processes of capital, associated with more violent—disjunctive—practices than most of us are ready to admit. A last reader is a figure of schizo culture, which comes out of use and abuse of rhetorical and cognitive devices that absorb past and future schizzes. In addition, the notion of a schizo time that disturbs identity, subjectivity, and related concepts is a probe of new disjunctions. For instance, in Lyotard's construction of historiographical discourse's shift from metanarrative inclusion to sign interpretation, a contemporary subject has no option but to work the schizophrenia, what history says versus what experience might teach. Deleuze's equally jarring arguments about habit and memory and a subject's experience of the abyss and the formless, destiny something like an "eye of the needle" that reveals processes affirmed and denied, asks that historiography embrace disjunctions, a hard thing to do.

The historiographer Reinhart Koselleck has drawn our attention to the fact that epistemological methods and concepts that have added to historical consciousness are inventions of the vanquished—from Thucydides to Augustine, from Commynes to the Scottish Enlightenment, from Marx to Humboldt to Weber. Their inventions, Koselleck writes, emerged from experiences of contestation and failure—epistemology is an effect of defeat.[2] The argument in this book is somewhat different—it emphasizes that historical epistemology is too dangerous in a society that uses historical telling to exclude claimants from the future. *Critical historical epistemology* is mostly an oxymoron in a social system in which different types of bonds are tested for investment and survival, making the future happen. Again, the case of Taiwan is instructive. One China—a highly restrictive story—is shared across the political spectrum, and circulates a tendentious political interpretation with strong economic and social interests, where misfiguration is normalized—to remove a claimant. It is not just liberals and conservatives that hew to restrictive narratives over Taiwan, but Marxists as well.[3] Another way of putting this is to stress that historiography's social promise, to offer syntheses by which its readers understand combinations of contingency and necessities, understanding deployed for perspectival orientation, becomes use and abuse precisely once social bonds do not hold—as schizo relations become facts on the ground.

In a sense, restrictive narratives continue the age-old despotic practice of ranking things—there are many past neocanonizations or past modernities, as Lyotard thought. The continuity of prose and despotism seems pertinent, but with a difference, which is ours: many of the narratives discussed above do not rank things because of their exemplary being in themselves, but for how they will add to a future that must occur. The narratives from the *Los Angeles Times,* Hollinger on the sixties, Dworkin, and Derrida come together as insistence on "must," disturbing in their narrative syntheses because used to idealize a restriction, to exclude further argument.

Prose discourse is the ground of historical narration, and brings its own entirely contentious genealogy to historiography. From Gorgias on discursive wizardry to Derrida's ghost hunter, the back and forth of prose and narrative is a movement to make names and naming *tell stories*—the victory of historical representation over the difficulty and murkiness of genealogical analysis, which makes every identity contestable. The former traces lines of continuity, from primitive marking devices that registered quantities of things and cosmological movements to the earliest barbarian narratives to pragmatic masters of history who turn all that happens into a resource. Modern historiography traces its core alliances to the eighteenth century, with of course Herodotus, Thucydides, Polybius, and a few others called upon to anchor basic, continuous practices—evidence testing, narrative inclusion, words that evoke spectacular conflict, worlds coming and going. Historical representation is secure so long as its readers identify with periodization of large-scale actions or small-scale ones made large (incident-history), periodizations that flow to a reader's ability to track some segment of a social bond, its ups and downs. Such representation alternates between innocence and irony—a sense of beginnings and outcomes that started well or badly and ended badly or better. Genealogy is a practice of critical thought that asks how readers, identities, and periodization are joined—and which processes are named and narrated *away* by any specific text of historical representation.

Finally, if historical representation cannot now generate a sense of inviting more discourse to contest narrated origins and ends, nor evoke the strategic and tactical possibility of conceiving events-as-difference, what happens to that historical consciousness out of which was to come social transformation? What would it say if historical consciousness were now more of a device to regulate competitions of all kinds, unable to sort through issues of goals and ends, taking these subjects into issues of social bonds? To close then with another beginning: what would it require in our "advanced" society—that has been historicized—to openly say that historical representation is just material for discussion—we wish to test ourselves with it instead of stepping into its comfort zones? What would one make of a society where history was actually taken seriously for its disjunctions instead of seeking identifications within it?

■ Notes

Introduction   Philosophical Prelude

1. See Niethammer, *Posthistoire*, p. 144.

2. Ibid., p. 151.

3. Janicaud, *Rationalities, Historicities*, p. 129.

4. Stephen Kinzer, "A Provocateur's Homecoming," *New York Times*, January 14, 2003, p. B1.

5. See Rodowick, "Introduction," p. 14.

6. See Turner, "Scientists as Agents," pp. 362–84.

7. Hill and Rubin, "The Genealogy of Normativity," p. 152.

8. See Rotman, "Going Parallel," p. 60.

9. See the analysis by Patricia Clough, "On the Relationship of the Criticism of Ethnographic Writing and the Cultural Studies of Science," p. 265.

10. See Biagioli, "From Book Censorship to Peer Review."

11. I am borrowing from Mario Biagioli's analysis of Galilean conflicts over the social status of mathematics and courtier society. See his *Galileo, Courtier*, pp. 16–17.

12. Cohen, *Passive Nihilism*, chapter 5.

13. See Krell, *Infectious Nietzsche*, pp. 5–7. Knowledge claims in the humanities can be negatively expressed: someone got their facts wrong. But positive bases are contestable, since one is dealing with rhetoric, logic, sense, and affect, or belief, opinion, grounds, support, and so on. Discourse and epistemology conflict because statements fall in and out of epistemic coherence or sense. Consequently, the humanities can never leave the plane of modeling—making concepts that are at once socially used, as discourse, and epistemically shaky. Further, these models are necessarily discontinuous with each other—what counts as a thesis in cultural studies is a bias from another discipline's perspective. The humanities articulate without foundations and have no option but to categorize and conceptualize existence treated as discourse. This makes the humanities an interesting version of *contamination*, where the object of study affects the subject doing the study, with numerous variations, including those of group discourse and behavior. See the introduction to Greimas and Fontanille, *The Semiotics of Passion*, for an important discussion of this issue.

14. Which Hannah Arendt, in *The Life of the Mind*, pp. 262–63, compares to

cultural incoherence, an idea not far from de Man's notion that language shows one side or face turned to possible hallucination and delirium.

15. Thanks to Gabrielle Spiegel for comments on this topic.

16. See McSherry, *Who Owns Academic Work?* p. 4.

17. See the recent essay by Lionel Gossman, "History and Anecdote."

18. Lyotard, *The Postmodern Condition,* p. 27.

19. Collingwood, *The Idea of History,* pp. 153–54.

20. Danto, *Narration and Knowledge,* p. 241.

21. Rancière, *The Names of History,* p. 89.

22. Koselleck, *Futures Past,* p. 200.

23. Greimas and Courtés, *Semiotics and Language.*

24. See Megill, "Historicizing Nietzsche?" pp. 115, 151.

25. See the mortified statements by Appleby, Hunt, and Jacob in their *Telling the Truth about History,* pp. 207ff.

26. Lyotard, "The Sign of History," in *The Lyotard Reader,* p. 399.

27. Ibid., p. 400.

28. To compete, the County Museum needs a "name = historic" architect, i.e., someone with a track record; the "history" of the architect underwrites, as it were, the legitimacy of the new building, which is not actually needed. Why isn't this seen as the confusion of name and thing that fuels competition?

29. Lyotard, "The Sign of History," in *The Lyotard Reader,* p. 404.

30. Deleuze, *Difference and Repetition,* p. 1. All further references are given in parentheses within the text.

31. Luc Ferry and Alain Renaut, in their *French Philosophy of the Sixties,* write that Deleuze and Guattari "contributed greatly to the methodological divestment of the 'I,'" the human subject's relations to temporality turned into the "pulverized or disintegrated Ego," a project that Ferry and Renaut make into a "will to annihilation," refusing to grant to Deleuze and Guattari's text any affirmative theses or projects (p. 66). Thomas Pavel, in a 1989 book, *The Feud of Language,* writes that *Capitalism and Schizophrenia* "is hedonistic and violent, often degenerating into intellectual acrobatics . . . theoretical ejaculations devoid of any preparation" (p. 133).

32. See Conley, "The Film Event," p. 308. Conley uses the phrase "evention" to characterize Deleuze's account of invention and event.

33. Royce, *Lectures on Modern Idealism,* p. 244.

34. Deleuze and Guattari, "May '68 Did Not Take Place."

35. Deleuze and Guattari, *Anti-Oedipus,* p. 86. See During, "Deleuze et apres?" p. 305.

Chapter 1   Nietzsche and Us

1. Giorgio Agamben, *Remnants of Auschwitz,* p. 148.

2. Ibid., p. 155.

3. Ibid., p. 52.

4. Koselleck, *The Practice of Conceptual History,* p. 135.

5. Ronell, *Stupidity,* p. 3.

6. Megill, "Historicizing Nietzsche?" pp. 115, 151.

7. These comments are based on Agamben, *The Man without Content,* pp. 85–92.

8. See the exemplary analysis by Sarah Kofman, *Nietzsche and Metaphor,* pp. 89–90.

9. No one has pursued this unreliability further than Paul de Man. See his *Allegories of Reading,* p. 20.

10. Felix Guattari, "I Am an Idea-Thief."

11. "The mythologist is excluded from this history in the name of which he professes to act. The havoc which he wreaks in the language of the community is absolute . . . he must live this assignment without any hope of going back or any assumption of payment." Barthes, *Mythologies,* p. 157.

12. Gorgias, "Encomium on Helen," p. 134.

13. Alain Badiou, *Manifesto for Philosophy,* pp. 118–19.

14. Heidegger, *What Is Called Thinking?* p. 29.

15. Cited in Grube, *The Greek and Roman Critics,* p. 9.

16. These remarks are drawn from Kenneth Burke's *A Grammar of Motives,* pp. 408ff.

17. Harris, *The Origin of Writing,* pp. 117–19.

18. See Barilli, *Rhetoric,* p. 5.

19. Benveniste, *Indo-European Language and Society,* pp. 411–13.

20. See Pinker, *How the Mind Works,* p. 81.

21. I am drawing upon Heidegger, "The Origin of the Work of Art," pp. 180–81.

22. Scarry, *Resisting Representation,* pp. 173ff.

23. See Genette, *Mimologics,* pp. 333–35.

24. Burke, *Language as Symbolic Action,* pp. 460ff.

25. See Bakhtin, *Rabelais and His World,* pp. 150ff.

26. Gorgias, "Encomium on Helen," p. 129.

27. Barthes, "The Old Rhetoric," p. 14.

28. Pinker, *The Language Instinct,* p. 28. Unfortunately, Pinker's views will become dominant, blending linguistic scientism with the affirmation that everyday language is fine as it is. This is called evolutionary psychology (it used to be called historicism).

29. Deleuze and Parnet, *Dialogues,* p. 86. Also see Deleuze and Guattari, *A Thousand Plateaus,* introduction.

30. Vico, *The New Science,* pp. 343, 126.

31. Ibid., pp. 14, 109.

32. Nietzsche, *Philosophy and Truth,* p. 85.

33. This section echoes part of Adorno's argument in *Negative Dialectics.*

34. Bloom, *The Map of Misreading,* pp. 68–69.

35. Vico, *The New Science,* pp. 342–43.

36. See Hillis Miller, "Dismembering and Disremembering," p. 50.

37. Paul de Man, *The Rhetoric of Romanticism,* p. 240.

38. Nietzsche, "On Truth and Lies in a Nonmoral Sense," in *Philosophy and Truth,* pp. 80–81.

39. Johnson, *The Critical Difference,* p. x.

40. The political theorists Laclau and Mouffe insist that discourse must be an attempt "to dominate the field of discursivity, to arrest the flow of differences, to construct a centre." Is this proposition moral-political or aesthetic, a chimera of satisfaction? See Laclau and Mouffe, *Hegemony and Socialist Strategy,* pp. 112–14.

41. Kofman, *Nietzsche et la metaphore,* p. 44.

42. Nietzsche, *Joyful Wisdom,* p. 220.

43. See Paul de Man, *Allegories of Reading,* pp. 153–54.

44. Thomas Pavel, *The Feud of Language,* p. 134.

45. See *Emergences* 12, no. 1 (2002), an issue on academic disjunctions and their social messiness.

46. Nietzsche, *Joyful Wisdom,* p. 328.

47. Ibid., p. 330.

48. De Man, *Allegories of Reading,* p. 111.

49. Ibid., p. 113.

50. Megill, "Grand Narrative and the Discipline of History."

51. Deleuze and Guattari, *A Thousand Plateaus,* p. 84.

52. Nietzsche, *The Genealogy of Morals,* p. 112.

53. Ibid., p. 181.

54. Deleuze and Guattari, *Anti-Oedipus,* p. 190.

55. These comments are a reflection on some ideas of Hayden White.

56. Butler, *Bodies that Matter,* p. 188. Thanks to Vicky Kirby for this reference.

57. See the writing of Paul Mann on all this, especially his *Theory Death of the Avant-Garde.*

58. See the great work by the Kneales, *The Development of Logic.*

59. See Haar, "Nietzsche and Metaphysical Language," pp. 5–36.

60. Ellis, "The Many-Minded Man," p. 11.

61. Nietzsche, *Philosophy and Truth,* p. 83.

62. As quoted in the *Chronicle of Higher Education,* February 10, 1995, p. A7.

63. Nietzsche, *Philosophy and Truth,* p. 90.

64. Nietzsche, *The Birth of Tragedy,* section 8.

65. See During, "Deleuze et apres?"

66. Deleuze, *Nietzsche and Philosophy,* pp. 111ff.

67. See chapter 4 of Deleuze and Guattari's *A Thousand Plateaus.*

68. Žižek, *Tarrying with the Negative,* p. 234.

69. See Paul Mann, *Masocriticism*. Also, on Žižek, see Kriss Ravetto, "Frenchifying Film Studies," and Ravetto-Biagioli, "Film according to Žižek."

70. See Hollier, *The College of Sociology*, p. viii.

71. See Greimas and Fontanille, *The Semiotics of Passion*, p. xxiv.

72. Nietzsche, *The Birth of Tragedy*, sections 8, 10.

73. Deleuze, *Nietzsche and Philosophy*, pp. 73–74.

74. Kaplan, "The Economics of Family and Faith," p. 5.

75. See Sloterdijk, *Thinker on Stage*, p. 83.

76. Kant, *Critique of Judgment*, section 27.

77. Barthes, *Elements of Semiology*, p. 9.

78. Quoted in Stambaugh, *Nietzsche's Thought of Eternal Return*, pp. 53, 55.

79. Nietzsche, *Philosophy and Truth*, pp. 88–90.

Chapter 2   How to Make an Ahistorical People

1. Unfortunately, the ahistorical is related in Western historiography to the pre-historic, as in groups without Statist writing; to the historical, as in the persistence of traditions commingled with fashion and the arbitrary, with its concomitant theories of mourning and loss; and to the posthistorical, which Deleuze calls the sovereign individual. Deleuze, *Nietzsche et la philosophie*, pp. 155ff.

2. Deleuze and Guattari, *A Thousand Plateaus*, p. 99.

3. The editorials after the ousting of the KMT in the spring of 2000 used the occasion to raise Taiwan's history. The *New York Times* called Taiwan a "murky" and "unruly" island, and the *Los Angeles Times* offered a piece that emphasized that any Taiwanese claim to independence is an "historical . . . accident of China's turbulent history," dissolving Taiwan into China. See Nicolas Kristof, "The Murky Tale of Taiwan: Island with an Unruly Past," *New York Times*, March 21, 2000, p. A8; and M. Meisner, "The Historical Basis for a Free Taiwan," *Los Angeles Times*, March 26, 2000, p. M1.

4. One of the best books on the topic of who represents what (what Deleuze once called the problem of who selects in representation, not what is selected) is Chow, *Writing Diaspora*, p. 13, where the author notices the tendency toward "self-subalternization" on the part of Westerners speaking about anything Asian.

5. Lyotard, *The Differend*, p. xi.

6. See the comments by J. J. Clarke, in *Oriental Enlightenment*, p. 27. My sense of Taiwan is, in Clarke's idiom, constructed by my sense of "cultural disquietude" about the West.

7. See Knapp, "The Shaping of Taiwan's Landscapes," p. 4.

8. See Spence, "Kissinger and the Emperor," p. 18.

9. See Stainton, "The Politics of Taiwan Aboriginal Origins," p. 34. I should say that I have relied on this and other pieces by Stainton, whose acute understanding of historiographic uses and abuses I find productive.

10. Ibid., p. 32.

11. Ibid., p. 35.

12. See Dixon, *The Rise and Fall of Languages,* p. 86.

13. Stainton, "The Politics of Taiwan Aboriginal Origins," p. 38.

14. Ibid., p. 39.

15. Quoted in ibid., p. 40.

16. See Shinkichi, "An Outline of Formosan History," p. 43.

17. See Davison and Reed, *Culture and Customs of Taiwan,* pp. 4–5.

18. Hsu, "From Aboriginal Island to Chinese Frontier," p. 5.

19. Ibid., pp. 22–23.

20. See Copper, *Taiwan,* pp. 22–23.

21. Hsu, "From Aboriginal Island to Chinese Frontier," p. 12.

22. Ibid., p. 15.

23. Many writers on Taiwan have something to say about this repetition or parallel. One of the best books on the subject is Crozier, *Koxinga and Chinese Nationalism,* p. 19.

24. Copper, *Taiwan,* p. 27.

25. See Weller, *Resistance, Chaos, and Control in China,* p. 114.

26. Davison and Reed, *Culture and Customs of Taiwan,* p. 18.

27. Copper, *Taiwan,* p. 33.

28. On the scary "identity" between communist and Kuomintang—their shared belief in corporatism, on securing the "national-will"—see Gold, "Taiwan's Quest for Identity in the Shadow of China," p. 170.

29. Copper, *Taiwan,* p. 35. See also Lai Tse-Han, Myers, and Wei-Wou, *A Tragic Beginning,* pp. 168–70.

30. *City of Sadness,* a film by Hou Hsiao-hsien, is one of the strongest representations of the Massacre.

31. Tsai, "Political Reorientation."

32. See Mosher, *China Misperceived.*

33. In particular, Henry Chu and Jim Mann. Each has written strong if implicit deflations of even the *Times'* editorial page.

34. In his *Oriental Enlightenment,* J. J. Clarke makes the point that a persistent sense of "disquietude" about the West, within the West, accompanies the sense of superiorism.

35. Todorov, *The Morals of History,* pp. 14–15.

36. Ibid., pp. 136–37.

37. See Kuan-Hsing Chen, "Problematizing 'Asia,'" e-mail, August 25, 1997, distributed worldwide.

38. Tom Plate, "Brainy Ideas from 'the Rome of the Rim,'" *Los Angeles Times,* March 25, 1997, p. B7.

39. Tom Plate, "On Taiwan, Beijing Learns to Yawn," *Los Angeles Times,* August 5, 1997, p. B7.

40. Todorov, *The Morals of History*, p. 35.

41. Tom Plate, "Asia's Politically Tone Deaf Leaders," *Los Angeles Times,* September 30, 1997, p. B7.

42. Tom Plate, "Left Behind, China Hopes for New Life," *Los Angeles Times,* May 17, 2000, p. B7.

43. Tom Plate, "In Praise of Advancing the Cause of Peace," *Los Angeles Times,* May 24, 2000.

44. Tom Plate, "In Praise of Advancing the Cause of Peace."

45. Tom Plate, "Beijing's 'Salesman' Makes an Offer of Hong Kong 'Plus,'" *Los Angeles Times,* May 3, 2000, p. B9.

46. Tom Plate, "Realism Tempers the 'One China' Principle," *Los Angeles Times,* March 25, 2000, p. B7.

47. Tom Plate, "Taiwan Has Anti-Corruption Fever," *Los Angeles Times,* March 22, 2000, p. B7.

48. Tom Plate, "The Press Shares Blame on China," *Los Angeles Times,* March 1, 2000, p. B7.

49. Tom Plate, "Goldilocks Policy on China May Be 'Just Right,'" *Los Angeles Times,* January 26, 2000, p. B13.

50. Tom Plate, "Hawk Plus Dove Makes Unpersuasive Policy," *Los Angeles Times,* September 22, 1999, p. B7.

51. On the Chinese slush funds to the Democratic Party and China's espionage of our technology, Plate takes the occasion to emphasize that China "knows" it has bigger problems than increasing its military capacity, "despite occasional pushy behavior in the South China Sea." "Pushy" is an amazing euphuism. "Is Clinton Losing China?" *Los Angeles Times,* May 26, 1999, p. B7.

52. While teaching in Xiamen in 1997, during the "return" of Hong Kong to the CCP, I watched the televised ceremony in which a male and a female ringmaster swooned the party leadership into chairs, seated before thousands in an auditorium, while patriotic songs burst forth all around. Jiang Zemin mouthed the words about Hong Kong's return—surrounded by dozens of top officials, all men, all with jet-black hair but one (a general, I was told), all in their sixties up, and it struck me as Communist Kitsch or Las Vegas meets History. It was remarkably like an American Democratic or Republican convention, minus the technology, perhaps minus the dread of not being cool, but sharing the same predicates—sincere, utopian, cynical, and pious, clear about the wrong things, right about nothing but vaguenesses.

53. Tom Plate, "China: Renounce Force on Taiwan," *Los Angeles Times,* July 7, 1998, p. B7.

54. Ibid.

55. Barthes, *Mythologies*, pp. 141–42.

56. Baudrillard, *The Mirror of Production*, pp. 165–67.

Chapter 3   Art Criticism and Intellectuals in Los Angeles

1. Susan Freudenheim, letter to Sande Cohen, October 23, 1998.
2. Quoted in Bellah, "Max Weber and World-Denying Love," p. 23.
3. Relyea, "Virtually Formal," pp. 116, 173.
4. Harvey, "Booster Shots," p. 38.
5. Harvey, "Jurassic Sequels," p. 35.
6. Hultkrans, "Surf and Turf," p. 105.
7. Suzanne Muchnic, "Things Are Popping Up at the Getty," *Los Angeles Times,* April 10, 2001, p. F1.
8. Suzanne Muchnic, "Rethinking a Think Tank," *Los Angeles Times, Calendar,* April 29, 2001, p. 6.
9. Suzanne Muchnic, "Ascent of the Early Risers," *Los Angeles Times, Calendar,* April 1, 2001, p. 6. See as well Israel, "Public Offerings," p. 189.
10. Wasserman, "The Latitude and Longitude of L.A. Lit," p. R3.
11. Shoshana Wayne press release, December 16, 2000–February 3, 2001, text by Jan Tumlir, curator.
12. Susan Anderson, "The Artistic Void in the Collections of L.A.'s Museums," *Los Angeles Times,* December 19, 1999, p. M1.
13. See Cohen and Zelevansky, "This Is Not an Opinion," pp. 139–64.
14. See Boyle, *Shamans, Software, and Spleens,* p. 28. Thanks to Mario Biagioli for this reference.
15. Deleuze and Guattari, *What Is Philosophy?* pp. 169ff.
16. The *New York Times* ran a story called "L.A. Gets Serious. Seriously," April 17, 1999, p. B9, and cited a writer *in* L.A. who writes *on* L.A.: "L.A. is as self-conscious about itself and generating as much literature about itself as any other city in the world." The writer *in* and *on* L.A. is modeled as a "public intellectual" because of an *identity* between place and writing, the writer not making ideas and critiques but "reflecting" on what is already here.
17. For example, see Neil Gabler, "The Deconstruction of Clinton," *Los Angeles Times* January 3, 1998, pp. M1, M6. Gabler teaches at USC and frequently writes cultural editorials, one leitmotiv being that of the indistinctness between culture and the social.
18. See McSherry, "Uncommon Controversies," p. 226.
19. See Barilli, *Rhetoric,* p. 126.
20. Wasserman, "L.A. Is Book Country," p. 3.
21. Wasserman, "Years of Hope, Days of Rage," p. 5.
22. Ibid., p. 6.
23. Ibid.
24. Jacoby, "Essential Adorno," p. 5.
25. Lehman, "A Language of One's Own," p. 10.
26. Appleby, "Danger, Historians At Work," p. 1.

27. Wasserman, "Why Read Marx?" p. 10.

28. Marx and Engels, *The Communist Manifesto,* pp. 21, 31. Italics added.

29. Eco, *The Role of the Reader,* p. 8.

30. Wasserman, "Years of Hope, Days of Rage," p. 5.

31. In a review of Al and Tipper Gore's new book on the family, Andrew Hacker shows that some statistics are so irregular as to defy the book's own conclusions. See Hacker, "Gore Family Values," p. 24.

32. Hobsbawm, "Making It," p. 5.

33. Mount, "Two-Eyed King," p. 4; Toulmin, "Prodigal Son," p. 6.

34. Eugene Genovese, "Restoring Dignity to Thucydides' Profession," *Los Angeles Times,* May 31, 1998, p. M2.

35. Ascherson, "How Could They?" p. 3.

36. Ibid.

37. See George Marcus, "Middlebrow into Highbrow at the J. Paul Getty Trust." As Marcus points out, it is the middlebrow that requests "a discourse and response of wonder, free of context, to sacred relics of art," a "middlebrow seriousness" that Marcus wittily calls into question.

38. Vivas, "A Natural History of the Aesthetic Transaction," p. 99.

39. Pagel, "Looking into Seeing," pp. 10–20; Hickey has an essay in this catalogue, and bases his assertions of antitheory on Gilbert-Rolfe's writings, so it seems fair to link these writers who have already joined in an alliance.

40. Hickey, "Simple Hearts," p. 11.

41. Ibid., p. 13.

42. Hickey, "David Reed's Coming Attractions," pp. 33–34.

43. Hickey, "Why Art Should Be Bad," pp. 16–17.

44. Hickey, "Hue and Cry," p. 7. This upsurge of ressentiment is co-coded in being placed side by side with an anecdote with and of Warhol, which is probably hagiographic: "one day" on the street, it's "'Hi, Andy,' I said. 'Oh, hi.' 'Whatcha up to?' 'You know, shopping.' 'Wha'd you get.' 'You want to see?' 'Yeah.'"

45. Ibid.

46. Hickey, "The Murmur of Eloquence," pp. 23–24. In this regard, see Pagel's review of Jeremy Gilbert-Rolfe's show, *Los Angeles Times,* September 25, 1998, p. F25, where he, some four years after *Plane/Structures,* writes that Gilbert-Rolfe's paintings "unfold in slow motion . . . Defying time . . . endlessly fascinating," verbal tags that are a model of the very thing detested, language's absorption of object.

47. Hickey, "The Murmur of Eloquence," p. 25.

48. Ibid.

49. Ibid.

50. Ibid., p. 31.

51. Todorov, *Theories of the Symbol,* pp. 64ff, 73ff.

52. Disclosure: David Pagel did some coursework and discussion with me while he was a Mellon Fellow at the California Institute of the Arts.

53. The argument is remarkably similar to any mode of intellectual cleansing, e.g., "left political cleansing" of the type associated with denunciations of beauty.

54. Pagel, "Designer Marxism," p. 19.

55. By using the rhetoric of *exuscitatio,* a trope of mobilizing emotions.

56. Pagel, "Designer Marxism," pp. 17–18.

57. All the citations of this paragraph are in Pagel, "Designer Marxism," p. 18.

58. Ibid., p. 19. Hickey insists that "irony" is European, whereas "cool" belongs to the virtues of American democracy. The perfect oration, like the best artworks, occurs when "the orator . . . need only mount the dais and stand before his fellow citizens to make the quality of his virtue and of his case visible through the presence of his body." That reads as less a defense of cool than the terrorism of the power of, say, Hitler as orator. See Hickey, "Simple Hearts," p. 12.

59. Pagel is unable to factor into his language that *Art Issues* is a privately held corporation paid for by the very foundations (Lannan, Annenberg Foundation, Getty Trust, et al.) denounced here as sustaining "Designer Marxism," or that what is published in *Art Issues,* where Pagel serves as reviews editor, is decided in the very same "secretive exchanges" of said Marxism in the universities. See my *Passive Nihilism,* chapter 1, for an analysis of high-standing American historians who try to eliminate cultural criticism because the latter challenges the *historical naturalism* of American values—criticism should not undercut Americans' acceptance of individualism, competitive capitalism, etc.

60. Bernard Holland, "Listen with the Ear, Not the Mind," *New York Times,* December 20, 1998, Arts and Leisure, p. 1. To "ear" equals to be able to say "I like / don't like," where "like" equals another blank term for "I like / don't like."

61. Hickey, "Why Art Should Be Bad," p. 16.

62. Pagel, "Designer Marxism," p. 17.

63. Hickey, "Why Art Should Be Bad," pp. 16ff.

64. Quoted in Christopher Knight, "It's All in What You See," *Los Angeles Times, Calendar,* September 14, 1997, p. 80.

65. Hickey, "Why Art Should Be Bad," p. 18.

66. David Pagel, "Baldessari Plays with Puzzles," *Los Angeles Times,* November 5, 2002, p. E22. David Pagel, "Eleven Artists at the Getty," *Los Angeles Times,* March 1, 2000, p. F1.

67. Baudrillard, "Objects, Images and the Possibilities of Aesthetic Illusion," p. 7.

68. Gilbert-Rolfe, "The French Have Landed."

69. Gilbert-Rolfe, *Beyond Piety,* p. 239.

70. Ibid., p. 239. The gnomicism of Gilbert-Rolfe's writing is very strong. To say that singularity = wrongness or that the nonsingular = multiplicity makes the key terms reversible, or undercuts all of them at once, returning them to tautology.

71. Ibid., p. 243.

72. In an interview with Christopher Knight, Baldessari also affirmed that "art is about money." *Los Angeles Times,* December 30, 1996.

73. Gilbert-Rolfe, *Beyond Piety,* pp. 273–74.

74. Ibid., p. 248.

75. Ibid., p. 171.

76. This crib the point of my *initial* letter to Susan Freudenheim at the *Times.*

77. Gilbert-Rolfe, *Beyond Piety,* p. 173. Pagel's essay is a clone of Gilbert-Rolfe's essay, cited above, on Baudrillard and the art world.

78. Ibid., p. 182.

79. Ibid., p. 187.

80. Ibid., p. 55. In the *Los Angeles Times,* August 30, 1998, p. 58, he professes shock at how "right-wing" America is.

81. Ibid., p. 73. This is amplified in a chapter on Frank Gehry's design for a restaurant/bar in Venice, California, called Rebecca's, where the contemporary bar, as such, is said to be a place so noisy that it is a place "of faces rather than voices." Without analyzing bar differences, it is insisted that "faces" over "voices" is to be compared with Manet's bar, with its internal distances (subjects in conflict) replaced by L.A.'s mere "faces." Assuming his readers have been to Rebecca's, the restaurant/bar mirrors Los Angeles, for the latter is nothing but "anteriority rather than interiority . . . movement between . . . rather than passage from outside to within. Looking and looking at must, in such a culture, similarly take place within the language of the anterior . . . of what lies behind rather than what lies within . . . an absence of good sense . . . frivolity rather than industry . . . display rather than conversation."

82. "Vision's Resistance to Language," which is cited in *Beyond Piety* as previously presented as a lecture in 1993 was also previously published in an Art Center journal, *More and Less* 1, no. 1 (Spring 1994).

83. Gilbert-Rolfe, *Beyond Piety,* p. 41.

84. See Christopher Knight, "A World Beyond Cherished Concepts," *Los Angeles Times,* November 28, 1999, p. 52. On the County Museum, only one of Knight's rants is necessary to cite. He denounces a show called "Made in California" as a "flea-market" with "pretensions," as a "novelty show," as an "academic parlor game" because of curatorial "recontextualization" of displayed objects, all of this due to "university education over the last 30 years." "Universities have replaced the traditional study of art history with cultural studies . . . sociological rather than artistic." "For five years, LACMA has been the largest American art museum headed not by an art historian but by a former university administrator, with no knowledge of the discipline. What should we expect?" Christopher Knight, "Thematically Overwrought," *Los Angeles Times,* October 23, 2000, p. F1.

85. Christopher Knight, "Art for School's Sake," *Los Angeles Times,* July 8, 2001, p. 67.

86. Christopher Knight, "Peering Beyond the Edge," *Los Angeles Times,* July 24, 2001, p. F1.

87. Christopher Knight, "A MOMA Retrospective," *Los Angeles Times,* April 6, 2002, p. F1.

88. Christopher Knight, "Like, Conceptual, Dude," *Los Angeles Times,* November 25, 2002, p. E3.

89. See Christopher Knight, "Andy Warhol, Properly Labeled," *Los Angeles Times,* April 13, 1997, p. 71; and "Lots of Sunshine, Little Light," July 27, 1997, p. 4.

90. Christopher Knight, "Art Exhibitions, Inc.," *Los Angeles Times,* June 20, 2004, p. E33; "Artworks with Wattage," *Los Angeles Times,* June 21, 2004, p. E1.

91. Deleuze, "On the New Philosophers," p. 40.

Chapter 4   Figuring Forth the Historian Today

1. See Sloterdijk, "Interview."

2. Deleuze, *Difference and Repetition,* pp. 77–78.

3. Lecercle, *Interpretation as Pragmatics,* p. 167.

4. This quote is from a spammed e-mail sent from Peter Lunenfeld to Recipient List Suppressed in 2000.

5. By invoking the notion of implosion, borrowed from Jean Baudrillard, I am suggesting that historical representation "has already left its own goals behind and thereby no longer has any remedies at hand," a proposition that tries to make sense of the actual diversity of historical writing. See Baudrillard, "The Anexoric Ruins," p. 30.

6. Ronald Dworkin, "Affirming Affirmative Action," *New York Review of Books,* October 22, 1998, p. 92.

7. Ibid., p. 94.

8. Which the authors of *Anti-Oedipus* locate as unconscious desire to thwart preconscious class interests. See Deleuze and Guattari, *Anti-Oedipus,* p. 104.

9. Dworkin, "Affirming Affirmative Action," p. 98.

10. Ibid., p. 99.

11. Theweleit, *Male Fantasies;* Kenneth Burke, *A Grammar of Motives,* p. 101.

12. Dworkin, "Affirming Affirmative Action," p. 100.

13. Ibid., p. 101.

14. Hayden White, "Historical Text as Literary Artifact," p. 49.

15. For research historians in particular, syntactic play with the reader that seriously undermines synthesis is taboo. The historical profession has not had to seriously write in a way that calls into question the equation between historical discourse = possession of reality. A further equation with discourse/possession is the authorization to make judgments, i.e., "wise people," and the vast connotations and branchings from there.

16. Barthes, "Historical Discourse," p. 145.

17. Ibid., p. 147.

18. Ibid., p. 148.

19. Ibid., p. 151.

20. Ibid. Surprisingly, even Barthes's astute readers do not focus on the cognitive aspects of assertion, or the phrase "reversion," which kicks off the "psychotic" dimension. Wulf Kansteiner, for example, emphasizes Barthes's idea of the "paradox" of historical representation, literary form taken for extradiscursive referent, but it is far stronger than paradox. "Hayden White's Critique of the Writing of History," p. 275.

21. The exception would be those metahistorical writings that do not assert but only multiply perspectives.

22. See Weil, *The Need for Roots,* pp. 45–52; Arendt, "The Concept of Culture."

23. Polan, "The Professors of History," pp. 237ff.

24. See Sharon Traweek, "Pilgrim's Progress."

25. See Mario Biagioli, "The Scientific Revolution Is Undead," pp. 141–48.

26. Polan, "The Professors of History," p. 245.

27. The Enola Gay exhibition in Washington in 1994 is an exception.

28. By comparison to their counterparts in Germany, Russia, France, Italy, Japan, etc.

29. Polan, "The Professors of History," p. 252; U.S. Department of Education, National Center for Education, Table 257, August 2001.

30. Rancière, *The Names of History,* p. 69. In Rancière's terms, the historian takes what is separated, the "dia-bolic," and gives words that cause "the place of truth to speak in place of the unconscious chatterers." For history to be possible, "it must settle its account with the devil. It must give him a place, attach him to his place" (p. 68).

31. Deleuze and Guattari, *Anti-Oedipus,* p. 260.

32. Christopher Rhoads, "Historians Researching the Nazi-Era Industry Find Their Reputations Are Also at Risk," *Wall Street Journal,* February 19, 1999.

33. Deleuze and Guattari, *Anti-Oedipus,* p. 202.

34. Ibid., p. 260.

35. Collini, "Against Utopia," p. 3.

36. Margalit, "Isaiah and the Jews," p. 19.

37. Ryan, "Wise Man," p. 29.

38. Marcus, "Both Fox and Hedgehog," p. 7; Ignatieff, "On Isaiah Berlin," p. 10; Collini, "Against Utopia," p. 3; Dabney, "The Philosopher and the Critic," p. 31; Ryan, "Wise Man," p. 29; and Williams, "The Reluctant Philosopher," p. 18.

39. Collini, "Against Utopia," p. 3.

40. Ibid.

41. Ibid.

42. Ryan, "Wise Man," p. 29.
43. Ibid., p. 32.
44. Ibid., p. 34.

Chapter 5   *A Critical Analysis of the Historiographic Anecdote*

1. White, *Figural Realism,* p. 3.
2. Ibid., p. 6.
3. Ibid., pp. 18–19.
4. Shotwell, *The History of History,* pp. 48–62.
5. Genette, *Figures of Literary Discourse,* p. 55.
6. Ducrot and Todorov, *Encyclopedic Dictionary of the Sciences of Language,* p. 228.
7. See Perelman and Olbrechts-Tyteca, *The New Rhetoric,* pp. 291, 417ff.
8. White, *Figural Realism,* p. 63.
9. Burke, *A Grammar of Motives,* pp. 59–61.
10. White, *Figural Realism,* pp. 72–73.
11. Danto, *Narration and Knowledge,* p. 152.
12. Shulevitz, "Keepers of the Tenure Track," p. 46.
13. Jameson, "The Politics of Theory," p. 65.
14. White, *Figural Realism,* p. 63.
15. Ibid.
16. See Andrea Loselle, "How French Is It?"
17. Fineman, "The History of the Anecdote," p. 49. All further references to this essay will be given in the text.
18. One of the best discussions of this is in Arthur Danto's *Narration and Knowledge.*
19. Kant, *Foundations of the Metaphysics of Morals,* p. 83.
20. See Lewis White Beck's remarks in Kant, "On History," p. xxvi.
21. See Genette, *Figures of Literary Discourse,* pp. 120–21.
22. Roudinescu, "Jacques Lacan—The Erasure of History," pp. 87–98.
23. Ravetto, "Frenchifying Film Studies."
24. Lacan, *The Language of the Self,* p. 193.
25. These remarks are based on Deleuze and Guattari, *Anti-Oedipus,* pp. 60, 82.
26. Starns, "Introduction," p. 2. "New Erudition" is a subcoding within European historiography often pursuing the "rights of the connoisseur," favoring a "penchant" for the "telling" anecdote.
27. Koselleck, *The Practice of Conceptual History,* p. 76.
28. Hollinger, "The Disciplines and the Identity Debates," p. 333. All further references to this essay will be given in the text.
29. See Hayden White's comments on New Historicism in *The New Historicism,* p. 301.

30. In Appleby, Hunt, and Jacob's *Telling the Truth about History,* p. 7, a "lack of confidence" in the knowledge proffered by humanistic "experts" stems from the "relativism . . . that the truth of a statement is relative to the position of the person making the statement . . . a questioning of the ideal of objectivity." For a more extensive critique, see my "Reading the Historian's Resistance to Reading," pp. 1–28.

Chapter 6   Derrida's "New Scholar"

1. In this regard, see Palti, "The 'Return of the Subject' as a Historico-Intellectual Problem," pp. 72–73, 78. Palti notes certain problems in Foucault's conceptions of an *episteme,* and some arguments against them. He notices that Foucault's use of *episteme* derived from Heidegger's emphasis that subject and modernity go together in representation, separation of I/self from the world, the subject in charge of the dispersions of life. Those markers of a classical *episteme* were disturbed with a *modern episteme:* "History comes from within . . . Time contains within itself the principle of its own transformation." Palti goes on to add that for Foucault, the correlation of modern plus subject plus time as transformation meant the subject was both empirical and transcendental, a paradox, at once a principle of formation yet unknowable. Palti thinks we now occupy a new *episteme,* which he calls neostructuralism, represented by Derrida: the radical contingency of all things, where "that which founds a given horizon but cannot be objectified within it without destroying itself (its condition of possibility-impossibility)."

2. Carter, "Telling Times," pp. 12–13.

3. Krell, *The Purest of Bastards,* pp. 113, 203.

4. Hobson, *Jacques Derrida,* p. 121.

5. These comments are drawn from Genette, *Figures of Literary Discourse,* pp. 137–43.

6. Nowhere is this more evident than in Appleby, Hunt, and Jacob's *Telling the Truth about History,* wherein the authors actually write that historical consciousness is continuous with a human "craving" for narrative, that there is a "cry" by humans for historical identity and that such "amour propre" makes historical consciousness something *natural* (pp. 258ff). Their critique of Derrida comes from a reactionary attempt to close historiography to anything that smacks of what they call postmodernism's "stripping" of human beings of their very humanity (p. 224).

7. See William Spanos's critical remark that "Derrida's appropriation of Saussure's assertion that 'in language there are only differences without positive terms' in effect translates the temporal difference that Heidegger locates in material being . . . into a transcendental/universal that operates in the free-floating, leveled-out space of textuality." Spanos, *Heidegger and Criticism,* p. 121.

8. White, "The Absurdist Moment in Contemporary Literary Theory," pp. 402–3.

9. Spanos, *Heidegger and Criticism,* p. 88.

10. White, "The Absurdist Moment in Contemporary Literary Theory," p. 403.

11. De Man, *Blindness and Insight,* pp. 131–32.

12. Ibid., p.135.

13. Rheinberger, "Experimental Systems," p. 65. Thanks to Mario Biagioli for showing me this essay.

14. Ibid., p. 68.

15. Ibid., p. 69.

16. Ibid.

17. Ibid., p. 77.

18. See Weber, "Piecework."

19. Derrida, *Specters of Marx,* p. xviii. All further citations from this will be given in parentheses in the chapter.

20. Nora, "Between Memory and History," p. 9.

21. Hamacher, "Lingua Amissa," p. 177.

22. See Richard Eder, "Giving Voice to an Awkward Silence in Germany," *New York Times,* February 5, 2003, p. B7.

23. See Koselleck, *Futures Past.*

24. Hamacher, "Lingua Amissa," p. 167.

25. Rodolphe Gasché, in *The Tain of the Mirror,* p. 205, has it that *différance* "promotes the plurality of difference, of a conflictuality that does not culminate in contradiction but remains a contradiction without contradiction." Rhetorical analysis sees in this the affirmation of a paradox, a one-sided demand for what Gasché calls the "quasi-transcendental" status of *différance.*

26. See the brilliant remarks by Karl Löwith, *Meaning in History,* pp. 18ff.

27. See Descombes, *Modern French Philosophy.*

28. See White, *Figural Realism,* pp. 38–40.

29. The historian L. P. Curtis once wrote that the English use of images for social control over things Irish consistently played off the confusion of "guerilla"/ "gorilla" in the newspaper imagery of the nineteenth century.

30. See Gasché, *The Tain of the Mirror,* pp. 197, 244.

31. See, in this regard, Hamacher, "Lingua Amissa," pp. 166–67.

32. Löwith, *Meaning in History,* pp. 44–46.

33. See Ermarth, *Sequel to History,* p. 149.

34. See Benveniste, *Indo-European Language and Society,* pp. 410ff.

35. Deleuze and Guattari, *Anti-Oedipus,* pp. 6–8.

36. One of the best treatments of this subject is found in G. A. Kelly, *Idealism, Politics and History,* introduction.

37. Hamacher, "Lingua Amissa," p. 171.

38. See Ermarth, *Sequel to History,* pp. 151, 153.

39. Deleuze and Guattari, *What Is Philosophy?* pp. 70–83.

Chapter 7 The Use and Abuse of History according to Jean-François Lyotard

1. See Appleby, Hunt, and Jacob, *Telling the Truth about History,* pp. 209–10.
2. Lyotard, "Figure Foreclosed," in *The Lyotard Reader,* p. 74.
3. Readings, *Introducing Lyotard,* p. 57.
4. Lyotard, "Figure Foreclosed," in *The Lyotard Reader,* p. 95.
5. Baker, *The Image of Man,* p. 123.
6. Lyotard, "Figure Foreclosed," in *The Lyotard Reader,* p. 98.
7. See Koselleck, *Futures Past,* p. 204. Emphasis added.
8. See Biagioli, "The Scientific Revolution Is Undead," pp. 141–47.
9. Jon Weiner, "Historian with a History," *Los Angeles Times,* May 2, 2004, p. M1. Weiner criticizes the Bush administration's nomination of an historian with a "controversial history" due to the ethics of this historian's publisher paying ex-KGB Russian spies for documents and the historian's withholding of research materials from other scholars. He compares this to what he thinks is the excessive negative treatment received by the historian Bellesiles who was forced to resign from Emory University a few years ago over substantiated claims of research fraud. The board that investigated Bellesiles, Weiner says, found "evidence of falsification only on one page." Weiner omits the actual report on Bellesiles, which noted that he had in fact falsified data and omitted factual information that undercut his thesis. Weiner neglects to say that the analysts of Bellesiles could not examine his research, Bellesiles claiming it had been destroyed in a flood, but what they did analyze was full of distorted claims concerning the documents he possessed. Why choose here between left and right? See *New York Times,* October 27, 2002, p. A25; Emory University, "Report of the Investigating Committee in the Matter of Michael Bellesiles," August 10, 2002.
10. Croce, *History as the Story of Liberty,* p. 20.
11. White, *Metahistory,* p. 399.
12. Croce, *History as the Story of Liberty,* p. 165.
13. Danto, *The Body-Body Problem,* pp. 181–82.
14. Lyotard, *Peregrinations,* p. 35.
15. Marquand, *Farewell to Matters of Principle,* pp. 94–97. Thanks to Elie During for sending me this volume, as well as for some discussions on this topic.
16. Benn, *Primal Vision,* pp. 87, 100; de Certeau, "The Historiographical Operation," p. 85.
17. De Certeau, "The Historiographical Operation," pp. 90, 98.
18. Nietzsche, *The Use and Abuse of History,* p. 10.
19. "Save the future" is heard more and more these days. While it can have a reactionary edge to it (e.g., eco-purists), the intellectual problem of the future is as undescribed as ever.
20. Cited in Descombes, *Modern French Philosophy,* pp. 112–13.
21. Lyotard, "Lessons in Paganism," in *The Lyotard Reader,* p. 127.

22. Ibid., p. 133.

23. See Hebdige, *Hiding in the Light,* p. 81.

24. Lyotard, "Lessons in Paganism," in *The Lyotard Reader,* p. 148.

25. Lyotard, "Philosophy and Painting in the Age of Their Experimentation: Contribution to an Idea of Postmodernity," in *The Lyotard Reader,* p. 190.

26. Lyotard, *The Postmodern Condition,* p. 73.

27. Ibid., p. 75.

28. Ibid., p. 80.

29. This is the argument made by Deleuze and Guattari in their last joint work, *What Is Philosophy?*

30. Nietzsche, *The Use and Abuse of History,* pp. 24–25.

31. Ibid., p. 9.

32. Nietzsche, *Philosophical Writings,* p. 6.

33. Lyotard, "Judiciousness in Dispute, or Kant after Marx," in *The Lyotard Reader,* p. 325.

34. See Ravetto, "Shaking Down LA Cool," pp. 207–27.

35. In terms complementary with those of Lyotard, Michel de Certeau has argued that historical concepts are now *inside scientific protocols* in terms of research and setting of problems, while its mode of presentation serves the interests of making a place for death, of writing as satisfaction. See de Certeau, "The Historiographical Operation," p. 100.

36. Lyotard, *The Postmodern Condition,* pp. 46–47.

37. Lyotard, *Just Gaming,* p. 9.

38. Ibid., p. 10.

39. Lyotard, *The Differend,* pp. 137–38.

40. Ibid., p. 13. Thanks to John Tagg for this reference.

41. Lyotard, "Universal History and Cultural Differences," in *The Lyotard Reader,* p. 414.

42. See de Man, *Allegories of Reading,* p. 116, for a cogent analysis.

43. Lyotard, "Universal History and Cultural Differences," in *The Lyotard Reader,* p. 318.

44. Ibid., p. 321.

45. Lyotard, "The Sign of History," in *The Lyotard Reader,* p. 394.

46. Ibid., p. 386.

47. Ibid., p. 397.

48. Ibid., p. 399.

49. Ibid., p. 400.

50. Ibid., p. 404.

51. Nietzsche, *The Use and Abuse of History,* p. 52.

52. Carroll, *Paraesthetics,* p. 182.

53. See Appleby, Hunt, and Jacob, *Telling the Truth about History,* p. 235.

54. Lyotard, *Postmodern Condition,* p. 81.

Chapter 8   The Genealogy of History according to Deleuze and Guattari

1. Foucault, *Language, Counter-Memory, Practice,* pp. 139–40.
2. Danto, *Narration and Knowledge,* pp. 12–15.
3. See Appleby, Hunt, and Jacob, *Telling the Truth about History,* p. 7. They write: "The experience of ww2 with its horrendous new weaponry and the genocidal policies of the Nazi regime temporally forestalled the progress of skepticism and relativism. The killing of the Jews seemed to show that absolute moral standards were necessary, that cultural relativism had reached its limits in the death camps. But the lull was only temporary." Such statements are both professionally sanctioned and illiterate.
4. Niethammer, *Posthistoire,* p. 148–49.
5. See Fineman, "The History of the Anecdote: Fiction and Fiction"; Rancière, *Names of History,* pp. 84–85; de Certeau, *The Writing of History,* p. 88.
6. Carlo Ginzburg's narration of ancient hunter into Greek semiotician into early modern antiquarian into modern connoisseur is a key instance of antigenealogical idealism. See my "Desire for History," pp. 57–75.
7. Wood, "Creating the Revolution," p. 41.
8. Foucault, "Nietzsche, Genealogy, History," p. 76.
9. De Certeau, *The Writing of History,* pp. 84–85.
10. Ankersmit, "Danto, History, and the Tragedy of Human Existence," p. 304.
11. Deleuze and Guattari, *Qu'est-ce que la philosophie?* p. 96. All future references to this text will be given in the chapter as *WP.*
12. Shotwell, *The History of History,* p. 170.
13. See Breisach, *Historiography,* p. 33.
14. See the comments by Daniel Smith, Introduction to *Essays Critical and Clinical,* p. xxxix.
15. Shotwell, *The History of History,* p. 82.
16. Lingis, "The Society of Dismembered Body Parts," p. 6.
17. Baker, *The Image of Man,* p. 115.
18. Deleuze and Guattari, *Anti-Oedipus,* p. 143. All further references to this text will be given in the chapter as *AO.*
19. See Massumi, *A User's Guide to Capitalism and Schizophrenia,* p. 44.
20. Kelley, "Vico's Road," p. 23.
21. Massumi, *A User's Guide to Capitalism and Schizophrenia,* p. 4.
22. Breisach, *Historiography,* p. 76. Also see Shotwell, *The History of History,* p. 60.
23. See Lyotard, *Just Gaming,* p. 62.
24. See Breisach, *Historiography,* pp. 8–9.
25. Shotwell, *The History of History,* pp. 168–69.
26. "Although Rauschenberg can be seen to have prefigured early 'post-modernist' positions that sought to subvert overarching social power structures, his own project was ultimately compromised in that it did not take into account the

emergent, decentralized forces of control that began to characterize late-capitalist society at precisely this time . . . The essential insight Warhol brought to bear on the older artist's work was that the centralized, hierarchical forms of social control Rauschenberg attempted to subvert were already superseded in an era of increasing commercialism and mass media." Joseph, "'I'll Be Your Mirror,'" p. 117. Thanks to Howard Singerman for this reference.

27. The writings of Howard Singerman, *Art Subjects* (Berkeley: University of California Press, 1999) and Tom Lutz, *Cosmopolitan Vistas* (Ithaca, NY: Cornell University Press, 2004), are exemplary.

28. De Landa, *A Thousand Years of Nonlinear History,* pp. 190–91.

29. Nietzsche, *The Genealogy of Morals,* section 26.

30. See Hardt, *Gilles Deleuze,* pp. 120–21.

31. Ibid., p. 107.

32. Deleuze, *Nietzsche et la philosophie,* pp. 1–2. All future references to this text will be given in the chapter as *NP.*

Chapter 9   Nothing Affirmative Ever Dies

1. See Boundas, "Deleuze-Bergson," p. 102.
2. Hardt and Negri, *Empire,* p. 367.
3. See Winfree, "The Repetition of Eternal Return," pp. 21–22.
4. See During, "Blackboxing in Theory," pp. 177ff.
5. See Ansell-Pearson, *Philosophy and the Adventure of the Virtual,* p. 159.
6. See Hardt, *Gilles Deleuze,* p. 18.
7. Deleuze and Guattari, *Anti-Oedipus,* p. 134.
8. Ferry and Renaut, *French Philosophy of the Sixties,* pp. 66, 69.
9. Pavel, *The Feud of Language,* p. 33.
10. See Lotringer, "Doing Theory," p. 138.
11. Lotringer, "Better than Life," p. 252.
12. Alliez, foreword to *Capital Times,* p. xxiii.
13. Laing, *The Bird of Paradise,* p. 150.
14. This is the argument of Lyotard's *The Differend,* which has been virtually ignored by mainstream American philosophy.
15. Deleuze, *Difference and Repetition,* p. 1. All further references to this text will be given in parentheses.
16. See Massumi's *A User's Guide to Capitalism and Schizophrenia,* p. 84.
17. Winfree, "The Repetition of Eternal Return," pp. 19–20.
18. Deleuze, *The Logic of Sense,* pp. 287–89.
19. Ansell-Pearson, *Philosophy and the Adventure of the Virtual,* pp. 168–69.
20. Salanskis, "Idea and Destination," pp. 69–70.
21. Deleuze, *The Logic of Sense,* pp. 289, 292.
22. Deleuze and Guattari, *Anti-Oedipus,* p. 86.

23. This is the confused and confusing argument of Frank Ankersmit, in "Danto, History, and the Tragedy of Human Existence," p. 304, cited above, chapter 8, note 10.

24. Ansell-Pearson, *Philosophy and the Adventure of the Virtual*, pp. 172, 182.

25. See the nasty comments by Ankersmit against Lyotard or "French Philosophy" in his book review of Pieters' *Moments of Negotiation*, in "Danto, History, and the Tragedy of Human Existence," pp. 255ff.

26. Ansell-Pearson, *Philosophy and the Adventure of the Virtual*, p. 189.

27. Descombes, *Modern French Philosophy*, pp. 158–59.

28. Deleuze and Guattari, *What Is Philosophy?* pp. 169–70.

29. It should be emphasized here that *Difference and Repetition*, with its references to Kant and Holderlin and "catastrophe," plays off a Romanticism *not encoded* as reconciliation, as desire, as longing for unity, as allegory.

30. For a critique of the contemporary making of irony into a transcendental condition of any historicity whatsoever, see Cohen, *Passive Nihilism*, chapter 1, part 1.

31. Rancière, *The Names of History*, pp. 89, 91.

32. Ferry and Renaut, *French Philosophy of the Sixties*, p. 89.

33. Badiou, *Manifesto for Philosophy*, p. 38. For an interesting criticism of Badiou and an argument for schizophrenia as process, see Eric Alliez, "Anti-Oedipus—Thirty Years On."

34. Ansell-Pearson, *Philosophy and the Adventure of the Virtual*, p. 182.

35. See the interesting if sketchy arguments of R. M. W. Dixon, *The Rise and Fall of Languages*, p. 82.

36. Berlin, *Historical Inevitability*, pp. 55, 57.

37. Lenci and Bertinetto, "Aspects, Adverbs, and Events," pp. 252–53.

38. Ansell-Pearson, *Philosophy and the Adventure of the Virtual*, p. 169–70.

39. Ibid., p. 179.

40. Murphy, "The Theatre of (the Philosophy of Cruelty) in *Difference and Repetition*," pp. 107–9, 131.

41. Malabou, "Who's Afraid of Hegelian Wolves," p. 132.

42. Deleuze, *Bergsonism*, p. 107.

43. Ansell-Pearson, *Philosophy and the Adventure of the Virtual*, p. 169.

44. Deleuze and Guattari, *What Is Philosophy?* pp. 50, 111.

45. Deleuze and Guattari, *Anti-Oedipus*, p. 267.

46. So writes Jonathan Kirsch: the author under review "rarely injects himself into his book, but when he does, he succeeds in making his points more sharply than in the more cerebral passages." "Native Cultures, Imported Myths," *Los Angeles Times Book Review*, July 18, 2004, p. R2.

47. Deleuze and Guattari, *Anti-Oedipus*, p. 48.

48. See Deleuze and Guattari, *A Thousand Plateaus*, chapter 4.

49. See the remarks of Massumi, *A User's Guide to Capitalism and Schizophrenia*, pp. 96–98.

50. Royce, *Lectures on Modern Idealism,* p. 35.

51. See the work of Manuel de Landa, *A Thousand Years of Nonlinear History,* pp. 257ff.

52. For Deleuze's analysis of sense, see his *Logic of Sense,* p. 22.

53. The many writings of Gérard Genette are exemplary on narrative temporality.

54. De Man, *The Rhetoric of Romanticism,* pp. 93–124.

55. Deleuze and Guattari, *Nomadology,* p. 121.

56. Deleuze, *The Logic of Sense,* pp. 55–56.

57. Cohen, *Passive Nihilism,* pp. 42–44.

58. Deleuze and Guattari, *Anti-Oedipus,* p. 382.

Conclusion

1. Ankersmit, "Danto, History, and the Tragedy of Human Existence," p. 297.

2. Koselleck, *The Practice of Conceptual History,* p. 76.

3. See Perry Anderson's recent mythmaking in "Stand-Off in Taiwan." Anderson, without offering any evidence, regards Taiwan as a former province of China as he makes baleful comments about gangsters and the current leadership of the DPP. For a Marxist to omit such *historical facts* as the rebellion of the Tai Republic declared in early twentieth-century Taiwan against the Japanese is indicative of the politics involved—a Western Marxist fear that the PRC will go to the scrapheap of history. As this book goes to press, the leader of Taiwan's KMT Party met in China with President Ho Jintao. Declaring consensus against Taiwanese independence, the CP and KMT "close" their contested "history," as Taiwan is again isolated.

Bibliography

Adorno, Theodor. *Negative Dialectics.* New York: Seabury Press, 1972.
Agamben, Giorgio. *The Man without Content.* Stanford: Stanford University Press, 1999.
———. *Remnants of Auschwitz.* New York: Zone Books, 1999.
———. *Stanzas: Word and Phantasm in Western Culture.* Minneapolis: University of Minnesota Press, 1993.
Alliez, Eric. "Anti-Oedipus—Thirty Years On." Paper presented at Birkbeck College, London, November 29, 2003.
———. Foreword by Gilles Deleuze, *Capital Times,* translated by Georges Van Den Abbeele. Minneapolis: University of Minnesota Press, 1996.
Anderson, Perry. "Stand-Off in Taiwan," *London Review of Books* 26, no. 11 (June 3, 2004).
Ankersmit, Frank. "Danto, History, and the Tragedy of Human Existence." *History and Theory* 42, no. 3 (2003).
———. Review of "Pieters' Moments of Negotiation." *History and Theory* 42, no. 2 (2003).
Ansell-Pearson, Keith. *Philosophy and the Adventure of the Virtual.* New York: Routledge, 2002.
Appleby, Joyce. "Danger, Historians At Work." *Los Angeles Times Book Review,* August 4, 1996.
Appleby, Joyce, Lynn Hunt, and Margaret Jacob. *Telling the Truth about History.* New York: Norton, 1994.
Arendt, Hannah. "The Concept of Culture." In *Between Past and Future: Six Exercises in Political Thought.* New York: Viking, 1961.
———. *The Life of the Mind.* New York: Harcourt Brace Jovanovich, 1979.
Ascherson, Neal, "How Could They?" *Los Angeles Times Book Review,* May 10, 1998.
Badiou, Alain. *Manifesto for Philosophy.* Albany: State University of New York Press, 1999.
Baker, Herschel. *The Image of Man.* New York: Harper and Row, 1947.
Bakhtin Mikhail. *Rabelais and His World.* Bloomington: Indiana University Press, 1984.
Barilli, Renato. *Rhetoric.* Minneapolis: University of Minnesota Press, 1989.

Barthes, Roland. *Elements of Semiology.* New York: Hill and Wang, 1968.
———. "Historical Discourse." In *Introduction to Structuralism,* edited by Michael Lane. New York: Basic Books, 1970.
———. *Mythologies.* New York: Hill and Wang, 1972.
———. "The Old Rhetoric." In *The Semiotic Challenge.* New York: Hill and Wang, 1988.
Baudrillard, Jean. "The Anexoric Ruins." In *Looking Back on the End of the World,* edited by D. Kamper and C. Wulf. New York: Semiotext(e), 1989.
———. *The Mirror of Production.* St. Louis: Telos, 1975.
———. "Objects, Images and the Possibilities of Aesthetic Illusion." In *Art and Artefact,* edited by N. Zurbrugg. Thousand Oaks, CA: Sage, 1997.
Bellah, Robert N. "Max Weber and World-Denying Love." Lecture given at the University of California–San Diego, October 30, 1997.
Benn, Gottfried. *Primal Vision: Selected Writings of Gottfried Benn,* edited by E. B. Ashton. London: Bodley Head, 1961.
Benveniste, Emile. *Indo-European Language and Society.* Coral Gables, FL: University of Miami Press, 1973.
Berlin, Isaiah. *Historical Inevitability.* London: Oxford, 1955.
Biagioli, Mario. "From Book Censorship to Peer Review." *Emergences* 12, no. 1 (May 2002).
———. *Galileo, Courtier.* Chicago: University of Chicago Press, 1994.
———. "The Scientific Revolution Is Undead." *Configurations* 6, no. 2 (1998).
Bloom, Harold. *The Map of Misreading.* New York: Oxford University Press, 1975.
Boundas, Constantin. "Deleuze-Bergson: An Ontology of the Virtual." In *Deleuze: A Critical Reader,* edited by Paul Patton. London: Blackwell, 1996.
Boyle, James. *Shamans, Software, and Spleens.* Cambridge: Harvard University Press, 1996.
Breisach, Ernst. *Historiography.* Chicago: University of Chicago Press, 1983.
Burke, Kenneth. *A Grammar of Motives.* Berkeley: University of California Press, 1969.
———. *Language as Symbolic Action.* Los Angeles: University of California Press, 1968.
Butler, Judith. *Bodies that Matter.* London: Routledge, 1993.
Carroll, David. *Paraesthetics.* London: Methuen, 1987.
Carter, Jonathan A. "Telling Times: History, Emplotment, and Truth." *History and Theory* 42 (February 2003).
Chow, Rey. *Writing Diaspora.* Bloomington: Indiana University Press, 1993.
Clarke, J. J. *Oriental Enlightenment.* New York: Routledge, 1997.
Clough, Patricia. "On the Relationship of the Criticism of Ethnographic Writing and the Cultural Studies of Science." *Cultural Studies, Critical Methodologies* 1, no. 2 (May 2001).

Cohen, Sande. "Desire for History: Historiography, Scholarship, and the Vicarious." *Storio della Storiografia* 30 (1996).

———. "Hide Your Commodification: Art and Criticism in Los Angeles, or Language Denied." *Emergences* 9, no. 2 (November 1999).

———. *Passive Nihilism.* New York: St. Martin's, 1998.

———. "Reading the Historian's Resistance to Reading: An Essay on Historiographic Schizophrenia." *Clio* 26 (Fall 1996).

Cohen, Sande, and Paul Zelevansky. "This Is Not an Opinion." *Journal of Visual Culture* 1, no. 2 (2001).

Collingwood, R. G. *The Idea of History.* Oxford: Clarendon, 1946.

Collini, Stefan. "Against Utopia." *Times Literary Supplement,* August 22, 1997.

Conley, Tom. "The Film Event." In *The Brain Is the Screen,* edited by Gregory Flaxman. Minneapolis: University of Minnesota Press, 2000.

Copper, John. *Taiwan: Nation-State or Province?* Boulder: Westview, 1999.

Croce, Benedetto. *History as the Story of Liberty.* London: Allen and Unwin, 1949.

Crozier, Ralph. *Koxinga and Chinese Nationalism.* Cambridge: Harvard East Asian Research Center, 1997.

Dabney, Lewis. "The Philosopher and the Critic." *New York Times Book Review,* November 29, 1998.

Danto, Arthur. *The Body-Body Problem.* Berkeley: University of California Press, 1999.

———. *Narration and Knowledge.* New York: Columbia University Press, 1985.

Davison, Gary M., and Barbara E. Reed. *Culture and Customs of Taiwan.* Westport, CT: Greenwood, 1998.

de Certeau, Michel. "The Historiographical Operation." In *The Writing of History,* translated by Tom Conley. Minneapolis: University of Minnesota Press, 1988.

de Landa, Manuel. *A Thousand Years of Nonlinear History.* New York: Zone Books, 1997.

Deleuze, Gilles. *Bergsonism.* New York: Zone Books, 1988.

———. *Difference and Repetition.* New York: Columbia University Press, 1994.

———. *The Logic of Sense.* New York: Columbia University Press, 1990.

———. *Negotiations.* New York: Columbia University Press, 1995.

———. *Nietzsche and Philosophy.* New York: Columbia University Press, 1983.

———. *Nietzsche et la philosophie.* Paris: Presses Universitaires de France, 1962.

———. *Nomadology: The War Machine,* translated by Brian Massumi. New York: Semiotext(e), 1986.

———. "On the New Philosophers and a More General Problem." *Discourse* 20, no. 3 (Fall 1998).

Deleuze, Gilles, and Félix Guattari. *Anti-Oedipus.* Minneapolis: University of Minnesota Press, 1983.

———. "May '68 Did Not Take Place." In *Hatred of Capitalism: A Semiotext(e) Reader,* edited by Chris Kraus and Sylvère Lotringer. Los Angeles: Semiotext(e), 2001.

————. *Qu'est-ce que la philosophie?* Paris: Minuit, 1991.

————. *A Thousand Plateaus.* Minneapolis: University of Minnesota Press, 1987.

————. *What Is Philosophy?* New York: Columbia University Press, 1994.

Deleuze, Gilles, and Claire Parnet. *Dialogues.* New York: Columbia University Press, 1987.

de Man, Paul. *Allegories of Reading.* New Haven: Yale University Press, 1983.

————. *Blindness and Insight.* New York: Oxford University Press, 1971.

————. *The Rhetoric of Romanticism.* New York: Columbia University Press, 1984.

Derrida, Jacques. *Margins of Philosophy.* Chicago: University of Chicago Press, 1982.

————. *Specters of Marx.* New York: Routledge, 1994.

Descombes, Vincent. *Modern French Philosophy.* Baltimore: Johns Hopkins University Press, 1985.

di Leonardo, M. "It's the Discourse, Stupid." *Nation,* March 17, 1997.

Dixon, R. M. W. *The Rise and Fall of Languages.* Cambridge: Cambridge University Press, 1997.

Ducrot, Oswald, and Tzvetan Todorov. *Encyclopedic Dictionary of the Sciences of Language.* Baltimore: Johns Hopkins University Press, 1979.

During, Elie. "Blackboxing in Theory: Deleuze versus Deleuze." In *French Theory in America,* edited by Sylvère Lotringer and Sande Cohen. New York: Routledge, 2001.

————. "Deleuze et apres?" *Critique* 623 (April 1999).

Dworkin, Ronald. "Affirming Affirmative Action." *New York Review of Books,* October 22, 1998.

Eco, Umberto. *The Role of the Reader.* Bloomington: Indiana University Press, 1979.

Ellis, Joseph J. "The Many-Minded Man." *New York Times Book Review,* July 6, 2003.

Ermarth, Elizabeth Deeds. *Sequel to History: Postmodernism and the Crisis of Representational Time.* Princeton: Princeton University Press, 1992.

Ferry, Luc, and Alain Renaut. *French Philosophy of the Sixties.* Amherst: University of Massachusetts Press, 1990.

Fineman, Joel. "The History of the Anecdote: Fiction and Fiction." In *The New Historicism,* edited by H. Aram Veeser. New York: Routledge, 1989.

Foucault, Michel. *Language, Counter-Memory, Practice.* Ithaca, NY: Cornell University Press, 1977.

————. "Nietzsche, Genealogy, History." In *The Foucault Reader,* edited by Paul Rabinow. New York: Pantheon, 1984.

Gasché, Rodolphe. *The Tain of the Mirror.* Cambridge: Harvard University Press, 1986.

Genette, Gérard. *Figures of Literary Discourse.* New York: Columbia University Press, 1982.

———. *Mimologics.* Lincoln: University of Nebraska, 1995.

Gilbert-Rolfe, Jeremy. *Beyond Piety.* Cambridge: Cambridge University Press, 1995.

———. "The French Have Landed." Paper presented at the French Theory in America Conference, Drawing Center, New York, November 1997, organized by Sylvère Lotringer and Sande Cohen.

Gold, T. B. "Taiwan's Quest for Identity in the Shadow of China." In *In the Shadow of China,* edited by S. Tsang. Honolulu: University of Hawaii Press, 1993.

Gorgias. "Encomium on Helen." In *Ancilla to the Pre-Socratic Philosophers,* edited by Kathleen Freeman. Cambridge: Harvard University Press, 1978.

Gossman, Lionel. "History and Anecdote." *History and Theory* 42, no. 2 (2003).

Greimas, A. J., and J. Courtés. *Semiotics and Language: An Analytical Dictionary.* Bloomington: Indiana University Press, 1982.

Greimas, A. J., and J. Fontanille. *The Semiotics of Passion.* Minneapolis: University of Minnesota Press, 1993.

Grube, G. M. A. *The Greek and Roman Critics.* New York: Methuen, 1965.

Guattari, Félix. "I Am an Idea-Thief." In *Chaosophy,* edited by Sylvère Lotringer. New York: Semiotext(e), 1995.

Haar, Michel. "Nietzsche and Metaphysical Language." In *The New Nietzsche,* edited by David Allison. Cambridge: MIT Press, 1990.

Hacker, Andrew. "Gore Family Values." *New York Review of Books,* December 5, 2002.

Hamacher, Werner. "Lingua Amissa." In *Futures of Jacques Derrida,* edited by Richard Rand. Stanford: Stanford University Press, 2001.

Hardt, Michael. *Gilles Deleuze: An Apprenticeship in Philosophy.* Minneapolis: University of Minnesota Press, 1993.

Hardt, Michael, and Antonio Negri. *Empire.* Cambridge: Harvard University Press, 2000.

Harris, Roy. *The Origin of Writing.* La Salle, IL: Open Court, 1986.

Harvey, Doug. "Booster Shots." *Los Angeles Weekly,* September 17, 2001.

———. "Jurassic Sequels." *Los Angeles Weekly,* August 24, 2001.

Hebdige, Dick. *Hiding in the Light.* London: Routledge, 1988.

Heidegger, Martin. "The Origin of the Work of Art." In *Basic Writings,* edited by David Farrell Krell. New York: Harper and Row, 1977.

———. *What Is Called Thinking?* New York: Harper and Row, 1958.

Hickey, Dave. "David Reed's Coming Attractions." In *David Reed Paintings, Motion Pictures.* La Jolla, CA: Museum of Contemporary Art, San Diego, 1998.

———. "Hue and Cry." *Artforum* (Winter 2000).

———. "The Murmur of Eloquence: Intimations of the Full World." In *Plane/Structures,* edited by David Pagel. Los Angeles: Fellows of Contemporary Art, 1994.

————. "Simple Hearts: American Cool." *Art Issues,* January–February 1999.

————. "Why Art Should Be Bad." *Harper's Magazine,* January 1998.

Hill, Austin, and Jonathan Rubin. "The Genealogy of Normativity." *PLI* 11 (2001).

Hillis Miller, J. "Dismembering and Disremembering in Nietzsche's 'On Truth and Lies in a Nonmoral Sense.'" *Boundary 29,* no. 3 (Spring 1981), and 10, no. 1 (Fall 1981).

Hobsbawm, Eric. "Making It." *Los Angeles Times Book Review,* March 15, 1998.

————. "Why Read Marx?" *Los Angeles Times Book Review,* February 8, 1998.

Hobson, Marian. *Jacques Derrida: Opening Lines.* New York: Routledge, 1998.

Hollier, Denis, ed. *The College of Sociology, 1937–39.* Minneapolis: University of Minnesota Press, 1988.

Hollinger, David A. "The Disciplines and the Identity Debates, 1970–1995." *Daedalus* 126, no. 1 (Winter 1997).

Hsu Wen-Hsiung. "From Aboriginal Island to Chinese Frontier: Taiwan before 1683." In *China's Island Frontier,* edited by R. G. Knapp. Honolulu: University of Hawaii Press, 1980.

Hultkrans, A. "Surf and Turf." *Artforum* (Summer 1998).

Ignatieff, Michael. "On Isaiah Berlin." *New York Review of Books,* December 18, 1997.

Israel, Nico. "Public Offerings." *Artforum* (September 2001).

Jacoby, Russell. "Essential Adorno." *Los Angeles Times Book Review,* August 30, 1998.

Jameson, Fredric. "The Politics of Theory: Ideological Positions in the Postmodern Debate." *New German Critique* (Fall 1984).

Janicaud, Dominique. *Rationalities, Historicities.* Atlantic Highlands, NJ: Humanities Press, 1997.

Jay, Martin. "Of Plots, Witnesses, and Judgments." In *Probing the Limits of Representation,* edited by Saul Friedlander. Boston: Harvard University Press, 1993.

Johnson, Barbara. *The Critical Difference.* Baltimore: Johns Hopkins University Press, 1980.

Joseph, Branden. "'I'll Be Your Mirror': Robert Rauschenberg and Andy Warhol, 1952–1968." In *Center 18: Record of Activities and Research Reports, June 1997–May 1998.* Washington, DC: Center for Advanced Study in the Visual Arts, 1998.

Kansteiner, Wulf. "Hayden White's Critique of the Writing of History." *History and Theory* 32, no. 3 (1993).

Kant, Immanuel. *Critique of Judgment.* In *Philosophical Writings,* edited by Ernst Behler. New York: Continuum, 1986.

————. *Foundations of the Metaphysics of Morals.* New York: Liberal Arts, 1959.

————. "On History." In *Philosophical Writings,* edited by Ernst Behler. New York: Continuum, 1986.

Kaplan, Richard. "The Economics of Family and Faith." *Los Angeles Times Book Review,* July 30, 1995.

Kelley, Donald R. "Vico's Road." In *Giambattista Vico's Science of Humanity,* edited by Giorgio Tagliacozzo and Donald Phillip Verene. Baltimore: Johns Hopkins University Press, 1976.

Kelly, G. A. *Idealism, Politics and History.* Cambridge: Cambridge University Press, 1969.

Knapp, R. G. "The Shaping of Taiwan's Landscapes." In *Taiwan: A New History,* edited by Murray A. Rubinstein. Armonk, NY: M. E. Sharpe, 1999.

Kneale, William, and Mary Kneale. *The Development of Logic.* London: Oxford University Press, 1962.

Kofman, Sarah. *Nietzsche and Metaphor.* Stanford: Stanford University Press, 1993.

———. *Nietzsche et la metaphore.* Paris: Galilée, 1983.

Koselleck, Reinhart. *Futures Past.* Cambridge: MIT Press, 1985.

———. *The Practice of Conceptual History.* Stanford: Stanford University Press, 2002.

Krell, David Farrell. *Infectious Nietzsche.* Bloomington: Indiana University Press, 1996.

———. *The Purest of Bastards: Works of Mourning, Art, and Affirmation in the Thought of Jacques Derrida.* University Park: Pennsylvania State University Press, 2000.

Lacan, Jacques. *The Language of the Self.* New York: Delta, 1968.

Laclau, Ernesto, and Chantal Mouffe. *Hegemony and Socialist Strategy.* London: Verso, 1985.

Lai Tse-Han, R. H. Myers, and Wei-Wou. *A Tragic Beginning.* Stanford: Stanford University Press, 1991.

Laing, R. D. *The Bird of Paradise.* Middlesex: Penguin, 1967.

Lecercle, Jean-Jacques. *Interpretation as Pragmatics.* New York: St. Martin's, 1999.

Lehman, David. "A Language of One's Own." *Los Angeles Times Book Review,* October 10, 1993.

Lenci, Alessandro, and Pier Marco Bertinetto. "Aspects, Adverbs, and Events: Habituality vs. Perfectivity." In *Speaking of Events,* edited by J. Higginbotham, Fabio Pianesi, and Achille C. Varzi. London: Oxford University Press, 2000.

Lingis, Alphonso. "The Society of Dismembered Body Parts." *PLI: Warwick Journal of Philosophy,* edited by Joan Broadhurst (1992).

Loselle, Andrea. "How French Is It?" In *French Theory in America,* edited by Sylvère Lotringer and Sande Cohen. New York: Routledge, 2001.

Lotringer, Sylvère. "Better than Life." *Artforum* (April 2003).

———. "Doing Theory." In *French Theory in America,* edited by Sylvère Lotringer and Sande Cohen. New York: Routledge, 2001.

Löwith, Karl. *Meaning in History.* Chicago: University of Chicago Press, 1949.

Lyotard, Jean-François. *The Differend: Phrases in Dispute.* Minneapolis: University of Minnesota Press, 1988.

———. *Just Gaming.* Minneapolis: University of Minnesota Press, 1985.

———. *The Lyotard Reader,* edited by Andrew Benjamin. Oxford: Blackwell, 1989.

———. *Peregrinations: Law, Form, Event.* New York: Columbia University Press, 1988.

———. *The Postmodern Condition.* Minneapolis: University of Minnesota Press, 1984.

Malabou, Catherine. "Who's Afraid of Hegelian Wolves." In *Deleuze: A Critical Reader,* edited by Paul Patton. Oxford: Blackwell, 1996.

Mann, Paul. *Masocriticism.* Albany: State University of New York Press, 1999.

———. *Theory Death of the Avant-Garde.* Bloomington: Indiana University Press, 1991.

Marcus, George. "Middlebrow into Highbrow at the J. Paul Getty Trust." *Cultural Anthropology* 5, no. 3 (1990).

Marcus, Steven. "Both Fox and Hedgehog." *New York Times Book Review,* November 29, 1998.

Margalit, Avishai. "Isaiah and the Jews." *Times Literary Supplement,* May 29, 1998.

Marquand, Odo. *Farewell to Matters of Principle.* Oxford: Odeon, 1989.

Marx, Karl, and Friedrich Engels. *The Communist Manifesto,* edited by Samuel H. Beer. New York: AHM, 1955.

Massumi, Brian. *A User's Guide to Capitalism and Schizophrenia.* Cambridge: MIT Press, 1993.

McSherry, Corynne. "Uncommon Controversies: Legal Mediations of Gift and Market Models of Authorship." In *Scientific Authorship,* edited by Mario Biagioli and Peter Galison. New York: Routledge, 2003.

———. *Who Owns Academic Work?* Stanford: Stanford University Press, 2001.

Megill, Allan. "Grand Narrative and the Discipline of History." In *A New Philosophy of History,* edited by Frank Ankersmit and Hans Kellner. Chicago: University of Chicago Press, 1995.

———. "Historicizing Nietzsche? Paradoxes and Lessons of a Hard Case." *Journal of Modern History* 68 (March 1996).

Mosher, Steven W. *China Misperceived: American Illusions and Chinese Reality.* New York: Basic Books, 1990.

Mount, Ferdinand. "The Two-Eyed King." *Los Angeles Times Book Review,* August 30, 1998.

Murphy, Timothy S. "The Theatre of (the Philosophy of Cruelty) in *Difference and Repetition.*" *PLI* (October 1992).

Niethammer, Lutz. *Posthistoire: Has History Come to an End?* London: Verso, 1992.

Nietzsche, Friedrich. *The Birth of Tragedy and the Genealogy of Morals.* New York: Anchor Books, 1956.

———. *The Genealogy of Morals.* London: T. N. Foulis, 1913.

———. *Joyful Wisdom.* New York: Frederick Ungar, 1979.

———. *Philosophical Writings.* New York: Continuum, 1995.

———. *Philosophy and Truth,* edited by Daniel Breazeale. Atlantic Highlands, NJ: Humanities, 1979.

———. *The Use and Abuse of History.* New York: Bobbs-Merrill, 1957.

Nora, Pierre. "Between Memory and History: Les Lieux de Memoire." In *Representations* 26 (Spring 1989).

Pagel, David. "Designer Marxism." *Art Issues,* September–October 1998.

———. "Looking into Seeing." In *Plane/Structures,* edited by David Pagel. Los Angeles: Fellows of Contemporary Art, 1994.

Palti, Elias. "The 'Return of the Subject' as a Historico-Intellectual Problem." *History and Theory* 43 (February 2004).

Pavel, Thomas. *The Feud of Language.* Oxford: Blackwell, 1989.

Perelman, Chaim, and L. Olbrechts-Tyteca. *The New Rhetoric.* Notre Dame: University of Notre Dame Press, 1969.

Pinker, Steven. *How the Mind Works.* New York: Norton, 1997.

———. *The Language Instinct.* New York: Morrow, 1994.

Polan, Dana. "The Professors of History." In *The Persistence of History,* edited by Vivian Sobchack. New York: Routledge, 1996.

Rabinow, Paul. "For Hire: Resolutely Late Modern." In *Recapturing Anthropology: Working in the Present,* edited by Richard Fox. Sante Fe, NM: School of American Research, 1991.

Rancière, Jacques. *The Names of History.* Minneapolis: University of Minnesota Press, 1994.

Ravetto, Kriss. "Frenchifying Film Studies: Projecting Lacan onto the Feminist Scene." In *French Theory in America,* edited by Sylvère Lotringer and Sande Cohen. New York: Routledge, 2001.

———. "Shaking Down LA Cool: Hopping Up Neo-Noir." *Emergences* 9, no. 2 (1999).

———. *The Unmaking of Fascist Aesthetics.* Minneapolis: University of Minnesota Press, 2002.

Ravetto-Biagioli, Kriss. "Film according to Žižek: or Hitching and Lynching Sexuality." *South Atlantic Quarterly* (Fall–Winter 2005).

Readings, Bill. *Introducing Lyotard.* New York: Routledge, 1991.

Relyea, Lane. "Virtually Formal." *Artforum* (September 1998).

Rheinberger, Hans-Jorg. "Experimental Systems: Historiality, Narration and Deconstruction." *Science in Context* 7, no. 1 (1994).

Robins, Robert H. *A Short History of Linguistics.* Bloomington: Indiana University Press, 1970.

Rodowick, D. N. "Introduction: Mobile Citizens, Media States." *PMLA* 117, no. 1 (January 2002).

Ronell, Avital. *Stupidity.* Urbana: University of Illinois Press, 2002.

Rotman, Brian. "Going Parallel." *Substance* 29, no. 1 (2000).

Roudinescu, Elizabeth. "Jacques Lacan—The Erasure of History." In *French Theory in America,* edited by Sylvère Lotringer and Sande Cohen. New York: Routledge, 2001.

Royce, Josiah. *Lectures on Modern Idealism.* New Haven: Yale University Press, 1964.

Ryan, Alan. "Wise Man." *New York Review of Books,* December 17, 1998.

Salanskis, Jean-Michel. "Idea and Destination." In *Deleuze: A Critical Reader,* edited by Paul Patton. London: Blackwell, 1996.

Scarry, Elaine. *Resisting Representation.* New York: Oxford University Press, 1994.

Schjeldahl, Peter. "Desert Songs." *New Yorker,* August 13, 2001.

Shinkichi, E. "An Outline of Formosan History." In *Formosa Today,* edited by M. Mancall. New York: Praeger, 1964.

Shotwell, James. *The History of History.* New York: Columbia University Press, 1939.

Shulevitz, Judith. "Keepers of the Tenure Track." *New York Times Book Review,* October 29, 1995.

Singerman, Howard. "From My Institution to Yours." In *Public Offerings.* Los Angeles: Museum of Contemporary Art, 2001.

Sloterdijk, Peter. "Interview: 'Ich bin ein heiliges Monstrum.'" *Die Weltwoche,* September 16, 1999, www.weltwoche.ch.

———. *Thinker on Stage.* Minneapolis: University of Minnesota Press, 1989.

Smith, Daniel. Introduction to *Essays Critical and Clinical,* by Gilles Deleuze, translated by Daniel Smith and Michael Greco. Minneapolis: University of Minnesota Press, 1997.

Spanos, William. *Heidegger and Criticism.* Minneapolis: University of Minnesota Press, 1993.

Spence, Jonathan. "Kissinger and the Emperor." *New York Review of Books,* March 4, 1999.

Stainton, Michael. "The Politics of Taiwan Aboriginal Origins." In *Taiwan: A New History,* edited by Murray A. Rubinstein. Armonk, NY: M. E. Sharpe, 1999.

Stambaugh, Joan. *Nietzsche's Thought of Eternal Return.* Baltimore: Johns Hopkins University Press, 1972.

Starns, Randolph. "Introduction: The New Erudition." *Representations* 56 (Fall 1996).

Theweleit, Klaus. *Male Fantasies,* vol. 1. Minneapolis: University of Minnesota Press, 1987.

Todorov, Tzvetan. *The Morals of History.* Minneapolis: University of Minnesota Press, 1995.

———. *Theories of the Symbol.* Ithaca, NY: Cornell University Press, 1984.

Toulmin, Stephen. "Prodigal Son." *Los Angeles Times Book Review,* January 3, 1999.

Traweek, Sharon. "Pilgrim's Progress: Male Tales Told." In *The Science Studies Reader,* edited by Mario Biagioli. New York: Routledge, 1998.

Tsai Yuan-Huang. "Political Reorientation of the Taiwanese Intellectuals after 1987." Paper given at the Los Angeles County Museum of Art, June 1998.

Turner, Stephen. "Scientists as Agents." In *Science Bought and Sold*, edited by Philip Mirowski and Esther-Mirjam Sent. Chicago: University of Chicago Press, 2002.

Vico, Giambattista. *The New Science*. Ithaca, NY: Cornell University Press, 1968.

Vivas, Eliseo. "A Natural History of the Aesthetic Transaction." In *Naturalism and the Human Spirit*, edited by Yervant Krikorian. New York: Columbia University Press, 1969.

Wasserman, Steve. "L.A. Is Book Country." *Los Angeles Times Book Review*, April 19, 1998.

———. "The Latitude and Longitude of L.A. Lit." *Los Angeles Times Book Review*, October 27, 2002.

———. "Why Read Marx?" *Los Angeles Times Book Review*, February 8, 1998.

———. "Years of Hope, Days of Rage." *Los Angeles Times Book Review*, October 11, 1998.

Weber, Samuel. "Piecework." In *Strategies for Theory*, edited by Randy L. Rutsky and Bradley McDonald. Albany: State University of New York Press, 2003.

Weil, Simone. *The Need for Roots*. New York: Routledge, 1978.

Weller, Robert. *Resistance, Chaos, and Control in China*. Seattle: University of Washington Press, 1994.

White, Hayden. "The Absurdist Moment in Contemporary Literary Theory." *Contemporary Literature* 17, no. 3 (Summer 1976).

———. "Comments on New Historicism." In *The New Historicism*, edited by H. Aram Veeser. New York: Routledge, 1989.

———. *Figural Realism: Studies in the Mimesis Effect*. Baltimore: Johns Hopkins University Press, 1999.

———. "The Historical Text as Literary Artifact." In *The Writing of History*, edited by Robert H. Canary and Henry Kozicki. Madison: University of Wisconsin Press, 1978.

———. *Metahistory*. Baltimore: Johns Hopkins University Press, 1973.

Williams, Bernard. "The Reluctant Philosopher." *Times Literary Supplement*, May 29, 1998.

Winfree, Jason. "The Repetition of Eternal Return, or the Disastrous Step." *PLI* 11 (2001).

Wood, Gordon. "Creating the Revolution." *New York Review of Books*, February 13, 2003.

Žižek, Slavoj. *Tarrying with the Negative*. Durham: Duke University Press, 1993.

Index

"Absurdist Moment in Contemporary Literary Theory, The" (White), 155–56
accident: and anecdote, 135; and necessity/chance, 136
Adorno, Theodor, 41, 80, 81, 191, 252, 265n33
aesthetic: and aesthesis, 209; and belatedness, 33; and classical historiography, 106; and cognitive dissonance, 247; and commands, 34–35; and consolation, 29; as critique, 96; and epistemology, 41, 182; and experimentation, 190; and historicity, 184, 194, 201; and impact, 39–40; and judgment, 7; and knowledge, 25–26; and narration, 195, 202; and public language, 46; and reader, 203; and savage, 213; social cohesion of, 5; and status, 72; and "true" repetition, 235; and violence, 184
affirmative action, 109–12, 114–15, 118, 258–60; as historiography, 111
Agamben, Giorgio, 21–23, 40, 265n7
ahistorical, 48; and politics, 60
Alliez, Eric, 231, 283n33
Althusser, Louis, 146
Anderson, Susan, 75
anecdote, 126–50 passim; ambiguity of, 8; definition of, 129–32; and disruption, 128; laudatory, 129; and movement of language, 130; and the real, 131
Ankersmit, Frank, 207, 213, 283n23, 283n25
Ansell-Pearson, Keith: and abyss/formless, 243; on Deleuze, 229
anti-intellectualism, 86; and transpolitical, 101
antiproduction, 4, 7; and capitalism, 153; and difference, 239

Apollonian, 39, 43, 122
Appleby, Joyce, 264n25, 277n6 (chap. 6), 277n30 (chap. 5), 281n3
Arendt, Hannah, 104, 115, 120, 263–64n14
art: and criticism, 86–102; false affirmation of, 93; and irresponsibility, 96
Artforum, 74, 230
Art Issues, 91, 93, 272n59
Ascherson, Neal, 85
assertion, and primary historicization, 100
aternal, and untimely, 227

Badiou, Alain, 28, 283n33
Bakhtin, Mikhail, 30
Baldessari, John, 94–97, 273n72
Barilli, Renato, 78
Barthes, Roland, 265n11; on fascism in language, 35; on mass communication, 29; and myth, 69, 190; on narrative, 203, 210; on prose, 31; and schizophrenic writing, 105–6, 112–15, 118, 259
Baudrillard, Jean, 274n5; antihistoricism of, 193; and finalities, 70; misuse of, 230; on sign-value, 93; use of, 95–97
Beck, Lewis White, 276n20
Bell Curve, The (Murray and Hernstein), 34
Bellesiles, Michael, 279n9
Benjamin, Walter, 162–63
Benn, Gottfried, 187, 188
Benveniste, Emile, 130
Bergson, Henri, 244
Berlin, Isaiah, 236; as courtier, 84; on historical writing, 207, 243; as icon, 7, 201; as index, 106; representations of, 120–24
Beyond Piety (Gilbert-Rolfe), 94, 96, 272n70, 273n77

297

Index

historiospectography, 177–78, 181; and inheritance, 177
history: and coexistence, 246; and cultural disjunctions, 4; and destiny, 253;
end of, 209; fear of, 6; and foreclosure,
185; and future, 101; and haunting of
Europe, 163; as "house of correction,"
185; as misrepresentation, 60; as objectless singular, 9; and *posthistoire*,
188–91, 193; and posthistory, 1, 12, 173;
and public contention, 7; and subjectivity, 136–40, 142, 150
History as the Story of Liberty (Croce), 186
History of History, The (Shotwell), 129
"History of the Anecdote: Fiction and
Fiction, The" (Fineman), 133–45
Hitler, Adolf, 249, 272n58
hitlerism, 16–17
Hitler's Willing Executioners (Goldhagen),
237
Hobsbawm, Eric, 82–84, 101
Holderlin, Friedrich, 251, 283n29
Holland, Bernard, 92–93
Hollier, Denis, 44
Hollinger, David, 260; on "situated
knowledge," 145–50
Homer, 207, 211, 213
Hou Hsiao-hsien *(City of Sadness)*,
268n30
Humboldt, Wilhelm von, 260
Hunt, Lynn, 277n6 (chap. 6), 277n30
(chap. 5), 281n3

Idea of History, The (Collingwood), 9
identity-debates, and historiography,
145–49
Ignatieff, Michael, 84
image: and connoisseur, 124; disjunctions
of, 118; of historian and despotic,
118–19; and injunctive inscription, 213;
personification of, 122; and the popular, 119; and schizophrenic writing,
120, 124
incommensurable, 183, 195–96
inscriptive, and historiography, 208
insubordinate principle, and destiny, 254

Jacob, Margaret, 277n6 (chap. 6), 277n30
(chap. 5), 281n3
James, Jesse, 15, 107
Jameson, Fredric, 37, 52, 132, 192, 230
Janicaud, Dominique, 1
Jiang Zemin, 67, 69, 269n52
Joan of Arc, 16, 235
Johnson, Barbara, 36
*Jonah Will Be 25 in the Year Two Thou-
sand* (Tanner), 116
Just Gaming (Lyotard), 194

Kansteiner, Wulf, 275n20
Kant, Immanuel, 15, 244, 283n29; Arendt
and, 137, 139; Deleuze on, 234, 250–51;
Derrida on, 162; and imagination, 16;
Koselleck on, 185; Lyotard on, 13, 182,
192, 199–200; and savage appraisal,
213; and sublime, 46, 115
Kantian, 12, 136
Kaplan, Richard, 45
Kinzer, Stephen, 263n4
Kirsch, Jonathan, 283n46
Kissinger, Henry, 53, 60
Knight, Christopher, 72, 93, 99–100,
272n64, 273n72, 273nn84–85,
274nn86–90
Kofman, Sarah, 40
Kojève, Alexandre, 11, 173–74, 178,
189–90, 238
Koselleck, Reinhart: and diagnosis/progno-
sis, 252; and "house of correction," 185;
and openness to history, 257; and peri-
odizaton, 10; and vanquished, 144, 260
Koxinga (Cheng Ch'eng-kung), 57, 59
Krell, David, 154
Kristof, Nicolas, 267n3
Kuan-Hsing Chen, 268n37

Lacan, Jacques, 136, 140–41, 190
Lacanian, 39, 126, 140–42
Laclau, Ernesto, 266n40
Laing, R. D., 231
Landes, David, 83–84
language: aesthetics of, 26; and art, 92;
and belief, 28; concepts of, 26; fear of,

teleology, 142, 167; and eschatology, 167, 256; and public, 209; rationalization of, 251

temporality: and action/fatigue, 241; ambiguity of, 241; and contraction and habit, 244–45; and deferral, 158–59; and dynamics of active and passive synthesis, 244–45; and messianic, 174; and new timings, 251; and "now," 251; paradoxes of, 244; and present disjunctions, 247; and present memory, 244; restored by Derrida, 176; and Stoic notions of language, 251; syntheses of, 242–50 passim; time-conducts of, 231

Theory of the Avant-Garde (Berger), 95

Theweleit, Klaus, 110

Thousand Plateaus, A (Deleuze and Guattari), 212

Thucydides, 1, 73, 147, 214–15, 260–61; Deleuze and Guattari on, 212; and Fineman's theory of historical writing, 126, 133–39, 143, 144–45, 179, 184, 208; as local narrator, 85, 198; and performative onset, 119

Times Literary Supplement, 121

Titian, 88, 89

Todorov, Tzvetan, 61–62, 65, 70, 129, 259

Toichi, Mabuchi, 53

Toulmin, Stephen, 84

Toward a Speech Act Theory of Literary Discourse (Pratt), 126

Tristes Tropiques (Levi-Strauss), 187

Trust (Fukuyama), 45

Tsing-Hua University, 62

Turner, J. M., 221

uncanny, the, 180–81

Uncommon Valor (Kotcheff), 185

unidirectionality, and temporal synthesis, 244

University of California–Los Angeles (UCLA), 63, 74, 77

unmeasurable, and temporality, 251

van Gogh, Vincent, 222, 239

Vico, Giambattista, 5, 11, 30–33, 35, 123, 210

Virilio, Paul, 244

Wall Street Journal, 119

Wang Daohan, 67–68

Warhol, Andy, 3, 88–89, 98, 100, 119, 214, 271n44, 281–82n26

Wasserman, Steve, 270n10, 270nn20–23, 271n27, 271n30

Wayne, Shoshana, 270n11

Wealth and Poverty of Nations, The (Landes), 83

Weber, Max, 72–73, 260

Weber, Samuel, 160

Weil, Simone, 11, 115

Weiner, Jon, 279n9

What Is Philosophy? (Deleuze and Guattari), 207, 222, 238, 280n29

White, Hayden, 8, 136, 257, 266n55, 276n29; on anecdote, 131; and burden of history, 117, 240, 246; and contemporary reader, 112, 124; on Derrida, 155–57, 174; on modern event, 138; on narrative and perception, 127–28; on New Historicism, 130, 133

Who Owns Academic Work? (McSherry), 7, 264n16

Wittgensteinian, 134

Wood, Gordon, 168, 206, 210, 250

Zhu Rongji, 68–69

Žižek, Slavoj, 44